CASS LIBRARY OF AFRICAN STUDIES

AFRICANA MODERN LIBRARY

No. 7

General Editor: PROFESSOR E. U. ESSIEN-UDOM
University of Ibadan, Nigeria

# Apropos of Africa

*Sentiments of Negro American Leaders
on Africa from the 1800s to the 1950s*

Compiled and edited by

ADELAIDE CROMWELL HILL

AND

MARTIN KILSON

FRANK CASS & CO. LTD.
1969

First published in 1969 by
FRANK CASS AND COMPANY LIMITED
67 Great Russell Street, London, W.C.1

Coll 't̄ —
E
448
.H64

Printed in Great Britain by
Billing & Sons Limited, Guildford and London

# Preface

This book represents to a large extent a labour of love—an expression of our concern as Negroes and Africanists that much of relevance in the relation between Africans and Americans of African descent had never been fully appreciated and today was in danger of being totally forgotten or denied. We know very well that these selections do not represent all the examples of Negro American interest in and sentiment about Africa through the years. The unrecorded curiosity and yearning of those who wanted to but could not return to Africa when this or that project was ended or never materialized; the Negro sailors who felt excitement and joy in reaching African ports; and the many Negro missionaries who served and even died there—all of these experiences have had an effect on Africa in the minds and hearts of the Negro American.

We decided to begin with the leaders—those persons whose concern with Africa undoubtedly had a broad effect on others who accepted their leadership. In compiling what, in our opinion, were the most significant contributions, we sought and received the assistance of others. We wish to thank, therefore, particularly Mrs. Dorothy Porter of the Moreland Collection, Howard University; Mrs. Jean Blackwell Hutson, the Schomburg Collection of the New York Public Library; Mr. Svend Holsoe; Mr. Theodore Brown and Dr. Lawrence D. Reddick for bringing to our attention selections we might not have seen or in assisting us in our search for wanted but difficult to locate selections.

We wish also to thank the American Society of African Culture for its financial support which made it possible for us to do the original photostating and to have the clerical assistance of Vivian Johnson, and the African Studies Center of Boston University for the services of Jane Martin and Susanne Marcus, whose interest and efficiency made our task considerably easier.

We are indebted to J. Saunders Redding for helping us to present our ideas in the most acceptable English prose.

ADELAIDE CROMWELL HILL
MARTIN KILSON

v

# Contents

# PART II (a)

## How Negro Americans Can Help
### *As Individuals*

CONTENTS

# PART II (b)

## How Negro Americans Can Help
### *As Organizations*

ix

CONTENTS

# PART III

## When I was in Africa

# PART IV

## Negro Self-Identity and Pan-Africanism

CONTENTS

# Introduction

The post-war era in America simultaneously discovered Africa and the Negro American. To some persons African nationalism and the Negro American protest movement are but parts of the same process. For others, Africa and the Negro American are 300 years and 4,000 miles apart, with the possibilities of meaningful ties and common interests non-existent. No doubt the barriers between Africans and Negroes throughout the Western Hemisphere (North America, the Caribbean, and Brazil) have been significant; but the important fact is that means have always been found, on both sides of the ocean divide between the new world and old world Negro communities, to overcome these barriers and create ties of common interest.

The period of a conscious search among Negro Americans for an understanding of and identity with their African heritage began during the mid-1800's when there appeared the beginnings of a Negro American intelligentsia. With the end of the Civil War and the start of a measure of Negro social mobility within American society, this intelligentsia expanded the forms of its interests in the African heritage. In particular, there was an increasing concern for self-identity in a situation of social mobility toward the norms of a segregated American society. Such mobility necessarily rendered the Negro's sense of self, of racial or cultural identity, ambivalent. In resolving this ambivalence the intellectual elements among Negroes turned to the African heritage in one form or another.

Simultaneous with the Negro American intelligentsia's confrontation with the white supremacist forms of American institutions which impelled their search for their African heritage, there was occurring in Africa itself the full colonization of the continent by European powers. Among other things, European colonization in Africa established patterns of racial segregation comparable to those found in American society. In other words, modern colonialism brought the Negro African into precisely the same type of relationships with white-dominated industrial society that Negroes in America, the Caribbean, and South America were already experiencing. It therefore created the context within which the intelligentsia in both the old world and new world Negro communities could

xiii

identify their common needs and interests and seek their ameliora-
tion. This was the starting point of what became known as Pan-
Africanism, whose essence never received a better formulation than
in the verse of Countee Cullen, the Negro American poet:

> We shall not always plant while others reap
> The golden increment of bursting fruit,
> Nor always countenance, abject and mute,
> That lesser men should hold their brothers cheap; . . .
> We were not made eternally to weep.

This anthology attempts to fill in the variegated picture of the
long history of the relationship of Negro Americans to Africa, and
to assess its dimension as illustrated in the words and deeds, thoughts
and actions, of the Negro intelligentsia. Each person included in this
anthology had or has a position of some prominence among the
Negro American community. While some like Delany, Bruce,
Garvey, and DuBois had such prominence because of a special
African interest, others like Locke, Williams, Wright, and Diggs
had prominence for other reasons. In either case, whatever their
degree of concern with Africa may have been, it may be taken as a
reasonable measure of the concern of the Negro community in
general with questions and issues regarding their African heritage.

# PART I

# Let's Go Home to Africa

The sentiment of American Negroes toward Africa as a past or future home should not be considered out of the context of America in general, nor out of the context of the Negroes' politically and economically weak position in America in particular. To most of her inhabitants, except the Indian and the Negro, America has always seemed an enduring refuge voluntarily sought by troubled and burdened people. Having fled from oppressive situations in their homelands, the immigrants became Americans. Though not necessarily hostile to their fatherlands, they were emphatic as to their rightful positions as Americans on this continent and in their desire to remain here.

Africa as a homeland to American Negroes could mean freedom if nothing else. But this image would not be encouraged or strengthened by a society with a vested interest in slavery. With little information out of which to create an image of Africa, and with even less incentive to do so, most Negroes adopted the expectations of immigrants in general—that America was a new country for all, and that there was room in it for all. None the less, Africa remained a place to which some Negroes wished to return. For quite obvious reasons, Africa was also seen by many whites as a place to which Negroes should return, however much they preferred to remain in America.

Africa for the American Negro was and is a great dilemma. It is quite impossible to think of American Negroes as having the simple and direct attitude towards Africa that characterizes the immigrant's attitude toward his native country or a stranger's longing for a home. It is essential to consider Negroes' feelings toward Africa as an aspect of their struggle for survival and citizenship in America. Black Nationalism, as many nationalistic movements of Negroes are called, is nothing more than a failure of White Nationalism—a failure to include black people in its rewards, and a failure to stop black people from seeking these rewards elsewhere on this earth.

One segment of white opinion held that the enslavement of Negroes was a travesty upon Democracy and Christianity which could only be remedied by a wholesale deportation of Negroes, free and slave, back to Africa. This philosophy held by the American Colonization Society led in 1822 to the settlement of Liberia on the West Coast of Africa. But even before white Americans accepted emigration as a solution to or evasion of the Negro question, individual Negroes like Paul Cuffe saw Africa as a land of opportunity for American Negroes.

As the son of an African father and an American Indian mother, Paul Cuffe had a real tie with Africa. Yet he was never to leave the country of his birth. His was a normal interest in his native land, and this interest, implemented by financial competence, expressed itself in his efforts to exercise the rights of citizenship and in his assuming the burden of providing the first free schools in New Bedford, Massachusetts. Nevertheless, he felt, and tried to promote in others, a strong tie to Africa, and in the year 1815 transported 38 free Negroes to Africa in his own ship and at his own expense. When he died in 1817, Cuffe had planned yet other voyages to Africa and had a waiting list of 2000 Negroes who wished to sail with him.

Meanwhile, life in America did not improve either for slaves or black freemen, and colonization schemes, especially to Africa, seemed to promise relief. The rationale for these schemes varied from the belief that the Negro had both the obligation and the natural ability to redeem Africa, to the idea that only in Africa could black men achieve freedom and independence. There was also an economic motivation to colonization schemes which must not be overlooked. Fanciful or not, the hope in some quarters was to weaken the southern economy by removing slave labour, its most valuable commodity. Negro leaders themselves, however, generally scorned this evasive solution to their problems, and were emphatic in their demands for better treatment in this country. Surely, it would have seemed strange for any group of American immigrants to do otherwise. The Negroes' demand for recognition in the United States was independent of their knowledge of the real or imagined circumstances of "life in the old country". As a counter proposal to the unsolicited action in their behalf free Negroes began as early as 1830 to convene on an annual basis to call the nation's attention to their demands. Initially these conventions paid only incidental attention to emigration schemes and problems, and then simply with the intent to disparage them. The meetings concerned themselves with ways of improving the lot of the Negro in this country

4

and even those participants who felt immigration might provide relief for some Negroes and welcomed Africa as a possible location were not very vocal, lest they be considered in the camp of the colonizers. Resolutions and programmes to promote self-help, legislative battles to secure rights (education and so forth), were the main concerns. But when these failed to win sympathy and attention, the attitude toward colonization in Africa gradually began to change. Although there was no lessening of agitation for rights in this country, the National Emigration Convention of Colored Men meeting in Cleveland, Ohio, in August 1854 openly debated whether their condition could be worsened by emigration. Africa was not publicly discussed, for it was felt by the convention leadership that such a discussion would have implied its approval of the proposal by the American Colonization Society to solve the Negro question merely by returning Negroes to their original home. But in the secret sessions of this convention Africa was indeed the subject of discussion, as a report on the convention indicates.

Though our great gun was leveled, and the first shell thrown at the American Continent, driving a slave-holding faction into despair, and a political confusion from which they have been utterly unable to extricate themselves, but become more and more complicated every year, Africa was held in reserve until by the help of an all-wise Providence we could effect what has just been accomplished with signal success—a work which the most sanguine friend of the cause believed would require at least half a century.

Four years later, at the Executive Council Meeting of the Board of the Convention, three different emigration schemes—to Central America, to Haiti, and to West Africa—were discussed. Dr. Martin R. Delany was chosen as commissioner to explore Africa and was given full power to choose his own colleagues. The African venture, referred to as the Niger Valley Exploring Party, was ultimately composed of Dr. Delany and Mr. Robert Campbell. A segment of white, and later of Negro, opinion did not feel Negroes were capable or ready to assume such an undertaking, and from the first, efforts were made to sabotage it. But the venture was a success, treaties were signed, and truly the success it had is a credit to the remarkable dedication and fortitude of a small group of people.

The strategic potential of Africa for the Negro becomes most apparent in the life and works of Frederick Douglass. Douglass fought the battle of the Negro vociferously during the most critical

5

stages of American history, when the country was deciding whether it could survive half slave and half free, and the Negro was seeking strength from the soul of America, not as a gift or privilege, but as his right. To Douglass the issue was merely a pragmatic proposition that Negroes belonged in America as much as any other group. This feeling reflected neither a particular love for America or the American system nor any hatred of Africa. Douglass refused to let sentiment for homeland or other motivations weaken his position. His dislike for the American Colonization Society knew no bounds, and he regarded any plans for emigration of Negroes as ill advised. In his opinion such critical years were hardly the time to engage in dialectics or alternatives. Sentiments had to be mobilized. The battle ground was here and the time was upon them. Africa was both dispensable and irrelevant.

The issues of the Civil War thrust attention upon the position of Negroes in America. As part of the propaganda of war it became useful to publicize the ill-treatment of the Negroes under slavery and to promise great changes as a result of emancipation and Northern victory. No responsible segment of the Negro community could afford not to be involved in the controversy and not to cooperate with plans to bring a rapid end to slavery. Negro regiments participated in some of the bloodiest fighting in the war, thus pro-providing one more bit of evidence of their right to be full citizens of this country.

The Civil War and the issues it was fought to resolve minimized, if not eliminated, the interest of many Negroes in Africa as a homeland. Their energies turned back toward this country. Individuals like Dr. Delany and Henry McNeal Turner found it necessary and important to give their maximum support to the war with the expectation that, when it was won, the Negro would be a free man with all the benefits to which he was entitled.

It is not without importance, however, that not all Negroes during the Reconstruction ceased to be concerned with Africa. Men like Alexander Crummell and later Booker T. Washington felt that the Negro American should share his knowledge and skills with his brothers in Africa.

But the disillusionment following the realization that freedom had not brought equality or integration into American life stimulated the growth of Negro protest, which manifested itself in the organization of the National Association for the Advancement of Colored People in 1909 and the National Urban League in 1910. These protest organizations, however, sought no solution to the Negro's predica-

6

ment outside the United States. They continued to fight to achieve full citizenship for Negroes in America.

Even today few persons appreciate the effect of World War I upon the American Negro and his life in this country. As a war fought to save democracy abroad World War I was in many ways a mockery to Negroes in America. Race riots and lynchings, even of Negro soldiers in uniform, publicized the inability of Americans, in spite of their democratic values, to face the Negro problem. Negroes were also no longer under any illusions that more than second-class citizenship was available to them in "the land of the free and the home of the brave".

Having responded to changes wrought by the conditions of World War I, Negroes in the United States became a more organized and, as a result of immigration from the West Indies, a more hetero-geneous group. This mass of frustrated and mixed humanity sought in vain for solutions to its predicament in America. They found little solace in the Negro churches and little assistance or support from Negro protest organizations. They appreciated instead the fiery and imaginative solutions of Marcus Garvey, a West Indian immigrant. Garvey understood the feelings of the people. It was his opinion that Negroes should return to Africa, and he set about organizing the financing and execution of a large exodus of Negroes to Liberia. He appealed to the black urban masses, initially those of West Indian extraction, and subsequently to the Negro poor at large. He was disdainful of the middle class comfortable Negroes and of their leadership. This group, for its part, considered him as, at best, an embarrassment and, at worst, a dangerous buffoon whose activities could only retard racial progress in this country. Like the Board of the Convention of 1858, Garvey sent a mission to Africa. Its plans were not successfully implemented, but Garveyism left its mark on the thinking of American Negroes in all walks of life.

Garveyism was the first effective pronouncement of Black Nationalism as a movement: it rejected the go-slow, integrationist attempts of the familiar protest movements of American Negroes; it dramatized—even lionized—the blackness of Negroes, both in pigmentation and in origin. Africa, African, and Black became the rallying call and integrative force of the Garveyites.

It is not without significance that the ideological basis of Black Nationalism as exemplified by the Garveyites emerged at the same time as the feeling for political independence in Africa and pan-Africanism were also developing. Cross-fertilization of ideas, even of personalities, indicates a common source and readiness in time for such things. Potential African nationalists such as Kwame Nkrumah of Ghana, and Nnamdi Azikiwe, former President of Nigeria, freely acknowledge the influence of Garveyism on their thinking. At the same time the personal activities of W. E. B. DuBois were instrumental in organizing the Five Pan-African conferences, the first of which was held in England in 1919. That DuBois and Garvey were in disagreement can readily be understood, but that both of them contributed to the larger ideological thinking of the Negro in relation to Africa cannot be disputed.

The removal of Garvey from the American scene did not eliminate the frustration of the urban Negro nor minimize Africa as a force in their lives. The concern for Africa among Negroes in the thirties and forties was merely dormant, and the issues of the Italian–Ethiopian War did much to rekindle their interest. At the same time leaders were emerging to rescue the black urban masses through a spiritual renaissance based on non-Christian foundations.

One of the crucial factors determining the position of the Negro in contemporary America has been the failure of Christianity and Christian churches to function as an ethic in American life. It was for this reason that Negroes originally withdrew from white churches and formed their own churches, and then withdrew from their own formal Christian denominations and started sects or cults which more nearly met their spiritual needs and more clearly answered their personal frustrations. This rejection of Christianity and Christian churches assumed many forms, ranging from Daddy Grace's United House of Prayer for All People to the Moorish Science Temple of America, which was founded in 1913 by a North Carolinian named Timothy Drew. The Moorish Science Temple accepted Allah as God, Jesus as His prophet, and a special version of the Holy Koran as their religious book. They viewed themselves as Moslems with Morocco as their homeland. This cult had no conversion, sanctification, or unusual experience. Heaven was a figure of the mind, and they made their own heaven while on this earth.

The Moorish Science Temple was strongest in Chicago, Detroit, and Philadelphia, and it appealed primarily to rural Negroes who had recently migrated to these urban centres. Its strength rested with the personality of its leader, Noble Ali Drew, whose mysterious death in 1929 split the units into numerous sub-units.

The philosophy of the Moorish Science Temple has been largely incorporated into the Nation of Islam, which was founded in 1930 and has been led by Elijah Muhammad since 1933. This group, with an estimated membership of 50,000 to 250,000, is strongest in the urban centres of New York, Boston, Chicago, Los Angeles, and Detroit. Known popularly as the Black Muslims, the movement's ideology includes an acceptance of Allah as God, Mr. Muhammad as His prophet, the Koran or a version of it as text, a rejection of the word *Negro* as a name, and a determination to dignify the black man and woman and their accomplishments. The Black Muslims, perhaps reflecting conditions of present-day Africa, seek closer ties between American Negroes and their black Muslim brothers throughout Africa, not merely those in Morocco, North Africa, or Ethiopia, to which Parker in The Children of the Sun and the Moorish Americans were oriented. The Black Muslims' thought in respect to Africa is in many ways closer to that of Marcus Garvey than to that of Noble Ali Drew. However, as the selection in this anthology indicates, the Black Muslims—the strongest of the Black Nationalists groups—have not been willing to give highest priority to Africa's redemption or to African–Negro relations. The American and non-intellectual background of their leaders, as opposed to the West Indian and generally more sophisticated background of Garvey and many of his close associates, has no doubt given an uncertain ring to statements of doctrine about Africa and Africans. It is interesting, however, that in their newspaper, *Muhammad Speaks*, which was founded after the period covered here and apparently edited by intellectuals within or without the movement, devotes an extraordinary amount of space to African news. The Muslims' programme also includes the idea, prevalent as far back as the days of Martin Delany, that the Negro should control some part of this land or elsewhere as his just reward for years of labour. But the desire to give dignity and status to American Negroes seems to be a stronger feature of the Black Muslim creed than any organized plan they may have to emigrate either to Africa or to some specific section of this country.

Outside this trend of religion-oriented Negro nationalism is a sprinkling of groups concerned with Africa and the Negro with a desire to influence public opinion on these subjects. Small groups like the United African Nationalists, the African Freedom Movement, African Nationalist Pioneer Movement, Liberation Committee for Africa and the Cultural Association for Women of African Heritage are located in or receiving their main support from the New York area. While they are certainly a part of this main stream of the American Negro's identification with Africa, they do not actually propose at the present time any emigration plans for going back to Africa.

# Paul Cuffe,
## 1759–1817

Paul Cuffe was born of an African father and an Indian mother on the island of Cuttyhunk near Westport, Massachusetts. He had no formal schooling when, at the age of sixteen, he went to sea. On his third voyage he was captured by a British brig and held prisoner of war for several months. Cuffe spent his entire life as a sailor, captain, and shipbuilder. In the course of his business he owned at different times, besides smaller boats, the *Ranger*, a schooner of 60 or 70 tons, a half interest in a brig of 162 tons, the brig *Traveller* of 109 tons, the ship *Alpha* of 258 tons, and a three-fourths interest in a larger vessel.

Cuffe, a tall and imposing figure, was deeply religious. He was a member of the Society of Friends and a minister among them. He believed it to be his duty to sacrifice private interests rather than enter into any enterprise harmful to his fellow man. Before the end of the Revolutionary War he refused to pay a personal tax on the ground that free coloured people did not enjoy the rights and citizenship of other citizens. He petitioned the Massachusetts Legislature and thereby became the first citizen of African descent to make a successful appeal in behalf of his civil rights. In 1797 Cuffe built from his own funds a school for the Negro and Indian children at New Bedford. As he visited the various communities in connection with his work, he urged Negroes to start self-help and mutual benefit societies. He organized such societies in Philadelphia, New York, and in Sierra Leone.

After an exploratory trip to Sierra Leone and England in 1810–11, Cuffe sailed in 1815 from Westport to Sierra Leone with thirty-eight free Negroes, whose expenses he largely underwrote. He maintained them for two months after their arrival in Africa until they were properly settled and returned home with a plan of undertaking another voyage in which no fewer than 2,000 Negroes had expressed interest. Unfortunately, Paul Cuffe died before the plans for the second voyage were completed.

Westport   6 mo 10<sup>th</sup>   1809

Esteemed friends,
John James and Alexander Wilson,*

I have for some years had it impressed on my mind to make a voyage to Sierra Leon in order to inspect the situation of the country, and feeling a real desire that the inhabitants of Africa might become an enlightened people and be so favored as to give general satisfaction to all those who are endeavouring to establish them in the true light of Christianity. And as I am of the African race I feel myself interested for them and if I am favored with a talent I think I am willing that they should be benefited thereby. I have had an opportunity with our esteemed friend James Pemberton† on the subject (who is since deceased) and I received a letter from him which informed me that he had given information of my concern to the Sierra Leon Company. They wrote to him that if Paul Cuffe should make a voyage there that he should have every priviledge that its government could afford.—When this comes to your consideration, if you think it expedient to write to England to inform the concern that I have some concern in navigation which if I concluded to settle there I would wish to take with me so that the inhabitants might be benefited both with agriculture and commerce; —and that in case I engage in the whale fishery whether I could have encouragement such as bounty, or to carry the productions of the country duty free to England.—If times should be so settled between this by next fall so as to be advisable to undertake such a voyage it looks pretty clear to be put in execution in case there should be encouragement. I think there are several families of good credit that may like to go—

I am your assured friend,
PAUL CUFFE

**Minutes of Paul Cuffe's first voyage to Sierra Leone and England with Brig *Traveller* and of her return by the way of Sierra Leone to America, etc.**

Brig *Traveller* of 109 Tons built in Westport in the year 1806 to 1807.
Paul Cuffe Owner and Supercargo.

* Quaker businessmen in Philadelphia with whom Cuffe regularly did business.
† A member of the African Institution of London.

11

Thomas Wainer, Master.
John Wainer, Mate.
Michael Wainer Jr.
John Marsterns
Samuel Hicks
Zechariah White
Joseph Hemnaway
Charles Augustus Freeburg
Thomas Paton                                          were the crew.
Capt. Richard—a passenger from Philadelphia.
Left Westport for Philadelphia 11 mo 25th—1810.
4th of the 12 month arrived at Philadelphia. & discharged cargo
of barley.

1 mo 1 1811 left Philadelphia for Sierra Leone.

2 mo 2. The brig struck down on the beam ends—John Masterns
washed overboard, but regained the vessel.

2 mo 21. The dust of Africa lodged on the rigging; the land
supposed to be about 25 leagues off.

1811 2 mo 24. At 10 AM sounded and found bottom in 65 fathoms.
had the first dinner of fish since they sailed from America.

2 mo 28th. Saw the mountains of Sierra Leone. at 8 o clock PM
anchored.

3 mo 1. Came to in Sierra Leone road.

3 mo 4. Dined with the Governor. some talk about the unsuccessful condition of the Colony of Sierra Leone.

3 mo 13. Visit from King Thomas. He was served with food
"But it appeared that there was *Rum* wanting, but none was given."

3 mo 18. Visited King George.

5 mo 10. Paul Cuffe in command of the *Traveller* sailed from
Sierra Leone for Liverpool leaving Thomas Wainer at Sierra
Leone. He Paul had intended to return with the brig to America.
but when about to sail he received from England permission to
bring a cargo of African produce to that country. This was contained in a letter from Wm. Allen which he received 4 mo 22°—
He then changed his plans and left for Europe.

7 mo 7. Saw land which proved to be Cape Clear.

7 mo 12. Arrived at Liverpool—had three men impressed on the
day of his arrival—two were given up—one detained.

7 mo 13. Ship *Alpha* arrived this morning 52 days from New
Orleans. Endeavoring to procure the liberation of the impressed
man Aaron Richards.

7 mo 14. Took stage in the evening for London at 10th.

12

16. Arrived in London about 6 oclock AM. Went to Plough Court and was received by Wm. Allen.

17. Saw St. Paul's

18. Called upon Wm. Wilberforce

19. Visited Lancaster's School room. much gratified.

20. Went to Wm. Dillwyn's

20. Heard of the release of Aaron Richards

26. Went to T. Macaulay's

30. Visited the mint

31. Set out on his return to Liverpool.

8 mo 1. Arrived at Liverpool.

„ 7. Dined with Wm. & Richard Rathbone in company with Thomas Thompson, William Roscoe, & Lord John Russell.

„ 9. Took dinner with Wm. Booth & Capt. Pane, formerly Slave dealers. "but treated me politely"—

„ 15. *Alpha* ready for sea.

„ 18. Started again for London. arrived on the 20th.

„ 23. Dined in company with Capt. Ebu Clark of New Bedford.

„ 26. Visited the London Docks.

„ 27. Met the Committee of the African Institution. Made the Duke of Gloucester a present of an African robe, a letter box and a dagger.

„ 29. Left London for Manchester—arrived 30th.

9 mo 2. Arrived at Liverpool.

1811 9 mo 4. Visited Wm. Roscoe. much conversation on African concerns with him.

6. Visited the school for the blind.

20. Departed from Liverpool for Sierra Leone—

11 mo 12. Arrived at Sierra Leone.

13. Entered at the Custom House.

Selling cargo—through the month.

12 Trading tc.

2 mo 11. Left Sierra Leone for America.

15. Sent back to Sierra Leone by the capt of an English Sloop of war.

2 16. Dragged off by the nose by the Sloop of war *Sabrina*—

2 19. Left Sierra Leone again.

26. Observe the sail much covered with African dust . . .

4 18. Saw land

19. Went to Westport in pilot boat leaving the *Traveller* at sea.

13

20. Went to New Bedford.

21. On returning to the *Traveller* found her in possession of the Revenu Cutter. She was carried into Newport the next day—

23. Prepared a petition to the Secretary of the Navy.

24. With a recomendation signed by Simeon Martin gov.— —Constant Taber group—G. C. Champlan—John Coggerhall— I. Vernon—Thos. G. Pitman Walter Channing.

25. Went to Providence. Form letter of reccomand from

27. Left Providence.

29. Reached N. York on the morning and Phila on the evening.

1812

4 mo 30. Left Philadelphia.

5 1. Reached Baltimore.

Arrived at Washington at 2 oclock.

2. Waited on the President and afterwards on the Secretary. Was promised an answer on Second day at 12 oclock.

4. Vessel and cargo restored. The Secretary very friendly.

5. Left for Baltimore convention in the stage coach.

6. Spent the day in Baltimore.

8. Left for Wilmington.

9. Left Wilmington for Philadelphia.

11. Met with the people of color tc. on African Affairs.

13. Left for New York.

14. Met with colored people and others in N. York.

19. Departed from New York.

22. Reached Newport and went home in the evening.

A BRIEF ACCOUNT OF THE SETTLEMENT AND PRESENT SITUATION OF THE COLONY OF SIERRA LEONE IN AFRICA*

*Paul Cuffe*

Having been informed that there was a settlement of people of colour at Sierra Leone under the immediate guardianship of a civilized power, I have for these many years past felt a lively interest in their behalf, wishing that the inhabitants of the colony might become established in the truth, and thereby be instrumental in its promotion amongst our African brethern. It was these sentiments that first influenced me to visit my friends in this colony, and instead of repent-

* *A Brief Account of the Settlement and Present Situation of the Colony of Sierra Leone in Africa*, New York, 1812, no. 357.

14

ing, I have cause to rejoice in having found many who are inclined to listen and attend to the precepts of our holy religion. Nevertheless, I am convinced that further help will be requisite to establish them in the true and vital spirit of devotion; for although there are many who are very particular in their attendance of public worship, yet I am apprehensive that the true substance is too much overlooked; and by thus mistaking the form for the substance, that their religious exercise is rendered rather a burden than a pleasure. It is not however my object to extend these observations at present. I merely wish to convey a brief account of the situation of the colony as I found it, hoping the information may prove serviceable and interesting to some of my friends in the United States.

Sierra Leone is a country on the west coast of Africa. Its situation is inviting, and its soil generally very productive. A river of the same name passes through the country, and the land for a great extent on each side is peculiarly fertile, and with the climate well calculated for the cultivation of West-India and other tropical productions. In the year 1791 an act passed the British parliament incorporating a company called the Sierra Leone Company, whose object was to settle and cultivate these lands, and open a trade with other countries in the products of the soil. The first settlers amounted to about 200 white persons, and a number of free blacks or people of colour from North America; and their experiments in sugar, cotton, &c. soon convinced them that they would be abundantly rewarded for their labour. The promising appearance of the settlement soon attracted the attention of the neighbouring chiefs, who with their subjects generally, became very friendly. The colony is now considerably increased, and continues to be a flourishing situation. The population at present as taken by order of Governor Columbine in the 4th mo. 1811, is as follows, viz.

| | | | | | | |
|---|---|---|---|---|---|---|
| Europeans | ... | ... | ... | ... | 22 | 4 | 2 |
| Nova-Scotians | ... | ... | ... | ... | 188 | 295 | 499 |
| Maroons | ... | ... | ... | ... | 165 | 195 | 447 |
| Africans | ... | ... | ... | ... | 20 | 43 | 37 |
| | | | | | 395 | 537 | 985 |
| | | | | | | | 537 |
| | | | | | | | 395 |
| Making together | ... | ... | ... | ... | | | 1917 |

Besides which there are 601 Crue men, so called from their being

15

natives of a part called Crue Country, from which they have emigrated since the establishment of this colony.

These people have not yet been enrolled in the list of citizens, but are generally hired by the inhabitants as labourers. The disposition prevails very generally to encourage new settlers who may come amongst them either for the purpose of cultivating the land, or engaging in commercial enterprise. A petition, of which the following is an outline was lately presented to his excellency governor Columbine, and signed by several of the most respectable inhabitants, viz.

1st. That encouragement may be given to all our brethren, who may come from the British colonies or from America, in order to become farmers, or to assist us in the cultivation of our land.

2nd. That encouragement may be given to our foreign brethren who have vessels for the purpose, to establish commerce in Sierra Leone.

3rd. That those who may undertake to establish the Whale Fishery in the colony may be encouraged to preserve in that useful and laudable enterprise.

There are at this time 7 or 8 schools established throughout the colony. One of these is for the instruction of grown persons, and the others contain together about 230 children, who are instructed in all the necessary branches of education.

The inhabitants have likewise six places of public worship, which are generally well attended. Their times for meeting on the sabbath are at 5 o'clock in the evening. Also, the week through, many of their meetings are attended at 5 in the morning and 6 in the evening. There was also a society formed here some time since for the further promotion of the christian religion. I have met with one of their epistles, which I shall insert at the close of my communication.

An institution was formed on the 1st of the 12th mo. last for the relief of the poor and disabled. It is now regularly held on the 1st second day in every month, at which time proper persons are appointed to take charge of those under the care of the institution. A general meeting is held once every six months. Every one can judge of the happy effect of such institutions as these in improving the dispositions and softening the manners of our native brethren.

The colonists have instituted 5 courts, consisting, first, of the Court of the Quarter Sessions, which is held four times in the course of the year. The governor always presides as judge, and is attended by a justice of the peace, sheriff's clerk, messengers of the baliff and constables. The pettit jury consists of 12 men selected from the Europeans, Nova-Scotians, and Maroons.

2nd. Mayor's Court. This formerly sat on the 5th day of every week; but the time for holding it has since been prolonged to every three months.

3rd. The Court of Requests which is held on the 7th day of every week. The power of this court is confined to the trial of debts not exceeding two pounds. 12 men are selected for this purpose, and four out of the number transact the business of a sitting.

4th. The Police Court, which is likewise held on the 7th day of every week, and is constituted of the same number of persons as the court of requests. Their business is confined to the trial of persons for disorderly conduct.

5th. The Court of Vice Admiralty; which is held as occasion may require.

The inhabitants are governed entirely by the British law, and are generally peaceable and willing to abide by the decisions of their civil magistrates. Governor Columbine lately issued a proclamation in which he offers the protection of these laws to any slave who may arrive in the colony with the consent of his or her owners, and leaves them at liberty to remain or go elsewhere, as they may think proper.

On the 18th of the 3d month, I travelled in amongst the natives of Africa. The first tribe I met with was called the Bullone Tribe. Their king, whose name is George, appeared to be very friendly. He could speak but very little English himself, but had a young man with him by the name of Peter Wilson who received his education in England, and appeared to be a man of very good information. This tribe, from what I could gather have adopted the mode of circumcission, and seem to acknowledge by words the existence of a Deity. So accustomed are they to wars and slavery that I apprehend it would be a difficult task to convince them of the impropriety of these pernicious practices. I gave the king a Testament and several other books, and let him know by the interpreter the useful records contained in those books, and the great fountain they pointed unto.

The Mendingo Tribe professes Mahometanism. I became acquainted with two men of this tribe who were apparently men of considerable learning; indeed this tribe generally, appeared to be a people of some education. Their learning appeared to be the Arabic. They do not allow spirituous liquors to be made use of in this tribe. They have declined the practice of selling their own tribe; but notwithstanding this, they continue to sell those of other tribes, and thought it hard that the traffic in slaves should be abolished, as they were made poor in consequence thereof. As they themselves were not willing to submit to the bonds of slavery, I endeavoured to hold this out as a light to convince them of their error. But the prejudice of education had taken too firm hold of their minds to admit of much effect from reason on this subject.

# Address

*To my scattered brethren and fellow countrymen at Sierra Leone.*
Grace be unto you and peace be multiplied from God our Father, and from the Lord Jesus Christ, who hath begotten a lively hope in remembrance of you; and for which I desire ever to be humbled, world without end. Amen.
*Dearly beloved friends and fellow countrymen,*
I earnestly recommend to you the propriety of assembling yourselves together for the purpose of worshipping the Lord your God. God is a spirit, and they that worship him acceptably must worship him in spirit and in truth, in so doing you will find a living hope which will be as an anchor to the soul and support under afflictions. In this hope, may Ethiopia stretch out her hand unto God. Come, my African brethren and fellow countrymen, let us walk together in the light of the Lord—That pure light which bringeth salvation into the world, hath appeared unto all men to profit withall. I would recommend unto all the saints, and elders, and sober people of the colony, that you adopt the mode of meeting together once every month in order to consult with each other for your mutual good. But above all things, let your meetings be owned of the Lord, for he hath told us that "where two or three are gathered together in his name, there he would be in the midst of them". And I would recommend that you keep a record of your proceedings at those meetings in order that they may be left for the benefit of the young and rising generation. In these meetings let it be your care to promote all good and laudable institutions, and by so doing you will increase both your temporal and spiritual welfare. That the Prince of Peace may be your preserver, is the sincere desire of one who wishes well to all mankind.

PAUL CUFFE.

The following advice, though detached from the foregoing address, appears to be intended to accompany it.

## ADVICE

First. That sobriety and steadfastness, with all faithfulness, be recommended, that so professors may be good examples in all things; doing justly, loving mercy, and walking humbly.

Secondly. That early care be extended towards the youth, whilst their minds are young and tender, that so they may be redeemed from the corruptions of the world—such as nature is prone to —swearing, following bad company and drinking of spirituous liquors. That they may be kept out of idleness, and encouraged to be industrious, for this is good to cultivate the mind, and may you be good examples therein yourselves.

Thirdly. May servants be encouraged to discharge their duty with faithfulness; may they be brought up to industry; may their minds be cultivated for the reception of the good seed, which is promised to all that will seek after it. I want that we should be faithful in all things, that so we may become a people, giving satisfaction to those, who have borne the heat and burden of the day, in liberating us from a state of slavery I must leave you in the hands of him who is able to preserve you through time, and to crown you with that blessing that is prepared for all those who are faithful unto death.

Farewell, PAUL CUFFE.

**Catalogue of the families on board the Brig.** *Traveller* **going from America for Sierra Leon in Africa sailed 12 month 10 1815 from Westport.**

| | |
|---|---|
| Perry Locks | 30 years old |
| Margaret Locks | 30 ditto |
| John Locks | 11 ditto |
| William Locks | 9 ditto |
| Maryann Locks | 7 ditto |
| Sarah Locks | 5 |
| | |
| Thomas Jarvis | 50 years old |
| Judiath Jarvis | 40 years old |
| Judaith Jarvis | under 11 years old |
| Thomas Jarvis, Jr. | 9 years old |
| Alexander Jarvis | 7 ditto |
| Edward Jarvis | 5 years old |

C

| | |
|---|---|
| Sarah Ann Jarvis | 1½ ditto |
| William Guinn | about 60 years old |
| Elizabeth Guinn | 56 ditto |
| Nancy Guinn | 17 ditto |
| | |
| Peter Willcox | 40 years old |
| Cloe Willcox | 34 ditto |
| Eliza Willcox | 11 ditto |
| Sarah Willcox | 8 ditto |
| Caroline Willcox | 6 ditto |
| Clarise Willcox | 4 ditto |
| Sushanah Willcox | 8 months |
| | |
| Samuel Hewes | 50 years old |
| Ann Hewes | 40 ditto |
| Nancy Hewes | 14 ditto |
| Samuel Hewes | 10 ditto |
| Sarah Hewes | 6 ditto |
| Eliza Ann Hewes | 1½ ditto |
| | |
| Antone Servenee | 45 years old |
| Elizabeth Servenee | 45 ditto |
| | |
| Robart Rigsby | 36 years old |
| Ann Rigsby | 36 ditto |
| Catherine Booath | 12 ditto |
| | |
| Samuel Wilson | 36 years old |
| Barbery Wilson | 28 about — |
| | |
| Charles Calumbine | 50 about |
| Judith Calumbine | ditto |

# Martin Delany,
## 1812–1885

Martin Delany was born in Charleston, Virginia, of African parents; his father was a Golah and his mother was a Mandingo. Delany's earliest instruction came from a Yankee pedlar. In 1822 his mother moved the family to Pennsylvania, where in the 1830's he began the study of medicine under Dr. Andrew M. McDowell. In 1850 he entered Harvard Medical School for one year.

Martin Delany was always ardently proud of his birth and race. Frederick Douglass once said of him, "I have always thanked God for making me a man, but Martin Delany always thanks God for making him a black man." His racial interests always competed with his interest in medicine. In 1843 in Pittsburgh, Delany started a weekly, *The Mystery*, because he felt Negroes were never able to get their works published in other journals. In 1848 Delany was mobbed in Ohio as an abolitionist. Though ardently anti-slavery and pro-Africa, Delany was not in sympathy with the "Liberation Experiment". In 1854 he published a "Call for a National Emigration Convention", which met in August of that year in Cleveland, Ohio. As a result of its deliberations, Dr. Delany set sail in May, 1859 on the *Mendi*, a boat owned by three African merchants, to lead the Niger Valley Exploring Party to Africa, where he remained for one year, negotiating for land and for the settlement of American Negroes. Excerpts from his *Official Report of the Niger Valley Exploring Party* (1861) are included in this anthology.

Dr. Delany served in the Civil War and was mustered out as a major in 1865. After the War, he worked for three years for the Freedmen's Bureau, and later as an inspector in the Customs House and Trial Justice for four years in Charleston, South Carolina. In 1874 he was the unsuccessful independent Republican candidate for governor of South Carolina.

21

A PROJECT FOR AN EXPEDITION OF ADVENTURE, TO THE
EASTERN COAST OF AFRICA*

## APPENDIX

## Martin Robison Delany

Every people should be the originators of their own designs, the projector of their own schemes, and creators of the events that lead to their destiny—the consummation of their desires.

Situated as we are, in the United States, many, and almost insurmountable obstacles present themselves. We are four-and-a-half millions in numbers, free and bond; six hundred thousand free, and three-and-a-half millions bond.

We have native hearts and virtues, just as other nations; which in their pristine purity are noble, potent, and worthy of example. We are a nation within a nation—as the Poles in Russia, the Hungarians in Austria, the Welsh, Irish, and Scotch in the British dominions.

But we have been, by our oppressors, despoiled of our purity, and corrupted in our native characteristics, so that we have inherited their vices, and but few of their virtues, leaving us in character, really a *broken people*.

Being distinguished by complexion, we are still singled out—although having merged in the habits and customs of our oppressors —as a distinct nation of people; as the Poles, Hungarians, Irish, and others, who still retain their native peculiarities, of language, habits, and various other traits. The claims of no people, according to established policy and usage, are respected by any nation, until they are presented in a national capacity.

To accomplish so great and desirable an end, there should be held, a great representative gathering of the colored people of the United States; not what is termed a National Convention, represented en masse, such as have been, for the last few years, held at various times and places; but a true representation of the intelligence and wisdom of the colored freemen; because it will be futile and an utter failure, to attempt such a project without the highest grade of intelligence.

* From Martin Delany, *The Condition, Elevation, Emigration and Destiny of the Colored People of the United States, Politically Considered*, Philadelphia, 1852.

No great project was ever devised without the consultation of the most mature intelligence, and discreet discernment and precaution.

To effect this, and prevent intrusion and improper representation, there should be a CONFIDENTIAL COUNCIL held; and circulars issued, only to such persons as shall be *known* to the projectors to be equal to the desired object.

The authority from whence the call should originate, to be in this wise:—The originator of the scheme, to impart the contemplated Confidential Council, to a limited number of known, worthy gentlemen, who agreeing with the project, endorse at once the scheme, when becoming joint proprietors in interest, issue a *Confidential Circular*, leaving blanks for *date, time*, and *place of holding* the Council; sending them to trusty, worthy, and suitable colored freemen, in all parts of the United States, and the Canadas, inviting them to attend; who when met in Council, have the right to project any scheme they may think proper for the general good of the whole people—provided, that the project is laid before them after its maturity.

By this Council to be appointed, a Board of Commissioners, to consist of three, five, or such reasonable number as may be decided upon, one of whom shall be chosen as Principal or Conductor of the Board, whose duty and business shall be, to go on an expedition to the EASTERN COAST OF AFRICA, to make researches for a suitable location on that section of the coast, for the settlement of colored adventurers from the United States, and elsewhere. Their mission should be to all such places as might meet the approbation of the people; as South America, Mexico, the West Indies, &c.

The Commissioners all to be men of decided qualifications; to embody among them, the qualifications of physician, botanist, chemist, geologist, geographer, and surveyor,—having a sufficient knowledge of these sciences, for practical purposes.

Their business shall be, to make a topographical, geographical, geological, and botanical examination, into such part or parts as they may select, with all other useful information that may be obtained; to be recorded in a journal kept for that purpose.

The Council shall appoint a permanent Board of Directors, to manage and supervise the doings of the Commissioners, and to whom they shall be amenable for their doings, who hold their office until successors shall be appointed.

A National Confidential Council, to be held once in three years; and sooner, if necessity or emergency should demand it; the Board of Directors giving at least three months' notice, by circulars and news-

23

papers. And should they fail to perform their duty, twenty-five of the representatives from any six States, of the former Council, may issue a call, authentically bearing their names, as sufficient authority for such a call. But when the Council is held for the reception of the report of the Commissioners, a general mass convention should then take place, by popular representation.

### MANNER OF RAISING FUNDS

The National Council shall appoint one or two Special Commissioners, to England and France, to solicit, in the name of the Representatives of a Broken Nation, of four-and-a-half millions, the necessary outfit and support, for any period not exceeding three years, of such an expedition. Certainly, what England and France would do, for a little nation—mere nominal nation, of five thousand civilized Liberians, they would be willing and ready to do, for five millions; if they be but authentically represented, in a national capacity. What was due to Greece, enveloped by Turkey, should be due to Us, enveloped by the United States; and we believe would be respected, if properly presented. To England and France, we should look for sustenance, and the people of those two nations—as they would have everything to gain from such an adventure and eventual settlement on the EASTERN COAST OF AFRICA—the opening of an immense trade being the consequence. The whole Continent is rich in minerals, and the most precious metals, as but a superficial notice of the topographical and geological reports from that country plainly show to any mind versed in the least, in the science of the earth.

The Eastern Coast of Africa has long been neglected, and never but little known, even to the ancients; but has ever been our choice part of the Continent. Bounded by the Red Sea, Arabian Sea, and Indian Ocean, it presents the greatest facilities for an immense trade, with China, Japan, Siam, Hindoostan, in short, all the East Indies— of any other country in the world. With a settlement of enlightened freemen, who with the immense facilities, must soon grow into a powerful nation. In the Province of Berbera, south of the Strait of Babelmandel, or the great pass, from the Arabian to the Red Sea, the whole commerce of the East must touch this point.

Also, a great rail road could be constructed from here, running with the Mountains of the Moon, clearing them entirely, except making one mountain pass, at the western extremity of the Mountains of the Moon, and the south-eastern terminus of the Kong Mountains; entering the Province of Dahomey, and terminating on the Atlantic Ocean West; which would make the GREAT THOROUGH-FARE for all the trade with the East Indies and Eastern Coast of Africa, and the Continent of America. All the world would pass through Africa upon this rail road, which would yield a revenue infinitely greater than any other investment in the world.

The means for prosecuting such a project—as stupendous as it may appear—will be fully realised in the prosecution of the work. Every mile of the road, will thrice pay for itself, in the development of the rich treasures that now lie hidden in the bowels of the earth. There is no doubt, that in some one section of twenty-five miles, the developments of gold would more than pay the expenses of any one thousand miles of the work. This calculation may, to those who have never given this subject a thought, appear extravagant, and visionary; but to one who has had his attention in this direction for years, it is clear enough. But a few years will witness a development of gold, precious metals, and minerals in Eastern Africa, the Moon and Kong Mountains, ten-fold greater than all the rich productions of California.

There is one great physiological fact in regard to the colored race—which, while it may not apply to all colored persons, is true of those having black skins—that they can bear *more different* climates than the white race. They bear *all* the temperates and extremes, while the other can only bear the temperates and *one* of the extremes. The black race is endowed with natural properties, that adapt and fit them for temperate, cold, and hot climates; while the white race is only endowed with properties that adapt them to temperate and cold climates; being unable to stand the warmer climates; in them, the white race cannot work, but become perfectly indolent, requiring somebody to work for them—and these, are always people of the black race.

The black race may be found, inhabiting in healthful improvement, every part of the globe where the white race reside; while there are parts of the globe where the black race reside, that the white race cannot live in health.

What part of mankind is the "denizen of every soil, and the lord of terrestrial creation", if it be not the black race? The Creator has indisputably adopted us for the "denizens of *every soil*", all that is left for us to do, is to *make* ourselves the "*lords* of terrestrial creation". The land is ours—there it lies with inexhaustible resources; let us go and possess it. In Eastern Africa must rise up a nation, to whom all the world must pay commercial tribute.

25

# Report of the Niger Valley Exploring Party

## MARTIN ROBISON DELANY

. . . At an Executive Council Meeting of the Board, September 1st, 1858, the following resolution, as taken from the Minutes, was adopted: That Dr. Martin R. Delany, of Chatham, Kent County, Canada West, be a Commissioner to explore in Africa, with full power to choose his own colleagues.

### SECTION III

### HISTORY OF THE PROJECT

. . . In the winter of 1831–2, being then but a youth, I formed the design of going to Africa, the land of my ancestry; when in the succeeding winter of 1832–3, having then fully commenced to study, I entered into a solemn promise with the Rev. Molliston Madison Clark, then a student in Jefferson College, at Cannonsburg, Washington County, Pennsylvania, being but seventeen miles from Pittsburgh, where I resided (his vacations being spent in the latter place), to complete an education, and go on an independent and voluntary mission—to travel in Africa—I as a physician and he as a clergyman, for which he was then preparing.

During these vacations of about seven weeks each, Mr. Clark was of great advantage to me in my studies, he being then a man of probably thirty years of age, or more, and in his senior year (I think) at college.

This design I never abandoned, although in common with my race in America, I espoused the cause, and contended for our political and moral elevation on equality with the whites, believing then, as I do now, that merit alone should be the test of individual claims in the body politic. This cause I never have nor will abandon; believing that no man should hesitate or put off any duty for another time or place, but "act, act in the *living present*, act," *now* or *then*. This has been the rule of my life, and I hope ever shall be.

In 1850, I had fully matured a plan for an adventure, and to a number of select intelligent gentlemen (of African descent, of course) fully committed myself in favor of it. They all agreed that the scheme was good; and although neither of them entered personally into it, all

26

fully sanctioned it, bidding me God-speed in my new adventure, as a powerful handmaid to their efforts in contending for our rights in America.

In 1854, at the great Emigration Convention in Cleveland, my paper, read and adopted as a "Report on the Political Destiny of the Colored Race on the American Continent," set forth fully my views on the advantages of Emigration.

Although the Call itself strictly prohibits the introduction of the question of emigration from the American Continent or Western Hemisphere, the qualification which directly follows—"This restriction has no reference to *personal* preference, or *individual* enterprise"—may readily be understood. It was a mere policy on the part of the authors of those documents, to confine their scheme to America (including the West Indies), whilst they were the leading advocates of the regeneration of Africa, lest they compromised themselves and their people to the avowed enemies of the race.

The Convention (at Cleveland, 1854), in its Secret Sessions made, Africa, with its rich, inexhaustible productions, and great facilities for checking the abominable Slave Trade, its most important point of dependence, though each individual was left to take the direction which in his judgment best suited him. Though our great gun was leveled, and the first shell thrown at the American Continent, driving a slaveholding faction into despair, and a political confusion from which they have been utterly unable to extricate themselves, but become more and more complicated every year, *Africa was held in reserve, until by the help of an All-wise Providence we could effect what has just been accomplished with signal success*—a work which the most sanguine friend of the cause believed would require at least the half of a century.

. . . Immediately after the convention of 1856, from which I was absent by sickness, I commenced a general correspondence with individuals, imparting to each the basis of my adventure to Africa to obtain intelligent colleagues. During this time (the Spring of 1857), "Bowen's Central Africa" was published giving an interesting and intelligent account of that extensive portion of Africa known on the large missionary map of that continent as Yoruba. Still more encouraged to carry out my scheme at this juncture, Livingstone's great work on Africa made its appearance, which seemed to have stimulated the Africo-Americans in many directions, among others, those of Wisconsin, from whom Mr. Jonathan J. Myers, a very respectable grocer, was delegated as their chairman to counsel me on the subject. In the several councils held between Mr. Myers and

27

myself, it was agreed and understood that I was to embody their cause and interests in my mission to Africa, they accepting of the policy of my scheme.

At this time, I made vigourous efforts to accomplish my design, and for this purpose, among others, endeavoured to obtain goods in Philadelphia to embark for Loando de St. Paul, the Portuguese colony in Loango, South Africa, where the prospect seemed fair for a good trade in bees-wax and ivory, though Lagos, West Central Africa, was my choice and destination.

. . . I had but one object in view—the Moral, Social, and Political Elevation of Ourselves, and the Regeneration of Africa, for which I desired, as a *preference*, and indeed the only *adequate* and *essential* means by which it is to be accomplished, men of African descent, properly qualified and of pure and fixed principles. These I endeavored to select by corresponding only with such of my acquaintances.

At the Council which appointed me Commissioner to Africa, having presented the names of Messrs. Douglass and Campbell, asking that they also might be chosen; at a subsequent meeting the following action took place:

Whereas, Dr. Martin R. Delany, Commissioner to Africa, having presented the names of Messrs. Robert Douglass and Robert Campbell of Philadelphia, Pa., U.S., requesting that they be appointed Commissioners, the Board having made him Chief Commissioner with full power to appoint his own Assistants, do hereby sanction the appointment of these gentlemen as Assistant Commissioners.

A paper was then laid before the Council, presenting the name and scheme of the party, which was received and adopted.

### THE NIGER VALLEY EXPLORING PARTY

The object of this Expedition is to make a Topographical, Geological and Geographical Examination of the Valley of the River Niger, in Africa, and an inquiry into the state and condition of the people of that Valley, and other parts of Africa, together with such other scientific inquiries as may by them be deemed expedient, for the purposes of science and for general information; and without any reference to, and with the Board being entirely opposed to any Emigration there as such. Provided, however, that nothing in this Instrument be so construed as to interfere with the right of the Commissioners to negotiate in their own behalf, or that of any other parties, or organization for territory.

The Chief-Commissioner is hereby authorized to add one or more competent Commissioners to their number; it being agreed and understood that this organization is, and is to be exempted from the pecuniary responsibility of sending out this expedition.

Dated at the Office of the Executive Council, Chatham, county of Kent, Province of Canada, this Thirtieth day of August, in the year of our Lord, One Thousand Eight Hundred and Fifty-eight.

By the President,
WILLIAM HOWARD DAY.
ISAAC D. SHADD, *Vice-President*.
GEORGE W. BRODIE, *Secretary*.

So soon as these names with their destined mission were officially published, there arose at once from mistaken persons (*white*) in Philadelphia, a torrent of opposition, who presuming to know more about us (the blacks) and our own business than we did ourselves, went even so far as to speak to one of our party, and tell him that we were *not ready* for any such *important* undertaking, nor could be in *three years yet to come*! Of course, as necessary to sustain this, it was followed up with a dissertation on the *disqualification* of the Chief of the Party, mentally and physically, *external* appearances and all. So effectually was this opposition prosecuted, that colored people in many directions in the United States and the Canadas, were not only affected by it, but a "Party" of three had already been chosen and appointed to supersede us! Even without any knowledge on my part, claims were made in England in behalf of the "Niger Valley Exploring Party", solely through the instrumentality of these Philadelphians.

Such were the effects of this, that our preparatory progress was not only seriously retarded (I having to spend eight months in New York city to counteract the influence, where six weeks only would have been required), but three years originally intended to be spent in exploring had to be reduced to one, and the number of Commissioners from five to two, thereby depriving Mr. Robert Douglass from going. . . .

SECTION XI

WHAT AFRICA NOW REQUIRES

. . . From the foregoing, it is very evident that missionary duty has reached its *ultimatum*. . . .

. . . It is clear, then, that essential to the success of civilization, is

29

the establishment of all those social relations and organizations, without which enlightened communities cannot exist. To be successful, these must be carried out by proper agencies, and these agencies must be a *new element* introduced into their midst, possessing all the attainments, socially and politically, morally and religiously, adequate to so important an end. This element must be *homogeneous* in all the *natural* characteristics, claims, sentiments, and sympathies—*the descendants of Africa* being the only element that can effect it. To this end, then, a part of the most enlightened of that race in America design to carry out these most desirable measures by the establishment of social and industrial settlements among them, in order at once to introduce, in an effective manner, all the well-regulated pursuits of civilized life.

That no mis-step be taken and fatal error committed at the commencement, we have determined that the persons to compose this new element to be introduced into Africa, shall be well and most carefully selected in regard to moral integrity, intelligence, acquired attainments, fitness, adaptation, and, as far as practicable, religious sentiments and professions. We are serious in this; and, so far as we are concerned as an individual, it shall be restricted to the letter, and we will most strenuously oppose and set our face against any attempt from any quarter to infringe upon this arrangement and design. Africa is our fatherland and we its legitimate descendants, and we will never agree nor consent to see this—the first voluntary step that has ever been taken for her regeneration by her own descendants—blasted by a disinterested or renegade set, whose only object might be in the one case to get rid of a portion of the colored population, and in the other, make money, though it be done upon the destruction of every hope entertained and measure introduced for the accomplishment of this great and prospectively glorious undertaking. We cannot and will not permit or agree that the result of years of labor and anxiety shall be blasted at one reckless blow, by those who have never spent a day in the cause of our race, or know nothing about our wants and requirements. The descendants of Africa in North America will doubtless, by the census of 1860, reach five millions; those of Africa may number two hundred millions. I have outgrown, long since, the boundaries of North America, and with them have also outgrown the boundaries of their claims. I, therefore, cannot consent to sacrifice the prospects of two hundred millions, that a fraction of five millions may be benefitted, especially since the measures adopted for the many must necessarily benefit the few.

Africa, to become regenerated, must have a national character, and her position among the existing nations of the earth will depend mainly upon the high standard she may gain compared with them in all her relations, morally, religiously, socially, politically, and commercially.

I have determined to leave to my children the inheritance of a country, the possession of territorial domain, the blessings of a national education, and the indisputable right of self-government; that they may not succeed to the servility and degradation bequeathed to us by our fathers. If we have not been born to fortunes, we should impart the seeds which shall germinate and give birth to fortunes for them.

# Free Negroes

The considerable literature on "free Negroes" makes very clear that their position was precarious, particularly in the slave and border states. In the south their very existence was a threat to the institution of slavery, and they shared with poor whites the problems of competing with slave labour. A few surmounted these problems and owned slaves themselves. A considerably larger number made a comfortable living as skilled labourers and craftsmen.

But, if free Negroes were a threat to slavery, the obverse was equally true. They could not escape the daily fear that someone would challenge their freedom, and there were instances of free Negroes being handcuffed and sold into slavery. Indeed, there are many reasons why freedom elsewhere might seem more desirable than freedom anywhere in the United States. But, the desire to use colonization, especially in Africa, as a means of seducing free Negroes from this country was bitterly resented by many leaders, of whom Frederick Douglass was the outstanding example. Other leaders like Martin Delany and Henry Highland Garnett were, however, able to separate the needs and advantages of Africa for American Negroes from the questionable intentions of the promoters of the American Colonization Society.

The issue took various forms and localized around various events in different states. The problem was particularly acute in Maryland, where in 1830, 52,938 free Negroes comprised the largest community of this class in the country. In 1752 Maryland had passed legislation restricting manumission of slaves, yet the non-slave element of the population continued to grow. Frightened by the Nat Turner slave

31

revolt in 1831 in nearby Virginia, Maryland immediately adopted a plan of colonizing all free Negroes in Africa, but apparently public sentiment was not behind implementing this legislation, partly because of the persistent need for black labour power. 2,350 manumissions were registered with the authorities between 1831 and 1845, but only 70 per cent of those manumitted were sent to Africa.

The statement of the Free Persons of Colour included in this anthology reflects one segment of the thinking of free Negroes as to their future at this time in this country.

# A Memorial from the Free People of Colour to the Citizens of Baltimore*

We have hitherto beheld, in silence, but with the intensest interest, the efforts of the wise and philanthropic in our behalf. If it became us to be silent, it became us also to feel the liveliest anxiety and gratitude. The time has now arrived, as we believe, in which your work and our happiness may be promoted by the expression of our opinions. We have therefore assembled for that purpose, from every quarter of the City and every denomination, to offer you this respectful address, with all the weight and influence which our number, character and cause can lend it.

We reside among you, and yet are strangers; natives, and yet not citizens; surrounded by the freest people and most republican institutions in the world, and yet enjoying none of the immunities of freedom. This singularity in our condition has not failed to strike us as well as you: but we know it is irremediable here. Our difference of colour, the servitude of many and most of our brethren, and the prejudices which those circumstances have naturally occasioned, will not allow us to hope, even if we could desire, to mingle with you one day, in the benefits of citizenship. As long as we remain among you, we must (and shall) be content to be a distinct caste, exposed to the indignities and dangers, physical and moral, to which our situation makes us liable. All that we may expect, is to merit by our peaceable and orderly behaviour, your consideration and the protection of your laws.

It is not to be imputed to you that we are here. Your ancestors remonstrated against the introduction of the first of our race, who were brought amongst you; and it was the mother country that insisted on their admission, that her colonies and she might profit, as she thought, by their compulsory labour. But the gift was a curse to them, without being an advantage to herself. The colonies, grown to womanhood, burst from her dominion; and if they have an angry recollection of their union and rupture, it must be at the sight of the baneful institution which she has entailed upon them.

* From *African Repository and Colonial Journal*, published by order of The Managers of the American Colonization Society, Washington, D.C., 1827, Volume II, pp. 295–299.

How much you regret its existence among you, is shewn by the severe laws you have enacted against the slave-trade, and by your employment of a naval force for its suppression. You have gone still further. Not content with checking the increase of the already too growing evil, you have deliberated how you might best exterminate the evil itself. This delicate and important subject has produced a great variety of opinions; but we find, even in that diversity, a consolatory proof of the interest with which you regard the subject, and of your readiness to adopt that scheme which may appear to be the best.

Leaving out all considerations of generosity, humanity and benevolence, you have the strongest reasons to favour and facilitate the withdrawal from among you of such as wish to remove. It ill consists, in the first place, with your republican principles and with the health and moral sense of the body politic, that there should be in the midst of you an extraneous mass of men, united to you only by soil and climate, and irrevocably excluded from your institutions. Nor is it less for your advantage in another point of view. Our places might, in your opinion, be better occupied by men of your own colour, who would increase the strength of your country. In the pursuit of livelihood and the exercise of industrious habits, we necessarily exclude from employment many of the whites—your fellow-citizens, who would find it easier in proportion as we depart, to provide for themselves and their families.

But if *you* have every reason to wish for our removal, how much greater are *our* inducements to remove! Though we are not slaves, we are not free. We do not, and never shall participate in the enviable privileges which we continually witness. Beyond a mere subsistence, and the impulse of religion, there is nothing to arouse us to the exercise of our faculties, or excite us to the attainment of eminence. Though under the shield of your laws we are partially protected, not totally oppressed; nevertheless, our situation will and must inevitably have the effect of crushing, not developing the capacities that God has given us. We are, besides, of opinion, that our absence will accelerate the liberation of such of our brethren as are in bondage, by the permission of Providence. When such of us as wish, and may be able, shall have gone before to open and lead the way, a channel will be left, through which may be poured such as hereafter receive their freedom from the kindness or interests of their masters, or by public opinion and legislative enactment, and who are willing to join those who have preceded them. As a white population comes into fill our void, the situation of our brethren will be nearer to liberty;

34

for their value must decrease and disappear before the superior advantages of free labour, with which their's can hold no competition.

Of the many schemes that have been proposed, we most approve of that of *African Colonization*. If we were able and at liberty to go whithersoever we would, the greater number, willing to leave this community, would prefer LIBERIA, on the coast of Africa. Others, no doubt, would turn them towards some other region: the world is wide. Already, established there in the settlement of the American Colonization Society, are many of our brethren, the pioneers of African Restoration, who encourage us to join them. Several were formerly residents of this City, and highly considered by the people of their own class and colour. They have been planted at Cape Montserado, the most eligible and one of the most elevated sites on the western coast of Africa, selected in 1821; and their number has augmented to five hundred. Able, as we are informed, to provide for their own defence and support, and capable of self-increase, they are now enjoying all the necessaries and comforts and many of the luxuries of larger and older communities. In Africa we shall be freemen indeed, and republicans, after the model of this republic. We shall carry your language, your customs, your opinions and christianity to that now desolate shore, and thence they will gradually spread, with our growth, far into the continent. The slave-trade, both external and internal, can be abolished only by settlements on the coast. Africa, if destined to be ever civilized and converted, can be civilized and converted by that means only.

We foresee that difficulties and dangers await those who emigrate, such as every infant establishment must encounter and endure; such as your fathers suffered when first they landed on this now happy shore. They will have to contend, we know, with the want of many things which they enjoyed here; and they leave a populous and polished society for a land where they must long continue to experience the solitude and ruggedness of an early settlement. But "Ethiopia shall lift her hands unto God". Africa is the only country to which they can go and enjoy those privileges for which they leave their firesides among you. The work has begun, and it is continuing. A foothold has been obtained, and the principal obstacles are overcome. The foundations of a nation have been laid, of which they are to be the fathers.

The portion of comforts which they may lose, they will cheerfully abandon. Human happiness does not consist in meat and drink, nor in costly raiment, nor in stately habitations: to contribute to

D

it even, they must be joined with equal rights and respectability; and it often exists in a high degree without them. If the sufferings and privations to which the emigrants would be exposed were even greater than we imagine, still they would not hesitate to sacrifice their own personal and temporary ease, for the permanent advantage of their race, and the future prosperity and dignified existence of their children.

That you may facilitate the withdrawal from among you of such as wish to remove, is what we now solicit. It can best be done, we think, by augmenting the means at the command of the American Colonization Society, that the Colony of Liberia may be strengthened and improved for their gradual reception. The greater the number of persons sent thither, from any part of this nation whatsoever, so much the more capable it becomes of receiving a still greater. Every encouragement to it therefore, though it may not seem to have any particular portion of emigrants directly in view, will produce a favourable effect upon all. The emigrants may readily be enabled to remove, in considerable numbers every fall, by a concerted system of individual contributions, and still more efficiently by the enactment of laws to promote their emigration, under the patronage of the State. The expense would not be nearly so great as it might appear at first sight; for when once the current shall have set towards Liberia, and intercourse grown frequent, the cost will of course diminish rapidly, and many will be able to defray it for themselves. Thousands and tens of thousands poorer than we, annually emigrate from Europe to your country, and soon have it in their power to hasten the arrival of those they left behind. Every intelligent and industrious coloured man would continually look forward to the day, when he or his children might go to their veritable home, and would accumulate all his little earnings for that purpose.

We have ventured these remarks, because we know that you take a kind concern in the subject to which they relate, and because we think they may assist you in the prosecution of your designs. If we were doubtful of your good will and benevolent intentions, we would remind you of the time when you were in a situation similar to ours, and when your forefathers were driven, by religious persecution, to a distant and inhospitable shore. We are not so persecuted, but we, too, leave our homes, and seek a distant and inhospitable shore: an empire may be the result of our emigration, as of their's. The protection, kindness and assistance which you would have desired for yourselves under such circumstances, now extend to us: so may you be rewarded by the riddance of the stain of slavery, the extension of civilization and the Gospel, and the blessing of our common Creator!

WILLIAM CORNISH,
*Chairman of the meeting*
*in Bethel Church.*
ROBERT COWLEY,
*Secretary of the meeting*
*in Bethel Church.*
JAMES DEAVER,
*Chairman of the meeting*
*in the African Church,*
*Sharp street.*
REMUS HARVEY,
*Secretary of the meeting*
*in the African Church,*
*Sharp street.*

# Frederick Douglass,
# 1817–1895

Frederick Douglass was the foremost Negro in the anti-slavery movement. Cruelly treated as a young slave on the eastern shore of Maryland, where he was born, he was removed to Baltimore, where the wife of his new master taught him his letters. Later Douglass ran away and settled for a time in New Bedford, Massachusetts. Here he joined the Garrisonian branch of the abolition movement. Beginning in 1843 he carried the abolition message to many states of the Union and abroad. In England abolitionist sympathizers raised money with which Douglass procured his freedom.

Returning to the United States, Douglass founded his own paper, *The North Star* (later *The Frederick Douglass Paper*), in 1848. It was in continuous publication until 1863 and was recognized as a unique abolitionist journal. But Douglass himself was unique; he was for women's rights, organized labour, and prison reform, as well as for abolition. He was unequivocal in his stand against the Negro Colonization movement, as is revealed in the first of the two excerpts from his speeches which follow.

# Colonization*

In view of this proposition, we would respectfully suggest to the assembled wisdom of the nation, that it might be well to ascertain the number of free colored people who will be likely to need the assistance of government to help them out of this country to Liberia, or elsewhere, beyond the limits of these United States—since this course might save any embarrassment which would result from an appropriation more than commensurate to the numbers who might be disposed to leave this, our own country, for one we know not of. We are of opinion that the *free* colored people generally mean to live in America, and not in Africa; and to appropriate a large sum for our removal, would merely be a waste of the public money. We do not mean to go to Liberia. Our minds are made up to live here if we can, or die here if we must; so every attempt to remove us, will be, as it ought to be, labor lost. Here we are and here we shall remain. While our brethren are in bondage on these shores; it is idle to think of inducing any considerable number of the free colored people to quit this for a foreign land.

For two hundred and twenty-eight years has the colored man toiled over the soil of America, under a burning sun and a driver's lash—plowing, planting, reaping, that white men might roll in ease, their hands unhardened by labor, and their brows unmoistened by the waters of genial toil; and now that the moral sense of mankind is beginning to revolt at this system of foul treachery and cruel wrong, and is demanding its overthrow, the mean and cowardly oppressor is mediating plans to expel the colored man entirely from the country. Shame upon the guilty wretches that dare propose, and all that countenance such a proposition. We live here—have lived here—have a right to live here, and mean to live here.—F. D.

* *The North Star*, January 26, 1849. Reprinted by kind permission of International Publishers, New York, from *The Life and Writings of Frederick Douglass* by Philip S. Foner, 1950, Volume I, pp. 350–2.

*Excerpt from:*

## The Right to Criticize American Institutions—speech before the American Anti-Slavery Society, May, 11, 1847*

I cannot agree with my friend Mr. Garrison, in relation to my love and attachment to this land. I have no love for America, as such; I have no patriotism. I have no country. What country have I? The institutions of this country do not know me, do not recognize me as a man. I am not thought of, spoken of, in any direction, out of the anti-slavery ranks, as a man. I am not thought of, or spoken of, except as a piece of property belonging to some *Christian* slave-holder, and all the religious and political institutions of this country, alike pronounce me a slave and a chattel. Now, in such a country as this, I cannot have patriotism. The only thing that links me to this land is my family, and the painful consciousness that here there are three millions of my fellow-creatures, groaning beneath the iron rod of the worst despotism that could be devised, even in Pandemonium; that here are men and brethren, who are identified with me by . . . stripes upon their backs, their inhuman wrongs and cruel sufferings. This, and this only, attaches me to this land, and brings me here to plead with you, and with this country at large, for the disenthralment of my oppressed countrymen, and to overthrow this system of Slavery which is crushing them to the earth. How can I love a country that dooms three millions of my brethren, some of them my own kindred, my own brothers, my own sisters, who are now clanking the chains of Slavery upon the plains of the South, whose warm blood is now making fat the soil of Maryland and of Alabama, and over whose crushed spirits rolls the dark shadow of oppression, shutting out and extinguishing forever, the cheering rays of that bright sun of Liberty lighted in the souls of all God's children by the Omnipotent hand of Deity itself? How can I, I say, love a country thus cursed, thus bedewed with the blood of my brethren? A country, the Church of which, and the Government of which, and the Constitution of which, is in favour of supporting and perpetuating this monstrous system of injustice and blood? I have not, I cannot have, any love for this

* Reprinted by kind permission of International Publishers, New York, from *The Life and Writings of Frederick Douglass*, by Philip S. Foner, 1950, Volume I, pp. 236–7.

country, as such, or for its Constitution. I desire to see its overthrow as speedily as possible, and its Constitution shivered in a thousand fragments, rather than this foul curse should continue to remain as now. [Hisses and Cheers.]

In all this, my friends, let me make myself understood. I do not hate America as against England, or against any other country, or land. I love humanity all over the globe. I am anxious to see . . . Slavery overthrown here; but, I never appealed to Englishmen in a manner calculated to awaken feelings of hatred or disgust, or to influence their prejudices towards America as a nation, or in a manner provocative of national jealousy or ill-will; but I always appealed to their conscience—to the higher and nobler feelings of the people of that country. to enlist them in this cause. I always appealed to their manhood, that which preceded their being Englishmen, (to quote an expression of my friend Phillips,) I appealed to them as men, and I had a right to do so. They are men, and the slave is a man, and we have a right to call upon all men to assist in breaking his bonds, let them be born when, and live where they may.

# Henry McNeal Turner,
## 1834–1915

Henry McNeal Turner was born of free parents in Abbeville County, South Carolina. His maternal grandfather was an African prince and is reported to have secured his freedom in this country because of his acknowledged royal blood. Turner's early education was limited and casual, secured largely through informal instruction received from white lawyers in the court house of Abbeville, where he worked as a handyman. Turner soon left South Carolina for Baltimore and at the age of seventeen became a member of the Methodist Episcopal Church South. Having been licensed to preach in 1853, Turner was admitted to the Missouri Conference of the African Methodist Episcopal Church in 1858 and was immediately transferred to Baltimore. There Turner received further education at Trinity College and as a special student of Bishop Crimmins of the Protestant Episcopal Church. Bishop Turner was married four times, the first time in 1856 to Miss Eliza Ann Peacher of South Carolina, whose father had migrated to Liberia.

President Lincoln appointed Turner United States Chaplain to the Negro troops in the early part of 1863. After surviving several battles and skirmishes, Turner was mustered out with his regiment in the fall of 1865 and recommissioned a U.S. Chaplain of the regular army by President Johnson. After a brief period of working for the Freedmen's Bureau, he returned to the church and built up the largest conference in the A.M.E. Church in Georgia—indeed, in the world.

Turner was an active political figure most of his life. He called the first Republican State Conference in Georgia in 1867 and in the same year was elected a member of the Constitutional Convention of Georgia. The following year he was elected a member of the Georgia Legislature and re-elected in 1870. He retained his position as presiding elder in the Church until 1872.

From 1872 to 1876 Turner was pastor of churches in and around Savannah, Georgia. In 1876 he was elected by the General Conference of the A.M.E. Church as general manager of the publications department in Philadelphia, where he directed and wrote all papers and sunday school material. In spite of some opposition within the Church, especially from Bishop Payne, Turner was ordained Bishop in 1880.

In addition to his regular episcopal districts, Turner was assigned to overseas work in West Africa. He was in favour of colonization of Negroes in Africa and was a vice-president of the African Colonization Society. He established A.M.E. churches in Sierra Leone and in Liberia. In 1898 he went to Cape Town, South Africa, and opened the first A.M.E. Conference there. While in South Africa Bishop Turner started a new trend in the South African Christian Church by ordaining African ministers. During the previous one hundred and fifty years of Christian missions in South Africa very few Africans or Bantus had been ordained, as ordination was considered a privilege reserved for European or white preachers. Bishop Turner organized four Methodist Conferences in Africa during the eight years he served as the first Methodist Bishop of Africa.

Bishop Turner was the author of *Methodist Polity*, *The Negro in All Ages*, *Turner's Catechism*, *Turner's World Hymnal Book*, and *A.M.E. Musical Hymnal*. He not only edited and popularized the *Christian Recorder*, but he inspired the organization of Women's Foreign and Home Missioners Society in 1896 and was the founder of the *Southern Christian Recorder*, *Voice of the Missions*, and the *Women's Christian Recorder*. He was Senior Bishop from 1895 to 1915.

Throughout his life Bishop Turner was a strong commanding figure who was unqualified in his affection for Africa and the fostering of strong African–American Negro relations. Not infrequently he was in conflict on this point with the outstanding American Negroes who preferred, now that the Civil War was over, to think only of America and of themselves as citizens of it. Bishop Turner, more than any writer included in this anthology, related the attraction of Africa as the fatherland to the problem of the Negro in this country.

43

# Will it be Possible for the Negro to Attain, in this Country, Unto the American Type of Civilization*

## BISHOP H. M. TURNER
### D.D., LL.D., D.C.L.

This interrogatory appears to presuppose that the seventeen or more millions of colored people in North and South America are not a part of the American population, and do not constitute a part of its civilization. But the term "this country" evidently refers to the United States of America, for this being the largest and the most powerful government on the American continent, not infrequently, is made to represent the entire continent. So the Negro is regarded as a foreign and segregated race. The American people, therefore, who grade the type of American civilization are made up of white people, for the Indian, Chinamen, and the few Mexicans are not taken in account any more than the Negro is, by reason of their diminutive numbers, and not because they are regarded wanting in intellectual capacity, as the Negro is.

The above is an interrogatory that can be easily answered if the term "American" is to include the United States and the powers that enact its laws and proclaim its judicial decisions, as we have no civilization in the aggregate. Civilization contemplates that fraternity, civil and political equality between man and man, that makes his rights, privileges and immunities inviolable and sacred in the eyes and hearts of his fellows, whatever may be his nationality, language, color, hair texture, or anything else that may make an external variation.

Civility comprehends harmony, system, method, complacency, urbanity, refinement, politeness, courtesy, justice, culture, general enlightenment and protection of life and person to any man, regardless of his color or nationality. It is enough for a civilized community to know that you are a human being, to pledge surety of physical and political safety to you, and this has been the sequence in all ages

* From D. W. Culp, *Twentieth Century Negro Literature or A Cyclopedia of Thought on the Vital Topics Relating to the American Negro*, 1902, pp. 42–45.

among civilized people. But such is not the condition of things as they apply to this country, I mean the United States. True, we have a National Congress, State Legislature, Subordinate and Supreme Courts, and almost every form of government, necessary to regulate the affairs of a civilized country. But above these, and above law and order, which these legislative and judicial bodies have been organized to observe, and execute justice in the land, we are often confronted through the public press with reports of the most barbarous and cruel outrages, that can be perpetrated upon human beings, known in the history of the world. No savage nation can exceed the atrocities which are often heralded through the country and accepted by many as an incidental consequence. Men are hung, shot and burnt by bands of murderers who are almost invariably represented as the most influential and respectable citizens in the community, while the evidences of guilt of what is charged against the victims, who are so inhumanly outraged, are never established by proof in any court, and all we can learn about the guilt and horrible deeds charged upon the murdered victims comes from the mouth of the bloody handed wretches who perpetrate the murders, yet they are not known according to published accounts. But enough is known to get from their mouths some horrible statements as to why this and that brutal murder was done, and invariably, it is told with such oily tongues, and the whole narrative is polished over and glossed with such skillfully constructed lies, that the ruling millions lift up their hands in holy horror and exclaim "they done him right."

Why, the very judges surrounded with court officers are powerless before these bloody mobs. Prisoners are cruelly, fiendishly and inhumanly dragged from their very custody. Sheriffs are as helpless as newborn babes. I do not pretend to say that in no instance have the victims been guilty as a whole or in part of some blood-curdling crime, for men perpetrate lawless acts, revolting deeds, disgraceful and brutal crimes, regardless of nationality, language or color, at times. But civilization presurmises legal adjudication and the intervention of that judicial authority which civilized legislation produces. And when properly administered the accused is innocent till he gets a fair trial; no verdict of guilt from a drunken lawless mob should be accepted by a civilized country; and when they do accept it they become a barbarous people. And a barbarous people make a barbarous nation. Civilization knows no marauders, mobs or lynchers and any one adjudged guilty by a drunken band of freebooters is not guilty in the eyes of a civilized people. For the ruthless and violent perpetrators of lawless deeds, especially when they are incarnate, are murderers to all intents and purposes, and popular approval does not diminish the magnitude of the crime. Millions may say, "Well done", but God, reason and civilization stamp them as culprits.

I confess that the United States has the highest form of civilized institutions that any nation has had. Let us take a cursory glance at the institutions of this country. It has common schools by the tens of thousands; colleges and universities of every grade by the hundred; millions of daily newspapers are flying from the press, and weekly papers and monthly magazines on all imaginary subjects; it has a Congress and President, Governors and State Legislatures without end, judges, various courts and law officers in countless numbers. Hundreds of thousands of school teachers, professors, and college presidents, and Doctors of Divinity, thousands of lecturers and public declaimers on all subjects, railroads, telegraphs and telephones in such vast numbers as stagger imagination itself, churches and pulpits that are filled by at least a hundred and twenty-five thousand ministers of the gospel, and Bibles enough to build a pyramid that would almost reach to heaven; a land of books upon every subject scattered among the people by the billions, and in short, we have all the forms and paraphernalia of civilization. But no one can say, who has any respect for truth, that the United States is a civilized nation, especially if we will take the daily papers and inspect them for a few moments, and see the deeds of horror that the ruling powers of the nation say "well done" to.

I know that thousands, yea millions and tens of millions would not plead guilty of having a part in the violent and gory outrages which are often perpetrated in this country upon human beings, chiefly because they are of African descent, and are not numerically strong enough to contend with the powers in governmental control. But that is no virtue that calls for admiration. As long as they keep silent and fail to lift up their voices in protestation and declaim against it, their very silence is a world-wide acquiescence. It is practically saying, well done. There are millions of people in the country who could not stand to kill a brute, such is their nervous sensitiveness, and I have heard of persons who would not kill a snake or a bug. But they are guilty of everything the drunken mobs do, as long as they hold their silence. Men may be ever so free from the perpetration of bloody deeds, personally, but their failure to object to any outrageous crime makes them *particeps crimines*.

I forgot to say in cataloguing the crimes committed in the United States that persons for the simple color of their skins are thrust into what are called Jim Crow cars on the public highways and charged as much as those who are riding in rolling palaces with every comfort that it is possible for man to enjoy. This is simple robbery on the public highways and the nine United States judges have approved of this robbery and said, "well done", by their verdict.

Such being the barbarous condition of the United States, and the low order of civilization which controls its institutions where right and justice should sit enthroned, I see nothing for the Negro to attain unto in this country. I have already admitted that this country has books and schools, and the younger members of the Negro race, like the younger members of the white race, should attend them and profit by them. But for the Negro as a whole, I see nothing here for him to aspire after. He can return to Africa, especially to Liberia where a Negro government is already in existence, and learn the elements of civilization in fact; for human life is there sacred, and no man is deprived of it or any other thing that involves his manhood, without due process of law. So my decision is that there is nothing in the United States for the Negro to learn or try to attain to.

_- No room for advancement in U.S._
_Negro_
_- reaction to post-emancp. horrors_

# John Henry Smyth,
## 1844-1908

John Henry Smyth was born in Virginia in 1844. At about eight years of age he was sent to Philadelphia, where he attended a Quaker school, and in 1862 was graduated from the Institute of Colored Youth. After a year's independent study he was admitted to the Academy of Fine Arts in Philadelphia and in 1865 went to London to prepare for a career on the stage. Failing in this, he returned to America and entered the Howard University Law School in 1869. After graduation he held numerous government posts, including clerk in the Bureau of Refugees, Freedmen, and Abandoned Lands, the Census Department, the Revenue Department, and the Freedmen's Bank. Later he was a member of the North Carolina Constitutional Convention of 1875.

In 1879, on the recommendations of Frederick Douglass, B. K. Bruce, and M. W. Ransom, Smyth was appointed by President Hayes as Minister Resident and Consul General to Liberia. Before he was recalled by President Garfield, Smyth served successfully for four years in Liberia, being reappointed in 1882 by President Arthur. Smyth was awarded the LL.D. by Liberia College and appointed Knight Commander of the Liberia Order of African Redemption by His Excellency H. Richard Wright Johnson, President of the Republic of Liberia.

## The African in Africa
## and the African in America*

### THE HON. J. H. SMYTH,
LL.D.

The fact will be readily admitted by those most familiar with the sentiment of a large and not unimportant portion of our American citizenship, who, by the fortunes and misfortunes of war, viewed from the standpoint of one or the other combatants of the sanguinary struggle of 1861–62–63–64, were made equal before the law with all other citizens, that as a class they are averse to the discussion of Africa when their relationship with that ancient and mysterious land and its races is made the subject of discourse or reflection. The remoteness of Africa from America may be a reason for such feeling; the current opinion in the minds of the Caucasians, whence the American Negroes' opinions are derived, that the African is by nature an inferior man, may be a reason. The illiteracy, poverty, and degradation of the Negro, pure and simple, as known in Christian lands, may be a reason in connection with the partially true and partially false impression that the Negroes, or Africans, are pagan and heathen as a whole, and as a sequence hopelessly degraded beings. These may be some of the reasons that make the subject of Africa discordant and unmusical to our ears. It is amid such embarrassments that the lecturer, the orator, the missionary must present Africa to the Negro in Christian America.

In view of recent newspaper articles about migration of Negroes to Liberia, so much has been recently said by men of African descent of prominence, and by men of like prominence of uncertain descent, and by men of other races than the Negro, of Liberia and Africa generally, that I deem it a duty as an American citizen and a Negro, in vindication of the men and women of like descent with myself, citizens of the United States, to state some facts explanatory of and in rebuttal of much that has been said, ignorantly, unwisely and un-

* Professor J. W. E. Bowen, Ph.D., D.D., Editor, *Africa and the American Negro*. Addresses & Proceedings of the Congress on Africa held under the auspices of the Stewart Missionary Foundation for Africa of Gammon Theological Seminary in connection with the Cotton States and International Exposition, Dec. 13–15, 1895. Atlanta: Gammon Theological Seminary, 1896. pp. 73–83.

sympathetically, to the detriment of the effort being made at self-government in Liberia, West Africa. The people who constitute the inhabitants and citizenship of Liberia (the largest portion of the latter class are American Negroes from the Southern part of the United States) are possessed of and imbued with the sentiment and the civilization peculiar to this section of our country. That these immigrant Negroes who migrated to West Africa, or began migration as far back as 1820, and who continue to go thither, have a better field there, with less embarrassing environment, to prove their capacity for self-government, for leadership in State-craft than their brethren in the northern, western and southern portions of the United States, will scarcely be seriously denied or questioned. This conceded, it seems to me that wisdom, self-respect, race loyalty, and American patriotism would show themselves richer to withhold judgment as to the success of the experiment being made in Africa for self-government until such time as this immigrant people and their descendants have lived in Liberia, Sierra Leone, the Gold Coast, the Camaroons and other parts of West Africa long enough to assimilate the sentiment of liberty and rule, the general heritage and possession of the native African, than it has shown itself in echoing the expression of opinion of white men, whatever their learning or literary capacity, who estimate the progress of the Negro by the standard of their own race with its superior opportunities, advantages and facilities.

Until we have demonstrated ability for organization, for government, and have shown effective cohesiveness and leadership here in the United States, it may be a little immodest to hastily and unadvisedly make up the record adverse to our immediate kith and kin, who less than sixty years ago made the first step on lines of independent form of government of themselves, and have successfully maintained themselves against the greed of Spain, the aggrandizement of France, and the envy and cupidity of the merchant class of England without active assistance or defense of our formidable North African squadron; without an army and without more than one gunboat, the property of the Republic.

Liberia is the only democratic republican form of government on the continent of Africa of which we have any knowledge. The civilization of the people constituting the majority of the citizenship of Liberia is American. It embraces that phase of our American system which has made the autonomy of the south distinct from that of all other parts of our common country. This is the resultant of the outgrowth of the laws and customs of the severalty as well as the jointness of that system of government which exists in the South. In so far as the civilization of the United States on analysis is differentiated as northern, southern, eastern, and western, and in the south as Virginian, Carolinian, Georgian, it may be said, that the people composing the nation have transferred such American phases of government to this part of Africa.

The pioneers of this colony, the descendants of them, and the immigrants that have gone from here at varying periods of time within sixty years, like those of us who have remained, have been the unhappy victims of the influences of an alien, racial oppression; are fragments of races and tribes, and lack much in capacity for maintaining a stable form of government without the aid which comes from the moral support of the United States. But notwithstanding the embarrassments and difficulties of this youthful nation, the elements of success are being gradually, surely and deeply laid in industrial and agricultural concerns. The masses of the people are directing their effort to agriculture, the development of the soil, and are leaving the matter of coast-commerce or barter to the few.

No epitome or summary of Liberia would be worthy of the name which failed to take note of the renaissance of education under the scholarly Blyden and Freeman, both of whom have been presidents of Liberia College. When the former scholar came to the presidency of the college, then was commenced the work of the adaptation of the training of the youth for the definitive and distinct purpose of advancing the nation on the line of race. This institution has sent forth strong Negro men, who are unperverted in their instincts, strong in their race loyalty, and unhampered by a civilization upon which the individuality of the race is not stamped. Such a civilization, unmodified, is unsuited to the African in Africa, or out of Africa and although it may develop him religiously, in manly, self-reliant feeling, it will make him a weakling and will be destructive of true manhood, self-respect and race integrity.

It is lamentable that two hundred and fifty years have removed us to a far greater distance from Africa than the geographical measurement which separates America from Africa, and to-day that continent is perhaps of less interest to the educated and refined Negro of America than to his thrifty, industrious and adventurous white fellow-citizen. . . .

The wrong done us here in America, the wrong done us in Turkey in Asia, and Turkey in Europe, and Constantinople, is being recognized at the center of Anglo-Saxon civilization, as is honestly indicated by utterances such as these: "It is too late to ask, 'Are we our brother's keeper?' " Three centuries ago the plea might have seemed specious, but since then Europe has made itself guilty towards Africa of the blackest series of crimes that stain the foul record of civilized history. The actual appalling state of things in Africa is the result of the policy of Europe towards the African races. European contact has brought in its train not merely the sacrifice, amid unspeakable horrors, of the lives and liberties of twenty million Negroes for the American market alone, but political disintegration, social anarchy, moral and physical debasement, the decay of the simple arts and industries which had been developed during centuries of undisturbed and uneventful existence. Christian Europe, it is true, no longer openly tolerates the slave trade, but Christian Europe furnishes the arms by means of which the slave trade is carried on. The European explorer paves the way for the Arab man-hunter; in his track follow not the blessings of civilization, but conflagration, rapine, and murder, and European trade, while extinguishing native handicrafts, places within the African's grasp the power of self-destruction by spirits and of mutual destruction by firearms.

I am aware that it will be insisted by some who have failed to give this matter the consideration which it merits, that we are a part of the greatest composite nationality, and therefore, any influence that would make the Negro less American and more African than he is, would be injurious to the best interest of our American nation. I would gladly impress upon persons entertaining such thoughts, that race allegiance is compatible with patriotism, with love of the land that gave us birth. This has been abundantly shown to be true with reference to the Jews. Whatever doubts may be entertained upon this point on account of their wide religious divergence from other religionists, must undergo a change in the presence of the admonition given in a missive sent to Israel by the Prophet Jeremiah, and which has been faithfully conformed to by Israel and the descendants of Israel: "Serve the King of Babylon, and live. Build ye houses and dwell in them; and plant gardens and eat the fruits of them. And seek the welfare of the city whither I have caused you to be carried away captives, and pray unto the Lord for it; for in the peace thereof shall ye have peace."

Though we are a part of this great national whole, we are a distinct and separate part, an alien part racially, and destined to be so by the immutable law of race pride, which is possessed by our white fellow-citizens, if not by us. The sentiment, the something stronger than sentiment which makes an English American proud of his connection with Britain, a French American proud of his connection with La Belle France, and a German American fondly attached to the memories of the fatherland, and all European races of their Aryan descent, has something that partakes of the moral sublime. Truly "language and religion do not make a race."

The characteristics, peculiarities, idiosyncrasies and habits have been determined by what has been displayed and noted of Negroes under influences foreign to them and beyond their control. This has been the cause of inaccurate knowledge of the races of Africa on the part of the whites, and inaccurate knowledge on the part of the Negroes themselves. . . .

The Civilized Negro here has but recently emerged from slavery and been recognized a freeman; and though guaranteed in the possession of political rights, is still hampered by his inability to understand himself, by the conviction that on account of the political unity of the races here, his end must be reached by pursuit of the same line followed by the controlling races.

The condition of the race past and present here makes the American Negro African, without the peculiarities of his race; and African only as to the hue of his skin and his blood. The black man here is Americanized, and as a sequence, sectionalized.

Now the difference between Africa in America, and Africa in Africa being recognized, let us look to Africa in Africa. The races of Africa have not been a subject of Caucasian study.

The Egyptian, Carthaginian, and Moorish people are imperfectly known, and the interior, eastern, western races, are still more imperfectly understood, and for very prudential reasons,—the uncompromising conditions of climate toward European peoples, and the almost insuperable difficulties of ingress to the country. . . .

The testimony of Africans, distinguished for their knowledge of their countrymen, for their learning and character, should be looked to, and consulted as authorities in these matters. The Arku and Ebo races are not to be known through the flippant and inconsiderate statements of some ignorant European who finds to his surprise and annoyance that he cannot successfully take advantage of them in a business transaction, and as a consequence declares the former people a deceptive, ignorant class, and the latter an insolent, lazy set. You are to read the history of these races in the light of what the learned Dr. Africanus Horton has written in his "Africa and the Africans," and what his lordship Bishop Crowther experienced in his successful labor of love among his own and other races.

A comprehensive knowledge of the Christian, Mohammedan, and heathen Africans of Central and West Africa must be read in the light of the full and exhaustive information to be found in the writings of Edward W. Blyden, D.D., LL.D., late president of Liberia's college. Christianity in the third and fourth centuries among the Africans must be studied, in the Africans' fathers, and in Lloyd's North African Church and in Abyssinian traditions.

The missionary work in West Africa in the fifteenth century may be read in the voluminous Spanish and Portuguese and Italian state papers and travels. A few most valuable ones as to the Congo races are to be found in an English translation made during the reigns of Henry VIII. and Elizabeth. Bishops Crowther and Colenso may be read on African character with profit. There are two classics, African, which should be read: A. H. L. Heeren, African Researches, and a portion of Herodotus.

For quite fair treatment of African character, French and German explorations are interesting, and in English, Mungo Park, Livingstone, and Gordon Pasha.

Having directed attention to the means and some of the sources to be relied on for facts concerning native African character, I now point to some illustrations of error and wrong in dealing with the African in Africa.

It is not to our century alone that we are to look for active but mistaken effort to christianize Africa. There has existed no African mission, which, in the same period of time, attained to such proportions as the Portuguese mission in the Congo region during the fifteenth century. A cathedral and churches adorned, beautified, and glorified that portion of West Africa, and a Congo gentleman, after pursuing the necessary course of study in Spain prescribed for the priesthood, was made a bishop, and returned to his country to carry on the work of christianizing his people through the religion of Catholic Rome. All this work passed away. The ships which brought priests as outward passengers took the human product of the race back as homeward cargo. The theory and practice of the European being in opposition, the one to the other, the work perished. The fetich of the cross in the hands of the Portuguese, did not deter them from knavery and theft and murder, and the Congoes concluded that their fetiches were less harmful than the alien Portuguese.

Africans cannot be influenced by aliens, who, however Christian, seek to subvert their manhood. With the African at home, service to God and service to his fetich will not be yielded if manhood be the sacrifice.

He may be forced to accept a dogma or a religion, but will not receive either under such circumstances. Alien races can aid the progress of Christianity and civilization among Africans, but cannot control it with hope of ultimate success in Africa. . . .

In the British colony of Sierra Leone opportunity is afforded to study native character, as at no other place with which I am acquainted. The representatives of not less than a hundred tribes may be seen here and of not a few races. Here one may see the stately and grave Mandingo, the diplomatic Sosoo, the frail but handsome Foulah, and the paragon of men, the magnificent Jollof, "his complexion free from any taint of Abyssinian blue or Nubian bronze, intensely, lustrously, magnificently black."

Of the foregoing races there has been no acceptance of anything of foreign civilization. These races represent a very high and unique type of Mohammedanism and Arabic training. They have adopted the religion of the Prophet and made it to conform to themselves. They have written their own commentaries on the sacred book. They are not controlled by the Arab, the Persian, or the Turk as to their conception of the Koran. Their women share in common with the men in the instructions of the masters. But there are two distinct races here, and some of each of them in Liberia, the Ebo and Arku races, among whom is displayed the highest type of English civilization, with their free, unhampered peculiarities and idiosyncrasies. These two races control and direct commercial interest in Sierra Leone, on the Gold Coast and at Lagos, and have brought peace to war and order from confusion in the independent Negro nations of Abbeokuta.

Among these races, in religion are the Crowthers; in medical and surgical science, the Davises and Hortons; in jurisprudence, the Lewises and McCarthys; in pure scholarship, the Blydens, Coles, and Quakers; in the mercantile profession, the Boyles, Williams, Grants, and Sawyers. The time was when these two races were opposed to each other, but happily much of the tribal hatred has been destroyed by contact and education. These people are distinct in their bent of character. The Arku race is marked by a suavity of manner, a disposition to please, which borders on obsequiousness, and are industrious. They live upon a very little that they may save very much. They are never found to be improvident. The women make most affectionate wives, and have no peers in the world in their disposition to prove themselves helpmeets. It is said that the refusal by a husband to allow an Arku wife to help him, not infrequently causes marital difficulties. She prefers to trade than to remain indoors attending to her domestic affairs and babies. In complexion this race represents the average dark complexion of the American Negro.

The Ebo is a proud, daring race. They are always industrious, are fond of display, and in their hospitality are ostentatious. It may be asserted that there exists no evidence to show these people ever to have been pagan, in their home on the Niger or elsewhere. As a race they have never received either Christianity or Mohammedanism, but claim to believe sincerely in God. Those in the British colony have assimilated Christianity and some have attained to the highest culture and refinement. The first Negro graduate of Oxford was an Ebo. The most distinguished physician—Negro physician—living up to 1884 was Dr. Horton, an Ebo. The knowledge of reading, and writing and ciphering, in short, rudimentary training in this colony, has been very thorough. To Wilberforce and Venn be lasting honor and praise for their effective work in the British colonies of West Africa. . . .

The principal races here are Mandingos, Kru and Graybo and Bassa people, cognate races; Veys, Golas and Pesseys. My contact has been with these races in the civilized settlements, and in their own towns and villages. It would be a task to describe them with the accuracy their tribal and racial differences merit. . . .

The Golas as a race are courageous and intrepid, and kindly in their relation with the Americo-Liberian, preferring peace with them to war. The Pesseys, once a martial race, have by internal dissension and wars with other races, to an alarming extent lost their independence and many of that once noble race have been made captives to other peoples and slaves. As slaves they are highly valued, being indefatigable laborers, and therefore admired bondsmen by their masters. Their language has the softness and liquid sweetness of Italian, being in striking contrast to the harshness of the Kru and Greybo tongue. . . .

I should perhaps leave an impression which would be misleading as to Liberia and Africa unless I be more explicit. If you have observed, in any utterance of mine, anything about Africa which seems to possess in itself, or as to the races of that continent, a roseate hue, be pleased to remember that I have faintly, and with unartistic hand, shown you a part of this garden of the Lord and limned its inhabitants with the pencil and brush of an amateur; and I appeal to Mungo Park, the sainted Livingstone, Barth, Schweinfurth, Nachtigal, and I may risk Stanley in the rear of this galaxy of friends of Africa, for more accurate data and for larger and fuller experiences. But I may astound you when I say that Africa fears not the invasion of her shores by Europe and the rightful acquisition of her territory, and that no Negro who knows Africa regards the European's advent there as a menace to the progress and advancement of her races, except when they bring with them rum and fire-arms. I am pronouncedly, and have been since I first stepped upon the soil of my fatherland in 1878, an African colonizationist, but I am so in a strictly qualified sense, as is shown in the official statement made to my and your government—made from the United States Consulate General, Monrovia, under the date of February 21, 1883.

It may not be inopportune or out of place to say, in the interest of the prospective immigrant and in the interest of Liberia, that it is perhaps unwise for persons to emigrate here simply for the purpose of being free and enjoying complete civil liberty and social equality. The State is young, and, though poor in developed resources, is vigorous in purpose and effort, and needy only of additional influences of civilization which are possessed by those who, at their homes, have displayed the ability of independent labor and proprietorship. That is to say, that the man needed as an immigrant here is one who, in his home, displays industry and fixedness of purpose sufficient to cause him to stick at work of some kind until he has earned and saved enough to purchase a comfortable home, is competent to control it and does control it, or a man who has entered upon a business and has self-denial enough to continue in it to the end of respectably supporting himself and family, or who has made himself a boss of some supporting trade—a man who is not directly dependent upon being a common servant, and who is not an ignorant laborer incapable of turning up something by his innate good sense and the God-given push within him. . . .

As a clear understanding of the conditions of labor here is important to that class of foreign Negroes who contemplate settlement here. The possession of a few hundred dollars, skill in labor, and executive ability, constitute a capital that cannot but secure a most confortable living here with a probability of wealth.

Unless the Negro out of Africa goes to Africa seeking a home because he has none; goes of his own volition, with as correct a knowledge of Africa as may be obtained from the writings of trustworthy African travelers and explorers and missionaries, reinforced by race loyalty, and with greater confidence in himself and his race than in any alien self and alien race; goes from a sense of duty imposed by his Christian enlightenment, and not unprovided with ability and previous experience to organize and control labor, with as ample means as he would go with from the Atlantic coast of the United States to the Pacific slope for the purpose of engaging in business, he is wholly and entirely unsuited for Africa, and would impede by his presence not only the progress of Liberia (if he went thither), but any part of Africa by his unprofitable presence, and ought to be denied the right to expatriate himself.

If by anything that I have said you have been impressed with the fact that you are descendants of African races and as a consequence that you are a separate and distinct people from Caucasian races, and that the highest excellence to which an individual can attain must be to work according to the best of his genius, and the other to work in harmony with God's design in his creation, on his race line; if I have impressed you at all with the wisdom or propriety of confiding in the highest Negro authorities and the best alien writings, for reliable data respecting our race in the fatherland, and thereby awakened in you an interest and sincere desire for the well being of Africa and her races, for our people, and for accurate information concerning that most ancient, and most mysterious of lands; then I feel conscious of having made a contribution of information not wholly valueless to my countrymen that may tend to modify and dissipate general ignorance of us and of our antecedents and their country; and I have done something toward awakening your dormant self-respect, and given you some conception of the dignity which attaches to Negro manhood, and created in you a preference for your race before all other races; and this sentiment, if produced, will place you *en rapport* with the Negroes in Africa, who have no conception of any land greater, more beautiful than their own; any men braver and manlier than themselves, any women better, lovlier, and handsomer than African women. Then you will retire from this place with a feeling of stimulus rather than of satiety, of unrest rather than of repose; then shall I retire from my effort to interest you in Africa in Africa, and Africa in America with satisfied pride in having performed something of duty as a Negro—clear in his conviction of the high destiny in reserve for Africa and its races, and of your duty to be loyal to the race, since true allegiance will make us sharers in that glory which the sacred writing declares shall come, when Ethiopia shall stretch forth her hand unto God.

58

# Marcus Garvey,
# 1887-1939

Marcus Garvey was born in St. Ann's Bay, Jamaica. His father was said to be descended from the "Maroons," a name given slaves who escaped to the uninhabited districts of Jamaica and Latin America and who, because of their resourcefulness, power, and military organization, were greatly feared by the surrounding white communities. Marcus Garvey's early education was sketchy, but he was apprenticed to a printer, became a master printer, and finally foreman of one of the largest printing plants in Jamaica.

As a young man, Garvey became involved in all sorts of disputes, which he tried to clarify by establishing a periodical called *Garvey's Watchman*, and a political organization, The National Club. In 1912 Garvey went to London, where he became associated with Duse Mohammed Ali, a Negro Egyptian and editor of the *African Times and Orient Review*. Ali broadened Garvey's perspective considerably and gave him much background on Africa, its culture, and its problems. Garvey also met many West Indians and Africans in London, but what moved him most during those years was his reading of Booker T. Washington's *Up from Slavery*.

Garvey returned to Jamaica in 1914 and established the Universal Negro Improvement Association and African Communities League to attract "all people of Negro or African parentage to join the crusade to rehabilitate the race . . . to promote the spirit of race pride and love, to reclaim the fallen of the race, to administer to and assist the needy, to assist in civilizing the backward tribes of Africa, to strengthen the imperialism of independent African states."

In 1915 Garvey came to the United States to enlist the support of American Negroes. He hoped, with the help of Booker T. Washington, to gain an instant audience, but the Titan of Tuskegee died at about the same time that the West Indian arrived. Garvey stayed on, however, and captured and held the imagination of thousands of black Americans, until his deportation in 1927 following his conviction for mail fraud.

Through his publication, *The Negro World*, which he founded in 1918, and his promotion of various ambitious schemes, Garvey sought to lift the black man from submission and insignificance in the

United States and to harness his energies and hopes to the redemption of the black man in Africa. More than any other leader, Garvey sought to establish a bond of identity between the Negroes of Africa and the Negroes of the New World.

Because of his philosophy, his activities, and his personality, Marcus Garvey was an extremely controversial figure. Unquestionably, however, his appeal to the black masses was on a secular, this-world basis, which not only gave them a sense of personal worth but a programme for action; Garvey is entitled to a position of mass leadership as yet unexcelled in Negro America.

# Examples of White Christian Control of Africa*

The world has seen many fair examples of white Christian control of Africa:

The outrages of Leopold of Belgium, when he butchered thousands of our defenceless brothers and sisters in the Belgian Congo, and robbed them of their rubber.

The natives of Kenya South East Africa armed with sticks and stones rebelled against the injustices and brutality of the English, and were hewn down by machine guns, because they did not supply the demands of the invaders.

The Hottentots of South West Africa in rebellion against similar brutality and exploitation, using spears and leather shields to protect themselves, were bombed from aeroplanes by the Christian(?) whites.

The above are but few examples of the many atrocities committed on our defenceless brothers and sisters in Africa by white exploiters and invaders. Surely the introduction of chemical gas among the natives of Africa would place them in a better position to handle "the alien disturbers of African peace".

It strikes me that with all the civilization this Western Hemisphere affords, Negroes ought to take better advantage of the cause of higher education. We could make of ourselves better mechanics and scientists, and in cases where we can help our brothers in Africa by making use of the knowledge we possess, it would be but our duty. If Africa is to be redeemed the Western Negro will have to make a valuable contribution along technical and scientific lines.

* *Philosophy and Opinions of Marcus Garvey*, second edition, Frank Cass, 1967, Part I, p. 43.

# Africa's Wealth*

## (*Written April 18, 1923*)

Gradually we, as Negroes, are witnessing an increasing encroachment upon our rights on the continent of Africa by the adventurous European races. Already the great colonizing governments of Europe have established themselves all over Africa by way of political control, and we find that they are calling upon their different nationals to go out and take up their residence on the continent for the purpose of exploiting the country and its natural resources. . . .

Africa today is the biggest game in the hunt of nations and races. Africa today is regarded, as I have always said, as the richest spot in the world, to be exploited by those who are keen enough and appreciative enough to invest their money and their interests in the development of that continent.

An open appeal is now being made to the white capitalists of different countries to invest in the exploitation of the oil fields, diamond, gold and iron mines of the "Old Homeland". This means that in a short time Africa will become the centre of the world's commercial activities, at which time the black man will naturally be relegated to his accustomed place of being the "underdog" of the New African civilization. This is about to happen in the face of a highly-developed Negro civilization in the Western world, wherein men of the Negro race seek the same opportunities in things economic as the other races of the world.

### WHITE CAPITALISTS LOOKING TOWARD AFRICA

Can we not realize that we of the Negro race have slept for hundreds of years, allowing during that period of time the great Caucasian race and the other great races to develop their own countries, their own homes and habitats until they have reached the point of exhaustion? They have practically extracted from their own countries all the wealth those countries could produce, whilst we have remained dormant for 300 years, ignoring the possibilities of our own country, ignoring the wealth of our own country. Now these other peoples are leaving their own countries—over-exploited and over-developed— and going into Africa to develop and rob its vast resources. What does that mean? It means that in another fifty or one hundred years,

* *Ibid.*, Part II, pp. 63–68.

if European and American capital develops and exploits Africa, it will become like Europe and the United States of America—the future home of the white man. Wherein with a small amount of investment, with a small amount of capital, they will have so exploited the country as to cause it to produce an abundance of wealth and make Africa the wealthiest country and continent in the world, with probably the greatest civilization that the world will see in another one hundred or two hundred years, which will be a civilization owned and controlled by white men, where Negroes in that period of time, will fall back into the natural life of that country, (just as we are in the United States of America at the present time) as a secondary part of the civilization when we will have to beg for a chance, as we are now doing in the United States of America. Because when the white man invests his money for the development of Africa it means that he is going to employ labor in doing this, and the same Negroes who say they have lost nothing in Africa, when men like John D. Rockefeller are ready to develop the oil resources there, they will carry them by the thousands to Africa. They will go as quickly as they went from the West Indian Islands to dig the Panama Canal, and West Indian Negroes know well the treatment they received at the hands of white Americans after the Panama Canal was completed. When men like Gary are ready to develop the coal and iron mines they will carry Negroes by the thousands to Africa, and they will go as readily as they go to Pennsylvania to work in the mines. Yet we say we have lost nothing in Africa; while Africa offers to us its possibilities, its untold opportunities. Why should we not go there and take an interest in its development, not for white men, but for Negroes. The white man is now doing it, not with the intention of building for other races, but with the intention of building for himself—for the white race.

### THE VALUE OF MINERALS

Most of us know, or ought to know, the value of minerals and oil. In Oklahoma, Texas and some of the Western States of America, men wake up over night and find themselves millionaires and rich men because oil happens to be discovered on their property. An acre or two of land with oil represents thousands of dollars, every day, according to the quantity of oil the well produces; because oil is being consumed all over the world in every line of industry. As of oil, so of coal, iron, copper and all the other minerals, which are to be found in Africa in abundance. Lately parsonite, a new radium-bearing mineral, has been found in the Belgium Congo. Radium is the most precious mineral in the world. It is sold at $120,000 per gram and is used extensively in scientific experiments, so we can readily realize the vast amount of wealth lying buried in Mother Africa awaiting development.

## NATIVE AFRICANS EXPLOITED BY WHITE MAN

The native Africans unfortunately have not been schooled in the appreciation of the valuable mineral wealth of Africa. They have not been schooled in the methods of exploiting mineral wealth. For a long time they were unable to appreciate the value of diamonds, until the white man went there with his scientific commercial knowledge and took away the diamond fields of Kimberley, Johannesburg and the entire Union of South Africa, where the greatest quantity of diamonds is found. The native Africans once owned all the wealth of South Africa, but Cecil Rhodes and other white men robbed and exploited them, and today the diamond fields are owned by white men, who have practically reduced the native Africans (who once owned the lands) to slavery, and by the system of forced labor, compelled them to mine the diamonds and other minerals and to live on reservations, herded together like cattle, under conditions wholly unsuited to human beings. The British Empire today owes its present financial existence to the wealth which has been recruited from Africa, the wealth that we Negroes could have controlled fifty years ago, when there was not so much interest in Africa. It is only within this period of time that Italy, France, England, Portugal and Belgium have started a wholesale colonization and exploitation of Africa. As for Belgium's contact with the native African in the Congo Basin, every Negro who knows anything about the "Leopoldian System" shudders at the mention of the word Belgian. This system out-rivals any of the most fiendish wholesale massacres and atrocities ever committed by human beings, and all for rubber and ivory. Villages were compelled to furnish a certain amount of rubber every week as a tax. Natives were not allowed to cultivate the soil, all their time was spent in getting rubber. Men, women and children were utilized in rubber getting, hence they died in large numbers from starvation and over work. When certain areas became non-productive by being over-worked, the inhabitants of these areas were massacred by the soldiers who were sent out to collect the rubber, and instead of returning with the rubber, they returned with trophies of hands and other parts of the human body, to prove that they had done their work. This system in its entirety lasted for twenty years, with a loss of life of over twenty million black men, women and children. In the last world war Negroes from every clime were called out to protect "poor Belgium" from the "brutal Hun". In the coming struggle of the "survival of the fittest", we may be able to repay "poor Belgium" measure for measure for her colonization of over one million square miles of African territory.

### ALL NEGROES SHOULD PROTECT AFRICA

Europe today is bankrupt and cannot advance much capital for the development of African industries, and therefore they are trying to interest American capitalists in the exploitation of the wealth of the great Continent. There is absolutely no reason why the 400,000,000 Negroes of the world should not make a desperate effort to re-conquer our Motherland from the white man, in that, whether he be English, French, German, Italian or Spanish, his one and only interest is selfish exploitation and domination. If native Africans are unable to appreciate the value of their own country from the standard of Western civilization, then it is for us, their brothers, to take to them the knowledge and information that they need to help to develop the country for the common good.

Why should we allow Belgium, Portugal, Spain, Italy, France and England to build up and rehabilitate their bankrupt nations and civilization out of the wealth and resources of our country? They have no room for us in their countries, and surely we have absolutely no room for them as exploiters in our country. We have allowed cowardice and fear to take possession of us for a long time, but that will never take us anywhere. It is no use being afraid of these nations and peoples. They are human beings like ourselves. We have blood, feelings, passions and ambitions just as they have. Why, therefore, should we allow them to trample down our rights and deprive us of our liberty? Negroes everywhere must get that courage of manhood that will enable them to strike out, irrespective of who the enemy is, and demand those things that are ours by right—moral, legal and divine.

### BLACK MILLIONAIRES A POSSIBILITY

Let us as Negroes, prepare ourselves throughout the world for the conflict that is bound to ensue between the rivalling forces for the ultimate domination of our country—Africa. For we are not going to give up easily, and allow these European intruders to rob, exploit and dominate the land of our fathers.

If the oil of Africa is good for Rockefeller's interest; if iron ore is good for the Carnegie Trust; then surely these minerals are good for us. Why should we allow Wall Street and the capitalist group of America and other countries to exploit our country when they refuse to give us a fair chance in the countries of our adoption? Why should not Africa give to the world its black Rockefeller, Rothschild and Henry Ford? Now is the opportunity. Now is the chance for every Negro to make every effort toward a commercial, industrial standard that will make us comparable with the successful business men of other races.

Africa invites capital to develop its resources. Let not that capital, whether it be financial or man-power, be supplied by white men, but let us as Negroes make our contribution. All that Africa needs is proper education. The Western Negro has much of that, and it is our duty to so prepare our brothers as to place them on guard against the tricky exploiters of Europe who have been deceiving and robbing them of their possessions.

# Elijah Muhammad,
# 1897–

Elijah Muhammad was born Robert Poole, one of twelve children of a Baptist minister on a tenant farm in Sandersville, Georgia. His formal education did not extend beyond the elementary grades. Muhammad worked as a common labourer in the south until 1923, when he migrated to Detroit with his wife and two children.

In Detroit Muhammad's fate seemed similar to that of many rural migrants. His employment was marginal, and from 1929 to 1931 he was the recipient of public assistance. For a time he was a Baptist minister as well as an assistant minister and close confidant to Prophet Fard. Fard, at one time leader of the Moorish American Science Temple, founded by Noble Ali Drew, himself founded a Temple in Detroit in 1930. According to one source, Eric Lincoln, Fard chose Elijah Muhammad to preside over the Nation of Islam. Muhammad, in turn, has been largely responsible for the deification of Fard and the perpetuation of his teaching. Even before Fard's mysterious disappearance, Muhammad showed himself to be a forceful personality. In 1934 he was arrested for refusing to send his children to the public schools of Detroit. Later that year he moved to Chicago and organized a second Temple. He built the movement by encouraging the growth of temples, schools, apartment houses, and small businesses of all sorts. Perhaps most significantly, he imbued his followers with a sense of pride in themselves.

While Fard has become identified with Allah in the minds of the reportedly 200,000 followers of the Nation of Islam, Elijah Muhammad is regarded as "the messenger of Allah, directly commissioned by Allah himself who came in the person of Fard to wake the sleeping black nation and rid them of the white man's age-old domination". The Nation of Islam is a form of Black Nationalism reflecting the combined ideologies of the Moorish Science Temple of America as well as the Garvey movement. Though the movement stresses Islam as a unifying factor for American Negroes, it does not neglect the appeal of the back-to-Africa idea with which Garvey mesmerized a large following.

From 1942 to 1946 Elijah Muhammad was in the federal correctional institution at Milan, Michigan, convicted of avoiding the draft and inciting others of his membership to do likewise. According to Essien-Udom this period in jail gave Muhammad an added quality of leadership and identification with the most unfortunate of American Negroes. Certainly, upon his release and return to Chicago in 1946 the Nation of Islam became one of the strongest organized groupings of Negroes in this country.

# Mr. Muhammad Speaks*

"ROBBED AND SPOILED" (Isaiah 42:22)

Seventeen million so-called American Negroes—the lost-found members of the Tribe of Shabazz, the original black nation of the earth—have been so successfully robbed and spoiled that today they do not know that they have been robbed, and now do not recognize their loss even when it is offered to them. They even prey upon each other. They are ever ready to help someone who should be helping them. They will open their purses to all of the independent nations of the earth, while dependent slaves, themselves, and will give without even asking for a receipt.

Just say, "Africa needs help", and you will see their dollars poured into the hands of a collector without even questioning the sincerity of the collector nor demanding to see a receipt from Africa showing the amount of money or charity given. This makes it so easy for the robbers of our people to rob you.

Millions of pennies are given in charities every week throughout the so-called Negroes' churches for foreign mission work in Africa. How do you know that these pennies are going for foreign mission work in Africa? There are some now giving their money to help Ghana's independence. Is the Government of Ghana sending you a receipt by the Secretary of that state saying "Thanks" to you, that they received your gift, or do those to whom you give it here receive one from over there? Has Africa ever sent you any help for the past 400 years? The Prime Minister of Ghana was here visiting a few days ago, and we have not heard him asking private people for anything.

It would be a shame on the part of any independent nation's government to come here begging for help from the so-called Negroes whose status is that of *free slaves*—the most foolish of all people on earth. No one gives you nor seeks you. As Isaiah says of you (42: 22): "They are for a prey, and none delivered, for a spoil, and none saith restore." But yet you are willing to help restore all except your own self here in America. Why not awaken to the knowledge of the robbers? If you have extra money to send abroad, why not use it on SELF, and your people here in America, for a good home on this good

* *Pittsburgh Courier*, September 3, 1958, and reprinted by kind permission of the editor.

68

earth where they can live in peace without being afraid that someone will say, "Move over, this is a white man's country".

*You are picked* up off the streets in the South, beaten or shot by a mob of devils without even making any attempt for justice. None pity *you*, nor do you pity yourself. Nevertheless, you are foolish enough to have pity for those who beat and kill you. Have you any sense at all? *First,* help yourself, and then if you are able, help others if you want to.

It is written and it is proven that God helps those who help themselves. Let us first help ourselves to be free and independent and with the help of Almighty God Allah, who has come to free us from our tormenters. Accept Him and the good religion Islam that makes true friendship with God and the righteous. Do not be satisfied with empty promises. Let us have some earth, and PEACE in it.

The day has arrived that you will have to help yourselves or suffer the worst. Unite and get some of this earth for a home, like other nations.

Hurry and join on to your own kind. The time of this world is at hand.

# PART II(a)

## How Negro Americans Can Help

### As Individuals

# How Negro Americans Can Help

## AS INDIVIDUALS

In her relations to the rest of the world Africa has been explored and conquered, converted and bartered. The Negro experience in America can be described in similar terms; the Negro could rarely negotiate as a free and equal member of society. If this limitation has been socially disastrous, it has also served to strengthen the Negro's identification with Africa and to cause him to seek ways of helping Africans. His concept of help is itself a product of his western and new world culture; it is a religious and Christian concept.

No doubt there are many reasons why Christianity was the vehicle most frequently employed to establish ties between Negroes and Africans. The church is the strongest institution developed by Negroes in this country. It represents their greatest wealth and the source of some of their most viable talent. At the same time there could be comparatively little objection by American whites to Negroes peacefully assisting in the religious conversion of their African brothers. Indeed, a white American congregation, the Richmond Baptist Missionary Society, sent the first practising Negro missionaries, Lott Cary and Collin Teague, to Liberia in 1822—although American Negro ministers representing several denominations accompanied the Negro settlers from Nova Scotia to Sierra Leone in the late eighteenth century. Cary later became an assistant to Jehudi Ashmun, a white American agent of the American Colonization Society. Lincoln University in Pennsylvania, long known for its role in the education of African students, was originally named Ashmun Institute in honour of the Colonization Society's principal agent. Before Cary's untimely death in 1828, he had expressed the desire to return as a settler to Liberia upon the expiration of his contract with the Colonization Society.

Alexander Crummell, born in New York of an African father and a free coloured mother, was educated for the Episcopal ministry and is second only to Edward Blyden as a Negro scholar from the West concerned with Africa. Dr. Crummell, addressing himself to the important men of colour in 1861, spoke realistically of the inhibi-

73

tions of Negroes but principally of their obligations to serve Africa. Dr. Crummell was no romanticist, and his plea (included in this anthology) reflects his direct and realistic approach to the problem.

A more sanguine statement was given at the Negro Christian Student Conference in New York a half century later by John W. Gilbert, then President of Miles College in Birmingham, Alabama. Mr. Gilbert felt strongly that American Negroes as Christians and as people of African descent owed a debt to Africa. Negroes, in his opinion, were obligated to convert and to educate their African brothers.

No account of the desire of American leaders to help Africa is complete without an assessment of the opinions of Booker T. Washington and Frederick Douglass. Washington, the great advocate of industrial education for Negroes and of a pattern of race relations harmonious with the separate but equal philosophy of the post-Reconstruction South, was unquestionably the most influential Negro in the United States for more than twenty years. Like Frederick Douglass, a leader of comparable stature a generation earlier, Washington is rarely thought of as having concerned himself with Africa. Yet both were concerned, and neither thought his concern to be an impairment of the quality and effectiveness of his leadership on behalf of American Negroes.

Although some of the selections from Douglass included in this anthology are on the theme of returning to Africa, perhaps the most thought-provoking of his statements related to Africa are those in the editorial in the *North Star* expressing his reaction to the African Civilization Society. In debating the merits of this organization with his good and esteemed friend, Henry Highland Garnett, Douglass' philosophy and strategy are clear. Africa is "the land of my fathers" to which anyone, including Negroes, is free to emigrate, but the energy expended to organize such a return on a mass basis as a solution to the problems of slavery or the slave trade "plants its guns too far from the battlements of slavery". This debate deserves greater familiarity as it sharply draws the lines of thought and action which have frequently characterized the philosophy of Negroes as they ponder the reality of Africa and their relation to it.

Dr. Washington's position was less forthright, as the following anecdote suggests:

Sometime ago a young coloured man, about twenty-two years old, came to see me in New York with tears in his eyes. He said "Dr.

74

Washington, I may not see you again, I have come to tell you good-bye. I am going to sail across the waters; I feel it my duty to go to Africa and give my life—yes, die if need be—for the salvation of my race." I said to him, "Yes, young man, are you willing to do something for your race?" He said, "Yes sir." I then said to him: "I am not going to ask you to *die* for the Negro race in the South, but I am going to ask you to go down there and *live* for your race."

But, influenced perhaps by Emmett Scott, Dr. Washington did express an interest in the affairs of the Africans in South Africa and considered the possibility of establishing a school similar to Tuskegee in Liberia. He served as host at Tuskegee to an International Conference of the Friends of Africa in April, 1912. At his invitation representatives of eighteen foreign countries or colonies of foreign countries and twenty-five different missionary societies representing twelve different religious denominations came to this conference. The British African Society, Sierra Leone, Liberia, and the Gold Coast were all represented. According to a report of the conference in *The Southern Letter*, a considerable part of the proceedings was devoted to Africa and the future of the peoples of Africa.

Adding a fascinating and little documented dimension to the story of the American Negro and Africa are the many isolated examples of help from lesser known individuals. An example is Mr. Loudin's concern, during his trip abroad with the famous Fisk Jubilee Singers, that the American Negro should assume some responsibility in in-influencing world opinion on behalf of the English because of their friendship to the Africans at the time of the Boer War. More surprising, perhaps, is the opportunity afforded Mr. J. B. Bruce to provide letters of introduction for Dr. Aggrey of the Gold Coast to Africans from Nigeria and Sierra Leone. Bruce, an American Negro, knew Africans from many countries intimately, while Aggrey, having spent most of his adult years in this country, knew only the Africans from his own country.

In addition, it is interesting that there is little to differentiate the ideas of James H. Robinson in 1956 from those expressed in 1914 by John W. Gilbert. Mr. Robinson, like Gilbert, feels that Negroes have a peculiar role to play as missionaries in Africa. His statement, written perhaps more for a white than a Negro audience, places the primary responsibility for employing Negroes upon the shoulders of the Foreign Mission Boards of the United States. He also suggests that such action on their part might be an effective weapon in the battle against communism in Africa.

Carter Godwin Woodson as an individual scholar and as the founder of the Association for the Study of Negro Life and History merits a special place in this anthology. Dr. Woodson, as a rule, always appeared to be the involved but objective scholar. However, by his endeavours to carry the subject of Negro history, including its African roots, to every corner of this land with almost no funds but always at the level of highest scholarly respectability, Dr. Woodson established a unique academic beachhead. In the appendix to this anthology we have described the long concern of Negro scholars for Africa, but unquestionably Woodson, by his prolific output, his scholarly quality, and his organizational ability, deserves special emphasis. His role bridges the gap between individual contribution and organizational development. The selection from Dr. Woodson included in this anthology reflects perhaps the real, but not so well known, side of his interest in Africa. The biographical sketch of Dr. Woodson is the contribution of Professor Kelly Miller of Howard University, long a close and intimate friend of Dr. Woodson.

## AS ORGANIZATIONS*

The most effective way in which the American Negro has been able to express his identification with and interest in Africa has been through the special groups organized over the years for this particular purpose. The tendency of Americans in general and Negroes in particular to join organizations for mutual assistance, recreation, and education is well known. Considering that Negroes have had the long interest in Africa indicated in this anthology, it is to be expected that this interest should be reflected in the existence within the Negro community of a number of organizations dealing with Africa.

Various kinds of African identification are manifest in voluntary organizations among Negroes. There is the simple identification expressed in such names as the African Society, the Sons of Africa, the African American League, or, more subtly, the Children of the Sun. Another form of identification is reflected in organizations devoted to scholarly or cultural pursuits relative to Africa or to Africa and Negroes, such as the American Negro Academy, the Negro Society for Historical Research, the Association for the Study of Negro Life and History, and the American Society of African Culture. Yet another form of identification is expressed in associations organized to help Africans either on a project basis in this country or in Africa,

* See pp. 155–225.

as, for example, the African Union Company, the Council of African Affairs, and the Lynchburg Improvement Society, or by encouraging a return to Africa as the homeland of American Negroes, as, for example, the African Civilization Society and the Universal Negro Improvement Association.

The Negro Church itself is actually the outgrowth of African Societies formed as mutual aid groups by American Negroes. The African Methodist Episcopal Church is the direct outgrowth of the Free African Society started in Philadelphia in 1787 by Richard Allen and Absalom Jones. Certainly over the years the most sustaining and obvious form of help that American Negroes have given Africa has been in the area of mission work there and in the education of Africans in this country in schools supported by the Negro Church. The African Methodist Episcopal Church particularly has maintained its deep involvement in Africa and represents the strongest organization of African identification on the part of American Negroes. Essien-Udom has reminded us, however, that all Negro segregated Protestant churches do have some components of black nationalism which in turn found their source in African identification. For particularly in the churches do the Negroes find success, a broad base of participation, independent black leadership, and sociability—all incipient ingredients of nationalism.

As mentioned above, some individual Negroes have been sent by white congregations as missionaries to Africa; but there is some evidence that white mission bodies changed their policies and in fact preferred not to send Negroes as missionaries. Therefore, the African Methodist Episcopal Church, the Colored Methodist Episcopal Church, and the Negro Baptist Church have been the organizations largely responsible for the role played by Negro missionaries in Africa and have generously spent their resouces on mission work. These missionary activities were found in such African areas as Sierra Leone, Ghana, Congo Leopoldville, Congo Brazzaville and Kenya, and were particularly vigorous in Liberia and the Republic of South Africa.

The help American Negro churches have given Africans in church-supported schools in America has also been of tremendous importance. Before the decade of the fifties most Africans who studied in this country attended the all-Negro schools like Lincoln, Howard, and Fisk. The importance of some contemporary political leaders like Nkrumah of Ghana or Azikiwe and Mbadiwe of Nigeria—all graduates of Lincoln—has caused us to forget Aggrey and Chilembwe of Livingston or the long procession of students who studied at Wilberforce, which is supported entirely by the African Methodist Episcopal Church. In a preliminary study of this subject Horace Mann Bond tells us that between 1894 and 1950, of the 431 African students coming to the United States for education, 64, or 15 per cent, attended Wilberforce and, therefore, were being supported by the Negro Church. Unfortunately, Bond did not include statistics for Bethune-Cookman, Livingston, Storrer, and Morris Brown in his listings. But the facts speak for themselves.

One must note here again the existence of the so-called black nationalist groups who see in Africa a tangible symbol in solving the problems of Negroes in this country. These groups do provide a potential source of help for Africa, but at this time there is little evidence that it is being offered. However, such groups definitely serve as a bridge of understanding between the Negro masses and Africa. These so-called black nationalist organizations, of which, according to a 1961 survey published in the *New York Times*, there were thirteen in New York City alone, should facilitate the establishment of meaningful ties, communications, and possible assistance from various levels of the Negro community to comparable groups in the countries of Africa.

In this anthology the existence and role of all these types of organizations is presented in varying ways, from the inclusion of a constitution or statement of principles to letters of introduction and detailed plans for organization as part of programming or organizational functioning.

# Lott Cary,
## 1780–1828

Lott Cary was born in Virginia about 1780 and worked first as a tobacco packer in a warehouse in Richmond, Virginia. Having taught himself to read, Cary became interested in African mission work in 1815 and played an important part in founding the African Missionary Society in Richmond in that year.

Cary saved his money and bought his freedom. Sponsored by the Baptist Board of Foreign Missions of the United States, he sailed for Africa with the Reverend Collin Teague in 1820. Cary is reported to have expressed an interest in Africa by saying, "I am an African, and in this country, however meritorious my conduct and respectable my character, I cannot receive the credit due to either. I wish to go to a country where I shall be estimated by my merits, not by my complexion, and I feel bound to labor for my suffering race."

Cary served as physician for the settlers in Sierra Leone and in 1828 was appointed acting governor of Liberia. He was also active as a preacher and became an agent for the American Colonization Society. He died in 1828 as a result of an explosion of cartridges he was making to protect the colonists from unfriendly Africans.

TO THE REV. DR. STAUGHTON                       *Free Town*,
*of the Baptist Board of Missions\**            *March 13th*, 1821

Rev. and dear sir,

I am happy that an opportunity is now afforded, to inform the board through you, that we all arrived safe in Africa. We had a long passage of forty-four days, yet we were wonderfully preserved by the great ruler of the winds and seas. Our captain informed us that he was never so long out with less apparent danger. I suppose we had as much sea sickness as common, but no deaths, except a child about a year old, the youngest child of Mrs. Coker. It is not common to see a ship's crew as orderly during a long passage, as those on board of the brig Nautilus. You must know, that any captain having on board, men, women, and children, has a great deal to encounter;

\* James Barrett Taylor, *Biography of elder Lott Cary*, Baltimore 1837, pp. 28–32.

and unless he has the fear of God or his own credit at heart, he will follow the too common habits among seamen. But notwithstanding captain Blair had his beckets lost, and the men, women and children in his way, I must say, that from his lips, I never heard one word of profane swearing during the passage. He often received things more like a Christian than a seafaring captain, I hope the board will pray for him.

I am truly sorry that the hopes of the board, cannot be realized, as to our missionary labors, for, as it pleased you to have us connected with the Colonization Society, and the agents of the society upon their arrival here, finding their prospects of getting lands very gloomy, so much so, that they disowned us as colonists; and the government's agent had captured Africans, for whom he was bound, by the laws of the United States, to procure a place, in order to settle them, or until there can be a more permanent settlement obtained, the agent received us as laborers and mechanics, to be settled with them, in order to make preparation for the reception of others; we are therefore bound to the government's agent. He has rented a farm, and put us on it, and we must cultivate it for our support, and for the support of these Africans; and pay as much of the rent as we can. And as this obligation will last until lands are purchased by the agents of the Colonization Society, I am greatly afraid it will not end soon; and until it does, our mission labors will be very few. Jesus Christ our Saviour when he came on his mission into this world, was often found with a broad axe in his hand; and I believe a good many corn field missionaries would be a great blessing to this country, that is if they were not confined to the field by the law and by necessity. We are bound by both. I converse very freely with you on this subject, because with me, it is a very important one, and because of the interest which the board has taken in this mission. Africa suffers for gospel truth, and she will suffer, until missionaries can be sent, and settled in different parts of her continent.

I have not been able to write any information relative to the state of the country, which can be of much use to the board. I intend taking a small excursion in the country, but cannot promise when that will be, as the rains will set in soon, my wife is sick, and we are desirous to get a small crop on the way, as early as possible. These things I presume will be a sufficient preventive to my leaving home for six months to come. I however have the promise of some friends to take me down as far as the Bagroo, as soon as I am ready to go. I believe that just over on the Bullom side is a beautiful field for missionary labors, among the Mandingoes, and that labors might be extended at once to advantage, because there is a regular trade carried on with the natives of that country, and the people of this place. They have not only acquired some knowledge of the English language, but some of their habits also; and as they are dependant on this place for trade, any traveller or any settler among them, would be perfectly safe, so long as they fear that the injuring of the missionary or settler would have a tendency to interupt their trade with this place. A missionary, therefore, settled among them, would have every means in his hands, and would have a right, under the blessing of God, to expect a rapid spread of the gospel truth. It is strange that a subject of so much importance, and which appears to be so practicable, should be so much neglected. If you intend doing anything for Africa, you must not wait for the Colonization Society, nor for government, for neither of these are in search of missionary ground, but of colonizing grounds; if it should not sow missionary seeds, you cannot expect a missionary crop. And, moreover, all of us who are connected with the agents, who are under public instructions, must be conformed to their laws whether they militate against missionary operations or not.

I have been wonderfully blessed, as to my health; for I have not had a day's sickness since I left America. But my wife left America sick; she has not had her health since, and it is very doubtful with me, how her sickness will terminate. My children are all very well. Please, sir, to make my respects to the board.

Before we left the United States, we formed ourselves into a church, consisting of seven members. We adopted the constitution of the Sansom street church. This little body, small as it is, has appointed Lord's day, 22d, to commune.

TO MR. WILLIAM CRANE,       *Monrovia, (Africa,)*
*Richmond Baptist Missionary Society*\*    *January 16th, 1825*

Dear Brother,

I am glad that an opportunity is afforded to hand you a few lines, which leave me and mine in good health; and, I hope, may find you enjoying the blessings of a favorable Providence. I have not much (but still something, I think) worth communicating. Since I wrote you last, the Lord has in mercy visited the settlement, and I have had the happiness to baptize nine hopeful converts; besides, a number have joined the Methodists. The natives are more and more friendly; their

\* *Ibid.*, pp. 46–47.

confidence begins to awaken. They see that it is our wish to do them good, and hostilities have ceased with them. I have daily applications to receive their children, and have ventured to take three small boys; to find clothes, and pay for their attendance at the day school—two from Grand Cape Mount, and one from Little Bassa; the two former are very promising, but the other is slow to learn, yet a fine boy. Two of them, I was obliged to send home, ten days ago, in consequence of sores, which they had; but they will return as soon as they are cured; and, in order to establish my confidence in their returning, they refused to take their clothes with them. Our Sunday school still goes on, with some hopes that the Lord will ultimately bless it to the good of numbers of the untutored tribes. The natives attend our Lord's day worship, quite regularly. We have commenced bringing out our timbers for the building of our meeting house, and have got all the large timbers on the ground, but we shall want boards, shingles, nails, window glass, etc., of which you will please to collect what you can, and send out. Please make my respects to the board, and accept of the same for yourself and family.

I am yours, very dearly,

LOTT CARY

TO FRIENDS IN VIRGINIA*                                    *Monrovia,*
                                                          *April 24, 1826*

Dear Brother,

Your letters and all the articles you mentioned, arrived safe, and were very thankfully received. I expected, until Friday last, that the return of the ship would have enabled me to present personal thanks to you; but the agent was of opinion that I had better defer it a little longer. I am of the same opinion, as the last emigrants have not as yet got entirely over the fever, and my services cannot be dispensed with, without very great risk; but I hope that, if not before, I shall see you next spring, if the Lord permit.

We dedicated our meeting-house last October; it was four weeks from the time we raised it to the time it was dedicated. It is quite a comfortable house, thirty by twenty feet, and ceiling inside nearly up to the plates, with a decent pulpit, and seats. I feel very grateful to you for your services, and to brethern and friends for their liberal contributions. We may say, that "hitherto the Lord has helped us",

* *Ibid.*, pp. 61–63.

therefore we have gone on middling well. We have no particular revival at present, but still we labor in hope that the Lord will, in answer to prayer, yet favor Zion. Our native schools still go on under hopeful circumstances. I think the slave trade is nearly done in our neighborhood. The agent, with our forces, has released upwards of one hundred and eighty from chains, since the first of October, which has added greatly to our strength. If the colored people of Virginia do not think proper to come out, the Lord will bring help to the colony from some other quarter, for these recaptives are ready to fight as hard for the protection of the colony, as any of the rest of the inhabitants. I mention these circumstances that you may look through them to the time foretold in prophecy; i.e. Ethiopia shall stretch out her hands unto God. We have very few meetings but that some of the native born sons of Ham are present, and they begin to learn to read and sing the praises of God. I should think that among your large population of colored people, if love of themselves did not bring them out, the love of God would, for here is a wide and extensive missionary field.

My respects to all. Please let the colored brethren in your church hear this letter read. Farewell.

Very respectfully, yours,
In the bond of Christian affection,

Lott Cary

LETTER TO MR. CRANE*　　　　　　*Monrovia, (Liberia,) Africa,*
*June 15, 1825*

Dear Sir,

The arrival of the Fidelity, gives me an opportunity to hand you a few lines, which, I hope, may find you in good health. Nothing very interesting has taken place since I wrote you last, only that among the last emigrants that came out, there has been some considerable sickness and death, the precise account I cannot give at this time. I do believe, that the sickness on new comers hitherto has been greatly increased in consequence of the very unfavourable season of the year in which they leave America. You know that they have long been accustomed to have their system prepared for the summer heat; but to leave in the winter, and be suddenly introduced into a warm climate, it is natural to conclude that they will be sooner attacked,

* *Ibid.*, pp. 55–57.

G　　　　　　　　　83

and that it will generally terminate more seriously. Send them out in the fall, and I think that the sickness will be very light, and, in some constitutions, altogether avoided. Please to use your influence to have a physician sent out, as I must, of necessity, quit the practice of medicine. It occasions a greater consumption of time than I can possibly afford. We begin now to get on with our farms and buildings middling well. I have a promising little crop of rice and cassava, and have planted about 180 coffee trees this week a part of which, I expect, will produce the next season, as they are now in bloom. I think, sir, that in a few years, we shall send you coffee of a better quality than you have ever seen brought into your market. We find that the trees, of two species, abound in great quantities on the capes, both of the large and small green coffee, of which I will send you a specimen by the first opportunity. The Sunday school goes on and prospers, we have now on the list forty, two of them can read in the New Testament quite encouragingly, George and John, from Grand Cape Mount. In addition to that, I have got under way a regular day school. We began with twenty-one, and now have on our list thirty-two. This is called the Missionary School, because established in the name of the African Missionary Society. My respects to all the brethren and friends.

Yours, with respect,

LOTT CARY

TO THE BOARD*    *Monrovia, (Liberia,) Africa,*
*June 15th, 1825*

Very dear patrons,

I know that it will be a source of much gratification to you to hear, that on the 18th day of April, 1825, we established a missionary school for native children. We began with 21, and have increased since up to the number of 32; and as I knew it to be the great object which the society had had in view, I felt that there was no risk in furnishing them with a suit of clothes, each. Upon the credit of the board, I purchased 165 yards of domestic, of brother J. Lewis, which the board will please to pay to his order. We teach from eleven in the morning, until two in the afternoon, that being as much time as I can spare at present. You will see from the list, that Grand Cape Mount will soon be a field for missionary labor, as that nation is

* *Ibid.*, pp. 53–55.

most anxious for improvement. I wrote to the king, some time in May, to send me five or six girls to school; and have since received an answer, informing me that their mothers, and all, were in the Grigory bush, and their girls with them, of course, and when they returned I should have them. According to their custom, they have to remain six months. I intend writing to him again on the subject, and as soon as in the judgement of the board, they can support such an establishment, to get up a school there. To furnish clothes and books, for the children, and support a teacher, is what the board would have to do. I think that after one or two years, such an establishment would be of no expense to the board; but that they would very gladly support a school themselves. I wish the board would deliberate on the subject, and write by the first opportunity, as I expect to go up the next dry season; and probably might succeed in getting on the way such a school; and appoint some one of our young men to take charge of it. The assortment of books, which have been hitherto sent out, has not been adapted to the nature of our infant schools, as we found but very few of them that contained the first principles. You will please to improve our supply of schools books, such as the American, or Webster's spelling book. I have some hope of meeting you in your next annual meeting, if the Lord will. We are told to expect great things, and attempt great things. You must know, that it is a source of much consolation to me, to hear the word of God read by those native sons of Ham, who a few months ago were howling in the devil's bush. May the Lord direct and protect you in all your movements.—Amen.

Yours, etc.

LOTT CARY

# Alexander Crummell, 1819–1898

Alexander Crummell was born in New York City. His father, Boston Crummell, was the son of a Temne chief. Forced to leave an academy in New Hampshire in 1835 because of neighbourhood sentiment against Negroes, Crummell, Henry Highland Garnet, and Thomas S. Sidney entered the Oneida Institute in New York.

When Crummell's petition to be admitted to the general Theological Seminary of the Protestant Episcopal Church in New York was refused, he went to Boston, where he was ordained to the Deaconate in 1842. Two years later he was ordained a priest in Philadelphia. Following this education, Crummell conducted a private school, which was financially unsuccessful. Then he went to England, where he entered Queen's College, Cambridge University, in 1851 and took his B.A. degree in 1853.

Crummell then spent twenty years in West Africa working as a clergyman and educator. In 1873 he returned to Washington and was placed in charge of St. Mary's Protestant Episcopal Mission, which became St. Luke's Episcopal Church during his leadership. Dr. Crummell was pastor there for twenty-two years, and from his pulpit and in the community he exercised leadership over the Negroes in their relation to their position in their own communities and in their relation to Africa.

In 1862 Dr. Crummell published *The Future of Africa* and in 1891 *Africa and America*. For many years he was President of the Colored Ministers' Union of Washington and a member of the Commission for Church Work among Colored People. On March 5, 1897, he founded the American Negro Academy, "an organization of authors, scholars, artists, and those distinguished in other walks of life; men of African descent, for the promotion of letters, science and art, for the promotion of scholarly work, the aiding of youth of genius in the attaining of the higher culture at home and abroad and the gathering into its archives of valuable data." Dr. Crummell has been described as the "ripest literary scholar, the writer of the most graceful and flawless English, and the most brilliant conversationalist the race produced in the nineteenth century."

# The Relations and Duties of Free Colored Men in America to Africa*

*A Letter to Charles B. Dunbar, M.D., Esq., of New York City*

## THE REV. ALEXANDER CRUMMELL

*High School, Mt. Vaughan,*
*Cape Palmas, Liberia*
*1st September, 1860*

. . . I address the "Free Colored Men of America," because I am identified with them; and not because I feel that *they*, especially, and above all the other sons of Africa, in distant lands, are called upon for zeal and interest in her behalf. It is the exaggeration of the relation of *American* black men to Africa, which has turned the hearts of many of her own children from her. Your duties, in this respect are no greater than those of our West Indian, Haytian, and eventually our Brazilian brethern. . . . But I am not the man to address them.

. . . I need not insult the intellect and conscience of any colored man who thinks it his duty to labor for his race on American soil, by telling him that it is his duty to come to Africa. If he is educated up to the ideas of responsibility and obligation, he knows his duty better than I do. . . .

My object in writing this letter is not to vex any of our brethren by the iteration of the falsehood that America is not their home; nor by the misty theory, "that they will all yet have to come to Liberia". . . . I am not putting in a plea for Colonization. . . . But believing that *all* men hold some relation to the land of their Fathers, I wish to call the attention of the sons of Africa in America to their "Relations and Duty to the Land of Their Fathers".

And even on such a theme I know I must prepare myself for the rebuff from many—"Why talk to *us* of Fatherland? What have we to do with Africa? We are not Africans; we are Americans. You ask no peculiar interest on the part of Germans, Englishmen, the Scotch,

* Alexander Crummell, *A Letter to Charles B. Dunbar*, Case Lockwood and Co., 1861.

the Irish, the Dutch, in the land of their fathers; why then do you ask it of us?"

Alas for us, as a race! so deeply harmed have we been by oppression, that we have lost the force of strong, native principles, and prime natural affections. Because exaggerated contempt has been poured upon us, we too become apt pupils in the school of scorn and contumely. Because repudiation of the black man has been for centuries the wont of civilized nations, black men themselves get shame at their origin and shrink from the terms which indicate it.

Sad as this is, it is not to be wondered at. "Oppression" not only "makes a wise man mad", it robs him also of his self-respect. . . .

When these colored men question the duty of interest in Africa because they are not Africans, I beg to remind them of the kindred duty of self-respect. And my reply to such queries as I have mentioned above is this: 1. That there is no need of asking the interest of Englishmen, Germans, Dutchmen and others in the land of their Fathers, because they have this interest, and are always proud to cherish it. And 2nd, I remark that the abject state of Africa is a most real and touching appeal to *any* heart for sympathy and aid. It is an appeal, however, which comes with a double force to every civilized man who has Negro blood flowing in his veins.

. . . There seems to me to be a natural call upon the children of Africa in foreign lands, to come and participate in the opening treasures of the land of their fathers. Though these treasures are the manifest gift of God to the Negro race, yet that race reaps but the most partial measure of their good and advantage. It has always been thus in the past, and now as the resources of Africa are being more and more developed, the extent of *our* interest therein is becoming more and more diminutive. . . .

For three centuries and upwards, the civilized nations of the earth have been engaged in African commerce. Traffic on the coast of Africa anticipated the discoveries of Columbus. . . .

Africa is as rich in resources as India is; not as yet as valuable in products, because she is more unenlightened, and has a less skillful population. But so far as it respects mineral and vegetable capacity, there seems to me but little, if any doubt that Africa more than rivals the most productive lands on the globe. . . .

Now all of this flows into the coffers of the white men. I mean nothing invidious by this. I state a fact, and am utterly unconscious of any unworthy or ungenerous feeling, in stating it. . . . If the black man, I mean, civilized and enlightened, has lying before him a golden heritage, and fails to seize upon and to appropriate it; Providence,

88

none the less, intends it to be seized upon, and wills it to be used. And if the white man, with a keen eye, a cunning hand, and a wise practicalness, is enabled to appropriate it with skill and effect, it is his; God gives it to him; and he has a right to . . . the use of it—responsible, however, both to God and man for the use of right means to the ends he has before him, and for the moral features of his traffic.

But while conceding that the white man has, in the main, fairly won the present trade of Africa; I can not but lament over non-participation therein; for the larger advantages of it, go to Europe and America, and help to swell the broad stream of their wealth, luxury, and refinement. . . .

And now perhaps you ask—"How shall the children of Africa, sojourning in foreign lands, avail themselves of the treasures of this continent?" I answer briefly—"In the same way white men do." *They* have pointed the way; let us follow in the same track and in the use of the like (legitimate) agencies by which trade is facilitated and money is made by them.

Perhaps this is too general; let me therefore attempt something more specific and distinctive.

FIRST, then, I remark that if individuals are unable to enter upon a trading system, they can form associations. . . . If ever the epoch of Negro civilization is brought about in Africa; whatever *external* influences may be brought to bear upon this end; whatever foreign agencies and aids, black men themselves are without doubt to be the chief instruments. But they are to be men of force and energy; men who will not suffer themselves to be outrivaled in enterprise and vigor; men who are prepared for pains, and want and suffering; men of such invincible courage that the spirit cannot be tamed by transient failures, incidental misadventure, or even glaring miscalculations; men who can exaggerate the feeblest resources into potent agencies and fruitful capital. Moreover, these men are to have strong moral proclivities, equal to the deep penetration and unyielding tenacity of their minds. No greater curse could be entailed upon Africa than the sudden appearance upon her shores of a mighty host of heartless black buccaneers . . . . only regarding Africa as a convenient goldfield from which to extract emolument and treasure to carry off to foreign quarters. . . .

Happily for Africa, most of the yearnings of her sons towards her are gentle, humane and generous. When the commercial one shall show itself, it will not differ, I feel assured, from all the others her children have showed. God grant that it may soon burst from many warm and ardent and energetic hearts, for the rescue of a continent.

SECOND. I proceed to show the whole coast offers facilities for adventurous traders. There are few, if any localities but where they can set up their factories and commence business. . . .

But aside from all of this, I may remark here, 1st, that of all rude and uncivilized men, the native African is the mildest and most gentle; and 2nd, that no people in the world are so given to trade and barter as the Negroes of the Western coast of Africa.

THIRDLY. Let me refer to the means and facilities colored men have for an entrance upon African commerce. And 1st, I would point out the large amount of capital which is lying in their hands dead and unproductive. There is, as you are doubtless aware, no small amount of wealth possessed by the free colored population of the United States, both North and South. Notwithstanding the multitudinous difficulties which have beset them in the pathway of improvement, our brethren have shown capacity, perseverence, oftentimes thrift and acquisitiveness. As a consequence they are, all over the Union, owners of houses, farms, homesteads, and divers other kinds of property; and stored away in safe quarters, they have large amounts of gold and silver; deep down in large stockings, in the corners of old chests, in dark and undiscoverable nooks and crannies; besides larger sums invested in banks, and locked up in the safes of city savings banks. . . .

The greater portion of their wealth, however, is unproductive. As a people we have been victimized in a pecuniary point of view, as well as morally and politically; and as a consequence there is an almost universal dread of entrusting our monies in the hands of capitalists, and trading companies, and stock; though in the great cities large sums are put in savings banks. There are few, however, who have the courage to take shares in railroad and similar companies, and in many places it could not be done. . . .

2nd. I turn now to another of their facilities for engaging in African commerce. I refer to NAVIGATION. And here I might rest the case upon the fact that money will purchase vessels, and command seamen and navigators. But you already have *both*. . . . There are scores, if not hundreds of colored men who own schooners, and other small craft in those localities; pilots and engineers, captains and seamen, who, if once moved with a generous impulse to redeem the land of their fathers, could, in a brief time, form a vast commercial marine, equal to all the necessities of such a glorious project.

. . . At an early day whole fleets of vessels, manned and officered by black men from the United States and Liberia, would outrival all the other agencies which are now being used for grasping West African commerce. Large and important houses would spring into existence among you, all through the states. . . .

These are some of the material influences which would result. . . . the moral and philanthropic results would be equally if not more notable. The kings and tradesmen of Africa, having the demonstration of Negro capacity before them, would hail the presence of the black kinsmen from America, and would be stimulated to a generous emulation. To the farthest interior, leagues and combinations would be formed with the men of commerce, and thus civilization, enlightenment and Christianity would be carried to every state, and town, and village of interior Africa.

. . . those men whose feelings are the most averse to anything like colonization, cannot object to the promotion of trade and the acquisition of wealth. Indeed, I have no doubt that there are thousands who would be glad of a safe investment in anything wherein there is probability of advantage. . . .

I have nothing extravagant to say about Liberia. It is a theme upon which I never fall into ecstacies. I cannot find in it as yet place or occasion for violent raptures. . . . Liberia is a young country, hardly yet "in the gristle"—laying, as I dare to affirm, good foundations, but with much pain, great trials, consuming anxieties, and with the price of great tribulation, and much mortality. But is this not the history of all young countries? . . .

I have never been disappointed in anything moral, social or political that I have met with in this land. I came to the country expecting the peculiarities of struggling colonial life, with the added phase of imported habits, tinctured with the deterioration, the indifference, the unthriftiness, which are gendered by *any* servile system. . . .

These anticipations proved correct, save that I found a stronger and a more general disposition to labor than the sad history of our brethren warranted my looking for. . . . Development shows itself on every side. . . . Of course we have here stupid obstructions, men who cling tenaciously to the dead past; a few millinered and epauletted gentry,

> " . . . Neat and trimly dressed,
> And fresh as bridegrooms,"

who would civilize our heathen neighbors with powder and shot; and a few unthinking, unreasoning men, who verily believe that the foundations of all great states have been laid in barter and pelf. But these are by no means the *representative* men of the land. If they were, I should despair of any future for Liberia, and depart.

We have another, a larger class than these; a class which comprises awakened old men, and ardent youth; the minds, whose great object in life is not mere gain of comfort; but who feel that they have a great work to accomplish for their children, for their race, and for God; who feel that they have been called to this mission, and who wish to spend themselves in the expansion and compacting of this youthful republic, to save bleeding, benighted Africa, and to help redeem the continent. . . .

. . . I have no wish to discourage those who are looking to the banks of the Niger. God bless them, every way, if that is indeed their mission! But, as an individual I have earnestly desired a non-sanguinary evangelization of West Africa. All empire, the world over, in rude countries, has been cemented by blood. In Western Africa the tribes, universally, save in Liberia, are strong, independent, warlike. Even British prowess, both at Sierra Leone, and on the Gold coast, succumbs, at times, to their indomitable spirit. And thus you see that for the establishment of a strong black civilization in central Africa, a strong and a bloody hand must be used. Color is nothing, anywhere. Civilized *condition* differences men, all over the globe. Besides this, I have had a prejudice that *that* field God had given to the freed and cultivated men of Sierra Leone,— that they were better fitted to the evangelization of the Niger than we; we with our peculiarities, bred amid American institutions, might prove a disturbing element to the great work, for which, by blood, training, lingual capacity, and the sympathy of character and habits, they were peculiarly fitted; and that our governmental proclivities might jar with what seems a manifest providence, that is, that Christianity is to be engrafted upon such strong states as Dahomey and Ashantee; whose fundamental *governmental* basis, it seems to me, it is not for the interests of civilization and of Africa to revolutionize or to disturb.

I would not pretend to argue these points, much less to dogmatize upon them; for the need of a civilizing element at LAGOS, especially, at Abbeokuta, and on the Niger, is so great that I fear even to state the above impressions. And I stand ready to hail, at any time, any nucleus of freedom and enlightenment that may spring up anywhere on the coast of Africa. . . .

I have heard the poverty of our particular locality contrasted with the richness of other parts of West Africa. Well, this may be the case; but I think there can be no doubt that there is no

92

nobler, more commanding position in West Africa, than that of Liberia. . . .

. . . We *need* immigration. We are poor in men and women. We do not number over 14,000 emigrant citizens . . . we need, I say, not less than 50,000 *civilized* men. I have had the fear that some of my fellow-citizens accustomed themselves to look upon Liberia as a "close corporation". . . . But we, in common with you, are becoming awake to the conviction that, *as a race*, we have a great work to do. The zeal of England and of America, for Africa, is opening our eyes. Our own thoughtful men begin to feel the binding tie which joins them in every interest and feeling, with the Negro race, all over the globe. . . . Let us therefore call our skillful and energetic brethren to come to us and share the suffering and the glory of saving Africa. . . .

As members of the church of Christ, the sons of Africa in foreign lands are called upon to bear their part in the vast and sacred work of her evangelization. . . . It is the duty of black men to feel and labor for the salvation of the mighty millions of their kin all through this continent. I know there is a class of her children who repudiate any close and peculiar connection with Africa. They and their fathers have been absent from this soil for centuries. In the course of time their blood has been mingled somewhat with that of other peoples and races. They have been brought up and habituated to customs entirely diverse from those of their ancestors in this land. And while the race here are in barbarism, they, on the other hand, are civilized and enlightened.

But not withstanding these pleas there are other great facts which grapple hold of these men, and bind them to this darkened wretched Negro race, by indissoluble bonds. There is the fact of kinship, which a lofty manhood and a proud generosity keeps them now, and ever will keep them from disclaiming. There are the strong currents of kindred blood which neither time nor circumstances can ever entirely wash out. There are the bitter memories of ancestral wrongs, of hereditary servitude, which cannot be forgotten till "the last syllable of recorded time". There is the bitter pressure of legal proscription, and of inveterate caste, which will crowd closer and closer their ranks, deepening brotherhood and sympathy, and preserving, vital, the deep consciousness of distinctive race. There still remains the low imputation of Negro inferiority, necessitating a protracted and an earnest battle, creative of a generous pride to vindicate the race, and inciting to noble endeavor to illustrate its virtues and its genius. . . .

How then can these men ever forget Africa?

93

## Dispatches from United States Ministers to Liberia, 1863–1906.

### Roll 7–9, Vol. 9, May 9, 1882–October 7, 1884.

*No. 12.   Jno. H. Smyth\* to Frelinghuysen,*
*October 2, 1882.*

Sir:

Very recently I had an interview with His Excellency the President of the Republic of Liberia, at which meeting that gentleman took occasion to express serious apprehensions with respect to his government being able to retain possession of the north western territory of Liberia, on account of the threatening demonstration made in the naval armament attendant upon the visit of Her Britanic Majesty's Consul for Liberia, the Governor of the West African Settlements, Hon. Arthur E. Havelock, C.M.G., but these apprehensions were augmented by the conference held here in Monrovia March 1st, when it was developed that the purpose of England was to take from the Liberian nation their purchased territory unjustly, wrongfully, upon the pretext that the native races were dissatisfied with Liberia's control, and that by his instructions, Her Majesty's Government had long desired that Sierra Leone and Liberia should be conterminous, that the colony of Sierra Leone needed elbow room on the coast, and being able to satisfy the need, England was determined to make the territories conterminous, by fixing the boundary and that in him (the Governor) had been vested the authority of the "solution of the long pending North Western Boundary of the Republic."

The papers with reference to the conference and subsequent correspondence, copies of the originals in the archives of Sierra Leone and the Liberian Foreign Office being enclosed herewith obviate the necessity of anything more than a passing allusion, since you Sir, will be competent to make comment and approach a proper decision as to the matter; and if not incompatible with the relation of a foreign mutual friend of England and Liberia, you will make such suggestions favorable to the Negro nation's rights as may tend to a final and speedy settlement of the matter in justice and equity to both nations, should you feel called upon to interpose, and your suggested views should be heeded.

This, I am advised, is the desire of the President.

\* See p. 48 for biographical sketch of John H. Smyth.

Since you have ample knowledge of this boundary matter, and I am in possession of facts which may not have before been known to the Department, I improve this occasion to very briefly call attention to such as have become known to me.

England has never had nor does she now pretend to have any right or color of claim to the territory in dispute. Being the self constituted censor in matters of title as to weak and heathen peoples, she feels it to be her high mission to go beyond the limitations of other nations by interference with the concerns of weak and heathen peoples, where such interference is most likely to be followed by material benefits to England. In this particular instance, it is indubitable that if Liberia be ousted of her possession and right, the aboriginal races, with the territory will become vassals and the land, the property of Her Majesty's colonial government of Sierra Leone, and the rich oil and forest possessions will be guarded and protected for the enrichment of England with little reference to whether the Negro is benefitted or not. While there can be no doubt from West African precedent but that England will, should she take this territory (in this instance) afford more immediate and ample facilities for cultivation among the native races of Western civilization than Liberia can now afford, yet she is likely to make the Negroes here subservient to her too frequently incompetent and unsympathetic British representatives and traders, and thereby destroy that self dependence that heathen and barbarous races must in a measure retain in taking upon themselves alien civilizations; if they are to amount to anything more than a servile and an imitative class. In other words, the benefits of such control will be on the side of the civilizer, England, and the civilized will possess doubtful good, questionable advantage. With nations as with the individuals, elevation should be from within—by growth, not from without—by mounting upon others.

The native races are not dissatisfied with the control of the civilized Negro state. And, if they were, neither England nor any other nation has a right, unless injured by such control, to relieve them of it, or by consent of the governing state. Three years ago it was my pleasure to visit, incognito, some of the native races resident in the disputed territory, and I found contentment and plenty among them in the towns and villages. It was a year of successful crops, and although native wars were then in action, yet the Liberian citizen had immunity from molestation so long as his relation was that of a neutral. Trade in the civilized settlements suffered in consequence of the wars, but the same condition of affairs existed then in the native settlements to the east of Sierra Leone, and the military force at command was not competent to stop the wars, and trade languished at times in Freetown. These temporary suspensions of trade will continue to occur from time to time until the influence of civilization shall gradually destroy heathenism and though the work of peaceful change be slow, it is all the more permanent. War force cannot but pander to the worst instincts of heathen races, as it does to the baser instincts of civilized nations.

But the enclosure of the convention made between the Liberian Peace Commission and the native chiefs of the disputed territory (No. 8) speaks with more force than I can against the statement made on the side of the British officer, (No. 7) in refutation of the assertion that the native races are dissatisfied with Liberia's control. The agreement entered into by Governor Havelock and the natives, stripped of the glamour which surrounds it, is but a cajoling of the people into a sale of what is not theirs, for a deferred consideration, and the contingency upon which it depends may happen at any time, and cause a discontinuance of the stipendiary bribes offered and given.

A better lesson in duplicity was never given than the one taught in the convention betweeen Governor Havelock and the native chiefs of the disputed territory.

To say the least, the Commissioners of 1879, with our distinguished naval officer, Commodore Shufeldt, with persons and papers produced, and in the soil in dispute, were, in the opinion of any unbiased mind, more competent to pass upon the subject than the Governor in the absence of the original testimony.

As to the proposal of President Gardner, I am advised that it was made under duress, and with a consciousness that the nation in its representative capacity would oppose it, and hence the effort made to gain time by referring it to the Senate, which will convene in December next.

While European nations have done much for Africa and the world by affording information concerning the ancient and mysterious land—geographically and as to its native races, still seizure was not the controlling motive in the researches of these people. Europe needed a means of perpetuating her own material well being, which overcrowded communities denied. And if to attain the end in view, Africa has suffered in proportion as she has been benefitted, it is not surprising. In the light of the foregoing, it is but reasonable to conclude that, when our country shall be induced to take an active interest in Liberia, or any other portion of the African continent that interest will be unselfish, philanthropic and sincere; or when America shall seek the commerce of Africa, she will do so with no design of acquiring colonial possessions, and she will be more just than others in her dealings with native races.

Please find the following enclosures: number 1 a note as to the prospective conference and its object; number 2, proposition of the British Governor, number 3, the reply to the Governor's proposition by the Secretary; number 4, the President's proposal; number 5 & 6, letters to Morannah Sandoh by Governor Havelock and G. M. Macaulay, number 9 the consent of H.M.'s Government to wait the action of the senate.

With sentiments . . .

JNO. H. SMYTH.

P.S. There is a prospective result that may be looked for to follow the taking from Liberia of this long possessed disputed territory; the lowering of her prestige among the native races within Liberia and contiguous to Liberia. Power always commands respect. Denude Liberia of any portion of her territory, and she so far is injured, and falls in the estimation of native races. Should England take the disputed territory, and the native races be forced into a recognition of a foreign, alien power, they will never *feel* any respect for it. The change must affect injuriously Liberia, and injuriously the aboriginal Negroes' self respect.

The civilized Negro in Africa under foreign domination, as the civilized Negro out of Africa under like control, suffers in his liberty, because it has not the element of imperium. "Imperium et Libertas" must be the motto and the practice of the Negro, if he is to have self respect; if he is to merit the respect of others.

I hope it may be found in consonance with the foreign policy of our Government to aid Liberia in a retention of her self respect unimpaired, her control of her territory, her prestige which is the consequence of her control.

J. H. S.

# George Washington Williams,
## 1849–1891

George Washington Williams was born in Pennsylvania of free parents and was of mixed Negro, German, and Welsh ancestry. He received his early education in Pennsylvania and at the age of fourteen enlisted in the Union Army. After the war he attended the Newton Theological Seminary, from which he was graduated in 1874. His first pastorate was the Twelfth Baptist Church of Boston, the oldest Negro religious community in that city.

During his lifetime, George Washington Williams had several careers. He was the editor of two newspapers, the *Commoner* in Washington, and the *Southwestern Review* in Cincinnati, and for most of his life he combined the roles of scholar, minister, politician, and lawyer, having studied law in the office of Judge Alfonso Taft and later at the Cincinnati Law School. Mr. Williams was author of the first encyclopedic history of the Negro, *The Negro Race in America*, published in 1883, and he was nominated as the first Negro member of the Ohio legislature in 1877. His interest in Africa, however, goes back many years to his valedictory address entitled "Christianity in Africa", given at Newton Theological Seminary. Toward the end of his life, George Washington Williams was commissioned by the United States government to make an investigation of conditions in the Congo, and he was also at one time Minister to Haiti.

AN OPEN LETTER TO HIS SERENE MAJESTY LEOPOLD II, KING OF THE BELGIANS AND SOVEREIGN OF THE INDEPENDENT STATE OF CONGO BY COLONEL, THE HONORABLE GEO. W. WILLIAMS, OF THE UNITED STATES OF AMERICA

*Good and Great Friend,*
I have the honour to submit for your Majesty's consideration some reflections respecting the Independant State of Congo, based upon a careful study and inspection of the country and character of

the personal Government you have established upon the African Continent. . . .

It afforded me great pleasure to avail myself of the opportunity afforded me last year, of visiting your State in Africa; and how thoroughly I have been disenchanted, disappointed and disheartened, it is now my painful duty to make known to your Majesty in plain but respectful language. Every charge which I am about to bring against your Majesty's personal Government in the Congo has been carefully investigated; a list of competent and veracious witnesses, documents, letters, official records and data has been faithfully prepared, which will be deposited with Her Brittannic Majesty's Secretary of State for Foreign Affairs, until such time as an International Commission can be created with power to send for persons and papers, to administer oaths, and attest the truth or falsity of these charges. . . .

There were instances in which Mr. HENRY M. STANLEY sent one white man, with four or five Zanzibar soldiers, to make treaties with native chiefs. The staple argument was that the white man's heart had grown sick of the wars and rumours of war between one chief and another, between one village and another; that the white man was at peace with his black brother, and desired to "confederate all African tribes" for the general defense and public welfare. All the sleight-of-hand tricks had been carefully rehearsed, and he was now ready for his work. A number of electric batteries had been purchased in London, and when attached to the arm under the coat, communicated with a band of ribbon which passed over the palm of the white brother's hand, and when he gave the black brother a cordial grasp of the hand the black brother was greatly surprised to find his white brother so strong, that he nearly knocked him off his feet in giving him the hand of fellowship. When the native inquired about the disparity of strength between himself and his white brother, he was told that the white man could pull up trees and perform the most prodigious feats of strength. Next came the lens act. The white brother took from his pocket a cigar, carelessly bit off the end, held up his glass to the sun and complaisantly smoked his cigar to the great amazement and terror of his black brother. The white man explained his intimate relation to the sun, and declared that if he were to request him to burn up his black brother's village it would be done. The third act was the gun trick. The white man took a percussion cap gun, tore the end of the paper which held the powder to the bullet, and poured the powder and paper into the gun, at the same time slipping the bullet into the sleeve of the left arm. A cap was placed upon the nipple of the gun, and the black brother was implored to step off ten yards and shoot at his white brother to demonstrate his statement that he was a spirit, and, therefore, could not be killed. After much begging the black brother aims the gun at his white brother, pulls the trigger, the gun is discharged, the white man stoops . . . and takes the bullet from his shoe!

By such means as these, too silly and disgusting to mention, and a few boxes of gin, whole villages have been signed away to your Majesty. . . .

When I arrived in the Congo, I naturally sought for the results of the brilliant programme: *"fostering care"*, *"benevolent enterprise"*, an *"honest and practical* effort" to increase the knowledge of the natives *"and secure their welfare"*. I had never been able to conceive of Europeans, establishing a government in a tropical country, without building a hospital; and yet from the mouth of the Congo River to its head-waters, here at the seventh cataract, a distance of 1,448 miles, there is not a solitary hospital for Europeans, and only three sheds for sick Africans in the service of the State, not fit to be occupied by a horse. Sick sailors frequently die on board their vessels at Banana Point; and if it were not for the humanity of the Dutch Trading Company at that place—who have often opened their private hospital to the sick of other countries—many more might die. There is not a single chaplain in the employ of your Majesty's Government to console the sick or bury the dead. Your white men sicken and die in their quarters or on the caravan road, and seldom have christian burial. With few exceptions, the surgeons of your Majesty's Government have been gentlemen of professional ability, devoted to duty, but usually left with few medical stores and no quarters in which to treat their patients. The African soldiers and labourers of your Majesty's Government fare worse than the whites, because they have poorer quarters, quite as bad as those of the natives; and in the sheds, called hospitals, they languish upon a bed of bamboo poles without blankets, pillows or any food different from that served to them when well, rice and fish.

I was anxious to see to what extent the natives had *"adopted the fostering care"* of your Majesty's "benevolent enterprise" (?), and I was doomed to bitter disappointment. Instead of the natives of the Congo "adopting the fostering care" of your Majesty's Government, they everywhere complain that their land has been taken from them by force; that the Government is cruel and arbitrary, and declare that they neither love nor respect the Government and its flag. Your Majesty's Government has sequestered their land, burned their towns, stolen their property, enslaved their women and children, and committed other crimes too numerous to mention in detail. It is natural that they everywhere shrink from "*the fostering care*" your Majesty's Government so eagerly proffers them.

There has been, to my absolute knowledge, no "*honest and practical effort made to increase their knowledge and secure their welfare.*" Your Majesty's Government has never spent one franc for educational purposes, nor instituted any practical system of industrialism. Indeed the most unpractical measures have been adopted *against* the natives in nearly every respect; and in the capital of your Majesty's Government at Boma there is not a native employed. The labour system is radically unpractical; the soldiers and labourers of your Majesty's Government are very largely imported from Zanzibar at a cost of £10 *per capita*, and from Sierre Leone, Liberia, Accra and Lagos at from £1 to £1/10 *per capita*. These recruits are transported under circumstances more cruel than cattle in European countries. They eat their rice twice a day by the use of their fingers; they often thirst for water when the season is dry; they are exposed to the heat and rain, and sleep upon the damp and filthy decks of the vessels often so closely crowded as to lie in human ordure. And, of course, many die.

Upon the arrival of the survivors in the Congo they are set to work as labourers at one shilling a day; as soldiers they are promised sixteen shillings per month, in English money, but are usually paid off in cheap handkerchiefs and poisonous gin. The cruel and unjust treatment to which these people are subjected breaks the spirits of many of them, makes them distrust and despise your Majesty's Government. They are enemies, not patriots.

There are from sixty to seventy officers of the Belgian army in the service of your Majesty's Government in the Congo of whom only about thirty are at their post; the other half are in Belgium on furlough. These officers draw double pay—as soldiers and as civilians. It is not my duty to criticise the unlawful and unconstitutional use of these officers coming into the service of this African State. Such criticism will come with more grace from some Belgian statesman, who may remember that there is no constitutional or organic relation subsisting between his Government and the purely personal and absolute monarchy your Majesty has established in Africa. But I take the liberty to say that many of these officers are too young and inexperienced to be entrusted with the difficult work of dealing with native races. They are ignorant of native character, lack wisdom, justice, fortitude and patience. They have estranged the natives from your Majesty's Government, have sown the seed of discord between tribes and villages, and some of them have stained the uniform of the Belgian officer with murder, arson and robbery. Other officers have served the State faithfully, and deserve well of their Royal Master. . . .

From these general observations I wish now to pass to specific charges against your Majesty's Government.

FIRST.—Your Majesty's Government is deficient in the moral, military and financial strength, necessary to govern a territory of 1,508,000 square miles, 7,251 miles of navigation, and 31,694 square miles of lake surface. In the Lower Congo River there is but one post, in the cataract region one. From Leopoldville to N'Gombe, a distance of more than 300 miles, there is not a single soldier or civilian. Not one out of every twenty State-officials know the language of the natives, although they are constantly issuing laws, difficult even for Europeans, and expect the natives to comprehend and obey them. Cruelties of the most astounding character are practised by the natives, such as burying slaves alive in the grave of a dead chief, cutting off the heads of captured warriors in native combats, and no effort is put forth by your Majesty's Government to prevent them. Between 800 and 1,000 slaves are sold to be eaten by the natives of the Congo State annually; and slave raids, accomplished by the most cruel and murderous agencies, are carried on within the territorial limits of your Majesty's Government which is impotent. There are only 2,300 soldiers in the Congo.

SECOND.—Your Majesty's Government has established nearly fifty posts, consisting of from two to eight mercenary slave-soldiers from the East Coast. There is no white commissioned officer at these posts; they are in charge of the black Zanzibar soldiers, and the State expects them not only to sustain themselves, but to raid enough to feed the garrisons where the white men are stationed. These piratical, buccaneering posts compel the natives to furnish them with fish, goats, fowls, and vegetables at the mouths of their muskets; and whenever the natives refuse to feed these vampires, they report to the main station and white officers come with an expeditionary force and burn away the homes of the natives. These black soldiers, many of whom are slaves, exercise the power of life and death. They are ignorant and cruel, *because* they do not comprehend the natives; they are imposed upon them by the State. They make no report as to the number of robberies they commit, or the number of lives they take; they are only required to subsist upon the natives and thus relieve your Majesty's Government of the cost of feeding them. They are the greatest curse the country suffers now.

THIRD.—Your Majesty's Government is guilty of violating its contracts made with its soldiers, mechanics and workmen, many of whom are subjects of other Governments. Their letters never reach home.

FOURTH.—The Courts of your Majesty's Government are abortive, unjust, partial and delinquent. I have personally witnessed and examined their clumsy operations. The laws printed and circulated in Europe "for the protection of the blacks" in the Congo, are a dead letter and a fraud. I have heard an officer of the Belgian Army pleading the cause of a white man of low degree who had been guilty of beating and stabbing a black man, and urging race distinctions and prejudices as good and sufficient reasons why his client should be adjudged innocent. I know of prisoners remaining in custody for six and ten months because they were not judged. I saw the white servant of the Governor-General, CAMILLE JANSSEN, detected in stealing a bottle of wine from a hotel table. A few hours later the Procurer-General searched his room and found many more stolen bottles of wine and other things, not the property of servants. No one can be prosecuted in the State of Congo without an order of the Governor-General, and as he refused to allow his servant to be arrested, nothing could be done. The black servants in the hotel, where the wine had been stolen, had been often accused and beaten for these thefts, and now they were glad to be vindicated. But to the surprise of every honest man, the thief was sheltered by the Governor-General of your Majesty's Government.

FIFTH.—Your Majesty's Government is excessively cruel to its prisoners, condemning them, for the slightest offences, to the chain gang, the like of which cannot be seen in any other Government in the civilised or uncivilised world. Often these ox-chains eat into the necks of the prisoners and produce sores about which the flies circle, aggravating the running wound; so the prisoner is constantly worried. These poor creatures are frequently beaten with a dried piece of hippopotamus skin, called a "chicote", and usually the blood flows at every stroke when well laid on. But the cruelties visited upon soldiers and workmen are not to be compared with the sufferings of the poor natives who, upon the slightest pretext, are thrust into the wretched prisons here in the Upper River. I cannot deal with the dimensions of these prisons in this letter, but will do so in my report to my Government.

SIXTH.—Women are imported into your Majesty's Government for immoral purposes. They are introduced by two methods, viz., black men are dispatched to the Portuguese coast where they engage these women as mistresses of white men, who pay to the procurer a monthly sum. The other method is by capturing native women and condemning them to seven years' servitude for some imaginary crime against the State with which the villages of these women are charged. The State then hires these woman out to the highest bidder, the officers having the first choice and then the men. Whenever children are born of such relations, the State maintains that the women being its property the child belongs to it also. Not long ago a Belgian trader had a child by a slave-woman of the State, and he tried to secure possession of it that he might educate it, but the Chief of the Station where he resided, refused to be moved by his entreaties. At length he appealed to the Governor-General, and he gave him the woman and thus the trader obtained the child also. This was, however, an unusual case of generosity and clemency; and there is only one post that I know of where there is not to be found children of the civil and military officers of your Majesty's Government abandoned to degradation; white men bringing their own flesh and blood under the lash of a most cruel master, the State of Congo.

SEVENTH.—Your Majesty's Government is engaged in trade and commerce, competing with the organised trade companies of Belgium, England, France, Portugal and Holland. It taxes all trading companies and exempts its own goods from export-duty, and makes many of its officers ivory-traders, with the promise of a liberal commission upon all they can buy or get for the State. State soldiers patrol many villages forbidding the natives to trade with any person but a State official, and when the natives refuse to accept the price of the State, their goods are seized by the Government that promised them "protection". When natives have persisted in trading with the trade-companies the State has punished their independence by burning the villages in the vicinity of the trading houses and driving the natives away.

EIGHTH.—Your Majesty's Government has violated the General Act of the Conference of Berlin by firing upon native canoes; by confiscating the property of natives; by intimidating native traders, and preventing them from trading with white trading companies; by quartering troops in native villages when there is no war; by causing vessels bound from "Stanley-Pool" to "Stanley-Falls", to break their journey and leave the Congo, ascend the Aruhwimi river to Basoko, to be visited and show their papers; by forbidding a mission steamer to fly its national flag without permission from a local Government; by permitting the natives to carry on the slave-trade, and by engaging in the wholesale and retail slave-trade itself.

104

NINTH.—Your Majesty's Government has been, and is now, guilty of waging unjust and cruel wars against natives, with the hope of securing slaves and women, to minister to the behests of the officers of your Government. In such slave-hunting raids one village is armed by the State against the other, and the force thus secured is incorporated with the regular troops. I have no adequate terms with which to depict to your Majesty the brutal acts of your soldiers upon such raids as these. The soldiers who open the combat are usually the bloodthirsty cannibalistic Bangalas, who give no quarter to the aged grandmother or nursing child at the breast of its mother. There are instances in which they have brought the heads of their victims to their white officers on the expeditionary steamers, and afterwards eaten the bodies of slain children. In one war two Belgian Army officers saw, from the deck of their steamer, a native in a canoe some distance away. He was not a combatant and was ignorant of the conflict in progress upon the shore, some distance away. The officers made a wager of £5 that they could hit the native with their rifles. Three shots were fired and the native fell dead, pierced through the head, and the trade canoe was transformed into a funeral barge and floated silently down the river. . . .

TENTH.—Your Majesty's Government is engaged in the slave-trade, wholesale and retail. It buys and sells and steals slaves. Your Majesty's Government gives £3 per head for ablebodied slaves for military service. Officers at the chief stations get the men and receive the money when they are transfered to the State; but there are some middle-men who only get from twenty to twenty-five francs per head. Three hundred and sixteen slaves were sent down the river recently, and others are to follow. These poor natives are sent hundreds of miles away from their villages, to serve among other natives whose language they do not know. When these men run away a reward of 1,000 N'taka is offered. Not long ago such a recaptured slave was given one hundred "chikote" each day until he died. Three hundred N'taka—brassrod—is the price the State pays for a slave, when bought from a native. The labour force at the stations of your Majesty's Government in the Upper River is composed of slaves of all ages and both sexes.

ELEVENTH.—Your Majesty's Government has concluded a contract with the Arab Governor at this place for the establishment of a line of military posts from the Seventh Cataract to Lake Tanganyika territory to which your Majesty has no more legal claim, than I have to be Commander-in-Chief of the Belgian army. For this work the Arab Governor is to receive five hundred stands of arms, five thousand kegs of powder, and £20,000 sterling, to be paid in several instalments. As I write, the news reaches me that these much-treasured and long-looked for materials of war are to be discharged at Basoko, and the Resident here is to be given the discretion as to the distribution of them. There is a feeling of deep discontent among the Arabs here, and they seem to feel that they are being trifled with. As to the significance of this move Europe and America can judge without any comment from me, especially England.

TWELFTH.—The agents of your Majesty's Government have mis-represented the Congo country and the Congo railway. Mr. H. M. STANLEY, the man who was your chief agent in setting up your authority in this country, has grossly misrepresented the character of the country. Instead of it being fertile and productive it is sterile and unproductive. The natives can scarcely subsist upon the vege-table life produced in some parts of the country. Nor will this con-dition of affairs change until the native shall have been taught by the European the dignity, utility and blessing of labour. There is no improvement among the natives, because there is an impassable gulf between them and your Majesty's Government, a gulf which can never be bridged. HENRY M. STANLEY's name produces a shudder among this simple folk when mentioned; they remember his broken promises, his copious profanity, his hot temper, his heavy blows, his severe and rigorous measures, by which they were mulcted of their lands. His last appearance in the Congo produced a profound sensation among them, when he led 500 Zanzibar soldiers with 300 campfollowers on his way to relieve EMIN PASHA. They thought it meant complete subjugation, and they fled in confusion. But the only thing they found in the wake of his march was misery. No white man commanded his rear column, and his troops were allowed to straggle, sicken and die; and their bones were scattered over more than two hundred miles of territory. . . .

## CONCLUSIONS

Against the deceit, fraud, robberies, arson, murder, slave-raiding, and general policy of cruelty of your Majesty's Government to the natives, stands their record of unexampled patience, long-suffering and forgiving spirit, which put the boasted civilisation and professed religion of your Majesty's Government to the blush. During thirteen years only one white man has lost his life by the hands of the natives, and only two white men have been killed in the Congo. Major

BARTTELOT was shot by a Zanzibar soldier, and the captain of a Belgian trading-boat was the victim of his own rash and unjust treatment of a native chief.

All the crimes perpetrated in the Congo have been done in *your* name, and *you* must answer at the bar of Public Sentiment for the misgovernment of a people, whose lives and fortunes were entrusted to you by the august Conference of Berlin, 1884–1885. I now appeal to the Powers which committed this infant State to your Majesty's charge, and to the great States which gave it international being; and whose majestic law you have scorned and trampled upon, to call and create an International Commission to investigate the charges herein preferred in the name of Humanity, Commerce, Constitutional Government and Christian Civilisation.

I base this appeal upon the terms of Article 36 of Chapter VII of the General Act of the Conference of Berlin, in which that august assembly of Sovereign States reserved to themselves the right "to introduce into it later and by common accord the modifications or ameliorations, the utility of which may be demonstrated experience".

I appeal to the Belgian people and to their Constitutional Government, so proud of its traditions, replete with the song and story of its champions of human liberty, and so jealous of its present position in the sisterhood of European States—to cleanse itself from the imputation of the crimes with which your Majesty's personal State of Congo is polluted.

I appeal to Anti-Slavery Societies in all parts of Christendom, to Philanthropists, Christians, Statesmen, and to the great mass of people everywhere, to call upon the Governments of Europe, to hasten the close of the tragedy your Majesty's unlimited Monarchy is enacting in the Congo.

I appeal to our Heavenly Father, whose service is perfect love, in witness of the purity of my motives and the integrity of my aims; and to history and mankind I appeal for the demonstration and vindication of the truthfulness of the charge I have herein briefly outlined.

And all this upon the word of honour of a gentleman, I subscribe myself your Majesty's humble and obedient servant,

GEO. W. WILLIAMS

*Stanley Falls, Central Africa,*
*July 18th, 1890.*

107

# Booker T. Washington,
## 1859–1915

Booker T. Washington was born a slave near Lynchburg, Virginia. After a childhood of extreme deprivation he moved with his mother and stepfather to Meldon, West Virginia. In 1872, after almost literally giving himself his early education, Washington gained admittance to Hampton Institute in Virginia and studied to be a teacher. After teaching for a short period at Hampton, he was recommended by General Armstrong of Hampton to start a similar industrial school at Tuskegee, Alabama. Tuskegee was opened on July 4, 1881, and Washington proved himself to be an able administrator and negotiator as well as teacher. Stressing the need for the Negro to learn the trades necessary for self-sufficiency, Washington's philosophy was congenial to the political and social climate of the South and the country as a whole.

As an able orator, Washington was invited to speak before distinguished audiences in this country and in England. His speech at the opening of the Atlanta Exposition in 1895 was a landmark, described by some as instigating a moral revolution and by others as an infamous retreat on the issue of equality for the Negro. Because of his famous formulation that in all things purely social the races can be separate as the fingers of the hand and in things economic as joined as the hand, Washington delineated a policy in race relations that was to dominate America for several decades.

The American public accepted Washington as the leader of his race, lavishing honours on him and, more significantly, giving him the power to make decisions affecting the position of the Negro in America. Like Douglass, Washington was concerned with the position of the Negro in this country during his lifetime. In addition to the founding of Tuskegee he organized in Boston the Negro Business League, which aimed to bring businessmen of the Negro race together to stimulate growth and development of their business activities by example.

However, Booker T. Washington was not unaware of Africa. As the following selection shows, he was willing to include Africa as a fertile soil for his ideas of education. There is now in Liberia a Booker T. Washington Institute. He also saw Africa as a field of
108

development for Negro business interests, but for Booker T. Washington Africa in its entirety, whether as an outlet for Negro skills or as a field for missionary endeavour, was only to be considered after progress in race relations had been made in this country.

REV. A. E. LE ROY ADAMS, M.S.*          *April 28, 1908*
*Natal, South Africa*

Dear Mr. LeRoy,
    I thank you for your kind letter of March 28th.
    I received the pamphlets on the "Educated Zulu" you sent me sometime ago and hope to use them. I have tried to keep in touch as much as I could with the public opinion of South Africa and to learn as much as possible of the condition, the hopes and the aspirations of the natives of that section. I still have a dream of visiting South Africa before many years.
    I am still sorry that it was not possible for me to accept the invitation some time ago which came from Lord Gray. I have since talked with Lord Gray who is now as you may know the representative of the English Government in Canada, and he again expressed the wish that I should make a visit to South Africa at some time in the future. It is one of the things I am going to keep in mind.
    With sincere regards and thanks for your kindness in writing me as you have, I am

Very sincerely yours,

BOOKER T. WASHINGTON

*January 30, 1911*

REV. JOHN H. HARRIS,†
*Denison House, Vauxhall Bridge,*
*London, S.W., England.*

Dear Mr. Harris,
    We are planning to hold the Conference of friends of Africa at Tuskegee Institute during the month of April, 1912. I shall write

* Reprinted by kind permission of the Washington family.
† Organizing secretary of the Anti-Slavery Aborigines Protection Society. This letter reprinted by permission of the Washington family.

you more fully when our plans are more thoroughly matured. I am very glad to learn that there is a possibility of your being able to attend this meeting. Nothing would give us greater pleasure than to welcome you there.

Yours very truly,

BOOKER T. WASHINGTON

LETTER TO MR. WASHINGTON FROM EMMETT SCOTT*

*July 2, 1910*

The Tuskegee Normal and Industrial Institute
For the Training of Colored Young Men and Women
Tuskegee Institute, Alabama

Dear Mr. Washington:

Sometime ago you suggested that I should submit some suggestions for the establishment of an industrial school in Liberia.

It occurs to me, to start with, that a study of the Tuskegee Institute catalogue as well as a study of the course of study formulated for the Children's House might be of substantial value to the person selected to undertake the establishment of such an institution.

At the very start I must record my conviction that vocational instruction, to be associated in the closest way possible with agricultural training, is the obvious need of the Liberian people; so obvious in fact is this need that it requires no elaboration.

As to academic instruction, I should say, first, that hygiene should have a very large place in the course of instruction. The Medical Attache of the Commission found that one of the gravest needs of the Liberian people is instruction in the most fundamental things that concern proper sanitary and health regulations. A person of strong individuality could do much to help the people along this line. This extract from the report to which I have referred may be worthy of attention:

> The medical conditions in Liberia are deplorable in the extreme, the amount of preventable or relievable suffering very great and the mortality undoubtedly much higher than it should be. This state of affairs is due to several causes, chief among which may be mentioned the total absence, from most parts of the country, of skilled

* See p. 322 for biographical sketch of Emmett J. Scott. This letter reprinted by kind permission of the Washington family.

or educated medical men, with consequent non-treatment or mistreatment of many cases of illness; climate and sanitary conditions; ignorance of hygiene and superstition. . . .

In my opinion it is safe to say that quite 90 *per cent* and possibly all, of the population of Monrovia has malaria. . . .

There are probably few places in the world where medical practitioners and hospitals are more needed and few that offer much poorer monetary inducements for them. If I may judge from my own observations I would say that most Liberians are very poor and therefore unable to pay decent fees for medical service. . . .

A drug store as a side issue to a medical practice should be very profitable, and it would certainly do great good if quinine and other standard drugs were sold at a moderate profit. At present the usual retail price of quinine is one shilling for 12 pills of 2 or 3 grains each, and as the laborer's wage is about a shilling a day, it may be seen that this price places the drug almost or quite out of his reach. . . .

There should be, I think, instruction in natural science adapting it, of course, to the essential needs of the people. In geography and history the attention of the people needs to be directed for instance to a study of their own country. I found a great deal of silliness in some of the instruction being given in Liberia, for instance: in a school being conducted by a well-intentioned woman who was able to have her children most glibly reply to questions as to the largest cities in America, the most important rivers, the capital of the United States, and the names of the Presidents of the United States, etc. When we in turn sought some replies, the children were unable to tell us even the most elementary things regarding Liberia and Africa itself. Some of the ludicrous replies I think I have in person mentioned to you. There should be it seems to me a special course similar to the one we have at Tuskegee on the "Negro in Africa".

It is not to be expected that in the beginning of such a work that everything can be done for the people but a course in physical training for both the boys and girls would be most helpful. Simple "setting-up" exercises for the boys and modified Swedish exercises for the girls would help much.

In selecting appropriate subjects for instruction in the mechanical industries it is hard to get away from the general idea that the trades at present needed in Liberia are those that are primarily associated with construction. To illustrate what is in my mind I would say that carpentry should have a fundamental place with a leaning toward the making of furniture and the construction of houses. Associated with carpentry should be elementary work in materials particularly in tinning, for the construction of water-spouts drains, and masonry. A great deal of attention might be given to the development of cement in masonry both of foundation and for construction purposes. The Liberians already are able to do some work in masonry but it is particularly crude. Greater skill is needed in making cement blocks and infinitely more skill is needed in laying the blocks.

Associated with this construction it seems to me should go instruction as to drainage. A great deal of attention might be given to the location of houses with respect to natural drainage and the means of diverting moisture through drains of all kinds. This should extend undoubtedly to the disposal of sewerage and, also, to the disposal of kitchen refuse. In a country which is so well watered it would be possible by means of proper pumps and cisterns to have sinks and running water in the houses, and this instruction might be included in the work of the school.

Aside from the special instruction which is above mentioned it seems to me that Liberia offers the opportunity, also, for the development of specific industries. Liberia is a country rich in fibers of all kinds. Instruction might be given in a way to introduce into the country some useful manual industries. I have in mind especially the weaving of these fibers. If such a scheme were practicable it should also lead to the better preparation of raw material for export because the use to which the raw material used could be put would, in a measure, be known to the people. The local market necessarily would be a small one, but there is no reason why the people should not manufacture all of the piassava baskets and hats which they need, and some besides for export. If this suggestion is practicable you can readily see that the weaving would offer especial opportunities for girls.

Industrial schools for girls are commonly confined to cooking, sewing, and to dress-making. Mr. Falkner, an associate Commissioner, who had charge of the Department of Education in Porto Rico, tells me that they had very great success there in introducing instruction in millinery. They made and trimmed hats which were in demand among the patrons of the school, and established a department for making women's hats on a more or less modern style for the relatively well-to-do people. This could be done in Liberia.

Of course with the carpentry there should go, it seems to me, some instruction in woodturning and woodworking. A sawmill also would be of undoubted value in teaching the Liberians, natives and others, how to turn the forests into lumber for the building of houses, etc.

Printing should not be overlooked. There are newspapers to be printed, government reports to be printed, and in fact the need for a printing department is so obviously necessary that I need not elaborate upon it.

I, also, think that there should be some training in painting so that the people might learn the value of preserving their houses from the hard rains which are a part of that climate.

Training in agriculture I consider a fundamental need of the Liberians. There is no reason why they should not raise all of their food supplies at home; and no reason why they should not raise hogs, and why efforts should not be made to improve the present breed of cows. In a country as rich as Liberia is as to fertility of soil, there is not the slightest reason, so far as I can imagine, why they should have to import one single thing to eat. There are many importations, even of rice, and this I think should be discouraged. By all means I think that one of the strongest men on the Faculty should be a man trained in agriculture.

There are other needs, of course, which may occur to you. I have only tried to sketch in detail some of the things that immediately occur to me. As above stated, I have had the privilege of talking with Mr. Falkner, and he is of the opinion that if a school somewhat after the above can be established for the Liberians it will prove of incalculable help to them.

Yours truly,

(signed) EMMETT SCOTT

M.H.

SPEECH

BEFORE THE BROOKLYN INSTITUTE OF ARTS AND SCIENCES,

*February 22, 1903\**

. . . Two thousand years later—in round numbers—another explorer and historian writing of the Africans—the stock out of which my race

* E. Davidson Washington (ed.), *Selected Speeches of Booker T. Washington*, Double, Doran & Co., Inc., 1932, pp. 268–69, and reprinted by kind permission of the Washington family.

grew—has this to say of them and I quote from Dr. Livingstone: "I had been in closer contact with heathenism than I had ever been before; and although all, including the chief, were as kind and attentive to me as possible, and there was no want of food, oxen being slaughtered daily, more than sufficient for the wants of all of us, yet to endure the dancing, warring, and singing, the jesting, anecdotes, grumbling, quarreling and murdering of these children of nature, seemed more like a severe penance than anything I had ever before met with in my course. . . ."

. . . If one had asked Caesar when he first discovered your forefathers in the condition that has been described, if in two thousand years they could be transformed into the condition in which they are now found in America, the answer doubtless would have been an emphatic 'No'. If one had asked Livingstone, when he first saw my forefathers in Africa, if in fifty years that have elapsed since then, or even in the two hundred and fifty years that have passed since the first African was brought to this country, a young Negro would be the class orator at Harvard University, the answer doubtless would have been a 'No'—as emphatic as Caesar's.

EDUCATION OF SOUTHERN NEGRO—DELIVERED AT 43RD ANNUAL MEETING OF THE NATIONAL EDUCATION ASSOCIATION, HELD AT ST. LOUIS, MO. IN CONNECTION WITH THE LOUISIANA PURCHASE EXPOSITION, JUNE 27–JULY 1, 1904

. . . Upon many vital points affecting the Negro the nation has been divided from the first. As far back as the 17th century a portion of the nation sent ambassadors to the natives in Africa, saying: "Come hither and we will do thee good." While another portion said to the African, "It is best for you and for us that you remain away." Later came slavery and the division of American sentiment was still more evident. One portion of the country said that slavery was righteous and best for the Negro and the nation; another said it was sinful and hurtful to the Negro and the nation. Still later came freedom, another division appears. One element said that the Negro could not be educated; another said he was capable of education; another element claimed that whenever a mulatto exhibited qualities of executive ability, of organizing power, it was the white blood that should have the credit; still another element just as emphatically claimed that the mixing of races tended to weaken the Negro. Another element claimed that the salvation of the South would only come

114

when the Negro departed from its cotton, rice and cane fields, still whenever the emigration agent appeared, he was usually met and virtually forbidden to take a Negro from Southern fields. One element argued that the future hope of the Negro consisted in keeping in close touch with the American white man, another said that it was the part of wisdom to keep the race as completely separated as possible. One element argued that the Negroes should return to Africa; another, that they should remain in America. One element contended that with the ballot the Negro was doomed. Another, that without the ballot destruction awaited him. . . .

These most bewildering contentions and differences at least prove two points: one, that the white man, at least on this subject, is not omniscient; and the other, that the Negro deserves the greatest credit for having kept his head and courage in the midst of such confusing contentions and differences.

LAST ANNUAL ADDRESS AS PRESIDENT, DELIVERED BEFORE
THE NATIONAL NEGRO BUSINESS LEAGUE, BOSTON, MASS.,
*August 19, 1915*

. . . We can learn a lesson, a serious lesson for our race in this country from the past experiences of those two Negro republics—Liberia and Haiti. For a number of years those people have devoted themselves to literary education and have been mostly concerned over political and religious matters. And the stress has been laid upon propositions largely abstract in character. In a large measure they have neglected to apply their education and energy to the development of the soil, to the development of the forests, mines and other natural resources of their respective countries, and the result is that instead of going forward they have gone backward from an economic point of view, until now both of those governments are so deeply in debt that white foreign nations have had to take practical charge over their financial and fiscal affairs. What economic development means for a nation in enabling it to be self-supporting, self-governed, and respected applies equally to any race and to any individual. . . .

# John Wesley Gilbert,
# 1865–1923

John Wesley Gilbert was born in Hephzibaha, Georgia, and was educated in the public schools of Augusta, the Atlanta Baptist Seminary (Theological Department of Morehouse College), Paine College, and Brown University. While at Brown, Gilbert was awarded a special scholarship for excellence in Greek, which enabled him to attend the American School of Classics in Athens. He travelled extensively in Europe and in Africa. Later he was sent to Africa and together with Bishop Walter Russell Lambuth of the Southern Methodist Church he founded the mission of Wembo-Nyama in the Republic of the Congo, the same mission which gave Patrice Lumumba his early education. This establishment represents the first missionary work of Southern Methodism in Africa.

Mr. Gilbert began his teaching in 1888 as the first Negro on the faculty of Paine College in Augusta, Georgia. In 1895 he entered the ministry of the Colored Methodist Church, which is composed of the families of those Negroes who were former slaves and who had been members of the Methodist Church South until 1870. In 1901 he was a member of an Ecumenical Congress which assembled in London. In 1913 he was elected the third president of Miles College, where he served for one year.

# The Southern Negro's Debt and Responsibility to Africa*

## JOHN W. GILBERT

*Birmingham, Ala., President Miles Memorial College, Colored Methodist Episcopal Church*

This meeting is none other than an epoch-making endeavor with the avowed purpose of bringing about such a missionary awakening among the Negro students of this country as to cause them to study seriously their obligations to Africa. If possible, it is to find young Christian men and women in this gathering, or as its results who will go to that land to help Christianize it in every sense of that word. Therefore, I am more than glad to be identified with it.

Once for all be it said that from nearly every viewpoint the pre-pared Southern Negro is the very best Negro, perhaps the very best person in the world, for African missionary work. This is true not only for climatic and purely physiological reasons, but because the Negro of the South has larger opportunities for development along all lines of Christian civilization than he has anywhere else in the world. Here are, according to the best available statistics, nine-tenths of all his churches, nearly all his schools, and most of his best homes, farms, and money. His opportunities to learn and ply most of the mechanical trades and professions are found in well nigh every section of the South. Whatever may be said against the South, it is here that the Negro flourishes best. Thank God, more and more the spirit and work of Christian cooperation between white and black people of the South in Church and school are growing every day that we move further forward from the "bloody 60's". Southern whites and Southern blacks are working together in Church and school for the uplift of the weaker brother both here and in Africa. And so it ought to be. Yea, more. So it *must* be, if we are ever to reach that proper adjustment of our inter-racial relationships which we call the "Race Problem". Christ at work with white and black men is what my country here and my fatherland over the seas are praying and working for to-day. Others ought to help us. We must help ourselves.

* A. M. Trawick (ed.), *The New Voice in Race Adjustments*, Addresses and Reports Presented at the Negro Christian Student Conference, May 14–18, 1914, pp. 129–133.

Now, in view of the advantages which the Negroes enjoy in the South where eight millions of them live, what are some of the debts which they owe to Africa and its 161,000,000 of heathens and pagans? Before enumerating any of these debts, we must fix well in our minds the Christian principle that the opportunity to pay them is the unvarying measure of our responsibility so to do. We Southern Negroes are responsible to God and good men for Africa's redemption according as we have opportunity.

The least binding debt that we owe Africa is that, because we are descendants of that Continent we ought, in the spirit of the descendants of all other lands, to do whatever we can for its uplift. This is race pride. It is natural. The most binding debt that we owe Africa and all men comes from Christ: "Go ye into all the world and preach the gospel to every creature." This is the Christ-love. Nature and law make men into races, and nations. Grace came by Jesus Christ, and grace makes us "neither Greek nor Jew—Barbarian, Scythian, bond nor free: but Christ is all and in all."

> All men are equal in God's sight.
> There is no black, there is no white.
> The petty distinctions of race and caste
> Are shriveled and shrunk in the
> Furnace blast of God's great love.

This theory is the ideal Catholicity of Christian ethics; nevertheless, the Southern Negro is bound to pay his obligations to Africa first and most; for that is very nearly the only mission field in which he has opportunity to labor. His white brother can go as a missionary to all heathen and pagan lands of the earth. However, it yet remains, that the measure of our obligation is in direct proportion to our opportunity.

What are some of the obligations that we American Negroes are under to Africa? The foremost seems to me to be the giving to the African a Negro ideal of all that is best in Christianity. When a man sees another of his own race who lives a true life and does a noble deed the chords of all his being are stretched and attuned by inspiration toward similar attainments. He sees his own future self mirrored in his ideal. No people can reach their best who have not inspiration from faith in themselves. This is righteous race pride. This is the background whence hope is projected into the future.

We owe it to the African to teach him that his continent and his people had proud representatives in the early morning of sacred

118

and profane history. Let him know that Egypt was introduced into history by dynasties of Hamitic, most probably Negro, kings; that hoary Mt. Berkel and Meroe, two large cities down the Nile, peopled and governed solely by wooly haired Negroes before Homer or Virgil sang the fall of Troy, had reached the acme of the world's sculpture and architecture. The African must learn that, omitting the Jew, his country and countrymen were more closely connected with biblical history than any other land and people. Africa has figured next to Palestine in "Sacred Story". Abraham, Jacob, Israel, Moses, Aaron, the pillar of cloud by day, the pillar of fire by night, the crossing of the Red Sea—Oh, how many men and miracles of God found their stage of action in the black man's land! Isaiah prophesied of it, "The land of the rustling of wings which is beyond the rivers of Ethiopia". Ebedmelech, the Ethiopian, received from God the reward of deliverance from peril for rescuing the prophet Jeremiah from a miry dungeon into which his own countrymen had cast him. "Africa cradled the Messianic race" thousands of years before it sheltered the infant Son of God. An African bore the cross of Christ. Africans, "dwellers in Egypt and the parts of Libya about Cyrene", were present at Pentecost. The book of Acts tells of two Africans that were leaders, a prophet and a teacher, in "the first Missionary Church". I pass by the many eminent African scholars and Church Fathers connected with early Church History. Nobody can by example more effectively teach the Negro his connection with the Bible and the possibilities of his own development under Christianity than the Negro himself. The native Africans have faith in the white man. They believe he can do anything. But they need to have faith in themselves and knowledge of themselves as a once great race. The Negroes of this enlightened country owe it to them to teach them that, although the fortuitous events of history, such as the slave trade and the fire and sword of Mohammed, have sunk their land into the darkest vice and degradation during the last ten or twelve centuries, nevertheless, according to biblical story and Church History, the Africans are one of heaven's most highly favored peoples. By nature the American Negroes—only the very best of them, I mean—are better prepared to do this work than any other people on earth.

Evangelization alone is not what the Southern Negro owes to Africa. But since all the virtues of Christ should enter into all forms of human activities and human relationships, and since true Christianity fosters the highest industrial, intellectual and spiritual culture, we owe it to the African to develop him in this threefold manner—owe it to him in a certain sense more than do any other people in the world. The Southern Negro's debt to Africa is obligatory from every point of view.

He ought to carry to his own "Brother in Black" industrial training. The ability to learn industries is native to the Africans, if their crude manufactures are to be taken as evidence. The native cloths of the Bakubas in Congo, Belge, knives, spear points, and many other articles made of the iron and copper of the Sankuru and Katanga districts, the dug-out canoes that ply the Congo and the Nile, the many hard woods of finest grain that constitute the African forests, the trees and vines that drip liquid rubber, copal, and oil, by day and by night, the unsurpassed fertility of the soil, the cassava and grain, and the very clay of the earth call to Hampton, Tuskegee and Cheyney Institutes more loudly than to white schools anywhere for factories, trades and scientific agriculture. For obvious reasons this cry could not in the past be answered by us; but more and more both in numbers and efficiency, as the opportunities come, we as a race must embrace them.

God is calling for the Christian Negro physicians of the South to go to Africa. The present King of Belgium is offering 125,000 francs to any physician who discovers a specific for "Sleeping Sickness", the scourge of Africa. No mission can be operated without a practicing physician and a pharmacy. The "witch doctor" kills more than he cures with his liquids, herbs, roots, charms, and fetiches. Meharry, Howard and Leonard ought to regard this condition a call from Africa more directly to them than to any of the white medical schools. The frightful mortality of the country (the second largest continent in the world with only 161,000,000 inhabitants) is due to the fact that there are generally no physicians there. The death rate of infants, child bearing women, and victims of one form and another of all the malarious and paludal diseases are calling for the Negro Christian physician every day.

Then Africa is calling for teachers—especially those possessing linguistic ability. Besides the actual work of teaching, the Scriptures and text books, their folklore told in song and story, must be put into at least one of the 160 dialects of the continent, according to whatever part of Africa the teacher may be in. The native dialects must be reduced to writing. To Africa Negro scholarship owes this debt in the name of Christ, who is not dead on earth, but whose biography is being lived out by us, if so it be that we are his in deeds as well as in creeds. Africa needs thousands of teachers, graduates of Atlanta, Fisk, Moorehouse, Paine, and similar institutions; for, besides possessing by nature, the race instinct, they are

120

better suited physically for work in Africa than their white brethren.

Now, coming to the preacher for the African mission, the Southern Negro with a burning passion for souls, a follower of Christ more than of creed, owes above all other men to the "Dark Continent" to redeem its women and men from the heathen and pagan thralldom of polygamy to the monogamy of the Christian religion. Polygamous Mohammedanism above the equator along with polygamous heathenism, and therefore the wrong estimate of women and children almost everywhere on the continent, ought to be met and overthrown by Negro preachers first of all.

The so-called civilization, tainted by the commercial corporations which have concessions from certain white governments to operate for financial profits in Africa, is worse in most respects than heathenism. These commercial companies exploit the land and the people for money, leaving in their wake rum and the prostitution of every innate sentiment of purity of life. Instead of bread they give them a stone, and instead of meat they give them a poisonous serpent.

"Come over and help us" ought to be heard by Negro Christians first of all.

This call has not been met heretofore by American Negroes in large numbers for such obvious reasons as financial inability, ignorance of the real conditions in Africa, and general unpreparedness in education and religion for mission work. Just here the white man's burden of duty to our race finds its ground of obligation not only to Africa in America, but also to Africa in Africa. To say nothing of the Christian duty of the strong to help the weak, without feeling anything but love for every man of whatever color, without finding fault with the ways of Providence in leading us through the schools of slavery and repression, it does seem, even from a human estimate of the equation of justice between man and man, that, whereas American white people held us in bondage for at least seven generations, they ought to feel bound to cooperate with us for at least that length of time in our Christianization. That is mere human justice. But Christ teaches that so long as one man is able to help another to material betterment and spiritual uplift, it is his duty to do so. Therefore it is the duty, especially of the Southern Negro to seek the help of the Southern white man in the interest of the race here and in Africa. When these two can get together on the broad plane of the "fatherhood of God and the brotherhood of man", all other men everywhere will follow their Christian example. Such cooperative Christian missionary work here and in the Dark Continent will do more real and lasting good than all other agencies combined.

# Frederic J. Loudin,
# 1840–1904

Frederic J. Loudin was born in Portage County, Ohio. Although his father had sufficient means to send him to a college in Ohio, Loudin was refused schooling in Ravenna and became a printer's apprentice. Later he joined the Methodist Church where he was refused a place in the choir because of his colour. Following the Civil War Loudin went to Tennessee, where he became interested in the work of the Fisk Jubilee Singers, which he joined previous to their second visit to Great Britain in 1875. He travelled abroad with this group for five years. Soon thereafter it disbanded, and in 1882 Mr. Loudin organized and directed his own group, which he called the Loudin Jubilee Singers. In 1888 his group made a world tour, travelling via the Mediterranean Sea through the Suez Canal to the Indian Ocean, the Pacific Ocean, and finally landing in San Francisco in June 1900. From 1900 to 1903 the group toured the British Isles. Mr. Loudin returned to the United States in 1903 after a final tour of the British Isles and died in his home in Ravenna, Ohio, in 1904.

*The Fisk University Jubilee Singers,*
*27 Paternoster Row,*
*London, E.C.*
*April 29, 1900*

Dear Mr. Bruce,*

I remember to have had the pleasure of meeting you once in Washington. I have read with much pleasure many articles from your pen and always with interest but none with deeper interest than the one I have just received in the Albany paper you so kindly sent me and I want to thank you for it for I am sure in "free"(?) America the Negro who is trying to hold up his head and do something for the race needs all the encouragement he is apt to get from those whom he

* See p. 126 for biographical sketch of John Bruce. This letter is in the Schomburg Collection and is reprinted by kind permission of the New York Public Library.

seeks to help as well as from those whose blows he is trying to ward
off. From my point of observation it seems as if the white people of
all political parties had hoisted the very floodgates of the lower regions to wipe us out. What does it all mean? I have been wondering
in what way "bloody McKinley" is going to appeal to the Negro
voter this time but he needs no appeal [to] get on the Republican
ticket that is all and he has pressed the button and the Negro will do
the rest. As you once very truly and aptly said "the Negro is the only
sure thing in politics". Had I a thousand votes to cast I would give
them all to Cleveland rather than one to McKinley or that other
whited sepulchre Roosevelt who slandered our brave soldiers who
saved him and his Rough Riders from annihilation. But I have little
faith or hope that the Negro has the manhood to resent the treatment
meted out to him by the so-called Republicans. They are for the
most part blindly Republicans which fact is in my opinion why the
Republicans ignore our wrongs and the other parties hate us and we
got or have ceased to receive the respect or defense of the Republicans and in my opinion nothing but a rebuke at the polls is going to
arouse the party who *owne us body and soule*. To a sense of their duty
we *say* they don't but the facts point the other way.

I wish you would start the ball rolling along another line.
America that owes the non-intervention of Europe in the late war
with Spain to Britain has turned her back on Britain now as she
turned her back on the Negro when the war was ended and the
white people are holding meetings all over the country passing resolutions of sympathy with those Boers who would enslave our people
the very moment they free themselves from British rule. In fact it is
well known that Britains refusal to allow that is in a great measure
responsible for the present outbreak. I grant you that British rule in
South Africa is not all we wish it were but it is a thousand times better than Boer administration. Britain has her missionaries there and
doing *something* to lift up the race while the Boers with all their religious hypocrisy dont believe we even have a *soul* to be saved and
only seek to repress and further degrade us. I need not tell you what
Britain has been to us and is the bare fact of the experience of
Coleridge Taylor the fact that there is a sentiment prevalent here to
render such a thing possible says more than all I could write in
months. Think of it one of the most exclusive and aristocratic musical
organizations in the world if not *the* most exclusive asking a Negro to
write a work for it and then to conduct their performance of it in the
finest and largest hall in Britain with orchestra of over 150 pieces
and choirs of over a thousand and singing a Negros music (not a

Coon song) and that Negro conducting it. Think of that and then tell me if the President Members of Congress of the Supreme Court and all the Legislatures would not resign if such a thing should occur in Free America and what is more I think Blanuelt and Whitney Mockridge are both Americans.

I am continually being asked how we stand on the war question "if *we* sympathise with the Boers". I think we ought to *speak out*. There has been no time in our history when speaking out on this question will count for half so much as the present moment. No time when our words will have such weight for the good of our race in all parts of the world so far as Britain is concerned as just *now* no time when we could make so many friends as now. It is well for us I think that the white people of America are talking with the oppressors of our race for it gives opportunity for our words to carry a weight with them they never would had the white Americans not acted so ungrateful. Then too the white Americans were *busy* over here sowing the seeds of sedition against us trying to undo the work of Douglass, Ida B. Wells and others. This country has passed resolutions at large and influential meetings condemning lynching. The press has spoken out against it but in recent years especially in the last year great efforts have been made to counteract that sentiment. Letters from Southerners and people from the North as well have frequently been published in various papers against us and to lead these people to believe they had not known the *real* facts in the case that the millions of money they have in the years gone by have been worse than thrown away and the effect was noticeable. But our time has come *now*. Have we the manliness to improve it?

All Europe and America sympathise with the Boers. *Surely these* people, the Britains are deserving of *our* sympathy, for they are and have been our friends. I have been under the British flag in nearly all quarters of the globe have never with the single exception of Canada —which draws its inspiration more from America than England— been denied any right a white man enjoys.

That which I would advise and *strongly* too is that mass meetings be held, resolutions—of which our people are very fond of passing— be passed and sent to the British Ambassador or to Lord Salisbury, but if sent to the British Ambassador requesting him to forward them to his government and dont be afraid to make them too strong and let them know *who* we are.

Please do not delay for *now* is the time. We will I am sure in this way make more friends—and God knows we need them—than in any other way. It will influence the treatment of our race in Africa

124

as well; the opportunity is one of a lifetime. It is the one time when the expression of opinion will have *great* weight.

This country is grievously disappointed over the attitude of the American people and press towards them and it opens a door to us that would otherwise have been closed.

I am fearful I may have to come to America this summer to look for singers. I am going to need a soprano an Alto and a Tenor. Good strong sweet voices and none but ladies or gentlemen. Do you know of any such who would be willing to stay over here at least two years if I wanted so long; nice looking and reasonably good disposition no drinkers or gamblers or profane people wanted. I shall be greatly obliged if you could put me in correspondence with any such people.

I am sending you another paper or two with criticisms on Coleridge Taylor in them.

Forgive me for trespassing so long upon your time. I should be glad of a line from you whenever you have the time and feel so inclined.

Faithfully yours in the great struggle,

F. J. LOUDIN

# John Edward Bruce,
# 1856–1923

John Edward Bruce was born a slave in Maryland, but was carried into the freedom of Washington by his mother, who worked as a cook to support him. Bruce received his early education privately and at quite an early age developed a taste for journalism. Beginning as Washington correspondent for the *Richmond Star*, he wrote under the *nom de plume* of "Rising Sun". Over the years he was editor of several newspapers: *The Argus* in Washington, D.C.; *The Sunday Item* in Washington; *The Republican* in Norfolk; and *The Commonwealth* in Baltimore. Later, writing under the name of Bruce Grit, given him by Thomas Fortune, he became a famous correspondent, contributing to a great number of papers of the Negro press, such as the *St. Louis World, The Indianapolis World, The Pittsburgh Virginia Herald, The Virginia Star, The Chicago Conservator, The Florida Sentinel, The New York Freeman, the New York Age, The Elevator, The Kansas City Call*, and *The Omaha Monitor*. He also contributed to *The Boston Transcript, The Albany Argus,* and *The Buffalo Express.* Mr. Bruce did not confine himself to papers in the United States, and occasionally contributed to *The New Age* of London, *The West African–Lagos Record, The South African Spectator* of Cape Town, *The Jamaica Advocate* of Kingston, Jamaica, and *The African Times and Orient Review* of London.

Having a long interest in Africa, Bruce was a member of the African Society of England, later becoming its Honorary Secretary, and in 1911 with Arthur A. Schomburg he organized and became the first president of the Negro Society for Historical Research of Yonkers, New York. The letters written by Bruce for Aggrey as he embarked on his famous trip to Africa for the Phelps-Stokes Foundation should be of particular interest to readers of this anthology. As an American Negro who had friends in many parts of Africa, Bruce at this time was able to introduce to his friends in Africa an African, then relatively unknown, whose name was to become for some synonymous with the modernization of Africa.

DR. MOSES DA ROCHA,                          *240 West 138th Street*
*Iron House,*                                   *New York, New York*
*Lagos, West Coast Africa*                          *July 29, 1920*

My dear old friend Da Rocha:*

This will be handed to you by Professor J. E. K. Aggrey, a professor in one of our leading Negro colleges—Livingstone at Salisbury, North Carolina. He is my warmest friend and I want you to know him well. Professor Aggrey is a native of the Gold Coast and has recently been appointed a member of a commission sent out by the Phelps-Stokes Fund to do important work in Africa and of which he will himself tell you. I am sure you will be glad to cooperate with him when you know the breadth and scope of the mission which has brought him to our beloved Fatherland and so I need not urge a *race patriot* to help a race patriot; that goes without saying.

You will find Professor Aggrey a Christian gentleman and a *scholar* of no mean ability. He has won high honors at Columbia University in New York City and ranks with the *best products* of that celebrated institution in the *force* that wins. Could you expect anything else of an *African*?

Yours sincerely,

BRUCE GRIT

* A similar letter was sent to Judge Dossen of Liberia, with the added comment, "*He is an African* of the African and is *working* for Africa. Help him." Professor Abayone Cole of Freetown also received a similar letter. This letter is in the Schomburg Collection and is reprinted by kind permission of the New York Public Library.

# Harry Dean,
## 1864– ?

Captain Harry Dean has been described as the Colored Trader Horn. He was born in Philadelphia and early came under the tutelage of Fanny Jackson Coppin, mentioned elsewhere in this volume as the Principal of the Institute of Colored Youth and the wife of Bishop Levi Coppin. Harry Dean was, however, largely self-taught. He learned the science of navigation in England, and, following a family tradition, he soon went to sea and became master of his own sailing vessel. He circumnavigated Africa eighteen times, crossed it from east to west three times, and from north to south once. Dean's life was one of great excitement and dedication. He visualized bringing Negroes back to Africa and motivating them to form a solid nation in co-operation with native Africans. He put his ideas into practice first by trying to unite African tribes in southern Africa and then by trying to acquire large tracts of land on which to settle the Negroes who might come. He was actually successful in uniting several tribes who had previously been enemies. From political motives the Portuguese offered to sell him Mozambique for £50,000, which he unsuccessfully tried to raise among affluent Negroes in America. Because of his perseverance and influence, Dean was regarded as a dangerous person in Africa. There were several attempts on his life, which he imputed to the connivance of the officials of the Union of South Africa and which forced him to leave Africa penniless.

As the following letter to Dr. Locke indicates, Dean never lost hope in his original plan to free Negroes in Africa. His autobiography, written jointly with Sterling North, a graduate student at the University of Chicago, and published under the title of *Pegro Gorino* (the name of his ship) *and Umbala* ("it is true") is a fascinating document.

Prof. Alain Locke
*Howard University*
*Washington, D.C.*

*Habashi Nautical College Incorporated,*
*1530 Lincoln Avenue,*
*Alameda [California].*
*April 17, 1925*

My dear and benificent Sir:*

We thank you for your article on that creature Sir Harry Johnson in the current "Opportunity" and your awakened insight and interest in our races dilemma. When in Uganda I handle some of the skulls of the thousands of noble Masis murdered by the fiends who have humbled our people and desecrated the sacred soil of our Motherland.

Give me leave to tell you that I am sensible of the fact that our Phila. boys think more of the honor of the race and the Motherland than of material things which makes your contribution to me so precious.

I am proud to see this day when we dark skins have set out to make our contributions to the cultural and economic organizations of mankind with the full measure of efficiency and when 50,000 of us are equipped with the arts and sciences of the sea and air and practice them then we will be able to again sing "no pilots aid Phonician vessels need, themselves instruct with life securely speed. Endowed with won'rous skill untaught they share, the purpose and the will of them they bear, To fertile relms and distant climats go, And where each relm and city lies they know. Swiftly they fly and through the trackless sea. Tho' wrapt in clouds and darkness find their way."

I too am a Cuffee the last of the Philadelphia Deans. I am glad to see you a real old timer take up the task of redeeming the Motherland.

I think we have met. I believe I met you at a smoker arranged by Levi Cottman when I passed through Phila. on my way to Abyssinia. Or at the Citizens Club or in London at the Colonial Institute or the British Museum Library. Some where it appears to me that I have met you. If convenient for you, I would like to exchange photos.

My oldest sister is Mrs. Alice Potts, 4759 Chestnut St. Perhaps you know of her daughters family, the Tysons, 4759 Chestnut St. I would like to get in touch with some of my old friends. Do you know the Bolivers, the Dutrells or any of the old timers. I spent the best part of my life in Africa especially the geographical center and the seven seas.

* Reprinted by kind permission of the Moorland Collection, Founders Library, Howard University, Washington, D.C.

We have started the Habashi Nautical College Inc. here. It is an outgrowth of our efforts to direct the efforts to the rehabilitation of the Motherland. After starting it at Djubili, Cape Town and Sinon we have succeeded in incorporating it here because there has never been a time in the history of our country when the youth of African blood have had access to an institution where nautical training is given. We are preparing to put a craft on between here and Africa soon. We propose to erect an observatory at Sinon more important than the work of Henry the navigator to us. Devilish opposition has obstructed the work but we shall resort to the Dondegentes the Macheavelli stunt and the almeadi technic. This work has to be done quickly for it is operative that our people are to be exterminated through a secret process of sterilizing our youth in two generations. That is the secret of the suppression of lynching. Our lords bishops and masters are agreeable and lending themselves to it. Our race group here in America have a larger per cent of traitors than any other group in history ever were cursed with and the husky youth with high ideals first class brains and bodies must get busy and work with high speed razor-like sharpness else all will be lost. Watch Standard Oil and the British Privy Council—It is possible that France could convince Spain and Italy that clearing the Nordic out of the Mediterranean or Latin America would follow or a combination of Russia Japan and China. Then when something breaks loose we must be prepared for "who knows." Heredatary bondsmen who would be free must themself strike the blow. I am convinced that national character does not change. I can see no change in the gringo from Tacitus to Heine, can you? Oh I wish DuBois could see the horrors I have seen in Africa and our poor people here enmeshed in this hypogogical environment for three hundred years. We cannot think straight. These religionists don't believe in their bible for there it says "if a man stealeth a man and selleth him or if he be found in his hands he shall surely be put to death." A plenary statement of law and some of our hypots are willing to become partially curious.

I see the Diety coming out here to make a pagent. I pity the interpretation of our history by that quashi rack movamus. The Catholics especially the Jew the gov. and in Britain, are moving heaven and earth to destroy us. They have adopted the diplomacy of Manoel de Alamedes and the sea alone offers safety. The psychology of the sea has never been explained in this country. I have 3 manuscripts and can't get them published. Oh Prof. Frederick Starr and Professor David P Barrow oh watch them. Can our people ever become sophisticated to meet and ward the Dondegentes and Machievellian diplomacy of this bleached Brahman or will we forever remain so naive and witless as the Indian. My uncle told me that when he came to California there were 200,000 Indians and Mexicans here. Now you must get a microscope to find one. Oh please excuse this scribble and believe me with most profound respect,

Very truly yours,

(Capt.) HARRY DEAN

# Paul Robeson,
## 1897–

Paul Robeson, one of five children of a Negro minister who had been a runaway slave, was born in Princeton, New Jersey. He received his pre-school and grammar school education in Princeton and his high school education in Somerville, New Jersey. Because of his athletic and scholarly abilities, Robeson was awarded a scholarship to Rutgers University, from which he was graduated in 1911 as an All-American and a member of Phi Beta Kappa. He then entered Columbia University Law School. He began his theatrical career in an amateur production of *Simon, the Cyrenian*, a production of the Provincetown Players at the Little Theater on MacDougall Street in Greenwich Village. In 1925 Robeson and his long-term associate, Lawrence Brown, gave the first professional concert of all-Negro music ever given.

From 1927 to 1939 Robeson and Lawrence Brown lived in England, where Robeson became particularly well known as a concert singer. However, with the gathering clouds of World War II he returned to New York. According to Robeson, the experience of living abroad was largely responsible for his discovery of Africa.

Tall, handsome, genial, and black, Robeson was always a popular figure, though from his earliest years he suffered the stigma of being a Negro. In the United States his artistic career continued to flourish. In 1939 he appeared in the revival of *Showboat*, and also he first sang the extremely popular "Ballad for Americans". In 1943 he opened on Broadway in the leading role of *Othello* and the same year was awarded the Spingarn medal.

However, Robeson found himself unable to keep silent on racial issues and on United States policies related to the war. His activities in such organizations as the Committee to Aid China, the Joint Anti-Fascist Refugee Committee, and the Council on African Affairs brought him under the scrutiny of the House Un-American Activities Committee. Although he had testified in 1946 that he was not a Communist, his passport was revoked in 1950 by the United States Department of State, which regarded him as being "under the direction, domination, and control of the Communist movement".

Robeson continued to be popular in Europe, and, when his passport was returned in 1958, he and his wife, Eslanda, left the United States and were well received in Europe, Great Britain, and the Soviet Union. As an ailing man Robeson returned to the United States with his wife in late 1963.

# African Culture*

## PAUL ROBESON

Critics have often reproached me for not becoming an opera star and never attempting to give recitals of German and Italian songs, as every accomplished singer is supposed to do. I am not an artist in the sense in which they want me to be an artist, and of which they could approve. I have no desire to interpret the vocal genius of half a dozen cultures which are really alien to me. I have a far more important task to perform.

When I first suggested singing Negro spirituals for English audiences, a few years ago, I was laughed at. How could these utterly simple, indeed, almost savage, songs interest the most sophisticated audience in the world? I was asked. And yet I have found response amongst this very audience to the simple, direct emotional appeal of Negro spirituals. These songs are to Negro culture what the works of the great poets are to English culture; they are the soul of the race made manifest. No matter in what part of the world you may find him, the Negro has retained his direct emotional response to outside stimuli; he is constantly aware of an external power which guides his destiny. The white man has made a fetish of intellect and worships the God of thought; the Negro feels rather than thinks, experiences emotions directly rather than interprets them by roundabout and devious abstractions, and apprehends the outside world by means of intuitive perceptions instead of through a carefully built-up system of logical analysis. No wonder that the Negro is an intensely religious creature, and that his artistic and cultural capacities find expression in the glorification of some deity in song. It does not matter who the deity is. The American and West Indian Negro worships the Christian God in his own particular way and

* *The African Observer, a Review of Contemporary Affairs*, Bulawayo, Vol. II, No. 5, March, 1935, Article 4, pp. 19–21. Reprinted with permission of the author.

makes him the object of his supreme artistic manifestation which is embodied in the Negro spiritual. But, what of the African Negro? What is the object of his strong religious sense, and how does his artistic spirit manifest itself? These are the questions I have set myself to answer.

As a first step I went to the London School of Oriental Languages and, quite haphazardly, began by studying the East Coast languages: Swahili and the Bantu group which forms a sort of Lingua Franca of the East Coast of Africa. I found in these languages a pure Negro foundation, dating from an ancient culture, but intermingled with many Arabic and Hamitic impurities. From them I passed on to the West Coast Negro languages and immediately found a kinship of rhythm and intonation with the Negro-English dialect which I had heard spoken around me as a child. It was to me like a home-coming, and I felt that I had penetrated to the core of African culture when I began to study the legendary traditions, folk-song and folk-lore of the West African Negro.

I hope to be able to interpret this original and unpolluted Negro folk-song to the Western world and I am convinced that there lies a wealth of uncharted musical material in that source which I hope, one day, will evoke the response in English and American audiences which my Negro spirituals have done; but for me this is only one aspect of my discovery.

Culturally speaking, the African Negro, as well as his American and West Indian brother, stands at the parting of the ways. The day is past when they were regarded as something less than human and little more than mere savages by the white man. Racial tolerance and political equality of status have taken the place of oppression and slavery for the greater part of the Negro race. But the sufferings he has undergone have left an indelible mark on the Negro's soul and at the present stage he suffers from an inferiority complex which finds its compensation in a desire to imitate the white man and his ways; but I am convinced that in this direction there is neither fulfillment nor peace for the Negro. He is too radically different from the white man in his mental and emotional structure ever to be more than a spurious and uneasy imitation of him if he persists in following this direction.

His soul contains riches which can come to fruition only if he retains intact the full spate of his emotional awareness, and uses unswervingly the artistic endowments which nature has given him.

It is astonishing and, to me, fascinating to find a flexibility and subtlety in a language like Swahili sufficient to convey the teachings of Plato, for example, and it is my ambition to make an effort to guide the Negro race by means of its own peculiar qualities to a higher degree of perfection along the line of their natural development.

Although it is a commonplace to anthropologists, these qualities and attainments of Negro languages are entirely unknown to the general public of the Western world and, astonishingly enough, even to the Negroes themselves. I have met Negroes in the United States who believed that the African Negro communicated his thoughts solely by means of gestures, that, in fact, he was practically incapable of speech and merely used sign language!

It is my first concern to dispel this regrettable and abysmal ignorance of the value of its own heritage in the Negro race itself. As a first step in this direction I intend to make a comparative study of the main language groups: Indo-European, Asiatic and African, choosing two or three principal languages out of each group, and indicate their comparative richness at a comparable stage of development. It may take me five years to complete this work, but I am convinced that the results will be adequate to form a concrete foundation for a movement to inspire confidence in the Negro in the value of his own past and future.

# James H. Robinson,
## 1907–

James H. Robinson was born in Knoxville, Tennessee. He attended
Lincoln University and the Union Theological Seminary. The
Reverend Mr. Robinson has served as minister of the Church of the
Master and has always been associated with social action on the
part of the church. He has served as the director of the Union
Neighbourhood Centre of Youth Work and as a director of the
Morningside Community Centre. As the article in this anthology
suggests, he has long been interested in supporting an active missionary presence, particularly on the part of Negroes. Since 1957,
however, he has been identified with Crossroads Africa, which he
founded as a "work-camp study seminar, friendship and aid program
which takes students, teachers, professors and other specialists to
countries in Africa for short term programs during the summer".
Operation Crossroads, which has functioned as a private voluntary
organization from its inception, has broadened Robinson's idea of
service to Africa to include not only Negroes but youth of both races
in this country as well as from Canada. According to the latest
statistics published on Operation Crossroads, 1,039 persons, representing forty-seven states, nine Canadian provinces, Mexico,
Uruguay, and Puerto Rico, have participated in eighty-five projects in
twenty-five African countries in five general categories: construction,
teacher training, and a broad miscellaneous category which would
include social work, libraries, etc. Dr. Robinson, as the founder,
remains chairman and director of the board of directors of Operation
Crossroads.

# What Africa Asks of Us*

## JAMES H. ROBINSON

If the church and missions are to meet Africa's grave social problems and the challenging opportunities created by the economic revolution there, they will have to reconstruct their thinking radically. We must move boldly into an urban ministry with Christian social and welfare centers, industrial evangelism, a vigorous youth work program. Above all we must build up strong African churches which will be capable of meeting the situation. Up to now, there is not a handful of Christian social and welfare centers in all Africa, although the expanding urban centers, choked with misery, destroyed families, disease, moral degradation, lost young people, have created social and religious problems of great magnitude. At present our missions are concentrated too largely in the villages. This was right years ago, when Africa's was wholly a rural agrarian society. But the villages have grown into towns, the towns have expanded into cities at a phenomenal rate, and now the cities leap into urban centers almost overnight. The whole process is hardly a quarter of a century old.

There is no Christian industrial evangelism, no ministry to labor, no youth work of any significance. Yet these are the areas where the communists are concentrating their forces and resources with marked success. Albert Hammerton, West African head of the International Confederation of Free Trade Unions, the outfit which is fighting communism in the labor unions, told me that the communists are underwriting their program in British West Africa to the extent of $80,000 annually. African industrialism and commercialism are still at the beginning. They will continue to expand, and labor forces will expand with them, as the West demands more and more of Africa's material wealth and the Africans themselves demand more and more of the consumer goods so necessary to an advanced civilization.

I

The communists are working overtime to win awakening African youth and students both at home and abroad. They are exploiting

* *The Christian Century*, February 1, 1956, pp. 137–39. This was the fourth in a series on Christianity and World Revolution and has been reprinted with the kind permission of the editor.

the sound idea that whoever wins Africa's youth wins its future leadership. Over against the skilled and seasoned leadership and the financial support the communists give to their nefarious work of subverting the youth, the churches and missions have almost nothing. There are less than a half-dozen, if that many, well trained and experienced church youth leaders in all the continent. Consequently, in most areas, the church and the missions no longer hold the youth they once had, nor even those who are being educated in mission schools. The youth of Africa is on the march, searching. What they find, where they end and whom they follow will depend largely on who works hardest to win their loyalty. These young people are dedicated to freedom and to Africa's future. It is up to us to help them make both Christian. One of the most important things missions must do, and do now, is to throw into the field the ablest and most experienced youth work people they can lay their hands on, and begin at once to train an African youth leadership.

Painfully but logically it follows that a Christian strategy to counteract communism must be developed at once. The communists are infiltrating most of the labor unions. They are organizing the mission hospital workers and the mission school teachers. They are spreading their noxious ideology among the masses and the young people in an effort to turn them against Christianity. Perhaps most serious of all, they are confusing the minds of some of the most seasoned African pastors. The need for personnel, resources and strategy to meet this most devastating challenge cries aloud.

Only a great joint effort into which we take Africans at the outset will be good enough. It must be an effort large in scope, both at home in the preparation of missionaries, and on the field with the African churches and their missionary colleagues. Communism may give us our hardest and very likely our longest battle in Africa. Whatever we do, it must be done not *for* Africans as wards but *with* Africans as partners.

II

The churches and missions have passed up a great reservoir of persons who could make a peculiarly effective witness in Africa— American Negroes. There are more Negroes of African origin in the United States than there are in all the rest of the world outside Africa, and more than in any African country or territory except Nigeria. Even Canada, with less than 50,000 Negroes, has more than any other country of the world, save ours and Brazil. But both our government and our churches have failed to make use of this potential to any extent. Outside Liberia, there are less than a dozen Negro missionaries in Africa from all the denominational boards combined. We may be sure that the Soviets would have trained and used hundreds by now if they had this resource. Mission board executives and missionaries or deputations returning from Africa rarely refer to the employment of Negroes there. Three or four boards once sent out a few Negroes, but most of them then abandoned the practice for various—and to a large degree valid—reasons. The great Negro denominations, sad to say, have never had a significant mission work outside South Africa, nor have Negro Christians as yet developed a real passion to Christianize the continent which is their original home. No matter what happened in days gone by, however, the situation now is far too advanced and the issues much too urgent to allow past experiences to determine our policy. We have the opportunity to prepare what I believe can be one of our most effective mission and fraternal resources for Africa. Chester Bowles, formerly our ambassador to India, in an article he wrote after visiting Africa (*Collier's* magazine, June 10, 1955) strongly recommended that our government send Negro citizens there to represent it in various capacities. If this is a right move for the government, how much more so for the churches! I do not suggest that American Negroes alone can work the redemption of Africa, but they can help mightily. To be sure, Negroes from this country are identified in the mind of Africans as Americans, but there are bonds of color, origin and suffering that tie the two groups together in ways so subtle that few whites can appreciate them. Given the right encouragement and training, hundreds of our Negro Christians will volunteer for this work. God has prepared our nation and our people for such a time as this, for the task awaiting us in swiftly changing Africa.

Everywhere I traveled in Africa I was implored to prevail on our churches to send Negro missionaries. In the French Cameroun an African pastor, the secretary of the Bass Synod mission committee, said in the presence of one of our missionaries, "I charge you to see that some of our people are sent by your board to work with us." In Southern Rhodesia Reverend Fred Rea, head of the British mission, asked me to come back and work with him. In the Congo an African pastor at Luebo said: "You American Negroes are the only group of our origin who have great experience, education and world respect. You, more than anyone else, can get our attention." In Kenya the secretary of the Christian Council, S. A. Morrison, urged me to do my utmost to get some Negroes out to help them as soon as possible. In the Gold Coast the director of social welfare, Robert Gardner, asked not only for Negro missionaries but for Negro doctors, nurses, teachers, social workers and technicians. In fact, within the last year Mr. Gardner has made two trips to the United States to explore the possibilities and is now arranging an agreement with Tuskegee Institute.

III

The use of American Negroes and also of Americans of Asian ancestry as missionaries and fraternal workers in Africa is not only wise; it is imperative. In color-conscious Africa, where hostility toward white people is increasing, what better way can we find to demonstrate the universality of the gospel than a multiracial witness? Professor Pierce Beaver, in his study *Race and Nationality in North American Foreign Missions*, states that as of now only thirteen boards in this country have agreed on a definite policy of appointing Negroes and only three are earnestly searching for Negro personnel. Fifty-one boards say they have no formal policy, and most of these add that the matter has never come before them. (Are they going to wait until Africa is lost?) Fifty-seven say they will consider all qualified applicants. (But will they seek out Negroes with the same diligence they employ in recruiting whites?). One board categorically states it will not accept Negro applicants, and two others say it is doubtful if they would do so.

The greatest liability to the spread of the gospel in Africa is racial discrimination and segregation, whether in Africa, Europe or the United States. The sin of racialism is, and will perhaps continue to be, the most difficult handicap to overcome. Racialism is a cancer within our society, within our Christian institutions, within ourselves, as well as in the colonial structure. Michael Blundell, cabinet member without portfolio in the Kenya government, told our party in Nairobi that European businessmen, settlers and government officials by both their attitudes and practices seriously obstruct the gospel. It is easy enough to condemn South Africans and other settlers, but we should remind ourselves that Americans in Africa make a very quick accommodation to European patterns of racialism, which are not greatly different from some of our American patterns.

In the mind of the African, racialism is identified with white people, and white people are identified with Christianity. Communists and Muslims and many of the nationalist leaders undercut the influence of African Christian leaders by charging that they perpetuate white racial patterns. On no other subject are Africans so greatly agitated and united as on racial attitudes and patterns of discrimination and segregation, and there is no greater hunger in Africa than the hunger for acceptance and brotherhood.

If they are to be true to the gospel of Jesus Christ, the churches and missions simply cannot evade this problem. This is not merely a question of the practical moves needed to win Africa or to hold back the evil hosts which seek to seduce Africa. All else we do will be of little avail if we do not face up to the obligation to abolish racialism. The African may not demand the accomplishment of miracles overnight, but unless he sees some convincing and practical demonstration now of our humility and sincere willingness to eliminate this racist denial of the gospel we preach, he will turn in revulsion against us and fall prey to doctrines destructive both to himself and to the rest of us.

There is no escape from the necessity of disciplining our deeds and making them conform to our professions. For Africa, the brightest or the darkest years lie just ahead. The outcome depends largely, if not wholly, on whether the churches and missions can understand the implication of their faith, whether they yield themselves up to the will of God. If they do so understand and obey, they can provide the moral and spiritual basis on which the African who will claim leadership and succeed to power, can build the New Africa soundly and wisely. Whether they can act with Christian resourcefulness, speed and power at the command of Christ to make disciples of all men by being true disciples themselves—this is the destiny-freighted question.

IV

Perhaps nothing is so important as the development and strengthening of an indigenous Christian leadership. In some African areas the Church of England and the Roman Catholic Church have taken some steps in this direction, but elsewhere very little has been done. Few missions have raised Africans to positions of partnership. An indigenous leadership, as the communists recognized at the outset of their efforts in Africa, will remain when all else has passed. Communists are staking their future on African communists, not on Europeans, because the former can move faster and more freely, without the hostility which encumbers Europeans and Americans, whom Africans think of as foreigners allied with colonial control.

They do not have to prove the genuiness of their concern with African problems, and they know the language. Since the continent's labor, nationalist and political forces are led chiefly by Africans who were largely educated in mission schools, it is fair to ask why missions have developed so few comparable leaders for Christian work. An African member of the Cameroun legislative body told me: "Missions did more for education than anyone else, yet they have so few African leaders for their own work. How long will it take you to learn that we are annoyed at this?"

Much more attention must be given to the preparation of African women for leadership roles. Of the more than 800 African students in the United States, less than 30 are women. Here again the labor and political leaders and the communists have shown greater readiness than the Christians to give responsibility to women. Surely these secular leaders are as well aware as the missionaries that the low status of women in Africa is a barrier perilous to surmount. A group of African women in Entebbe, Uganda, who asked to discuss this problem with me, pointed out among other things that one of the best ways to combat polygamy—one of Africa's greatest curses—is to educate and train more women for leadership roles. We know how an enlightened womanhood strengthens the social and moral fabric of our own country, and we see how women are helping to change the shape of things in India, Japan and the Philippines. We can at least be as ready as the communists to break with traditions which keep most of the women of Africa in the low estate of beasts of burden.

v

The preparation of leaders who can be partners with us and eventually assume full responsibility, so that we become their assistants, should be high on the list for early achievement. Training and educating Africans in Africa keeps them within a context where they are not confused by a multitude of conflicting ideas unrelated to their past, nor plagued by the large secondary adjustments to be made in foreign lands. In West and East Africa, the French and the British have recently begun to recognize the wisdom of such a policy. This will mean enlarging African educational institutions and bringing them up to first-class standards in all respects, but at the same time keeping them within the context of African thought and experience. (Too much of the present instruction is related to Europe and the United States.) This will mean personnel and support for African literature and textbooks, as Henry P. Van Dusen pointed out on his return from Africa two years ago.

There are many primary schools and a few good colleges and universities in Africa. The greatest weakness at present is in the secondary schools, which are far too few for the students coming up through the primary schools, and totally unprepared to take over graduates of the enlarged primary schools projected for the immediate future. We should provide the best possible equipment and facilities; most of our mission equipment is such that we should hang our heads in shame.

African students brought to the United States should be graduate students who have had their basic training and experience at home and who are being prepared for larger administrative leadership. But we should not be afraid to bring them when they are ready because some missionaries, businessmen and government officials think it "spoils" them. I found this to be a great fear among missionaries of all denominations as well as among colonial officials. Perhaps their fear is justified to some degree, but it springs also from the fact that they can no longer control Africans whose horizons have been lifted, whose education is as good as or better than theirs. The best results can be obtained by careful selection and proper preparation of candidates in Africa, and the provision of competent, friendly advisers who can give guidance and orientation once they are here.

VI

The West should be eternally grateful to the faculties of Lincoln University and the University of Pennsylvania and to the devout men and women in this republic who brought Prime Ministers Nkruma [sic] and Azikiwe and educators and clergymen like the famous J. E. K. Aggrey to these shores, guided their education and training, helped to deepen their respect for the democratic process, and conditioned them toward larger responsibilities and world-relatedness.

If we give Africans the tools, the inspiration and the confidence, we can trust them to achieve a church cut to the pattern of our Lord's will, but a church that, though absorbing the best we have to give, will be their own creation, not one imposed by us. African thinking should be given a larger determinative share in all decisions. In the final analysis, Africans themselves, not we, will have to bear the responsibility for Africa's future.

143

# Carter Godwin Woodson,*
## 1875–1950

Dr. Carter Godwin Woodson, the author, was born of ex-slave parents near New Canton, Buckingham County, Virginia, December 19, 1875. His father was James Henry Woodson, and his mother Anne Eliza (Riddle) Woodson. As he was one of a rather large family of nine children, his parents, who started life in poverty, could not provide him with the ordinary comforts of life and could not regularly send him to the five-months district school taught alternately by his two uncles John M. and James B. Riddle. He had never been as far as ten miles from his home nor had he seen a train to ride on it until he was seventeen years old. In this rural atmosphere, however, he managed largely by self-instruction to master the fundamentals of the common school subjects by the time he reached this age.

At this age, in 1892, he went with his brother Robert Henry Woodson to West Virginia, to which his parents were induced to move the following year. They settled at Huntington, but the young Woodson had to accept employment in the coalfields in Fayette County. There he labored as a miner for six years, while spending a few months annually in school in Huntington, West Virginia.

In 1895, this young man entered the Douglass High School of that city. At that time he came under the instruction of William T. McKinney, who inspired him to aspire to higher things. He completed the course in less than two years. He next entered Berea College in Kentucky. This institution was famous at that time because of its coeducation of the two races. He studied there a part of two years. He then began teaching at Winona, Fayette County, West Virginia, in 1898. From Winona he was called to the principalship of the Douglass High School, of Huntington, from which he had been graduated four years before. He then spent his summers studying at the University of Chicago. There he later obtained the degree of Bachelor of Arts.

He traveled and studied a year in Asia and Europe, spending one semester at La Sorbonne, the University of Paris, under the

* From: Kelly Miller, *An Estimate of Carter G. Woodson and His Work in Connection with the Association for the Study of Negro Life and History, Inc.*, Washington, D.C., The Association for The Study of Negro Life and History, 1926.

instruction of Professors Aulard, Diehl, Lemonnier, and Bouché-Leclère. In France he not only did graduate work in history, but in having contact with French as it is spoken, he learned to speak Spanish.

Returning to the United States, he resumed his studies at the University of Chicago. From this institution he received the degree of Master of Arts in 1908. After studying a little further at Chicago, he went to Harvard to continue his graduate work in history and political science. He specialized under Professors Charles Gross, Ephraim Emerton, W. B. Munro, and Edward Channing. In 1909 he accepted a position as instructor in Romance Languages in the Washington High Schools that he might engage in research in the Library of Congress. In this way he wrote his doctoral dissertation, *The Disruption of Virginia*, which was accepted at Harvard in 1912, in fulfillment of the requirements for the degree of Doctor of Philosophy.

Dr. Woodson served in the Washington Public School System ten years. During the last two years of this service he was an instructor in English and the History of Education at the Myrtilla Miner Normal School and principal of the Armstrong Manual Training High School. In 1919 he became Dean of the School of Liberal Arts of Howard University but resigned at the close of the year because he could not approve the policies of the administration. From 1920 to 1922 he served as Dean of the West Virginia Collegiate Institute, mainly to reorganize the college department.

... At the expiration of this last service, Dr. Woodson retired from teaching to devote all of his time to research in connection with the Association for the Study of Negro Life and History.

This Association was born in the brain of Carter G. Woodson. Its conception, inspiration, growth, and development are the outgrowth of his personal genius and energy. It was organized by him in Chicago on September 9, 1915, with only five persons. It was incorporated under the laws of the District of Columbia on the third of the following October. The purpose of this undertaking is to preserve and publish the records of the Negro that the race may not become a negligible factor in the thought of the world. The Association has endeavored to publish such materials in scientific form that facts thus properly set forth may tell their own story.

An important purpose of the Association is the publication of *The Journal of Negro History*, a quarterly scientific review of more than 100 pages of current articles and documents giving facts generally unknown. This publication has been regularly issued since

145

January, 1916, and has reached its twelfth volume. In bound form it constitutes a veritable encyclopaedia of information concerning the life and history of the Negro in this country and abroad. It circulates among scholars throughout the civilized world. It appeals especially to colleges and universities of both races as a desirable aid to social workers and students carrying on research.

During these years of painstaking research, Dr. Woodson has written a number of books dealing with neglected aspects of Negro history. The first of these, *The Education of the Negro Prior to 1861*, appeared in 1915. It evoked from the leading organs of thought in the United States most favorable comment to the effect that it showed both original treatment and independent research. His next work was *A Century of Negro Migration*, brought out in 1918 at the time of the culmination of the exodus of the Negroes to the North. Recently, Dr. Woodson has published through the Associated Publishers several very popular works, *The History of the Negro Church*, and *The Negro in Our History*. The former has reached its second edition and the latter its fourth in a revised and enlarged form. Dr. Woodson has recently produced also three important source books, *Negro Orators and Their Orations*, *Free Negro Heads of Families in the United States in 1830* and *The Mind of the Negro as Reflected in Letters written during the Crisis, 1800–1860*. He is now engaged in writing a comprehensive history of the Negro in six volumes. He is endeavoring to make this the monumental work of his life.

The importance of Dr. Woodson's work is better appreciated when we reflect that the literature of the race problem abounds mainly in propaganda based upon opinion and argumentation. The importance of collecting and collating exact and accurate material has not yet received the recognition which it deserves. We are so anxious to solve the race problem that we do not take time to study it. Infallible assumption and passionate dogma take the place of carefully ascertained fact and calm analysis. The largest measure of our admiration is due to the Negro who can divest himself of momentary passion and prejudice, and with self-detachment devote his powers to searching out and sifting the historical facts growing out of race relationship and present them to the world, just as they are, in their untampered integrity.

... Dr. Woodson has somewhere made a sharp distinction between the history of the Negro and the Negro in history. Too often the artist makes the mountain peaks suffice for the whole landscape. The infinite smaller eminences and depressions are apt to be ignored by the painter bent on exploiting dominant features. But not so with the scientific historian. The battle may be lost for the want of the horseshoe nail as well as for lack of the imperious general. It is said that the loss of the Battle of Waterloo, which turned the tide of European history, might have been attributable to the careless cook whose tough beefsteak affected Napoleon's usual alertness and enabled the Duke of Wellington to take advantage of his momentary dullness. Henson, the black attendant, accompanied Peary to the North Pole. The menial part played by this sable attendant was an important and essential part in polar discovery. Dr. Woodson is concerned in digging out every significant role which the Negro has played in the world's drama. This makes our history, not only full and complete, but true to the actualities of history happenings.

The Negro's pride of race is humiliated when he contemplates the great drama of this continent and finds that he is accorded no honorable part in the performance. The tendency is always to glorify the white man and to debase the Negro. The effect upon the spirit of the Negro is deplorably oppressive. If he must forever dwell upon a picture in which all worthwhile deeds are ascribed to white men and none to his own race, whence can he derive spirit and inspiration? So strong has been the tendency towards race belittlement, that even Negroes affect to disdain their own contributions. Some are even ashamed to study about themselves and the doings of their race. Negro students have been known to feel ashamed of the songs which welled from the heart of their race as the trill from the throat of the bird. How much more ennobling they feel to read about "how Achilles injured the Greeks" than to recount the lesser exploits of their own blood? But thanks to Dr. Woodson and the Association for the Study of Negro Life and History, all of this is being changed. The story of one's own blood and breed is naturally of keener interest and zest than the story of an alien. Every Jewish boy's heart feels a little bigger when he reads of the part his race has played in the drama of mankind. Not a single fact creditable to Jewry is ever allowed to escape his attention. See how the women delight to extol the part played by their sex; how the Catholics exploit the achievements of their co-religionists; and so the Negro must learn to know his own story and to love it.

Dr. Woodson is furnishing the material which will be of incalculable value to students and scholars of race relations, not only in the immediate future but in the remoter years to come. His work possesses what might be termed a strategic timeliness. America is just acquiring the scientific method of handling historical material. Dr. Woodson is, I believe, the second member of his race to receive complete university training and equipment for scientific historical inquiry. The facts involved in the contact of the African with the Western World are scattered throughout many sources which are growing less and less available as the years go by. Like the Sibylline books, the value increases as the volumes decrease. Many private libraries contain invaluable material, which will be disseminated or destroyed unless it is utilized during the lifetime of the compilers. Much invaluable material is now confirmable by living memory, which, within a few years, will pass beyond reach of consultation. Now is the time of all times to gather up the documents and to collect and collate the racial material which they contain. It is fortunate that some one has had vision enough to do this thing.

# African Superiority*

SURPASSES TRADUCERS IN RELIGIOUS CONCEPTS, SEXUAL
MORALITY, PUBLIC AND PRIVATE HONESTY AND IN ESSENTIAL
JUSTICE, HISTORIAN SAYS

## CARTER G. WOODSON

"I take exception to one of the things you said recently in referring to the Africans as having achieved more than the American Negroes when we have to send missionaries to civilize those heathens," said one of my friends to me last week.

That is the trouble with us in America today. We refer to the Africans as heathen when we should think of them as our brethren in black. Certainly we should send missionaries and other workers to help them, but most of those going to Africa are not properly informed as to the status of the people to whom they are sent and do not know the proper method of approach.

I have seen some of the so-called African heathen who might well undertake the task of enlightening the Europeans and Americans sent to them. I am sure that missionaries from Abyssinia can teach the Italians more about the principles of Jesus than that ilk can teach the Ethiopians.

* Undated clipping from Moorland Collection, Howard University, Washington, D.C., and reprinted with their kind permission.

148

Certainly the Holy Father of Axum comes nearer to being the representative of God on earth than that "Holy Father" in Rome, who has endorsed fire, pillage, and murder of an unoffending people that his hierarchy may have the privilege of singing psalms in a new area. If God has reached the low level thus proclaimed, Europe has nothing to offer Africa in righteousness.

### ROMAN "HOLY FATHER"

On this account, however, we should not discount merely the "Holy Father" in Rome. The Archbishop of Canterbury, the "Holy Father of England", and indirectly a "spiritual influence in America", took the same position with respect to the spoilation of Ethiopia immediately after having a conference with Baldwin who would give Mussolini practically all of Ethiopia if he will merely stop fighting in order to remove the danger of a much feared European war. The "Great Archbishop" said that Italy is at fault in resorting to bloodshed but that certain undeveloped parts of the world should be ceded Italy to provide for her much needed expansion.

In other words, Christianity is an adjunct of the armed-to-the-teeth Nordic exploiters, and it is carrying out God's will to dispossess others and exterminate them by segregation to clear the way for their enjoyment of the whole earth. I have made a special study of religion in Africa, but I have not yet discovered a tribe whose spiritual life is so low as to have such a dull sense of justice.

### HEATHEN IN EUROPE

When a white missionary tells me that he has been working among the natives of Africa I usually feel like suggesting that he direct his efforts to his own heathen fellowmen in Europe and America. The Nordic may teach the Africans how to build a railroad, develop a mine or administer a plantation, but in his own heathen state he cannot teach righteousness.

The customary lip service can be no more effective in Africa than elsewhere; and the Nordic cannot teach by example the principles of Jesus when he has never practiced them himself.

The African, just as alive to the situation as the Negro enslaved in America, has also learned to think that "Everybody talking about Heaven ain't going there." It is little wonder, then, that in spite of prolonged missionary effort not a single African tribe as a whole has yet accepted Christianity.

### SEXUAL MORALITY

Africans do not wear clothes like ours, do not live in the same sort of houses, and do not commit to memory facts from as many books as we do, but these so-called heathen can teach us many things which we think we know. For example, the African excels the European in the matter of sexual morality. A few princes, and the well-to-do may indulge in polygamy, but most men can support only one wife; and in some parts polygamy is unknown. All women, as a rule, are so connected as to have contact with one man only.

In Europe and America, however, both women and men may have and do have as many mates as their incomes and social prestige may enable them to obtain. Whereas sexual profligacy is generally unknown in uncontaminated Africa, it is as common in Europe and America as the inspiration and expiration of the human breath.

### THIEVING ELEMENT

Our very large thieving element in both public and private life could learn much from heathen Africa. Property there is both communal and personal, but no profiteer is allowed to grow rich at the expense of the poor. No one has to fear being dispossessed of what actually belongs to him. Locks and keys are unnecessary in that social and economic order.

Among us such protection avails little against the host of robbers organized as a government under a government. Our system is so influenced by the bribery of gangsters that not only a man's property is unsafe but even his life is ever in danger of being taken if that stands in the way of dispossessing him of what he has.

There is no record to show that Africa has ever descended to such depths. Hearing of our crimes of this sort, Africans have learned to pity us.

### TRUTH PARAMOUNT

The habit of lying so freely indulged in by both Europeans and Americans places them far below the Africans. When Africans dissemble to throw off their track invaders who seek to take their country soldiers and exploiters brand them as liars for thus acting in self-defence.

In the African scheme of life, however, nothing is emphasized more than truth. Referring to truth, the African, taught that "lies however numerous will be caught when it rises up. The voice of truth is easily known." Insisting that one should not be moved by tale-bearers the African said, "You condemn on hearsay evidence alone, your sins increase." No wonder then that the older people taught that of all things the liar is the worst on earth. You can turn the lock and key on a thief, but nothing can stop the liar. This great love for the truth is African.

The modern world may learn much from the African in the matter of justice. While it is conceded that the majority of Americans and Europeans have been most unjust to others, and even unjust to themselves, these Nordics after penetrating African life have to concede that in their uncontaminated state the Africans are the "most just" of all the people of the world.

Lady Lugard, whose opinion of the Negro is not very exalted, emphasizes in her book, "A Tropical Dependency", that while these people are spoken of as being "the most just they are likewise referred to as the blackest in Africa". Of all things which the African dislikes he detests injustice most. Give every man his just due. There can be no excuse for dealing with him otherwise. So highly developed is this desire for justice that African kings and emperors always permitted appeals to them from any lower judge. Some found the system so well developed among the Mossi as to say that they originated trial by jury.

# PART II(b)

## How Negro Americans Can Help

### *As Organizations**

* See p. 76.

# LAWS

## OF THE

## AFRICAN SOCIETY,

### *Instituted at*

## *BOSTON,*

### *Anno Domini.*

### 1796.

---

BOSTON:
PRINTED FOR THE SOCIETY, M,DCCII.

## A Lift of the Members names.

\*PLATO Alderſon.
\* Hannible Allen.
Thomas Burdine.
Peter Bailey. Joſeph Ball.
\* Peter Branch;
Prince Brown.
Boſton Ballard.
Anthoney Battis;
Serico Collens.
Rufus Callehorn.
John Clark.
Scipio Dalton.
Aurther Davis.
John Decruſe.
Hamlet Earl.
Ceazer Fayerweather.
Mingo Freeman.
Cato Gardner.
Jeramiah Green.
\* James Hawkins.
John Harriſon.
❋ Gloſaſter Haſkins.

\* Prince M. Harris.
Juber Howland.
Richard Holſted.
Thomas Jackſon
George Jackſon.
Lewis Jones.
Iſaac Johnſon.
John Johnſon.
Sear Kimball.
\* Thomas Lewis.
Joſeph Low.
George Middleton.
Derby Miller.
Cato Morey.
Richard Marſhal.
Joſeph Ocraman.
\* John Phillips.
Cato Rawſon.
\* RichardStandley.
Cyrus Vaſſall.
Derby Vaſſall.

🖙 Thoſe with a Star are

# Constitution of the African Civilization Society*

*Preamble*

It has pleased Almighty God to permit the interior of Africa to be made known to us during the last few years, by the efforts of missionaries and explorers, to an extent hitherto deemed almost impossible. The facts which have become public concerning its climate, soil, productions, minerals, and vast capabilities for improvements, are such, that we can no longer mistake the intention of the Divine Mind towards Africa.

It is evident that the prophecy that "Ethiopia shall soon stretch out her hands unto God", is on the point of fulfilment, and that the work, when commenced, shall be "soon" accomplished, when compared with the apparently slow progress of the Gospel in the other grand divisions of the globe. In order, therefore, to aid in this great work, and promote the civilization and christianization of Africa, as well as the welfare of her children in all lands, we have formed ourselves into an Association, to be known as the African Civilization Society, and we severally agree to be governed by the following

## CONSTITUTION

*Article I*

The Society shall be called the "African Civilization Society", and shall act in harmony with all other societies, whose objects are similar to those of this Association.

*Article II*

The object of this Society shall be the civilization and christianization of Africa, and of the descendants of African ancestors in any portion of the earth, wherever dispersed. Also, the destruction of the African Slave-trade, by the introduction of lawful commerce and trade into Africa: the promotion of the growth of cotton and other products there, whereby the natives may become industrious producers as well as consumers of articles of commerce: and generally, the elevation of the condition of the colored population of our own country, and of other lands.

* *The Anglo-African* (New York), Vol. 2, no. 33, March 14, 1863.

157

*Article III*

No one shall be sent out under the auspices of this Society, either as a religious teacher, agent, or settler, who shall uphold doctrines which shall justify or aid in perpetuating any system of slavery or involuntary servitude.

*Article IV*

The donation or subscription of not less than one dollar annually, shall constitute any individual of good moral character a member of this Society; and the payment at one time of twenty-five dollars shall make any person a life-member.

*Article V*

The officers of this Society shall be a President, Vice-President, a board of twenty Directors, a Recording Secretary, a Corresponding Secretary, and a Treasurer, who shall hold office for one year, and until their successors are regularly chosen.

*Article VI*

The members of this Society may be distinguished as either active, corresponding, or honorary members.

*Article VII*

The President shall preside at all meetings of the Society, and in the event of his absence, one of the Vice-Presidents shall discharge his duties. The Recording Secretary shall keep a regular and distinct account of the transactions of the Society. The Corresponding Secretary shall conduct the correspondence of the Society, and also act as its General Agent, under the direction, and with the consent of the Board of Directors.

The Treasurer shall keep the accounts, and have charge of the funds of the Society, holding them subject to the control of the Board of Directors.

The Board of Directors shall manage and regulate the affairs of the Society, and shall have power to make bye-laws for its own government, so as to fully control the business and funds of the Society.

Five members of the Board of Directors, when regularly convened, shall constitute a quorum for the transaction of business.

*Article VIII*

The President, Vice-Presidents, Secretaries, and Treasurer shall be ex-officio members and officers of the Board of Directors.

The Board of Directors shall manage and regulate the affairs of the Society, and shall have power to make bye-laws for its own government, so as to fully control the business and funds of the Society.

Five members of the Board of Directors, when regularly convened, shall constitute a quorum for the transaction of business.

*Article IX*

The Board of Directors shall have power to form special committees from among their own number, and to fill any vacancy occurring among the officers, for any time intervening before the regular election.

*Article X*

The Society shall hold an annual meeting during the month of May, on any day the Board of Directors may designate, to elect officers, receive reports, and transact its official business, not otherwise delegated to the Board of Directors.

Special meetings may be held at other times, as the Board of Directors may designate.

*Article XI*

The Annual Meeting shall consist of the regular officers and members of the Society at the time of such meeting, and of delegates from other co-operating Societies, each Society being entitled to one representative.

*Article XII*

The Constitution shall be altered only at an annual meeting of the Society, by vote of two thirds of the members present, upon a proposal to that effect transmitted to the Corresponding Secretary, and published in the City of New York, at least two months prior to the annual meeting.

SUPPLEMENT TO THE CONSTITUTION OF THE
AFRICAN CIVILIZATION SOCIETY

In order the better to make the origin and objects of the African Civilization Society known, and to define its designs, intentions, and true position, and to secure that harmony and co-operation originally designed with other similar institutions previously established by the colored people of the United States and Canada, as well as that by the friends of the African race in Great Britain, to aid these movements,

*Resolved*, That the succeeding articles be added as an essential and fundamental part of the Constitution:

*Art. 1.* The Society is not designed to encourage general emigration, but will aid only such persons as may be practically qualified and suited to promote the development of Christianity, morality, education, mechanical arts, agriculture, commerce, and general improvement; who must always be carefully selected and well recommended, that the progress of civilization may not be obstructed.

*Art. 2.* The basis of the Society, and ulterior objects in encouraging emigration, shall be—Self-Reliance and Self-Government on the principle of an African Nationality, the African race being the ruling element of the nation, controlling and directing their own affairs.

# African Civilization Society*

## FREDERICK DOUGLASS†

"But I entreated you to tell your readers what your objections are to the civilization and christianization of Africa. What objection have you to colored men in this country engaging in agriculture, lawful trade, and commerce in the land of my forefathers? What objection have you to an organization that shall endeavour to check and destroy the African slave-trade, and that desires to co-operate with anti-slavery men and women of every grade in our own land, and to toil with them for the overthrow of American slavery?—Tell us, I pray you, tell us in your clear and manly style. 'Gird up thy loins, and answer thou me, if thou canst.' "—Letter from Henry Highland Garnet.

Hitherto we have allowed ourselves but little space for discussing the claims of this new scheme for the civilization of Africa, doing little more than indicating our dissent from the new movement, yet leaving our columns as free to its friends as to its opponents. We shall not depart from this course, while the various writers bring good temper and ability to the discussion, and shall keep themselves within reasonable limits. We hope the same impartiality will be shown in the management of the *Provincial Freeman*, the adopted organ of the African Civilization Society. We need discussion among ourselves, discussion to rouse our souls to intenser life and activity.— "Communipaw" did capital service when he gave the subtle brain of Wm. Whipper a little work to do, and our readers the pleasure of seeing it done. Anything to promote earnest thinking among our people may be held as a good thing in itself, whether we assent to or dissent from the proposition which calls it forth.

We say this much before entering upon a compliance with the request of our friend Garnet, lest any should infer that the discussion now going on is distasteful to us, or that we desire to avoid it. The letter in question from Mr. Garnet is well calculated to make that impression. He evidently enjoys a wholesome confidence, not only in the goodness of his own cause, but in his own ability to defend it.

* *Douglass' Monthly*, February, 1859. Reprinted by permission of International Publishers, New York, from *The Life and Writings of Frederick Douglass* by Philip S. Foner, 1950, vol. 2, pp. 441–7.
† See p. 49 for biographical sketch of Frederick Douglass.

—Sallying out before us, as if in "complete steel", he entreats us to appear "in manly style", to "*gird up our loins*", as if the contest were one requiring all our strength and activity. "Answer thou me if thou canst?"—As if an answer were impossible. Not content with this, he reminds us of his former similar entreaties, thus making it our duty to reply to him, if for no better reason than respect and courtesy towards himself.

The first question put to us by Mr. Garnet is a strange and almost preposterous one. He asks for our "objections to the civilization and christianization of Africa". The answer we have to make here is very easy and very ready, and can be given without even taking the trouble to observe the generous advice to "gird up our loins". We have not, dear brother, the least possible objection either to the civilization or to the christianization of Africa, and the question is just about as absurd and ridiculous as if you had asked us to "gird up our loins", and tell the world what objection Frederick Douglass has to the abolition of slavery, or the elevation of the free people of color in the United States! We not only have no objection to the civilization and christianization of Africa, but rejoice to know that through the instrumentality of commerce, and the labors of faithful missionaries, those very desirable blessings are already being realized in [the land of my fathers] Africa.

Brother Garnet is a prudent man, and we admire his tact and address in presenting the issue before us, while we cannot assent entirely to its fairness. "*I did not ask for a statement of your preference of America to Africa.*" That is very aptly said, but is it impartially said? Does brother Garnet think such a preference, in view of all the circumstances, a wise and proper one? Or is he wholly indifferent as to the preference or the other? He seems to think that our preferences have nothing to do with the question between us and the African Civilization Society, while we think that this preference touches the very bone of contention. The African Civilization Society says to us, go to Africa, raise cotton, civilize the natives, become planters, merchants, compete with the slave States in the Liverpool cotton market, and thus break down American slavery, To which we simply and briefly reply, "we prefer to remain in America"; and we do insist upon it, in the very face of our respected friend, that that is both a direct and candid answer. There is no dodging, no equivocation, but so far as we are concerned, the whole matter is ended. *You* go there, *we* stay here, is just the difference between us and the African Civilization Society, and the true issue upon which co-operation with it or opposition to it must turn.

162

Brother Garnet will pardon us for thinking it somewhat cool in him to ask us to give our objections to this new scheme. Our objections to it have been stated in substance, repeatedly. It has been no fault of ours if he has not read them.

As long ago as last September, we gave our views at large on this subject, in answer to an eloquent letter from Benjamin Coates, Esq., the real, but not the ostensible head of the African Civilization movement.

Meanwhile we will state briefly, for the benefit of friend Garnet, seven considerations, which prevent our co-operation with the African Civilization Society.

1. No one idea has given rise to more oppression and persecution toward the colored people of this country, than that which makes Africa, not America, their home. It is that wolfish idea that elbows us off the side walk, and denies us the rights of citizenship. The life and soul of this abominable idea would have been thrashed out of it long ago, but for the jesuitical and persistent teaching of the American Colonization Society. The natural and unfailing tendency of the African Civilization Society, by sending *"around the hat"* in all our towns and cities for money to send colored men to Africa, will be to keep life and power in this narrow, bitter and persecuting idea, that Africa, not America, is the Negro's true home.

2. The abolition of American slavery, and the moral, mental and social improvement of our people, are objects of immediate, pressing and transcendent importance, involving a direct and positive issue with the pride and selfishness of the American people. The prosecution of this grand issue against all the principalities and powers of church and state, furnishes ample occupation for all our time and talents; and we instinctively shrink from any movement which involves a substitution of a doubtful and indirect issue, for one which is direct and certain, for we believe that the demand for the abolition of slavery now made in the name of humanity, and according to the law of the Living God, though long delayed, will, if faithfully pressed, certainly triumph.—The African Civilization Society proposes to plant its guns too far from the battlements of slavery for us. Its doctrines and measures are those of doubt and retreat, and it must land just where the American Colonization movement landed, upon the lying assumption, that white and black people can never live in the same land on terms of equality. Detesting this heresy as we do, and believing it to be full of all "deceivableness" of unrighteousness, we shun the paths that lead to it, no matter what taking names they bear, or how excellent the men who bid us to walk in them.

3. Among all the obstacles to the progress of civilization and of christianity in Africa, there is not one so difficult to overcome as the African slave trade. No argument is needed to make this position evident. The African Civilization Society will doubtless assent to its truth. Now, so regarding the slave trade, and believing that the existence of slavery in this country is one of the strongest props of the African slave trade, we hold that the best way to put down the slave trade, and to build up civilization in Africa, is to stand our ground and labor for the abolition of slavery in the U.S. But for slavery here, the slave trade would have been long since swept from the ocean by the united navies of Great Britain, France and the United States. The work, therefore, to which we are naturally and logically conducted, as the one of primary importance, is to abolish slavery. We thus get the example of a great nation on the right side, and break up, so far as America is concerned, a demand for the slave trade. More will have been done. The enlightened conscience of our nation, through its church and government, and its press, will be let loose against slavery and the slave trade wherever practiced.

4. One of the chief considerations upon which the African Civilization Society is recommended to our favorable regard, is its tendency to break up the slave trade. We have looked at this recommendation, and find no reason to believe that any one man in Africa can do more for the abolition of that trade, while living in Africa, than while living in America. If we cannot make Virginia, with all her enlightenment and christianity, believe that there are better uses for her energies than employing them in breeding slaves for the market, we see not how we can expect to make Guinea, with its ignorance and savage selfishness, adopt our notions of political economy. Depend upon it, the savage chiefs on the western coast of Africa, who for ages have been accustomed to selling their captives into bondage, and pocketing the ready cash for them will not more readily see and accept our moral and economical ideas, than the slave traders of Maryland and Virginia. We are, therefore, less inclined to go to Africa to work against the slave-trade, than to stay here to work against it. Especially as the means for accomplishing our object are quite as promising here as there, and more especially since we are here already, with constitutions and habits suited to the country and its climate, and to its better institutions.

5. There are slaves in the United States to the number of four millions. They are stigmatized as an inferior race, fit only for slavery, incapable of improvement, and unable to take care of themselves. Now, it seems plain that here is the place, and we are the people to

meet and put down these conclusions concerning our race. Certainly there is no place on the globe where the colored man can speak to a larger audience, either by precept or by example, than in the United States.

6. If slavery depended for its existence upon the cultivation of cotton, and were shut up to that single production, it might even then be fairly questioned whether any amount of cotton culture in Africa would materially affect the price of that article in this country, since demand and supply would go on together. But the case is very different. Slave labor can be employed in raising anything which human labor and the earth can produce. If one does not pay, another will. Christy says "Cotton is King", and our friends of the African Civilization movement are singing the same tune; but clearly enough it must appear to common sense, that "King Cotton" in America has nothing to fear from King Cotton in Africa.

7. We object to enrolling ourselves among the friends of that new Colonization scheme, because we believe that our people should be let alone, and given a fair chance to work out their own destiny where they are. We are perpetually kept, with wandering eyes and open mouths, looking out for some mighty revolution in our affairs here, which is to remove us from this country. The consequence is, that we do not take a firm hold upon the advantages and opportunities about us. Permanent location is a mighty element of civilization. In a savage state men roam about, having no continued abiding place. They are *"going, going, going"*. Towns and cities, houses and homes, are only built by men who halt long enough to build them. There is a powerful motive for the cultivation of an honorable character, in the fact that we have a country, a neighbourhood, a home. The full effect of this motive has not hitherto been experienced by our people. When in slavery, we were liable to perpetual sales, transfers and removals; and now that we are free, we are doomed to be constantly harassed with schemes to get us out of the country. We are quite tired of all this, and wish no more of it.

To all this it will be said that Douglass is opposed to our following the example of white men. They are pushing East, West, North and South. They are going to Oregon, Central America, Australia, South Africa and all over the world. Why should we not have the same right to better our condition that other men have and exercise? Any man who says that we deny this right, or even object to its exercise, only deceives the ignorant by such representations.

If colored men are convinced that they can better their condition by going to Africa, or anywhere else, we shall respect them if they go, just as we respect others who have gone to California, Fraser Island, Oregon and the West Indies. They are self-moved, self-sustained, and their success or failure is their own individual concern. But widely different is the case, when men combine, in societies, under taking titles, send out agents to collect money, and call upon us to help them travel from continent to continent to promote some selfish or benevolent end. In the one case, it is none of our business where our people go.—They are of age, and can act for themselves.—But when they ask the public to go, or for money, sympathy, aid, or co-operation, or attempt to make it appear anybody's duty to go, the case ceases to be a private individual affair, and becomes a public question, and he who believes that he can make a better use of his time, talents, and influence, than such a movement proposes for him, may very properly say so, without in any measure calling in question the equal right of our people to migrate.

Again it may be said that we are opposed to sending the Gospel to benighted Africa; but this is not the case. The *American Missionary Society*, in its rooms at 48 Beekman Street, has never had occasion to complain of any such opposition nor will it have such cause. But we will not anticipate the objections which may be brought to the foregoing views. They seem to us sober, rational, and true; but if otherwise, we shall be glad to have them honestly criticised.

# Lynchburg 'African Development Society', c. 1899*

Prof. G. W. Hayes, Pres., Lynchburg, Va.
Rev. J. A. Taylor, Vice Pres., Washington, D.C.
Rev. B. F. For, Sec., Salem, Va.
Rev. W. C. Hall, Asst. Sec., Danville, Va.
Mrs. Mary Hayes, Treas., Lynchburg, Va.
Rev. W. F. Graham, Asst. Tres., Richmond, Va.
CHE. JOHN CHILEMBWE, of EAST CENTRAL AFRICA, Gen. Solicitor.

PROSPECTUS
OF THE AFRICAN DEVELOPMENT SOCIETY
(To be incorporated) Capital $50,000 in $1.00 Shares.

*Whereas* certain Christian natives of East Central Africa have sent messengers to the Afro-American people, bearing a petition, asking their co-operation and direction in the development of the rich resources of their country, and

*Whereas* some of the tribes represented by the petitioners own vast areas of country in their own right of disposal, notably the Ajawa, Chipeta and Angoni peoples of Nyassaland, East Africa, and

*Whereas* certain very advantageous offers of extensive blocks of valuable plantation land have been made by certain of these Chiefs, at a cost of less than one cent per acre; and

*Whereas* it is beyond doubt that large fortunes have been made and are being made in that country from the production of coffee, sugar, tobacco, oil, nuts, cotton, rubber, etc., by a few enterprising Europeans; and

*Whereas* the climate has been proven to be temperate and healthy; the natives friendly and earnestly desiring Christian civilization; the

* George Shepperson and Thomas Price (eds.), *Independent African*, Edinburgh University Press, 1958, Appendix 2, pp. 533–35. Reprinted with permission of the author.

167

market easy of access and the present opportunities of vast importance to the Afro-American people,

*It is Proposed* to form the aforementioned society and conduct its
operations in a thoroughly Christian spirit, sending in the field only
men of an approved Christian standing who are believed to have the
best interests of the African race at heart. It is intended that the
transactions of the society in Africa shall be missionary in spirit,
though not in name.

The society proposes to take the following powers:

*1.* Power to acquire land in Africa by purchase or grants from native
Chiefs or others holding possession, and to retain, sell, or develop
the same, as the Directors, may see fit.

*2.* Power to establish manufactures, mining, or other industries,
or the cultivation of coffee, tea, sugar, tobacco, cotton, fruit, or
other profitable products, and to export or import, as they may desire.

*3.* Power to purchase, charter, or construct the means for transport
by land, river, lakes or ocean.

*4.* Power to provide, construct, or organize such means of defense
as the Directors may consider necessary in order to retain and develop the territories they may acquire in Africa by purchase or grant.

*5.* Power to increase the capital of the society at the discretion of a
two-thirds majority of the Board of Directors.

The society proposes to pay an interest not exceeding 7 per cent
yearly upon the paid-up shares, but does not guarantee to pay that
figure unless it be fully earned: any surplus profit earned to be
applied, first, to the creation and maintenance of a reserve fund
equal to one-fourth of the whole paid-up capital (such reserve fund
to be invested in government securities in the U.S. of America) and
second, to the founding of settlements of Afro-Americans desiring to
settle in Africa on the basis of Schedule D.* . . .

A special feature relating to the issue of the first 30,000 shares is

---

* This may well have been based on the Schedule D of Booth's *Africa for the
African*. This 'Negro Christian settlement programme' envisaged: ten families to
a settlement; each settlement to consist of 2000 acres; each family to have 200
acres of this; £3000 capital to be available for each settlement; 'during the first
seven years modest maintenance to be provided and such allowance further as
the executive considers to be merited'; after seven years, each 200–acre estate
and all its appliances becomes the absolute property of the settler.

that the Directors purpose giving each shareholder of not less than five paid-up shares a preferential right to a grant of 50 acres of land in East Africa under such title as the society may be able to furnish, with right to hold, occupy or sell to any Afro-American or African purchaser. Such preferential shareholders shall not be permitted to purchase more than 1,000 shares or be entitled to a grant of more than 10,000 acres of the society's estate: such preferential shares to be open only to Afro-American shareholders.

The registration and preliminary floating expenses to be paid by the Directors out of the sale of shares.

The following persons have agreed to act as provisional Directors and to take up the number of shares affixed to their respective signatures:

G. W. Hayes, 25 shares; T. J. Minton, 10 shares; H. T. Kealing, 10 shares; Matthew Anderson, 10 shares; Bernard Tyrrell, 10 shares; George W. Scott, 2 shares;

VIRGINIA SEMINARY PRINT

# American Negro Academy

## CONSTITUTION*

This Academy is an Organization of Authors, Scholars, Artists, and those distinguished in other walks of life, men of African descent, for the promotion of Letters, Science and Art; for the creation, as far as possible, of a form of intellectual taste; for the encouragement and assistance of youthful, but hesitant, scholarship; for the stimulation of inventive and artistic powers; and for the promotion of the publication of works of merit.

*Article 1*
The officers of the Academy, to be elected annually, shall be a President, four Vice-Presidents, a Corresponding Secretary, a Re-

* Reprinted by kind permission of the Moorland Collection, Founders Library, Howard University, Washington, D.C.

cording Secretary, a Treasurer, and an Executive Committee of five persons, who shall perform the usual duties of such offices.

When onerous duties are judged to demand it, the Secretaries may be salaried men.

*Article 2*

The membership of the Academy shall be limited to fifty persons.

*Article 3*

The conditions of membership shall be:

(a) Candidates shall be men of Science, Letters and Art, or those distinguished in other walks of life.

(b) Candidates must be recommended by six enrolled members, in a written application, through one of the Secretaries.

(c) Admission to membership shall be by ballot—by a two-thirds vote of all the membership, voting in person or by proxy—due notice having been given, two months before the balloting, to every member.

*Article 4*

The Academy shall endeavor with care and diligence:

(a) To promote the publication of scholarly work;

(b) To aid youths of genius in the attainment of the higher culture, at home or abroad;

(c) To gather into its Archives valuable data, and the works of Negro Authors;

(d) To aid, by publications, the dissemination of the truth and the vindication of the Negro race from vicious assaults;

(e) To publish, if possible, an "ANNUAL" designed to raise the standard of intellectual endeavor among American Negroes.

*Article 5*

The Academy may invite authors and writers, members and others, to submit their proposed publications to the criticism and judgement of the Academy: and if they shall receive its approval such publications may be issued under the recommendation of the Academy.

*Article 6*

The Annual Meetings of the Academy shall take place in the City of Washington, which shall be its seat, in the month of December, when papers shall be read, and such other exercises be held as the Academy, from year to year, may order.

*Article 7*

The admission fees to the Academy shall be $5.00 (including the first annual fee) and members shall be assessed annually $2.00; failure in payment of this or any other obligation voluntarily assumed for two years, shall cause membership to cease. Special assessments may be made for publications.

*Article 8*

In the publications of the Academy no titles of degrees shall be joined to the names of the members.

Organized March 5, 1897

## American Negro Academy*

### ALEXANDER CRUMMELL, *Founder*
#### Washington, D.C.

*July 27, 1920*

Mr. J. E. Kweggir-Aggrey,
London, Eng.

Dear Fellow Academician: The A.N.A. congratulates itself and the race on the high honor which is theirs on your mission abroad, especially to Africa the land of our fathers. While you are making observations as to conditions which doubtless have changed much since you left your home quite a generation ago and which have been modified by the world-wide war and the *influences* that followed in its train you are particularly commissioned to seek after and interest here and there the brightest minds you will find willing and eager to make contributions to our store of knowledge pertaining to our racial potentialities both here and throughout the world. In the discharge of this duty I trust you will leave no stone unturned, for much will grow out of what you observe and report from time to time.

Owing to the urgency of this letter I can not enter into details of the way you will therefore be governed by the spirit that, I am sure, you will interpret from what you have noted in our deliberations.

* From the Private Papers of John W. Cromwell. With the permission of the family.

171

Always you may count on the prayers of every member of the Academy as you journey among the sources of civilization and culture.

Very truly yours,

J. W. CROMWELL
*President*

CHILDREN OF THE SUN*

# The Hamitic League of the World

The Hamitic League of the World is open to every man and woman upon equal terms and every member has the same rights as any other. The definite work of the League is as follows:

To quicken the self-consciousness of our race and arouse in it a powerful race pride;

To spread the knowledge of the part played by Hamites in the development of human civilization;

To work for the revision of all text books that falsify and delete the truth concerning Hamitic races;

To strive for the universal admission of the equality of races;

To oppose all forms of prejudice against the race as well as all forms of prejudice within the race;

To rebuke all magazines and newspapers which endeavor to harm the race by inflamatory news, untruthful articles and disparaging dialect;

To fight for the capitalization of all terms used as an ethnic designation of our race;

To seek for all races the positive exercise of civil and political rights;

To promote the brotherhood of man.

* From the Private Papers of John W. Cromwell. With the permission of the family.

APPLICATION FOR MEMBERSHIP

The Hamitic League of the World,
   933 North 27th Street,
      Omaha, Neb.

I hereby enclose the sum of one dollar ($1.00) for life membership in the Hamitic League of the World, with the understanding that no other dues or assessments shall ever be made. I subscribe to the purposes of the organization and request that full information be sent me at once.

   Name  .............................................................

   Address................................................................

# Sons of Africa

## ADDRESS BY J. E. BRUCE*
### "DR. MARTIN OUR HOST"

Gentlemen:

About a year ago, I conceived the idea of organizing a society of Black and Colored men, to be known as the "*Sons of Africa*" and to be international in scope and to embrace in its membership men of all the darker races who have a grievance of any sort against the race which is now dominating the earth and reaping where it has not sown. In talking the matter over with Dr. Martin our *host*, he suggested, and I think well of the suggestion that we make the organization an *order* and enjoin upon the members secrecy. The psychological moment has I believe arrived for Negroes and colored men the wide world over to get together and to fight for every right with all

* See p. 126 for biographical sketch of J. E. Bruce. This address has been reprinted by kind permission of the New York Public Library.

173

our might. We must organize to secure uniformity of utterance and action among the darker races and to meet organized wrong with intelligently organized resistance.

The Slogan of the patriots of the American Revolution was: Eternal Vigilance is the Price of Liberty. The black and colored races can well afford to adopt it as their slogan for the liberties of both the wide world over were never more endangered by the grasping nations of the world than at the present time. The settled policy of the dominant race for the past one hundred years or more has been, and still is, to dominate and control all other races who wear "the shadowed livery of the burnished sun!" India, Africa, the West Indian Islands, the Phillipines, Cuba, Puerto Rico. And wherever the white man has been permitted or has forcibly inserted the thin edge of the wedge he has left a withering blight all along his pathway. His consuming desire is to pose as a world power at the sacrifice of the rights and interests of the so-called backward races. His cupidity and avarice have made him impervious to ordinary criticism of his dishonest methods, and it now becomes necessary for those ones who have been the victims of his greed and impulse to organize for self-protection in order to meet organized wrong with organized resistance intelligently directed and without the accompaniment of a Brass Band. This is, as I believe, the Psychological moment for Negroes all over the world to begin to touch elbows, exchange ideas and formulate plans for mutual protection for practical, racial and religious advantage. We are clearly within our rights in seeking here to found the Loyal Order of the Sons of Africa to bear a part in the revolution of ideas which usually preceeds a resort to physical force when reason and argument fail. The battle of the darker races is an intellectual one, and with *good* generals in command of the forces which are to do battle—the victory is all the more certain. An army divided is an army defeated. The reasons which we think make necessary such an organization as we have proposed may be briefly stated as follows: (1) the increase of race prejudice in Europe and America, (2) the denial of equal opportunities to black and colored men in countries supposedly their own but which have been preempted by cajolery or force by white men, (3) the growing tendency of white men to immunize the Negro influence in governmental affairs in this and in other countries by diplomacy, or brute force according to the exigencies of the case. (4) the deceit practiced by white men upon Negroes their peers in culture and character with whom they palter in a double *sense* to compass their reprehensive and dishonorable ends, (5) We all know what a treacherous

174

biped the white man is and how intensely selfish and hypocritical he is therefore it behoves us to play the game he is playing, but upon a loftier plane in the hope of saving to a future generation of black the heritage bequeathed to us by our fathers. Gentlemen the meeting is now open for full and free discussion.

# Negro Society for Historical Research

CONSTITUTION*

The name of this society shall be the Negro Society for Historical Research.

*Objects*
    *1.* The objects of this Society shall be: to encourage the study of Negro history: to collect books, MSS., photographs and portraits of noted Negroes; and from time to time to publish bulletins showing the achievements of Negroes in all the diversified walks of life, and to perform such other work as may best conserve the interest of the Negro race.
    *2.* The officers of this Society shall be a President, Secretary-Treasurer, Librarian, Art Director, Musical Director, who shall be elected on......of each month and serve for a period of...........
The duties of such officers shall be such as are performed by officers of similar societies.
    *3.* Committees. The President in his discretion may appoint from time to time from members in good standing such committees as may be necessary to carry out the wishes of the Society in the prosecution of its work and no committee shall consist of more than three members. The President being ex-officio shall not vote in committee.
    *4.* Membership shall be limited to..........and the joining fee shall be $10, payable one half with application and voucher and the remainder when admitted to membership. All applications for membership shall be voted on by ballot, and no rejected applications will be considered for a period of ...... years.
    The qualifications of members. Applicants for membership must

* The rough draft of a constitution drawn up by Mr. Bruce.

175

have had some reading in race literature, some knowledge of race achievement and be possessed of a desire for research.

It shall be the duty of the librarian to prepare and submit at slated meetings of the Society a journal, of which he shall be *editor*, which shall contain such articles and news items as may be gathered or sent to him by members of the Society bearing upon the work of the Society and subjects of a historical nature.

## MEMBERSHIP

King Lewanika of Barotseland, Honorary President
Prince Lubinda of the Barotse, son of King Lewanika, Hon. Member
Prince Akashambatwa of the Barotse, son of King Lewanika, Hon. Member
Hon. James J. Dossen, Vice-President of Liberia, Hon. Member
*Hon. Edward W. Blyden, Sierra Leone, W. A. Hon. Member
Hon. Casely Hayford Sekondi, Gold Coast, Africa, Hon. Member
Dr. Majola Agbebi, Lagos, West Africa, Hon. Member
E. Elliott Durant, Esq., Journalist, Barbadoes, W.I., Hon. Member
A. Rawle Parkinson, Esq., Educator, Barbadoes, W.I., Hon. Member
*Hon. A. White, Dean of the Law School, Louisville, Ky., Hon. Member
*General Evaristo Estenoz, Havana, Cuba, Hon. Member
Mr. F. Z. S. Peregrino, Journalist, Capetown, South Africa, Hon. Member
Matt Henson (Peary's Companion), Hon. Member
C. W. Anderson, Esq., New York City
Dr. T. E. S. Scholes, London, England, Hon. Member
Daniel Murray, Esq., Washington, D.C., Corresponding Member
William P. Moore, Brooklyn, N.Y., Corresponding Member
Prof. John W. Cromwell, Washington, D.C., Corresponding Member
Prof. Pedro C. Timothee, San Juan, Porto Rico, Corresponding Member
Moses de Rocha, Esq., Edinburgh University, Edinburgh, Corresponding Member
J. R. Clifford, Esq., Martinsburg, W. Va., Corresponding Member
C. A. Franklin, Esq., Denver, Colorado, Corresponding Member
Hon. James C. Smith, Killarney, Jersey, Channel Islands, Corresponding Member

176

W. E. Hawkins, Esq., Wilmington, N.C., Corresponding Member
Prof. W. E. B. DuBois, New York City, Corresponding Member
L. H. Latimer, Esq., Flushing, L.I., N.Y., Corresponding Member
Rev. E. D. L. Thompson, Freetown, Sierra Leone, W.A., Corresponding Member
Mrs. Veronica Nickelson, Ossining, New York.
Mrs. Lillian Urquhart, Newark, N.J., Corresponding Member
Mrs. Florence A. Bruce, Yonkers, N.Y., Corresponding Member
Mrs. Mary Butler, Yonkers, N.Y., Corresponding Member
Mrs. Marie Du Chatellier, Bocas del Toro, Panama, Corresponding Member
C. Carroll Clark, New York City, Corresponding Member
Mr. A. LeRoy Locke, Camden, New Jersey, Corresponding Member
Prof. J. S. Moore, Bahia, Brazil, Corresponding Member
Miss Emma Brown, Philadelphia, Pa., Corresponding Member
Rev. William Forde, Port Limon, Costa Rica, Corresponding Member
James B. Clarke, Esq., New York City, Corresponding Member
W. A. Lavalette, Washington, D.C., Corresponding Member
Duse Mohamed, Effendi, London, England, Corresponding Member
James A. Stephens, Yonkers, N.Y., Corresponding Member
F. J. Moultrie, Esq., Yonkers, N.Y., Corresponding Member
W. T. Jemmott, Esq., Brooklyn, N.Y., Corresponding Member
Thomas H. Knight, Wilmington, N.C., Corresponding Member
W. C. Bolivar, Esq., Philadelphia, Pa., Corresponding Member
John Edward Bruce, Yonkers, N.Y., Member
Arthur A. Schomburg, New York City, Member
David B. Fulton, New York City, Member
William Wesley Weekes, Brooklyn, New York, Member
Ernest W. Braxton, Brooklyn, N.Y., Member
Dr. York Russell, New York City, N.Y., Member
Dr. J. Frank Thorpe, New York City, N.Y., Member
W. P. Dabney, Cincinnati, Ohio, Member
Thomas I. Peregrino, Esq., Cape Town, S.A., Corresponding Member

# African Union Company Prospectus and Report

## WHAT THE AFRICAN UNION CO. HAS DONE IN ONE YEAR*

*Cincinnati, O., April 3, 1915*

### Organization

The African Union Company was organized December 3, 1913, and incorporated under the laws of New York for $500,000 in March, 1914. The stock is divided into twenty thousand shares of twenty-five dollars each. The shares sold in Africa are not all paid for in cash, many being sold for real estate and buildings in Africa, many for standing mahogany trees and a few for services rendered.

### Purpose

The purpose is to handle African produce on a large scale, establishing mercantile operations between Africa and the markets of the world, to ultimately establish an African Industrial School and to aid in the development of Africa generally.

We have three representatives in Africa—namely, Mr. C. W. Chappelle, of Pittsburg, Pa., our President and General Manager; Mr. I. S. Lee, of Pittsburg, and Assistant to the General Manager, and Mr. C. B. Ross, of Birmingham, Ala., as Financial Agent. We also have an auxiliary Board of Directors in Africa, composed of natives.

### Africans Interested

Our President has made three trips to Africa and has visited the various Kings and Chiefs, explaining the object of our Corporation. They have evinced remarkable interest in the movement, and have bought a large number of shares of stock, paying for them in standing mahogany trees, cocoa, palm oil trees, gum copal and other native products.

### Permanent Assets

The Corporation already owns and controls by way of leases vast mahogany and timber lands and oil palm plantations, four alluvial

* Reprinted by kind permission of the Washington family.

178

and three quartz gold mines, four completely equipped moving picture shows, an up-to-date photography establishment, several parcels of fee simple land for school building and agricultural purposes. No effort is now being made to operate any of the mining concessions because of the immense cost of operation.

*What It Will Pay Investors*
Your investment in this stock will pay from 20 per cent upward. It is an unparalleled opportunity for profitable investment.

The great European war has greatly hampered our operations owing to reduced shipping facilities, yet we are able to report the following shipments, viz.: November 19, 1914, of 4,928 pounds of cocoa; December 5, 146,844 feet of mahogany and 892 pounds of cocoa; January 19, 1915, 184 kid skins and 68 pounds ginger; February 23, 11,210 feet of mahogany. We have ready for shipment forty-five million feet of mahogany as soon as conditions will permit.

*The Directors*
Stronger evidence as to the prospects of this Corporation and the integrity of the men behind it could not be desired or obtained than are as follows: Chas. W. Chappelle, of Pittsburg, Pa., and New York, is President and General Manager. He has spent the greater part of three years in Africa. He is an Electrical, Mechanical and Architectural Engineer, a contractor and builder.

The late Dr. W. R. Pettiford, of Birmingham, Ala., was Vice President. He was founder and President of the Alabama Penny Savings Bank, with branches at Selma, Anniston and Montgomery, Ala. He was President of the National Negro Bankers' Association.

Jos. L. Jones, of Cincinnati, O., is Secretary and General Sales Manager. He is the founder and President of the Central Regalia Company, Vice Supreme Chancellor of the Knights of Pythias and Chairman of the Executive Committee of the National Negro Press Association.

John T. Birch, of Brooklyn, N.Y., is Treasurer. He is a large real estate owner of Brooklyn, and Treasurer of the Birch Realty Company.

Emmet J. Scott, of Tuskegee Institute, Ala., is a Director. He is Secretary of Tuskegee Institute, an ex-member of the United States Liberian Commission and Secretary of the National Negro Business League.

George M. Robb, of Pittsburg, Pa., is a Director. He is a large real estate owner of his city.

R. R. Jackson, of Chicago, Ill., is a Director. He is a member of the Illinois State Legislature, Major General of the Uniform Rank, K. of P., President of the Fraternal Press Printing Company, a Major in the Eighth Illinois National Guard, and a Commissioner of the Emancipation Exposition of Illinois.

Dr. D. W. Roberts, of St. Augustine, Fla., is a Director. He has large real estate holdings in Florida and is one of the leading physicians of the race.

Gilchrist Stewart, of New York, is a Director. He is a prominent New York counsellor-at-law.

Reeves & Todd, 165 Broadway, New York City, are the attorneys for the Corporation.

# Memorandum in re
# the Association for the Study of Negro
# Life and History*

*Its History*
1. Organized in Chicago, September 9, 1915.
2. Incorporated under the laws of the District of Columbia, October 3, 1915.
3. Brought out *The Journal of Negro History*, January 1, 1916.
4. Held the first biennial meeting, August 28, 1917.

*Its Purposes*
1. To collect sociological and historical documents.
2. To publish books on Negro life and history.
3. To promote the study of Negro life and history through clubs organized for intensive work.
4. To bring about harmony between the races by interpreting the one to the other.

*Its Promoters*
1. Well-known philanthropists like Harold H. Swift, Morton D. Hull, Moorfield Storey, Frank O. Lowden, William G. Wilcox, and Julius Rosenwald.

* Reprinted by kind permission of the Moorland Collection, Founders Library Howard University, Washington, D.C.

2. Distinguished scholars like Roland G. Usher, John M. Mecklin, Jerome Dowd, Kelly Miller, W. E. B. DuBois, Asa E. Martin, John H. Russell, Charles E. Chapman, and James F. Jameson.

3. Prominent persons like Henry Churchill King, William J. Schieffelin, Helen Adams Kellar, R. R. Moton, A. S. Frissell, and George Foster Peabody.

4. Some noted publicists, among whom are Talcott Williams, Frederick L. Hoffman, A. H. Stone, Mrs. L. Hammond, and Oswald Garrison Villard.

### What it has Accomplished
1. It has extended the circulation of *The Journal of Negro History* into South America, Europe, Asia, and Africa.
2. It has directed the attention of investigators to this neglected field.
3. It has published many series of documents giving facts which are generally unknown.
4. It has published valuable books, among which are *A Century of Negro Migration* and *Slavery in Kentucky*.

### Its Needs
1. A decided increase in revenue to extend the work by employing a number of trained investigators.
2. Adequate funds for publishing the results of their researches.

# Marcus Garvey,
## 1887–1939

No Negro in the United States before or since has been able to develop an organizational structure to rival in its size or impact that developed by Marcus Garvey as the Universal Negro Improvement Association and African Communities' League, of the World. Yet surprisingly little attention has been paid to examining the regulatory basis for this achievement. In 1920 Marcus Garvey issued a call for an international convention of Negroes to be held in New York City during August of that year. This Convention publicized for the first time Garvey's genius in involving the masses of Negroes in a mammoth organizational structure that not only met the expressed goals of the Universal Negro Improvement Association, but provided a sense of importance for the long downtrodden and ignored black men and women. From their parade down Lenox Avenue the surprised and impressed Negro world could gain a visual impression of the facets and goals of Garveyism. Revealing the discipline and pageantry so essential to a mass movement, the African Legion, the Black Cross Nurses, and the Juvenile Auxiliary paraded for all to see.

The foundation on which this organization was built is explained in the Constitution and Book of Laws made for the Government of the Universal Negro Improvement Association, Inc. and the African Communities' League, Inc., of the World. Only the Constitution is included in this anthology, but much of the detail and breadth of the organizational structure can only be understood from the Book of Laws. This part included the General Laws which consisted of three articles covering the procedure at Conventions, the electing of deputies to Conventions, and jurisdictional and divisional regulations. The third article, reflecting Garvey's appreciation of the need for expansion as well as the maintenance of control, had sixty-three sections. In addition to these three articles, the General Laws also included Rules and Regulations for Universal African Legions of the Universal Negro Improvement Association and African Communities' League having twenty-five articles which determined the form and character of this auxiliary body. It was to consist of men between the ages of eighteen and fifty-five who were to receive military training and discipline.

Also included are Rules and Regulations Governing the Universal African Motor Corps in four brief articles, Rules and Regulations Governing the Universal African Black Cross and Nurses in eight articles, Rules and Regulations for Juveniles from one year to eighteen years in four articles, and Rules for the Universal Negro Improvement Association Choirs in eight articles. At the end of the volume there are a Hymn for Opening of Meetings, a Prayer for the Opening of Meetings by John Bruce-Grit (see pages 126 ff. and 173 ff.), The Universal Ethiopian Anthem, which was the National Anthem of the Universal Negro Improvement Association and African Communities' League, and a Parting Hymn for Juveniles (the familiar 'Now the Day is Over').

The Agenda for the Sixth Annual International Convention of the Negro Peoples of the World, organized by Garvey to be held in the British West Indies and reported in the *Gold Coast Times* of June 1929, is a further example of the elaboration of Garvey's organizational structure and purpose, which he continued to pursue in spite of his imprisonment for mail fraud in 1925 and his commutation and deportation in 1927 to Jamaica. At this Convention too, as reported by Cronin,* "Jamaican Negroes were visibly impressed with the various units of the association—the smart marching bands, the elegantly uniformed African Legion, the Black Cross Nurses, the Universal Motor Corps, and the many delegates in their richly colored robes of office."

Although at the close of the Convention ten thousand persons attended the Court Reception for the Universal Negro Improvement Association and Garvey announced the inauguration of a worldwide campaign to collect six hundred million dollars for the new Universal Negro Improvement Association programme, a schism was developing within the organization between the United States delegates and others from which the movement as an international force never recovered.

* Edmund David Cronin, *Black Moses, The Story of Marcus Garvey and the Universal Negro Improvement Association*, Madison; The University of Wisconsin Press, 1955, p. 151.

# Constitution of the Universal Negro Improvement Association

PREAMBLE

The Universal Negro Improvement Association and African Communities' League is a social, friendly, humanitarian, charitable, educational, institutional, constructive and expansive society, and is founded by persons desiring to the utmost to work for the general uplift of the Negro peoples of the world. And the members pledge themselves to all in their power to conserve the rights of their noble race and to respect the rights of all mankind, believing always in the Brotherhood of Man and the Fatherhood of God. The motto of the organization is "One God! One Aim! One Destiny!" Therefore, let justice be done to all mankind, realizing that if the strong oppresses the weak confusion and discontent will ever mark the path of man, but with love, faith and charity towards all the reign of peace and plenty will be heralded into the world and the generations of men shall be called Blessed.

---

Made for the Government of the Universal Negro Improvement Association and African Communities' League

---

In Effect July,1918

---

Amended in August, 1920, August, 1921, and August, 1922

## Constitution

### ARTICLE I

*Jurisdiction*
  **Section 1.** This body shall be known as the Universal Negro Improvement Association and African Communities' League. Its

jurisdiction shall include all communities where the people of Negro blood and African descent are to be found. In it alone, and through the Potentate and Supreme Commissioner, hereinafter spoken of, and his successors, are vested powers to establish subordinate divisions and other organizations, whose objects shall coalesce and be identical with those herein set forth, and its mandates shall be obeyed at all times and under all circumstances. To the Universal Negro Improvement Association and African Communities' League, through the authority of the Potentate, is reserved the right to fix, regulate and determine all matters of a general or international nature as affecting the objects of the organization and the membership at large.

*Right to Reorganize Rebellious Branch or Division*
**Section 2.** The right is reserved to revoke charters and to re-establish jurisdiction over any division or subordinate organization whose affairs are conducted contrary to the welfare of the Universal Negro Improvement Association and African Communities' League as required by the Constitution and General Laws.

*Objects and Aims*
**Section 3.** The objects of the Universal Negro Improvement Association and African Communities' League shall be: to establish a Universal Confraternity among the race; to promote the spirit of pride and love; to reclaim the fallen; to administer to and assist the needy; to assist in civilizing the backward tribes of Africa; to assist in the development of Independent Negro Nations and Communities; to establish Commissionaries or Agencies in the principal countries and cities of the world for the representation and protection of all Negroes, irrespective of nationality; to promote a conscientious Spiritual worship among the native tribes of Africa; to establish Universities, Colleges, Academies and Schools for the racial education and culture of the people; to conduct a world-wide Commercial and Industrial Intercourse for the good of the people; to work for better conditions in all Negro communities.

*Seven Necessary Number for Charter*
**Section 4.** A charter may be issued to seven or more citizens of any community whose intelligence is such as to bring them within respectful recognition of the educated and cultured of such a community, provided there is no chartered division in such a community.

185

*Chapters*
**Section 5.** All additional Divisions created in the same cities shall be called Chapters. The Charters granted to such Divisions shall be called Chapter Charters, and all new Divisions so created shall be called Chapters instead of Divisions, and the Executive Secretary, who shall be a civil servant attached to the Division, shall be the Supervisor of such Chapters.

*Dominion, Provincial or Colonial Charters*
**Section 6.** In countries requiring the Provincial or Colonial registration of Charters, there shall be issued one Dominion, Provincial or Colonial Charter, as the law may require, and all Divisions within the Charter limits shall be designated as Branches. Nothing in this provision shall be construed as giving the original Division any jurisdiction over the others other than through the parent body.

ARTICLE II

*Laws*
**Section 1.** The Universal Negro Improvement Association and African Communities' League may enact and enforce laws for its government and that for subordinate divisions, organizations and societies and members throughout the jurisdiction.
**Section 2.** The laws of the Universal Negro Improvement Association and African Communities' League shall be comprised in (*a*) The Constitution which shall contain the outlines, fundamental principles and policies of the organization, its Jursidiction and that of local Divisions and societies, the list of officers and all matters pertaining to their duties; (*b*) The By-Laws, which shall contain the order of procedure in Convention, the specific duties of officers and committees, and the standing rules; (*c*) The General Laws, which shall contain all matters pertaining to the relations of members and local Divisions and societies to each other.

*Amendment to Constitution*
**Section 3.** The Constitution shall only be amended at times when such amendment tend absolutely to the further interest of the Universal Negro Improvement Association and African Communities' League and when carried by a two-thirds majority in Convention fully assembled.

186

*By-Laws and General Laws; How Enacted*

**Section 4.** By-Laws and General Laws may be enacted by the Convention of the Universal Negro Improvement Association and African Communities' League, and such laws shall be carried by a two-thirds majority.

### ARTICLE III

*Deputies to Convention*

**Section 1.** Divisions and all kindred organizations, societies and orders subordinate to the Universal Negro Improvement Association and African Communities' League are entitled to representation in Convention; such Divisions and societies sending a delegate or delegates, who shall be named deputies, as directed through the office of the President-General.

*Terms of Deputies*

**Section 2.** Each Deputy shall hold office for four years after election, and his office shall be honorary with his expenses paid for attending Convention by his own Division, organization, society or order. He shall be entitled to one vote in Convention and no proxy shall be allowed.

### ARTICLE IV

*Officials, Officers, Elections and Appointments*

**Section 1.** The rulers of the Universal Negro Improvement Association and African Communities' League shall be a Potentate and Supreme Commissioner, a Supreme Deputy, a President-General and Administrator, First Assistant President-General, Second Assistant President-General, who shall also be titular Leader of American Negroes; Third Assistant President-General, who shall also be titular Leader of the West Indies, South and Central America; a Fourth Assistant President-General, a Secretary-General, a First Assistant Secretary-General, a Second Assistant Secretary-General, and a High Chancellor; a Counsel General, an Assistant Counsel-General Auditor-General; a Minister of Labour and Industry, High Commissioner-General, A Chaplain-General, an International Organizer, a Minister of Legions and a Minister of Education, all of whom shall form the High Executive Council representing branches throughout the world, and

Be it resolved, That everything in the Constitution contradictory

187

to or in conflict with the above section, be and is hereby repealed and declared null and void.

**Section 2.** The offices of the Provisional President of Africa, the President-General and Administrator, the First Assistant President-General, the Second Assistant President-General, who shall also be titular Leader of American Negroes; the Third Assistant President-General, who shall also be titular Leader of Negroes of the West Indies, South and Central America; the Fourth Assistant President-General, all of whom shall be elected and their term of office shall be four years, providing their conduct conform to the best interests of the Universal Negro Improvement Association and African Communities' League.

**Section 2a.** All other officers forming the High Executive Council shall be appointed by the President-General and confirmed by the Convention, except the Potentate and the Supreme Deputy, whose term of office shall be permanent, and such appointments shall be for the same period as that of the Administration, providing their conduct conforms to the best interests of the Universal Negro Improvement Association, and have proven their confidence to the satisfaction of the administration, and

Be it resolved, That everything in the Constitution contradictory to or in conflict with the above section be and is hereby repealed and declared null and void.

*Failure of Official to Qualify*

**Section 3.** No person elected to a high office of the Universal Negro Improvement Association shall hold office until his credentials as to his character and qualifications have satisfied the High Executive Council. In case a person elected to a high office is rejected by the High Executive Council, the President-General and Administrator shall have the power to appoint a person to fill the position of the person rejected until the next session of the Convention.

*High Commissioners and Commissioners*

**Section 4.** A High Commissioner or Commissioner shall be appointed to represent the Universal Negro Improvement Association in every country where Negroes live. In parts where the country is divided up into large states and different sections a Commissioner shall be appointed to every state and section.

*Rank of Minister or Ambassador*

**Section 5.** There shall also be appointed High Commissioners who shall be given the rank of Ministers Plenipotentiary or Ambassadors, who shall be domiciled at the capitals of all regular governments. Their duties shall be to keep up friendly relations with the respective governments and to protect the interests of all Negroes.

## Appointment of High Commissioners

**Section 6.** The Potentate and Supreme Commissioner shall appoint High Commissioners on recommendation of the President-General and Administrator and commission them to represent the interests of the organization in all countries of the world, and they shall be controlled by the office of the High Commissioners-General.

## Election of Divisional Officers

**Section 7.** Divisions and subordinate organisations shall elect their officers (except President, who shall be appointed by the President-General) by majority vote to be approved of by the office of the President-General.

## Term of Office of Rulers

**Section 8.** The term of office of the Potentate and Supreme Commissioner and that of the Supreme Deputy shall be permanent. The term of all other officers of the parent body shall be four years, provided that their conduct conform with the interests of the Universal Negro Improvement Association and African Communities' League at all times.

ARTICLE V

## Potentate and Supreme Commissioner

**Section 1.** The Potentate and Supreme Commissioner shall be the invested ruler of the Universal Negro Improvement Association and African Communities' League and all its appendages. He shall be of Negro blood and race. He shall constitutionally control all affairs of the Association and League and all other societies. He shall institute social orders and societies and organizations in connection with the Universal Negro Improvement Association and African Communities' League, as determined by the said Association and League, and shall retain full power and control over their actions and jurisdiction. He shall have constitutional authority, through his high office, to suspend, reduce or relieve any officer other than the Supreme

Deputy of his commission or authority of service to the Universal Negro Improvement Association and African Communities' League and subordinate orders, societies and organizations. He shall issue "articles" or "messages" from time to time to the entire body of members of the Universal Negro Improvement Association and African Communities' League on questions of moment, and such "articles" and "messages" shall be respected by all those claiming allegiance to the Association and League. He shall appear in person to open the Convention and to deliver a speech which shall be called the "Potentate's Speech," and which shall be a review of the work and operations of the Association and League for the past year, as also advices for the conduct of affairs for the current or following year. He shall make his official residence at the place provided for him by the Universal Negro Improvement Association and African Communities' League. He shall marry only a lady of Negro blood and parentage, and his consort shall herself by virtue of her position be head of the female division of all organizations, societies and orders. He shall form an Executive Council to assist him in his administration out of the officials of the Universal Negro Improvement Association and African Communities' League and others elected by the Convention, and his colleagues shall be required to be loyal to him and to the Association and League. He shall be empowered to confer titles, honors, orders of merit, degrees, or marks of distinction on any person or persons who shall have rendered faithful service to the purposes of the Universal Negro Improvement Association and African Communities' League of whom he has been advised as being fit to bear such titles, honors, orders of merit, degrees or marks of distinction. He shall appoint or commission, through his office, any member or members to carry out any work in the interest of the Association and League. He shall be privileged to nominate his successor during his lifetime, and that nomination shall be handed in a sealed envelope to the High Chancellor, who shall preserve same until the time of his death, At the time of his death his nomination shall be handed over to the Executive Council, and the Executive Council shall make two other nominations before breaking the seal of the late Potentate's nomination; the nominations of the Executive Council shall be from among officials, officers, or distinguished members of the organization who have heretofore distinguished themselves in service to the Universal Negro Improvement Association and African Communities' League and whose honour, loyalty and devotion cannot be questioned. After breaking the seal of the Potentate's nomination the three nominations shall be announced to the world and the Supreme Deputy shall call an immediate session of the Convention and then and there elect the new Potentate from the three nominees by majority vote and ballot. The election of a new Potentate shall take place two months after the demise of the former, and his investiture shall take place one month after his election. On the death of the Potentate, and on the election of another, his consort shall vacate the official residence for another to be provided by the Universal Negro Improvement Association and African Communities' League, which shall support her until her death or marriage to another party.

*Potentate's Power Derived from Executive Council*
**Section 2.** The Potentate's power of action in all matters shall be derived from the advice received from his Executive Council and through the officers of the Universal Negro Improvement Association and African Communities' League, which advice shall be expressive of the will and sentiment of the people, and he shall not be empowered to act in any matter of great moment without first receiving the advice of the Executive Council.

*Court Reception or At Home*
**Section 3.** Immediately during the sitting of Convention of each year the Potentate and Supreme Commissioner shall cause to be given at his official residence or at some place of high moral and social repute an "at home" or "reception," which shall be called the "Court Reception," at which the Potentate and his Consort shall receive in presentation those distinguished ladies and gentlemen of the race and their male and female children whose character, morally and socially, stands above question in their respective communities. No lady below the age of eighteen shall be presented at "Court Reception," and no gentleman below the age of twenty-one. No one shall be received by the Potentate and his Consort who has been convicted of crime or felony, except such crime of felony was committed in the interests of the Universal Negro Improvement Association and African Communities' League, or whose morality is not up to the standard of social ethics. No one shall pay money to be presented at Court who is not known to the President or General Secretary, respectively, of the local Division to which he or she belongs. All recommendations for social recognition shall be made through local Divisions to the office of the High Commissioner-General, who shall edit a list of "social eligibles" and present said list to the Potentate, who shall cause commands from his household to be issued to the

respective parties to attend "Court Reception". Recognition for social or other distinctions shall only be merited by previous service to the Universal Negro Improvement Association and African Communities' League by the person or persons to be honoured, and no local Division shall recommend anyone to be honoured by the Potentate, who has never done some praiseworthy or meritorious service to the organization in the carrying through of its objects, and all persons honoured by the Potentate shall be so respected by all Negroes of all countries and climes.

### Impeachment of Potentate or Supreme Deputy

**Section 4.** The Potentate and Supreme Commissioner and Supreme Deputy, should they at any time act contrary to the good and welfare of the Universal Negro Improvement Association and African Communities' League in refusing or neglecting to abide by or carry out the commands of the Association and League through its Constitution and through the order of its Convention shall, on proper evidence of the fact, be impeached by any member of the Executive Council through the office of the Counsel-General, and they shall be tried for such irregularities, neglect, misconduct or disloyalty to the Association before the Convention, and if found guilty before the Convention by a two-thirds vote, they shall automatically forfeit the high office held by them, and the Convention shall take immediate steps to elect a new Potentate or Supreme Deputy.

### Counsel-General Must Prosecute

**Section 5.** If the Potentate and Supreme Commissioner or the Supreme Deputy shall be charged or impeached before the Convention, the Counsel-General shall prosecute them in the interest of the Universal Negro Improvement Association and African Communities' League, and the Potentate or Supreme Deputy shall have counsel to appear at the Bar of the Convention in his behalf, and such counsel shall be an active member or officer of the Universal Negro Improvement Association and African Communities' League.

### Defendant's Counsel

**Section 6.** No Counsel except an Officer or Active Member of the Universal Negro Improvement Association and African Communities' League shall be allowed to appear in behalf of any members charged before any "responsible body of trial" of the Association and League.

*Bribes*

**Section 7.** Should the Potentate and Supreme Commissioner or Supreme Deputy take or receive moneys or gifts from any person or persons by way of bribes or rewards for neglecting or selling out the interests of the Universal Negro Improvement Association and African Communities' League, he shall be guilty of high crime against the Association and League, and on conviction before the Convention shall forthwith be disgraced and dismissed from the high office he holds.

*Officials Found Guilty*

**Section 8.** Any officer or official of the Universal Negro Improvement Association and African Communities' League charged and found guilty of a similar offence shall be forthwith dismissed from the office of the Association and League through the office of the Potentate or his or her Superior Officer, on the approval of the Executive Council.

*Shall Not Receive Money or Gifts*

**Section 9.** No officer or official in the service of the Universal Negro Improvement Association and African Communities' League shall receive money or gifts on his or her account from anyone for services rendered for the Universal Negro Improvement Association and African Communities' League, but all such money and gifts shall be turned over to and shall be the property of the Universal Negro Improvement Association and African Communities' League; but a purse or testimonial may be presented publicly to any officer or official on his or her own account as appreciation of faithful services performed for the Association and League.

*All Active Members Must Approve Constitution*

**Section 10.** All officers, officials and active members of the Universal Negro Improvement Association and African Communities' League shall sign their names in approval and acceptance of the Constitution and By-Laws in a register provided for that purpose before they are installed into office.

ARTICLE VI

*Black Star Line Navigation and Trading Company*

**Section 11.** The Third International Convention of Negroes duly assembled ordains and establishes the Black Star Line Navigation & Trading Company for the purpose of carrying out the steamship programme of the Universal Negro Improvement Association in the interests of the race. The Universal Negro Improvement Association shall capitalize the new company, and no individuals shall be allowed to own any stock in said Company. All stocks shall be owned absolutely and exclusively by the Universal Negro Improvement Association.

**Section 11a.** The Executive Council of the Universal Negro Improvement Association is empowered by this Convention to invest its accumulated funds in the said new Steamship Corporation. And the said Executive Council shall be the incorporators of the new Company. And in the formation of the new Company, aside from the President-General, no other directors of the defunct Black Star Line Company shall be allowed to direct the affairs of the new Company. And that only competent persons be employed by the new Company.

*Black Star Line Redemption Corporation*

**Section 12.** The Universal Negro Improvement Association in Convention assembled does hereby authorize the Organization of an auxiliary to be known as the Black Star Line Redemption Corporation, for the purpose of redeeming the stocks and notes of the Black Star Line, Inc., now held by stockholders.

**Section 12a.** A period of five years shall be allowed for the complete redemption of the stock and notes of the Black Star Line, Inc., now held by stockholders, and two and one-half per cent. shall be paid on the stocks and notes of the Black Star Line, Inc., to the stockholders, from the time of the purchase of said stocks and notes to the time of their redemption.

**Section 12b.** The Universal Negro Improvement Association is hereby authorized to call upon all its Divisions and Chapters throughout the world to give an entertainment once per month to raise funds for the purpose of liquidating the stocks and notes of the stockholders of the Black Star Line, Inc. And the funds shall be remitted to the parent body for the purpose and intent so designed. The Parent Body is further authorized to print and distribute among its Divisions and Chapters, envelopes which shall be used by said Divisions and Chapters in soliciting twenty-five cents from all persons who frequent said entertainments, and the amounts collected, together with said envelopes, shall be immediately mailed to the Parent Body, and the funds so received shall be applied to the use for which they were collected.

*Supreme Deputy*

**Section 13.** The Supreme Deputy shall assist the Potentate in the discharge of his duties and shall perform the duties of the Potentate in his absence, incapacity or interregnum. He shall be the Potentate's special envoy to attend any function or ceremony that the Potentate may be unable to attend himself. He shall attend along with the Potentate the opening of the Convention and sit next to the Potentate. He shall be of Negro blood and his wife shall also be of Negro blood and parentage.

*President-General and Administrator*

**Section 14.** The President-General and Administrator shall be the working head of the Universal Negro Improvement Association and African Communities' League and he shall be held responsible to the Potentate for the entire working and carrying out of all commands. He shall attend Convention and make a speech in reply to that of the Potentate. He shall instruct minor officers on their duties and see that such duties are properly performed.

He shall be empowered to exercise a Veto Power on any financial matter initiated by any individual or by the Executive Council that may tend to jeopardize or ruin the finances of the organization. Such veto power shall only be used by the Administrator in financial matters, and where from his best judgment he is convinced that it is not to the best interest of the organization to permit the carrying out of such financial measures. An appeal may be made to the Convention against the veto of the Administrator, on any measure, and he shall be held responsible to the Convention for the exercise of his judgment on the matter.

*First Assistant President-General*

**Section 15.** The First Assistant President General shall assist the President General in the performance of such duties of his office as shall be assigned to him by the President General. He shall perform all the duties of the President General in case of absence, illness, permanent disability, resignation or death, until such time as the Convention shall have elected a new President General.

*Secretary General and High Commissioner*

**Section 16.** The Secretary General and High Commissioner shall have in his custody all correspondence of the Universal Negro Improvement Association and African Communities' League. He shall have under control all Divisional Secretaries and shall conduct the

o                                    195

general correspondence of the organization. He shall attend Convention and read reports and answer questions relative to the work of the organization. He shall be the spokesman of the Potentate and Executive Council in Convention.

### The Assistant Secretary General

**Section 17.** The Assistant Secretary General shall assist the Secretary General with the approval of the Executive Council, and in the event of absence, illness, permanent disability, resignation or death, he shall perform all the duties of the Secretary General until such time as the Convention shall have elected a new Secretary General.

### Second Assistant Secretary General

**Section 18.** It shall be the duty of the Second Assistant Secretary General to work in concert with the First Assistant and the Secretary General in the performance of the duties of that office.

### High Chancellor

**Section 19.** The High Chancellor shall be the custodian of the funds of the Universal Negro Improvement Association and African Communities' League and shall, under the direction of the President General, deposit all funds in some responsible bank. He shall give bond to the President General, which bond shall be well recognized. He shall attend Convention and deliver the Financial Speech of the year.

### Counsel General

**Section 20.** The Counsel General shall be the head legal officer of the Universal Negro Improvement Association and African Communities' League. He shall instruct all officials and officers of the Association on the law and shall conduct all cases or see to the defending of the Society before all courts of justice and appear on the Society's behalf at all times as directed by the President General.

### Assistant Counsel General

**Section 21.** The Assistant Counsel General shall assist the Counsel General in the performance of such duties of his office as shall be assigned to him by the Counsel General with the approval of the Executive Council, and in the event of absence, illness, permanent disability, resignation or death he shall perform all the duties of the Counsel General until such time as the Convention shall have elected a new Counsel General.

*Auditor General*

**Section 22.** The Auditor General and High Commissioner shall audit the accounts and books of the High Chancellor, and all accounts and books of other high officers and branches twice annually viz: For the six months ending January 31st within twenty-one days after that date, and for the six months ended Jan. 31st within twenty-one days after that date. He shall secure the assistance for this purpose of an expert accountant, and shall submit his report to the President General, who shall cause same to be published in the journal of the Association.

*High Commissioner General*

**Section 23.** The High Commissioner General shall be the head of the foreign High Commissioners. He shall receive their reports and report same to the Potentate and Executive Council through the proper officers. He shall recommend to the Potentate worthy individuals on whom commissions, titles, honours, social distinctions and degrees should be conferred.

*Chaplain General*

**Section 24.** The Chaplain General shall be the spiritual adviser of the Potentate and Council. He shall act as the representative of the Universal Negro Improvement Association and African Communities' League in conducting the investiture of all high officials and at the conferring of titles, honours and degrees by the Potentate. He shall attend Convention at its opening along with the Potentate and open the proceedings with prayer.

*International Organizer and High Commissioner*

**Section 25.** The International Organizer and High Commissioner shall be charged with the duty of organizing all the Negro communities of the world into the Universal Negro Improvement Association and African Communities' League, and shall have under his control all local organizers, who shall report to him monthly through the officers of their respective local Divisions the results of their various organizing campaigns. He shall make periodic visits to all countries to ascertain and to see to the proper bringing together of the world's corporate body of Negroes.

*Surgeon General*

**Section 26.** The Surgeon General shall disseminate by lectures, articles and circulars information to the members of our race, with regard to hygiene, eugenics, vital statistics and necessary precautions for the maintenance of health and the increase of life expectation, and shall perform the duties of a physician and surgeon as directed by the President General. He shall publish at least once monthly in the journal of the Association a statement of the physical conditions among Negroes. He shall examine the physical fitness of the Officers and Privates of the Legions and other auxiliaries.

### Minister of Labour and Industries

**Section 27.** The Minister of Labour and Industries shall be an Executive Officer of the Universal Negro Improvement Association, whose duty it shall be to regulate labour and industry of the parent body and among the Divisions and various members of the organization throughout the world. When feasible he should have representatives in each Division, and shall thereby inform himself of the labour conditions throughout the world and formulate plans to relieve the economic condition of Negroes everywhere. He shall also lend his assistance to all matters of immigration and to the establishment of avenues of industry for the members of the organization.

### Minister of Legions

**Section 28.** The Minister of the Legions shall be the Administrative Officer of the Universal African Legions of the Universal Negro Improvement Association. He shall be subjected to the commands of the Potentate, President General and Executive Council. He shall nominate his staff and Chief thereof with the approval of the President General and Potentate, who shall make the actual appointment. He shall use every means by travel, correspondence, and appeal to have a division of the legion formed in every city or district. He shall regulate all details as to uniforms, and shall give orders for other movements on the instruction of the President-General or Executive Council. He shall recommend Privates and Officers to the Commander-in-Chief for promotion.

### ARTICLE VII

### Requirements of Officials and High Officers

**Section 1.** All officials and high officers of the Universal Negro Improvement Association and African Communities' League shall be Negroes and their consorts or wives shall be Negroes. No one shall be admitted to the high offices of the Association whose life companion is of an alien race.

198

*Qualifications for High and Divisional Offices*

**Section 2.** The qualifications of candidates for high office of the Universal Negro Improvement Association and African Communities' League and for candidates for divisional offices shall be as follows:

Registered active membership with all dues paid up; shall be a Negro; shall be proven to be conscientious to the cause of racial uplift; he shall not be married to anyone of alien race, shall be free from criminal conviction, shall be of reputable moral standing and good education, and shall undergo a six months' course of instruction at any University of the Universal Negro Improvement Association, and that only when the student graduates that he be allowed to represent the organization; and for a correspondence course of one year shall be established for the same purpose, and this course shall be extended to all persons of the race who desire to take it.

### ARTICLE VIII

*Salaries and Expenses*

**Section 1.** The salary of the Potentate and Supreme Commissioner shall be in keeping with his high office and responsibilities, which salary shall be granted by the Convention. The Potentate shall labour for the good and welfare of the organization, irrespective of salary or other consideration.

**Section 2.** The Supreme Deputy shall be subjected to the same conditions on matter of salary as the Potentate.

*High Officers*

**Section 3.** All officials and high officers of the Universal Negro Improvement Association and African Communities' League other than the Potentate and Supreme Commissioner and Supreme Deputy shall be granted salaries commensurate with the work they perform, which shall be voted by the convention.

*Salaries of High Officials*

**Section 3a.** All officials of the Universal Negro Improvement Association shall be paid their salaries at the minimum which shall be half of the maximum, and each shall be allowed to earn the maximum by ability and fitness, which maximum shall be paid at the end of each month according to the record of such official.

## Salaries of Divisional Officers

**Section 4.** Officers of local Divisions who give their entire time to the working of their local Divisions shall receive salaries for their services according to the ruling of the membership of such local Divisions, and all such salaries shall be conditional on the local Division having at its disposal sufficient funds in its treasury to make payment of such possible.

## Transfer of Officers

**Section 5.** The President or any other officer of a local Division in the pay of the Universal Negro Improvement Association and African Communities' League shall be subjected to annual, bi-annual or tri-annual transfers, according to the advices of the office of the President General and Executive Council.

## Departmental Assistant

**Section 6.** No department of the Parent Body shall employ an Assistant for that Department without first obtaining the approval of the President General as to the fitness and desirability of the individual to be employed.

### ARTICLE IX

## Reveneue, Incomes, Etc.

**Section 1.** The Revenue of the Universal Negro Improvement Association and African Communities' League shall be derived from monthly subscriptions, which shall not be more that 25 cents per month, being authorized dues of each active member, donations, collections, gifts, profits derived from businesses, entertainments, functions or general amusements of an innocent nature, and a death tax of 10 cents per month.

## Division Responsible for Tax

That a tax of $1 shall be levied on every member of the U.N.I.A. each and every year, payable on the first of January, for the purpose of defraying expenses of the organization and its general upkeep, and said one dollar collected from each member shall be forwarded to the High Chancellor through the office of the Secretary General at headquarters.

## Annual Expense Tax

The One Dollar annual tax of each member shall be charged

against the local Division to which the member is attached, and shall be collected from the financial membership of the Division as by its report on the 31st December of each year.

**Section 2.** The revenue of the Universal Negro Improvement Association and African Communities' League shall be apportioned to the General Fund, which shall go to bear the general expenses of the organization for the carrying out of its objects.

### Remitting of Monthly Dues by Local Divisions, Societies, Etc.

**Section 3.** The Secretaries of all Divisions and subordinate organizations shall remit at the end of each month to the High Chancellor, through the Secretary General, one-fifth of all monthly subscriptions, joining fees, dues and net profits from local business under the control of the said Division, as also from donations, grants, gifts, amusements, entertainments and other functions for the general fund of the Universal Negro Improvement Association and African Communities' League for the carrying out of its general objects. That each person pay an entrance fee of twenty-five cents in joining the Association.

### Chancellor Deposits All Money

**Section 4.** All moneys of the Universal Negro Improvement Association and African Communities' League shall be lodged by the Chancellor in a responsible bank, and drawn only on the signatures of the President General, the High Chancellor and Secretary General.

### Donations to Charity by Potentates, Etc.

**Section 5.** The Potentate and Supreme Commissioner shall be empowered to make donations of charity to be created from the Charitable Fund of the Universal Negro Improvement Association and African Communities' League, to worthy causes in the name of the Association and League, with the approval of the Executive Council.

### Investing of Money

**Section 6.** The Universal Negro Improvement Association and African Communities' League and all its Divisions and allied societies may invest money in any business which to the best judgment of the members of the organization are of such as to yield profit in the interest of the Association, but no Division shall invest its funds without first getting the approval of the Parent Body.

*No Investments by Divisions*

**Section 7.** No investment of money shall be made by a local Division or society without the consent of the membership of the said Division or society with the approval of the Parent Body.

*Selling Outside Stock*

**Section 8.** No Division shall allow any of its officers or members to use the meetings of the organization for selling stocks or shares in any personal or private concern, and any such officer or member found guilty of such offence shall be suspended for three months.

**Section 9.** The Parent Body of the Universal Negro Improvement Association and African Communities' League may invest its money wholly or in company with others for the good of the organization.

**Section 10.** The funds of the Universal Negro Improvement Association and African Communities' League as derived from all sources herein mentioned shall be used for the carrying out of the objects of the Association.

*Net Proceeds to Divisions*

**Section 11.** Fifty per cent. of the proceeds of all entertainments given by auxiliaries of Divisions, Branches or Chapters shall be turned over to the Division, Branch or Chapter after all legitimate expenses incurred for such entertainments have been paid, and no auxiliary shall give any entertainment without the permission of the President of the Division, Branch or Chapter.

**Section 12.** All auxiliaries of Divisions must turn into the treasury of the Divisions to which they are attached all moneys derived from entertainments at the first meeting following such entertainments.

ARTICLE X

*Membership*

**Section 1.** All persons of Negro blood and African descent are regarded as ordinary members of the Universal Negro Improvement Association and African Communities' League, and are entitled to the consideration of the organization. Active members are those who pay the monthly dues for the upkeep of the organization, who shall have first claim on the Association for all benefits to be dispensed.

## ARTICLE XI

*Sitting of Executive Council*

**Section 1.** The Executive Council of the Universal Negro Improvement Association and African Communities' League shall assemble at the headquarters of the Association and shall consist of all the high officers of the Association and others elected thereto. The Potentate shall be its Chairman, and in his absence the President General and Administrator, and the Secretary General its Secretary. It shall decide all questions arising between Divisions and subordinate societies, appeals, international questions and all matters affecting the good and welfare of the organization and its members at large during the rising of the convention.

## ARTICLE XII

*Auditing Accounts*

**Section 1.** The President General shall cause the books and accounts of the High Chancellor and subordinate officers to be audited twice a year as follows: All accounts for the six months ending July 31st within 15 days after that date, and for the same period ending January 31st, within 15 days after that date. For this purpose he shall call upon the Auditor General and also appoint an expert accountant, who shall make a thorough examination and shall submit a report to the President General, who shall cause its publication in the regular journal of the society.

*Defalcation or Misappropriation*

**Section 2.** If said report should show any errors of importance or defalcation or misappropriation of funds of any officer so responsible, it shall be the duty of the President General, with the consent of the Potentate, to suspend such officer or officers, and he shall instruct the Counsel General to proceed at once, legally, to secure the Universal Negro Improvement Association and African Communities' League from loss, and in accordance with the bond or bonds of said officer or officers.

*Fiscal Year*

**Section 3.** The fiscal year of the Universal Negro Improvement Association and African Communities' League shall commence on the first day of June and end on the 31st day of May in each year.

ARTICLE XIII

*The Civil Service*

**Section 1.** A Civil Service shall be established by the Universal Negro Improvement Association. From this Civil Service shall be recruited all employees of the Association.

**Section 2.** A Civil Servant shall have precedence over and preference to all persons employed, or to be employed, by the Universal Negro Improvement Association.

*Lists*

**Section 3.** An official civil servants' list of the Universal Negro Improvement Association shall be compiled and designated as the Civil Service.

*Examination*

**Section 4.** All persons to be placed on the Civil Service shall first be obliged to pass an examination on general educational test as laid down by the official examiners, and in addition thereto such persons shall be required to give evidence of good moral character and honesty.

*Examiners*

**Section 5.** The official examiners shall be the Administrator of the Universal Negro Improvement Association and such other persons as he may appoint to serve with him.

*Civil Service Commission*

**Section 6.** The persons appointed by the Administrator to serve with him as official examiners shall be known as the Civil Service Commission; and the Civil Service Commission, together with the Administrator, shall compose the Board of Civil Service Examiners. They shall designate the subjects in which applicants shall be examined, and shall also prescribe the rules and regulations governing the examinations of applicants.

*Certificate*

**Section 7.** All applicants who have passed the Civil Service examination shall be given a certificate as proof thereof.

*Promotions*

**Section 8.** All promotions in the Universal Negro Improvement

Association shall be made from the Civil Service list of the Association.

**Section 9.** All Executive Secretaries of local divisions shall be members of the Civil Service.

ARTICLE XIV

*Passport Identifications*

**Section 1.** A Bureau of Passports shall be attached to the Secretary-General's office.

**Section 2.** Each and every member who desires a Passport Identification for the purpose of travel or for the purpose of receiving recognition, consideration and likely help from other branches, or for the purpose of proving connection with a regular organization or with a branch of the Universal Negro Improvement Association, shall be supplied with one of these Passports at any Division of the organization by the Executive Secretary of that Division at which application is duly made.

**Section 3.** Each passport shall have on its face a photograph of the bearer, the signature of the bearer, and such other details as may be provided in the rules and regulations of the Bureau of Passports and Identifications.

**Section 4.** Each passport identification shall be issued by the Universal Negro Improvement Association and African Communities' League from its Headquarters. It shall be signed and stamped by the Executive Secretary stationed at the Division where the passport has been secured.

**Section 5.** Before a passport identification can be secured each and every member shall be required to fill out a bill of particulars, and only financial members whose dues and assessments have been fully paid up and whose records are clean shall be supplied with a passport identification. No one shall be granted a passport identification until he or she shall have been in the organization for six months and shall have paid up all dues and assessments.

**Section 6.** The sum of two dollars shall be paid for the issuance of every Passport Identification. Renewals may be made annually against the payment of a fee of twenty-five cents.

**Section 7.** The Bureau of Justice, through the office of the President-General, shall see that each and every member who holds a passport identification is properly protected, in case of abuse, advantage or injustice committed upon such individual.

205

*African Redemption Fund*

**1.** The parent body shall be empowered to raise a universal fund from all Negroes for the purpose of the redemption of Africa. Every member of the Negro race shall be asked to contribute to this fund a sum not less than $5.00 (Five Dollars). This contribution to the African Redemption Fund shall not be a tax on active members, but shall be a voluntary contribution by all Negroes.

**2.** This fund shall be known as the "African Redemption Fund".

**3.** Each and every person who subscribes to this fund shall receive a certificate of loyalty to the cause "Afric". The certificate shall bear the signatures of the President-General, the High Chancellor and the Secretary-General of the Universal Negro Improvement Association.

**4.** The purpose of the African Redemption Fund shall be to create a working capital for the organization and to advance the cause for the building up of Africa.

## ARTICLE XV

*Bureau of Justice*

**1.** A Bureau of Justice shall be established by the parent body of the U.N.I.A. and A.C.L. for the protection of all Negroes.

**2.** The Bureau of Justice shall be composed of three members. It shall have for its head an attorney-at-law who shall be known as the chief of the Bureau of Justice. One of the members of the Bureau shall be its secretary.

**3.** The Bureau shall have to co-operate with it a committee of three from each Local Division, composed of the President and two members selected from the general membership. This committee shall be under the supervision of the Bureau.

**4.** The local committee shall have the power to dispose of all matters not of sufficient magnitude to require special attention of the Bureau and shall report to the Bureau their action therein.

**5.** The Bureau, with the consent and advice of the President General and High Executive Council, shall have the power to make such rules and incur such expenses as are absolutely necessary for the proper carrying out of its objects.

# Sixth Annual International Convention of the Negro Peoples of the World*

Under the Auspices of
The Universal Negro Improvement Association of the World
MARCUS GARVEY, PRESIDENT-GENERAL

To be held at
Kingston, Jamacia, B. W. I.
from
August 1st to 31st, 1929

———

THE PROGRAM TO BE DISCUSSED:

(1) The political and social freedom of the entire Negro race.

(2) The presentation of proper evidence before the League of Nations for an adjustment of the international race problem.

(3) The creating of a thorough educational system for the higher education of the Negroes of America, the West Indies and Africa, resulting in the founding of three Negro Universities of a purely technical character—one in America, one in the West Indies and one in Africa.

(4) The creating of general economic opportunities in agriculture, industry and commerce for the Negro people of the world whereby a brisk and proper trade relationship may develop between the Negroes of America, Africa, the West Indies and South and Central America to insure a stable economic status.

(5) The acquiring and controlling of agricultural lands for the scientific development of agriculture and also the establishment of factories and industrial institutions in various Negro communities to guarantee permanent employment to the Negroes of America, Africa, the West Indies and South and Central America, Europe and Canada.

* *The Gold Coast Times*, June 15, 1929, p. 5.

207

(6) The launching of a new line of steamships The Black Star Line—to facilitate Negro trade and commerce throughout the world.

(7) To establish in London, Washington, Paris, Berlin, Rome, Brussels, Geneva, Tokio-China, India, West Africa, South Africa, Embassies to represent the interest of the entire Negro race and to watch and protect their rights.

(8) The establishing of a daily paper in several large cities of the world to shape sentiment in favor of the entire Negro race, namely in London, Paris, Berlin, Capetown, New York, Washington, Gold Coast, West Africa, and the several important Islands of the West Indies.

(9) The practical effect of uniting every unit of the Negro race throughout the world into one organized body.

(10) The formulating of plans to unify the religious beliefs and practises of the entire Negro race.

(11) The establishing of a universal social code for the Negro race.

(12) To make practical and executive each and everyone of the above objects within ten years as a solution of the Negro problem, and as a means of saving the Negro race from further exploitation and possible extermination in the world.

(13) To budget for the expenditure of a Fund of six hundred million dollars in ten years to execute the above problem as shall be determined by the Convention.

(14) To elect the international officials of the Universal Negro Improvement Association and African Communities League of the world.

(15) To elect twelve delegates from the Convention to attend the tenth session of the League of Nations at Geneva, Switzerland.

(16) To take up all and such matters as affect the interest of the Negro race.

(17) To discuss and amend the Constitution of the Universal Negro Improvement Association and the A.C.L.

# Council on African Affairs

The Council on African Affairs merits a special explanation, as it was the first organization of Negro Americans actively to involve Africans in the United States within an institution whose specific purpose was to influence government policy toward Africa. In addition the Council's role is interesting because its decline was a result of conflict with the United States government.

Describing itself as a non-profit and non-partisan organization, the Council on African Affairs was established in 1937 under the guidance of Max Yergan* and Paul Robeson.† Its purpose was threefold: (1) to give concrete help to the struggles of the African masses; (2) to disseminate accurate information concerning Africa and its people; and (3) to influence the adoption of governmental policies designed to promote African advancement and freedom and preserve international peace. The Council held public meetings and forums and published a monthly bulletin, *New Africa*, as well as a number of pamphlets. Its motto was "Africa's Problems are Your Problems".

Stressing the fact that World War II, or the "war of liberation from Hitlerism", had not brought freedom to Africa, the Council promoted a programme of action toward Africa which could be understood

---

\* Max Yergan was born in Raleigh, North Carolina. He received his A.B. degree from Shaw University in Raleigh and later studied at Springfield College in Massachusetts, after which he entered the service of the International Committee of the Y.M.C.A. which sent him to India in 1914 and to East Africa in 1916. From 1916 to 1918 he served as chaplain at Camp Lee, Virginia, and from 1919 to 1920 as chaplain in France. After the war Max Yergan was sent to South Africa from 1921 to 1926 by the International Commission of the Y.M.C.A. When he returned to the United States in 1926 he was awarded the Harmon Award for outstanding social service in South Africa, and later the Spingarn medal for advancing inter-racial understanding in South Africa. He organized and directed the Council on Negroes in South African Affairs from 1937 to 1948 and was president of the National Negro Congress. In 1930 he published *Christian Students in Modern South Africa*, a report to the first congress dealing with problems in South Africa. In 1939 he published *Golden Poverty in South Africa*.

More recently Max Yergan has been identified with the American-African Affairs Association, Inc., as its co-chairman. This association was organized in 1966 to ". . . further the cause of knowledge concerning Africa among the people of the United States . . . without regard to the prevailing shibboleths, and from two viewpoints which we take to be similar in all essential respects: the cause of freedom in its struggle against Communism; and the best interests of the United States of America."

† See p. 132 for biographical sketch of Paul Robeson.

by Negro Americans and West Indians who faced similar problems in their own countries. The programme underscored the fact that the difficulties found on the African continent—colour bars to employment, inequality in wages for Africans, restrictions in participation in labour unions, the lack of the franchise, inadequate educational and health services, and discrimination against Africans in selection of members of regional economic, and policy-making commissions concerned with Africa—were also found in the Western hemisphere.

The Council's technique was to organize and support councils at the local level "to promote the cause of African freedom and progress", to petition governments, and to present to the United Nations a programme to implement its charter. Paul Robeson was the Council's first chairman and Max Yergan its first executive director. Members of the board were largely Negroes of liberal and academic interest, and some whites were also included.

The conference organized by the Council in 1944, the agenda of which follows, was attended by Negroes, Africans, and West Indians, as well as by white Americans. Organizations such as the African Students Association, the National Council of Negro Women, the National Maritime Union, the Club Employees Union of the American Federation of Labor, and the African Methodist Episcopal Church were among the co-sponsoring organizations. Perhaps the most prominent participating African was F. Nwi-Kofi Nkrumah, who, along with Ibango Udo Akapabio, represented the African Students Association.

As the Executive Director of the Council, Max Yergan opened the conference with a strong address urging the delegates to help strengthen Africa and increase that continent's contribution toward victory in the war by promoting the prompt elimination there of "land alienation, labour exploitation, social coercion and restriction which have followed from the economic penetration of the European into Africa . . . and by having our American labour movement, working in cooperation with the British and progressive forces of the world . . . aid in making the African people our full and equal ally in the struggle against fascism." Dr. Yergan also stressed the importance of solving territorial jurisdictional problems in the former African Italian Empire, the African mandated areas, the sovereign states of Liberia and Ethiopia, and the projected regional groupings of African territories as advocted by General Smuts. He stated that any change in jurisdictional lines should be made only when the dependent people themselves, not merely their governors, had a voice in making the decisions.

Dr. Yergan told the conference that "the breaking down of isolationist barriers between the various colonies in Africa has been one of the most significant changes which the war has brought to that continent. It has not only made for economic progress, it has also made possible, particularly in British West Africa, a new outlook for the unification of the African people. There is, however, the danger that these regional economic units may develop into institutions for furthering European domination of the continent." Yergan went on to say that planning for the social, economic, and political progress of the African people was the most important point to be considered, and he indicated that the Council view was that the future of Africa and of the other colonial areas must be worked out on the plane of world-wide international agreements and action. These would be implemented by an international agency comparable to the United Nations Relief and Rehabilitation Association which "would establish in cooperation with the representatives of the peoples affected, labor, social and civic standards and rights for the indigenous population of every dependent territory and would have the authority to hold the governments of such territories richly accountable for the maintenance of these standards and rights. . . . The agency in its direction and supervision of the economic development would guard against monopolistic restrictions and controls and would encourage public, cooperative and collective enterprise among the indigenous population. . . . It would have the further responsibility of the right of self-determination to the people of any dependent area and of promoting development of all such people towards self-government according to a specific time schedule."

Having been thus informed by Dr. Yergan that the position and expectations of the Council were clearly pro-African, pro-labour, and pro-international—which at that time and for this group implied pro-Soviet Union—the delegates turned to the agenda of the conference.

Four years later in 1948 the Council was branded as subversive by Senator Joseph McCarthy. In the same year Max Yergan was charged with frustrating the purposes of the council, mishandling its finances, and exercising illegal and high-handed control of its property and was removed from his post as Executive Director. He was replaced by Alphaeus Hunton*; Paul Robeson remained Chair-

* William Alphaeus Hunton was born in 1903 in Atlanta, Georgia. He was graduated from Howard University in 1924 and later received an M.A. from Harvard and a Ph.D. from New York University. From 1926 to 1943 he taught English at Howard and resigned to become Director of Information of the Council on African Affairs and Editor of *New Africa*, its monthly publication.

man, and W. E. B. DuBois* was named Vice Chairman. When the Council was dissolved in 1955, the *Daily Worker* stated that it was because of harassment by the United States government.

# Council on African Affairs

## "AFRICA—NEW PERSPECTIVES"

### *Proposed Agenda for Discussion†*

The following statement of principle and proposed agenda, which had been sent to the Conference participants in advance of the meeting, was agreed upon by the Conference as the basis for discussion.

What is the future of the dependent peoples of the world?

What is Africa's future?

The answer concerns us as well as the colonial peoples. A world of continuing colonialism will perforce be a world of economic scarcity, unemployment and want, since modern productive capacity and colonialism are as incompatible as were the wage and slave systems in the last century. A world of continuing colonialism can mean only increasing imperialist rivalries, the spread of fascism, and another world war. These are the inescapable alternatives to the world of the Atlantic Charter.

Africa, long the forgotten and "dark" continent, must have its proper place within the new post-war world. The principles postulated in the following outline, as a basis of our conference discussion, have been framed in accordance with the all-important perspective of international co-operation toward democratic goals. Within the framework of such co-operation there are boundless possibilities for

---

During this period, Hunton was a member of the Executive Board of the National Council of Arts, Sciences and Professions and the National Council for American Soviet Friendship. Later he went to Guinea as a teacher of English and from there to Ghana, where he resided until recently. While there, since its founding in 1962, he was Secretary of the Secretariat of the *Encyclopedia Africana*. Hunton is the author of *Decision in Africa, Source of Current Conflict*, which has a foreword by W. E. B. DuBois and was published in 1957.

  * See p. 310

  † Prepared for a Conference on Africa, sponsored by the Council on African Affairs, April 14, 1944. Reprinted by kind permission of the New York Public Library.

the future of all colonial peoples and of the world in general; without such cooperation there is no future for any of us. The American people, by virtue of their country's pre-eminent economic power, have a major responsibility for strengthening and giving direction to the United Nations coalition, thus insuring the security of a world free from imperialism.

### I. TO CONSIDER WHAT IS BEING DONE AND CAN BE DONE TO INCREASE AFRICA'S CONTRIBUTION TO VICTORY OVER FASCISM.

A. "Emergency" compulsory labor practices are unwarranted and harmful to African morale; such practices should be replaced by proper labor incentives.

B. Further immediate reforms needed to increase production are: abolition of the color bar in industry, provision of adequate wages and decent working conditions, and fair prices to small farmers and harvesters.

C. Further progress must be made in the rationalization of production through the use of machinery to replace human labor.

D. There is necessity for guarding against trends toward peace-time curtailment of production, already evident, for example, in the case of Rhodesian copper production.

E. Through United States economic missions and advisors, and through Lend-Lease assistance, much can be done toward correcting the conditions indicated in the preceding four points.

F. Organized labor in America, the projected World Trade Union Conference, and the International Labour Organization can all aid effectively in bringing about correction of these same conditions.

G. Though Africans have been and are being employed on the allied fighting fronts, the need still continues for doing away with barriers to their full participation in the armed services.

### II. TO DETERMINE THE BEST MEANS OF SOLVING JURISDICTIONAL AND TERRITORIAL PROBLEMS IN AFRICA.

A. The disposition of former Italian colonies or of other areas in

213

Africa must be in accordance with the first three points of the Atlantic Charter and in accordance with the agreement of a general world organization.

B. All projected regional councils and federations, whether having administrative or consultative powers, should be subordinate and subject to a world organization, should provide for the direct participation of African representatives, and should guarantee throughout the area under their jurisdiction the uniform observance of such social, economic and political principles as are set forth under the Atlantic Charter.

C. Ethiopia and Liberia, as sovereign states, should have the same direct representation as European colonial powers and other states in all regional councils and agencies, whether economic or political in function, in their respective areas.

D. Encouragement should be given to the unification of peoples who have been arbitrarily divided and separated by colonial boundaries and other barriers.

III. TO ESTABLISH PRINCIPLES UPON WHICH PLANS FOR THE
SOCIAL, ECONOMIC, AND POLITICAL ADVANCEMENT OF THE
AFRICAN PEOPLE SHOULD BE BASED.

A. It is impossible under traditional and current colonial policies and practices, both because of their general inadequacy and extreme variance, to bring Africa within any plan of world-wide economic abundance and political democracy.

B. The principle of mutual aid in mutual self-interest, which is guiding the United Nations to victory, must be maintained in order to win the peace; this international pattern must supplant the imperialistic pattern of exploiting and exploited nations; raising the standards of living in dependent areas, which can be accomplished only by large scale public and private investments and subsidies in such areas, is an essential requirement for the avoidance of a disastrous world-wide economic depression in the post-war-period.

C. Considerations of economy, efficiency, and international unity—in the spirit of Teheran—require that the planning and development of the education, economic stability, social welfare, and advancement of Africans toward self-government, be undertaken and supervised on a broad international basis—with African participation. (This assumes that individual states and governments would retain direct administration of their areas subject to international supervision and sanction: see "F" below.)

D. Such an international organization would make possible the uniform application of such progressive measures as the British Colonial Development and Welfare Fund (on a vastly enlarged scale), the Belgian industrial program, and the French social, economic and administrative reforms projected at the recent Brazzaville Colonial Conference.

E. Such an international organization would make possible the planning and adoption of a continent-wide system of education and health services, and the economic development of all areas of the continent.

F. Such an international organization would be responsible for guaranteeing full self-government and the right of self-determination to the people of any dependent area (even over the opposition of the suzerain state), and for setting definite dates at which time the peoples of each dependent area might achieve self-government. (The experience of the Soviet Union and the policy of the United States with reference to the Philippines provide proof and models of the practicability of setting specific time limits for the achievement of specific objectives.)

G. Parallel with equal access by all states to the trade and natural resources of Africa, as provided by point four of the Atlantic Charter, there must be progressive curtailment of the dominance of foreign interests over the economy of the people, with African public enterprise (government ownership and operations, co-operative industry, collective farming) taking the place of European private enterprise in the economic development of the continent—such economic autonomy is a guarantee (though not a preprequisite) of political autonomy.

H. As the first step toward the accomplishment of the social advancement of the African people, there should be the immediate abolition in all areas—colonial and non-colonial—of all restrictions of their civil, political, and trade union rights, to the end that democratic institutions and the responsibilities which these entail may be developed among the people.

# Constitution of the
# American Society of African Culture*

### PREAMBLE

American scholars, artists and writers of African descent join together in the American Society of African Culture to study the effect of African culture on American life, to examine the cultural contributions of African peoples to their societies; and to help the Western World and, more particularly, Americans to sweep away the prejudices that limit an appreciation of the cultural contributions of African peoples. Our purpose is also to study those conditions which effect the development of ethnic, national and universal culture and to acknowledge the ultimate immunity of the great cultural contributions of man to the distortions that result from political, economic and nationalistic bias.

### THE WORK OF THE
### AMERICAN SOCIETY OF AFRICAN CULTURE

The American Society of African Culture is an affiliate of the Société Africaine de Culture established in Paris in 1957. The American Society will cooperate with the international Society. It will send delegates to the General Assembly of that Society, and will select its members to be representatives on the Executive Council of the international Society. In America, the American Society will promote an inventory of the cultural achievements of American Negroes, will attempt to trace the African origins of American Negro art forms, will examine the economic, political and cultural status of American Negroes, and will examine the relations of the United States of America to Negro states and peoples throughout the world. The Society will also seek to promote the highest values inherent in American cultural life.

* Reprinted by kind permission of the Society.

## MEMBERSHIP

Membership in The American Society of African Culture is open to all persons of culture of Negro descent. Associate membership is open to persons of non-African descent and to Africans temporarily in the United States and to others who in all other respects qualify for membership. Such membership would carry all rights and privileges except voting rights. Application for membership shall be made to the Executive Director of the American Society and shall be approved by the Executive Director and any two other members of the Executive Council designated by that Council. Membership may be terminated by resignation or by action of the Executive Council by majority vote. Membership may also be terminated for non-payment of dues.

### ORGANS OF THE SOCIETY

1. *The General Meetings of the Society,* which shall be composed of the general membership of the Society, shall occur in June of each year and shall constitute the main legislative organ of the Society. However, the Executive Council shall have the authority to call meetings limited to voting members from time to time as they see fit. The General Meeting, in which proxy votes shall not be permissible, shall have the power to:

A. Determine the annual program of the Society by majority vote.

B. Nominate and elect the President of the organization by majority vote.

C. Nominate and elect by a majority vote ten of the eleven members of the Executive Council.

D. Propose by a 2/3 vote changes in the Constitution which shall in turn be adopted by a majority vote of a referendum of the entire membership.

E. Adopt the annual report of the President.

F. Determine upon the recommendation of the Executive Council the members to represent the American Society on the Executive Council of the international Society.

G. Upon the recommendation of the Executive Council or of 2/5 of the entire membership, adopt resolutions expressing the opinion of the Society on cultural matters or on relations with the international Society—all by majority vote.

H. Upon recommendation by the Executive Council, disband the Society or terminate affiliation with the international Society by a vote of 2/3 of the members present subject to ratification by 2/3 of the entire membership through referendum.

2. *The Presidency of the American Society of African Culture* shall be a position of honor. The President shall be elected for five years and shall preside at the General Meeting. He shall be the main ambassador of our relations with the Société Africaine de Culture in Paris and with other affiliates of that Society. All public statement of the American Society shall be made by him and in his name, and he shall be responsible for the Society's formal relations with other societies and with the public in general. The annual report to the General Meeting shall be made by the President.

3. *The Executive Council* shall make its decisions by a majority vote and shall be the policy determining organ of the Society between General Meetings. It shall be composed of eleven members; ten including the President elected by the General Meeting for five year terms with two retiring each year, and the Executive Director, who shall be chosen by the Executive Council and serve at its pleasure. Membership in the Executive Council may be terminated by resignation or by a 3/4 vote of the general membership.

The Executive Council shall have full power to decide all matters between General Meetings including the filling of its own vacancies subject to the approval of the General Meeting. It shall also fill the office of the President should this become vacant, subject to the approval of the General Meeting. In both cases the term of office shall run for the unexpired period. The Executive Council shall propose the members of the Executive Council of the international Society to represent America, who shall be chosen by the General Meeting by a majority vote. It shall choose its own Chairman who shall be the main executive of the organization and who shall in the name of the Executive Council and with its consent make all major policy decisions when the General Meeting is not in session. The Executive Council shall approve the annual report which the President makes to the General Meeting and shall prepare the proposed annual program to be adopted by the General Meeting. Individual members may make propositions to be included in the annual program, but such proposals must first be adopted by the Executive Council before presentation to the General Meeting. The Executive Council shall furthermore propose resolutions to the General Meeting.

4. *The Executive Director and the Assistant Executive Director* shall be appointed by the Executive Council and will serve at the pleasure of the Council. It shall be the function of these officers to carry out the orders of the Executive Council and more particularly its Chairman. They shall constitute the secretariat of the Society and shall take the main responsibility for the preparation of the annual program.

### AMENDING THE CONSTITUTION

The Constitution may be amended by a proposal of 2/3 of the General Meeting with adoption by a majority referendum of the entire membership. Whenever 2/3 of the membership shall propose it, the Executive Council shall call a national convention to draft a new constitution which shall in turn be adopted by sections (ad seriatim) by a 3/4 referendum of the entire membership.

# American Society of African Culture

## Program Activities 1958–59, A Summary*

### I. PUBLICATIONS

(a) *The AMSAC Newsletter*

On October 30, 1958, the American Society of African Culture initiated its AMSAC *Newsletter*. The newsletter appears monthly and is a roundup of news concerning the activities of the organization and its members. The newsletter has been extremely well received, with a readership far beyond those who are on the mailing list. Responses from all over the country as well as from Paris have been most enthusiastic. In January, 1959 the newsletter initiated as additional service a supplement published periodically. The supplements are works, preferably by AMSAC members, which are related either to the work of the Society and/or to African affairs.

(b) *The Special Issue*

The Special Issue of *Présence Africaine*, entitled *Africa Seen by American Negroes*, has been published and a limited number have already been distributed. The initial response has been entirely gratifying. The bulk shipment has only recently been received and a larger promotional campaign which is already planned is expected to increase sales substantially.

### II. REGIONAL PROGRAMS

So far, one pilot project has been held in Houston, Texas, under the auspices of the American Society of African Culture group in Houston. The program was a great success, with more than 1,000 persons participating. Additional projects are being planned for Georgia and California. The Society also participated in the World Affairs Institute held at Hampton, Virginia, June, 1958, and in the 40th American Conference of the Institute of International Education, April, 1959, Washington, D.C.

* Reprinted by kind permission of the Society.

### III. CONSULTATION AND ADVISORY SERVICES

The Society has rendered consultation and advice on several occasions to a number of organizations dealing with Africa. Among them are the John Hay Whitney Foundation, the Ford Foundation, the Rockefeller Foundation, the U.S. National Student Association, the Young Adult Council, World University Service, the American Committee on Africa, the African-American Institute, the African Studies Association, and the All African Students Union.

### IV. CONFERENCES, LECTURES AND SEMINARS

(a) The Society sent a delegation to the All Africa Peoples Conference in Accra in December of 1958. The delegation included Dr. John A. Davis, Dr. Horace Mann Bond, Dr. Mercer Cook, and also provided a grant for Mr. Michael Olatunji, President of the All African Student Union of the Americas, who traveled from New York representing his organization. In the course of their stay in Accra, AMSAC members were able to make contacts with a large number of important African leaders and had private talks with Prime Minister Nkrumah. In all there were about nine members of the American Society of African Culture present in Accra in one capacity or another. Dr. Cook, on his return from Accra, was received by President Sékou Touré of Guinea on which occasion Dr. Cook explained the work of AMSAC and invited His Excellency to visit this country.

(b) The Society has also been responsible for conducting seminars or parts of seminars related to Africa in cooperation with the United States National Student Association in New York, Philadelphia, and Boston.

(c) The Assistant Director of the Society assisted in presenting a series of lectures at the New School for Social Research on African Culture under the joint sponsorship of the School and the Society.

### V. CONFERENCE OF NEGRO WRITERS

On February 28 and March 1, 1959, the Society sponsored a conference of Negro writers at the Henry Hudson Hotel on the theme "The American Negro Writer and His Relationship to His Roots."

The conference was a great success and included many of the top Negro writers in the United States. There were some seventy writers who participated in the main body of the conference and about two hundred guests at the final session from publishing houses, television and screen industries. A series of recommendations coming from the conference are incorporated in the Executive Committee program recommendations. An excellent series of papers of high literary quality from this conference will be published in the near future and will be available for sale.

## VI. LIBRARY

The Society has continued the building up of its specialized library on Negro and African Affairs and African Culture. Works in the library now include a large selection of all publications of the Society of African Culture in Paris, as well as a growing collection of recorded African music.

## VII. BALLETS AFRICAINS

The Society, in correspondence with the European producers of Ballets Africains, was instrumental in helping set up the group physically in New York City and also in arranging other services such as the appearance of individual artists in New York night clubs and entertainment in private homes.

The principal service rendered by the Society to the Ballets was the conducting of four theatre parties in Chicago, Philadelphia, Boston and New York. All four parties were eminently successful and were responsible for bringing a large audience to the related performances of the Ballets. The enthusiasm of the AMSAC audiences is probably in no small measure responsible for the general acclaim with which the Ballets was received and the large success of their engagements.

## VII. ROME DELEGATION

The delegation which represented AMSAC at the Second Congress of Negro Writers and Artists in Rome from March 25 to April 2 included Dr. John A. Davis, Mr. James T. Harris, Jr., Dr. Mercer Cook, Mr. James W. Ivy, Dr. Horace Mann Bond, Dr. William T.

Fontaine, Mr. Saunders Redding, Mr. Samuel Allen, Mr. Robert Carter, Mr. Elton Fax, Dr. Adelaide Cromwell Hill and Miss Pearl Primus.

The conference was the seventh major conference since World War II bringing together Africans and people of African descent and perhaps was the turning point in the concerns of the men of culture in the Negro African world. For though it was clear that the all-important task of securing independence for areas still under colonial domination was unfinished, it was equally clear that the constructive work to be undertaken involved making "every effort toward . . . the enrichment of national cultures as well as . . . toward the coexistence of black men of culture in the context of their constituent civilizations . . . toward the universality of values through the contributions (of Negro culture) to human civilization."

More than two hundred delegates from some 30 countries were in unanimous agreement on the fundamental importance of freedom for Africa and Africans, without which indigenous culture could hardly survive, let alone grow.

## IX. THE JUNE CONFERENCE

Three meetings of a Special Preparatory Committee and three meetings of a Banquet Committee got underway plans for the Second Annual Conference of the American Society of African Culture. The meetings determined the sub-divisions of the conference, seminar discussion groups and the respective chairman, and planned a promotional campaign. The Conference took place June 26th to 29th at the Waldorf-Astoria Hotel and the public events ended with a banquet in the Grand Ballroom, June 28th.

## X. HOSPITALITY PROGRAM

(a) The Society has also provided hospitality programming for a number of African visitors to the United States, including Dr. J. J. Nguku from Swaziland; Mr. Patrick Hulede from Ghana; Mr. Martin Kuanda of Lusaka, in Northern Rhodesia; six student and youth leaders from French West Africa, and a special party for Mr. Tom Mboya of Kenya.

(b) In addition, several informal gatherings were sponsored during the year for the purpose of creating and maintaining liaison with African students, diplomats, educators and artists residing in the United States.

## XI. RADIO AND FILM PROGRAMS

(a) During the past three months the Society has undertaken an exploratory and experimental program to determine if there is a demand and use for radio program material taped in this country for use in Africa. These materials would largely be devoted to American Negro life and interests. At the moment negotiations are underway with Radio Conakry and Radio Djibouti.

(b) The Society has also been requested to cooperate in several film projects, both in Europe and in Africa, dealing with the making or distributing of film about Africa and the Negro. To date this has been only an exchange.

## XII. MEMBERSHIP AND ORGANIZATION

Membership in the Society is now about two hundred persons of outstanding caliber, with about fifty persons awaiting final action of the Executive Committee. Further expansion is expected as a result of a recent trip to the West Coast and the Midwest on behalf of the Society which resulted in enthusiastic reception of the Society from a substantial portion of the writers, artists and scholars in the Negro communities in Los Angeles, San Francisco and St. Louis.

Associate membership status for AMSAC was approved by the international society as a result of a meeting of the Executive Committee in Paris, October, 1958. Associate membership is open to persons of non-African descent and to Africans temporarily residing in the United States. It was also agreed that AMSAC could receive as Associate Members those of African descent from other countries in the Americas until such time as national committees in those countries are established. AMSAC representation in the Executive Council in Paris was also satisfactorily established.

## XIII. STUDENT AND INTERCULTURAL EXCHANGE

Under the sponsorship of the Council on Race and Caste in World Affairs, the Society has organized a limited student scholarship program for highly specialized scholars whose needs are clear and whose work is related to the Society's program and policies. To date, one grant has been made, and several are under consideration. In addition to these grants, the Society has several special research projects in the planning stage, including the work of Dr. Mercer Cook in Europe and that of Dr. St. Clair Drake in Ghana.

Dr. Cook has presently undertaken a study which will involve travel in Africa and interviewing a number of African leaders. A clear presentation of the men in positions of leadership as well as their estimates of the needs and aspirations of their countries is the purpose of the study. Dr. Cook also hopes to determine the position of the African leaders on the type of aid which they need to fulfill their objectives with particular emphasis on American aid.

# PART III

## When I Was in Africa

In most cases American Negroes have gone to Africa under the auspices of some particular organization or business and for some specific purpose. It is only within these last few years that Africa as a continent, aside from the southern portion, has acquired tourist attraction for more than the few persons who have been largely interested in safaris.

For the most part the American tourist abroad has been seeking general historic sites or cities rather than visiting or revisiting the land of his fathers. Over the years only those Americans of English descent or of the Jewish faith have seemed to have the desire to keep real or imaginary ties with ancestral homes strong by visits, marriages and organizational activities. It is certainly true that as the result of the two wars, particularly World War II, many American soldiers who had the opportunity to visit villages and countries from which their families stemmed have thereby discovered a desire to return, perhaps as tourists.

Through the years only Negro missionaries (the Bishop was also a missionary) have visited Africa or spent any considerable time there. In the pursuit of their tasks these persons have often been motivated to write generally of Africa. In another section of this anthology the writings of Cary, Crummell, and Gilbert illustrate how their exposure to Africa stimulated them to persuade other American Negroes to involve themselves in Africa or to accept responsibility related to Africa. However, just travelling in Africa has often affected some Negroes, compelling them to describe their reactions.

Henry McNeal Turner and Levi Coppin, the twelfth and thirtieth Bishops, respectively, of the African Methodist Episcopal Church, were among the religious leaders who felt motivated to publish their reactions to Africa. Bishop Turner, particularly, saw Africa and the work of the Negro church there as having the highest priority and as being a logical extension of the Negro's battle for equality in the United States. Turner felt wrongs committed here might be corrected there. For example, while serving in South Africa, he was able to ordain Africans as ministers in his church. At that time the ministers of the white churches there had denied this status to Africans in just the way that the white church in Philadelphia had refused ministerial recognition to Richard Allen, founder and first Bishop of the African Methodist Episcopal Church.

The opportunity for the individual Negro to visit Africa out of curiosity or general interest, either for a holiday or an extended

229

tour, has not been great. Nevertheless, whenever such Negroes have gone to Africa, it has had a great effect on them. Some, such as the austere DuBois and Dr. Delany, are reported to have bent down to kiss the soil as a measure of their reaction and feeling. For a Negro to go on his own to Africa argues particularly strong motivation—something in him to compel him to that continent, and something, therefore, which should have been satisfied as a result of the experience. The writing of Eslanda Goode Robeson as a scholar, Era Belle Thompson as a journalist, and Richard Wright as a writer express the quality of such reactions. Each of these extraordinary persons was dramatically affected by the experience.

Other American Negroes who have not had the inclination or ability to write of their reactions have also experienced Africa—as tourists, as students, as wives of Africans, or as employees of the United States government. The experiences of these Negroes have not all been equally satisfactory; their expectations of Africa and of Africans, or the effects they have on Africa, have not always been of a positive nature. Yet it is certainly true that increasing numbers of Negroes are voluntarily going to Africa. In some of the larger communities and towns of Africa it is now quite possible to discover several American Negroes having more or less permanent residence there. Naturally it would be impossible to determine with any finality how Negroes as a group react to Africa—as difficult as it would be to determine how American Jews visiting Israel or American Italians visiting Italy feel about the experience. In 1961, therefore, American Negroes noted with some annoyance the tendency on the part of some American writers, particularly journalists, to want to find a disproportionate amount of deprivation, frustration, and hostility towards Africa on the part of Negroes who voluntarily chose to live there. Comments and anecdotes to support these analyses were, Negroes felt, highly selective, taken out of context, and certainly not representative of the thinking of the great majority of American Negroes in Africa.

The included selection by Horace Mann Bond is a brilliant but bitter attack on two of these journalists, who were among those who foretold only gloom and disaffection among the Negroes who had chosen to live in Africa. This selection is an address given by Dr. Bond before an assemblage of Negroes and Africans at a conference of the American Society of African Culture. Although the speech is of more recent composition than the bulk of material included in this volume, it seemed important to include it because it represents a culmination of a trend of thought that has consistently been used in analyzing the relation of American Negroes to Africa; the wish to explain away the interest or positive feelings Negroes have expressed toward Africa or toward the African. One can only ponder the reasons for the rash of statements which prompted the speech of Dr. Bond. However, it would be naive not to note that they did rather neatly coincide with the embarrassment some American Negroes caused this country by demonstrating in the balconies of the United Nations at the time of the death of Patrice Lumumba.

# Henry McNeal Turner,*
## 1834–1915

*African Letters,*† from which excerpts follow, represent the reports which Bishop Turner wrote during his first trip to West Africa in 1891.

## Seventh Letter‡
### OF BISHOP TURNER

*Freetown, Sierra Leone, Africa,*
*November 16, 1891*

But why waste time and space with the topography of the country? Your readers will be more concerned about the people, their habits, customs, manners, etc. I find about everything here common to other cities. House builders, rock blasters, lime burners, stone chiselers and polishers, blacksmiths, wheelwrights, painters, white-washers, tailors, watch-makers, jewelers, finest kind of bootmakers, dress makers, glass polishers, boat caulkers, engineers, storekeepers, doctors, lawyers, judges, druggists, postmasters, custom house officers, schools, seminaries, colleges, cathedrals, publishers, editors, bookbinders, medicine makers, chemists, scholars and everything except horses and mules. Yes, I hear there are a few jackasses about —four legged I mean. We can find two legged asses anywhere. And what is grander to me than anything else, is the fact that the trades people are black men and women. Mixed bloods are not excluded, however. They have a share in everything. Several white men from England and some from France, Germany, Italy and America have come here and married black women and raised up families of mixed blood. Some have lived with their colored wives awhile and left them several children to look after, and disappeared; so mulattoes are not absent at all. But other white men have lived with their colored wives right along and died with them. A few black men have also gone to

* For biographical sketch see p. 42.
    † Bishop Henry McNeal Turner, *African Letters,* Nashville, A.M.E. Sunday School Union, 1893.
    ‡ *Ibid.,* pp. 37–41.

England and elsewhere, and married white ladies, and they have children, etc.

All the ministers here, except the Baptists, wear robes—the Catholics, Mohammedans, English Church, Wesleyan, Methodists, Presbyterians, Lutherans and African Methodist Episcopal. Elder Geda looks grandly in a robe, and the people here thought he was used to it. I smiled but said nothing. Of course I was at home in my robe. The Catholic and Mohammedan priests wear robes all over the city.

The dress of the people is not uniform at all. Some are dressed in fine broadcloth, some in silks, bonnets, jewelry and in the fashion; others in cheaper style; others in shirts, gowns, wraps; others also as God made them. The old settlers are the bloods or dignitaries; then comes in the tribal part according to grade. Tribal prejudice runs high in many cases. The bush crowd are the servants and domestics.

The bush or native heathen do all the drudgery work, such as pulling and pushing the carts, wheel chairs, sedan chairs, hammocks, hearses; carry all boxes, barrels, stones, mortar, bricks; row all the boats on the river, etc. The people are peaceable; I see or hear of no fighting; shooting is never heard of. Sometimes an African king may come from the bush, or country, and kill some runaway wife, then he is arrested and banished to some island, and made to work the balance of his life; but if a king comes to the city and kills a decent wife, he will likely kill himself before he will be arrested.

I learned that Bishop Crowther, of the Niger, has not been treated right somehow by the Church of England, and he and his ministers are about to set up an independent apostolic denomination. I am urged to go and confer with him, but the object might be misconstrued, therefore I shall not go. I do not blame the bishop for kicking, if what some of the ministers tell me be true.

A singular fact is, that anybody, white or colored, from America is welcomed out here in Africa, either on the coast or back in the interior, while Englishmen, French and Germans are mostly hated. The kings hate them especially about robbing them of their lands. The French are hated as the devil. Americans are looked upon as the guardians of Liberia and the friends of her black, and it modifies the prejudice somehow. I do not understand it yet. France is more intolerant in her claimed possessions than England it seems, and far less compromising, while the Mohammedans abominate Germany about the shiploads of rot-gut whisky they land along the coast to ruin the more heathen African. The English ships despise the German ships about the same; nearly every time they see a German ship at sea the entire crew will curse it about shipping poisoned liquor to Africa. The English ships carry a good deal, too, but they ease their conscience by saying, "Our whisky is all first-class. It is inspected before we leave Liverpool and London."

The African ladies who come in the city from the bush, for hundreds of miles, have to buy white doll-babies for their children. They want black, brown and yellow dolls. If some of our people will engage in their manufacture they can sell millions of colored dolls. England, France, etc., only send out white dolls. The black merchants out here (and they are plentiful) are crazy for a line of steamships to America, like England, France and Germany have, so they can deal in American goods, medicines, etc.; so the merchants can come over in ten or fifteen days and return in haste—the sail vessels are too slow.

These black Mohammedan priests, learned to kill, walking around here in their robes with so much dignity, majesty and consciousness of their worth, are driving me into respect for them. Some come for hundreds of miles from the country—out of the bushes—better scholars than in America. What fools we are to suppose these Africans are fools!

# Eighth Letter*

## OF BISHOP TURNER

*Freetown, Sierra Leone, Africa,*
*November 18th, 1891*

The native African has no fear, no cowardice, no dread, but feels himself the equal of any man on earth. The land, as far as I went, is rich, water streams in abundance, fruits of every kind, flowers of every beauty, and while I saw many doing nothing at all, I saw many hundreds at work, and hard at work, too. They need skilled labor, however, skilled farmers. Since I found out more, I find horses will live here and be fat. Dogs are like ours in every particular. The dogs, roosters, goats and sheep all talk like ours. I told the doctor they were all I could understand. I could not understand the people, but he could.

I have just had the honor of my life. King Kobbena Eljen of the Kromantic tribe, a powerful tribe on the Gold Coast, who was captured in the late war with England, and who is here as prisoner of

* *Ibid.*, pp. 42–45.

war, called to pay his respects, through me to his race, as he says "over the sea". He means in America. I kissed his hands a dozen times, and would have kissed his feet, had he not said, "No, no". The king is 64 years old. He is tall, erect and majestic, and is deeply concerned about the colored people in America. He wanted to know when we were coming home.

During the great Ashantee war, he was captured by the English army, and England tried to get him to sign away his territory and his people's land. He refused to do it and they brought him to Sierra Leone, as a prisoner, to be held until he signs away his kingdom. The king says he will die first. If he would sign the documents, England would send him back at once in a man-of-war. The African kings and nobility will make me hate England, grand as old England is in many respects. The king walks about town but cannot leave. He is loyal to his race and to his people. He will give his kingdom to his children in the United States, but not to England.

Well, the ship has arrived which is to carry me to Liberia, and having completed my work here, I must close this letter and begin to pack up. I have not written half, but all I could find time to write. . . .

# Eleventh Letter*
## OF BISHOP TURNER

*Muhlenberg, Liberia,*
*December 4, 1891*

Mr. Editor:

I have just strolled as far out in the direction of Boporo—the Eden of West Africa—as my strength and convenience would permit. I have seen the African in his native town and hut, rather dwellings, and I have just had a long weep or cry at the grand field for missionary operation here, and that I am too old now to engage in it. But if there were roads cut through the country and bridges for horses and wagons, I would try it, as old as I am. I am sure I could not stand the hills and valleys of this rolling country traveling on foot, at my age, and then the hammock system of travel is too cumbersome for regular locomotion. But Africa is the grandest field on earth for the labor of civilization and the Christian church. There is no reason under heaven why this continent should not or cannot be redeemed

* *Ibid.,* pp. 55–60.

and brought to God in twenty-five years—say thirty at most. Note the reasons:

First.—The African can beat the world in learning to speak the English language, in which all religious terms are found to convey Christian ideas.

Second.—The young African can come out of the bush, and in a few months at most, sing and play upon the organ any gospel song in print, even before he learns to wear clothes.

Third.—The Africans are the most honest people on earth. Where I am stopping at present, at the Training School of Rev. David A. Day, scores of wild and partly civilized Africans gather and sleep all about the yards as well as on the piazzas; not a door or window is shut all night, unless it is raining or windy.

Fourth.—The African is not a pagan, but a child of superstition; he worships no wooden or brass god, but believes more strongly in the invisible forces than we do; so it is an easy matter to have him transfer his faith from superstition to Christ Jesus the Lord.

Fifth.—And here is the crowning phase of this question: The Africans will give the god-man or god-woman millions of children to be instructed and trained to read, write, work, sing, pray, farm or do anything that will make them useful. When you approach the older ones, and begin to tell them about the benefits of a civilized life and the virtues of Christianity, they say: "You no change me now; take all my pickaninnies (children) and teach them, make them wise and great; not me, I be too old." And they will give you all their children, and frequently come once a week and bring food for them to eat. It makes one feel singular to see the almost naked native African father come out of the bush, and sit around the Training School, and watch their sons as they walk the yards in decent dress, and read, write, sing, march, use tools, etc. They are so fond of their children. Finally, they will walk off home, possibly having not uttered a word to their child or any one else. The African father seems to be solliloquizing thus: "Well, I suppose that will be the order of things in the future; my day will soon be gone, and another dispensation will be ushered in."

One thing stands to the everlasting credit of the African; he is anxious to learn; a seeker after knowledge; to-day he is the most susceptible heathen upon the face of the globe. He is ready to lay down any habit, custom or sentiment for a better, or have his children do it, which is the same thing. It is said, that often those that have been trained at schools, will return to the bush and strip off their clothes and go around like the others. That seems to be true from what I have seen in some cases. But what is the result? These very young men become the leaders and general instructors of their people; they do not forget their training by any means. They often become the diplomats of their tribes and negotiate with other tribes and civilized nations. Their education is not lost, if they go as naked as a "skinned coon".

# Twelfth Letter*

## OF BISHOP TURNER

*Monrovia, Liberia,*
*December 5, 1891*

Mr. Editor:

I have descended the St. Paul River and am now in Monrovia, stopping in the beautiful three-story brick residence of General R. A. Sherman, general-in-chief of the Liberian armies. Everything is superb in and outside of this spacious and finely-furnished palace. I would wager anything that General W. T. Sherman never lived in more style, and I am sure he never possessed anything like the social graces of the Liberian General Sherman. The general somewhat resembles ex-Senator B. K. Bruce in stature, color, hair and demeanor. He was born in Savannah, Ga., is about fifty years of age, and has been here some thirty-seven years. He has fought many battles, has been wounded repeatedly, and his name is a terror to the native heathen for hundreds of miles in the interior.

I have seen many sights of interest in the city. Dr. Blyden carried me through the Kroo Town, introduced me to the king, with whom I had a long talk. I was surprised at his intelligence and general information. He was dressed as a gentleman and very polite. His subjects, or people, treat him with great respect. The city is laid off in streets and squares, but not equal in extent; sometimes the streets curve and, in other cases, they so intersect one another as to form a triangle.

The houses are built of platted sheets of bamboo, which they plat upon the ground with taste and skill, and in some instances with peculiar art. Then they are set up and fastened to timbers, and rooms, kitchens, palaver halls, sitting-rooms and such like are made in the same building.

* *Ibid.*, pp. 61–65.

It is useless to talk about the African having no taste and pride.

I have found out another thing since I have come to Africa. I have traveled scores of miles through the interior and noted the tact, taste, genius and manly bearing of the higher grade of the natives. I have found out that we poor American negroes were the tail-end of the African races. We were slaves over here, and had been for a thousand years or more before we were sold to America. Those who think the receding forehead, the flat nose, the proboscidated mouth and the big flat-bottom foot are natural to the African are mistaken. There are heads here by the millions, as vertical or perpendicular as any white man's head God ever made. A straight rule laid upon the face of three-fourths of us in America will touch the nose and mouth only; here are native Africans, without number, whose nose and chin the rule would touch without touching the mouth, which is always indicative of the highest type of intellectuality. Some of the most neat and concave feet are found upon thousands of these Africans. I have seen specimens of 19 tribes, and I have not seen over 100 of them constructed on as low scale as I have seen in America. An African said to be 108 years old, said, "We no used to sell 'big blood' African to white man, except we capture him in war." I believe this old man tells the truth; that during the times of the slave trade there were no "big blood" (first class) Africans sold to the white man, unless they were war prisoners.

Monrovia far exceeds my expectations. Instead of being low, swampy and alluvial, it is on an elevated cape, three sides laved by the ocean and fanned by her breezes. It will average about 150 feet above the sea-level, I think. In the main, the houses are excellent, two, three and a few four-stories high, with sidewalks very good, but the streets proper are grassy and not kept in regular order. As they use no horses and wagons, the streets are not needed; but they are far superior to hundreds of streets I have seen where horses and mules are used.

In the rear of Monrovia, however, where a branch of the St. Paul River, called the Stockton Creek, and the Mesurado River form a confluence, there are some large mangrove swamps, alluvial, soft and lagoonish, which evidently emit a great deal of malaria and are highly productive of fever germs when the wind is blowing from the land side, just as we have in thousands of places in the United States. There is no remedy for this, for God is making these two rivers cart dirt from the high lands to fill up the low; the debris is gradually doing its work, and the people must await his time.

The Liberia College is situated on the side of Mount Mesurado;

the curriculum is high and the teachers are well informed. Two more learned professors are being looked for daily. The college is a credit to the government of Liberia, for it is a national institution.

I have had the honor of visiting the executive mansion of the Liberian government, was received with marked consideration, and the president, who is polished scholar, paid me special attention. I had seen nine presidents in the United States, but a real black president was to me a delightful sight. This administration is praised and blamed by friends and foes, just as is the case with our presidents. The Liberian government is in the hands of the following, who form the executive department: His Excellency H. R. W. Johnson, President, born in Liberia; Secretary of State, Hon. E. J. Barclay, born in Barbadoes, West Indies; Secretary of Treasury, Hon. H. W. Travis, born in Liberia; Postmaster-General, Hon. H. J. Moore, born in Liberia; Attorney-General, Hon. W. M. Davis, born in Philadelphia, Pa., Secretary of the Interior, not filled. The Secretary of the Treasury, for the present, does the duties of the War and Naval departments. Chief Justice, Hon. C. L. Parsons, born in Charleston, S. C.

The president-elect, who will take his seat early in January, 1892, is Hon. J. J. Cheeseman of Grand Bassa, born in Liberia; vice-president-elect, Hon. W. D. Coleman, born in Kentucky. Mr. Cheeseman is represented as an able man with progressive views.

I visited the Monrovia cemetery a few days ago, and was pleased with the tombstones, slabs and shafts I saw commemorating the dead. I counted nearly a hundred, some of which cost over a thousand dollars. I saw the grave of my aunt, "Hannah Greer," who died about the same time my mother did, some three years ago. She was about ninety years old. She was my oldest aunt of five, and the people here say she was a grand woman. I hope to send or bring her a marble head and foot slab from America. I visited also the graves of Hon. M. A. Hopkins, Hon. and Dr. Henry Highland Garnett, Hon. Alexander Clark, and Mrs. Mary Garnett Barboza, the distinguished daughter of Dr. Garnett. Hopkins, Garnett and Clark were the three American Ministers of State, who have died here. There is not a stone, or a shingle, at the foot or head of the grave of Dr. Garnett, —a shame, a shame, upon us American Negroes!

For forty years before Mr. Lincoln issued his proclamation of freedom, Dr. Garnett fought for his race as no other man could, except Douglass, when the lips of the Southern negro was sealed and he was gored by the slave-masters to the verge of death. Dr. Garnett periled life and everything for his freedom. Now for us American

239

negroes to allow his remains to lie here, as though he was a dog, is enough to make God blast the whole of us. As I looked at his grave I wept, and asked God if there was any hope for such an ungrateful people. If we do not send a tombstone here to mark his grave, the whole negro race in America deserves the contempt of perdition, to say nothing of heaven.

Hon. C. T. O. King is the agent of the Colonization Society here. He is a man of excellent parts and evidently understands himself. Mr. King thinks that some improvements could be made in the reception of emigrants from America, and I think so, too. But as I will speak about them at the proper place if I live, I will only say at present, that any persons coming out here should not come as paupers. While Liberia is the easiest place to make a living on earth and is the most paradisiacal spot in the world, all things considered; yet, there is a climatic change which most people must pass through (many do not), and while they are passing through it, they need rest and fresh food, which the Colonization Society does not provide, nor can it without steamships. Hence they need money to purchase the necessary food and often some medicine. Persons should not come here and expect to be hirelings; for the native African stands ready to do all kinds of work much cheaper and better than we can, except skilled labor. They till the ground and raise all the produce for twenty-five cents per day, or five dollars per month. A man coming here with two or three hundred dollars and good sense may be rich in four or five years. But this is no place for fools and paupers. The oldest man in Liberia at present is only one hundred and twenty-seven years; the oldest woman is one hundred and twenty. A young man twenty-seven years old has a wife seventy-two years old, and he is jealous of her and another fellow twenty-four years old.

The ministers of Monrovia are as follows: Rev. Garrison W. Gibson, of the Episcopal Church; Rev. Henry Cooper, M. E. Church; Rev. Robert J. Clark, Baptist Church; Rev. J. B. Perry, Presbyterian Church. All these ministers treat Geda and me with great courtesy. The Episcopal minister could not offer me his church to preach in, owing to the canons of his connection but he urged me to lecture in it. The M. E. Church pastor appropriated our service. He is a Christian and a gentleman of the highest type. Everybody seems to be overjoyed at the presence of the A. M. E. Church in Liberia. The welcome appears to be universal. Many desire that it shall be the National Church, others declare it will be the Continental Church. They have come after me to organize in Monrovia at once, but for reasons that I shall tell the bishops, I will not.

A minister of the A. M. E. Zion Church, who had united with us and claimed to be ordained by one Elder Cartright, maintained that his orders were valid, as Brother Cartright was superintendent of the church here and had been authorized by Bishop Hood to ordain. I denied the right of Bishop Hood to confer any such authority upon an elder and rejected his ordination. I ordained him a deacon, however, after due examination. I am sure Bishop Hood never did it.

The people here think I am a "rough," because I will sit in the draught, eat all kinds of African food, sleep with the windows open, walk around barefooted, etc., preach or speak every night. But I believe some people die here because of particularity. I never felt better in my life; but I cannot say how long this will continue.

They say Hon. Alexander Clark, who died here, had passed through the acclimating fever and would have lived easily enough had he not refused to eat food that would strengthen him; he confined himself to American hog soup, when the doctor and all begged him to eat other things. The people here say stinginess killed him. The report, however, that strong drink killed him is pronounced a base falsehood. People here say he was purely temperate.

# Fourteenth Letter*

## OF BISHOP TURNER

*York Island, Sherbro River, Africa,*
*December 9, 1891*

Mr. Editor:

I have left Monrovia and am now some seventy-five miles up the Sherbro River, interior-ward from the ocean. The native towns and vast population of our people living on each side of this river, and all through the bush, is simply wonderful. As you ascend the Sherbro, every now and then, small inlets can be seen flowing in from the land, while trees lock their branches across them, and flower-bearing vines festoon them with garlands of fragrant drapery. But, reverberating through and under these over-arched inlets, you can hear the voices of scores of natives, as they chant their rowing songs; for the native Africans sing as they work, especially as they row their boats, till they burst from under the green sceneries with small canoes laden with all kinds of fruit. Often a Mohammedan priest sits in front,

* *Ibid.*, pp. 72–74.

gorgeously robed, as though he was on watch for whisky; as the sixty millions of Mohammedans and their plurality of wives (which of course no Christian can endorse), I verily believe that God is holding these Mohammedans intact, and that they will serve as the forerunners of evangelical Christianity; in short, that the Mohammedan religion is the morningstar to the sun of pure Christianity. I have not spoken on any occasion against liquor-drinking in Africa but some Mohammedan has come and shaken my hand after service, and thanked me for fighting whisky. One thanked me "for cursing liquor", and said, "Our church and religion all curse it, too; it be our greatest foe". God save the Mohammedans, is my prayer, till the Christian Church is ready to do her whole duty. Beyond the fact that the Mohammedans allow more than one wife, they are as upright in conduct and civil behavior as any people in the land.

I regret to say what I am now going to write, but I promised to do it, and I suppose I had better keep my word.

The leading men, or a large number of them in Liberia, are disgusted with a majority of the representatives that our government sends over here. They say if our government cannot find sober, cool-headed, dignified and intelligent representatives of our own color to send here, ask the president to send white men. Dr. Henry Highland Garnett is the only man sent here, whom all join in complimenting, for many years. They say Dr. Garnett was a gentleman and a diplomat of high order. They also speak kindly of Hon. Alexander Clarke, so far as his sobriety and morality are concerned, but say that he had no knowledge of diplomacy. Some of our representatives have so far ignored the rule of diplomatic dignity or decorum that they have tried to force themselves into the President's Cabinet meetings. But I will tell no more, as I dislike gossip in any form; yet they prefer a white man to some of our colored men whom the Presidents have sent here.

It appears that the American minister is the Dean of the Diplomatic Corps at Monrovia, and in any formal meeting or reception he is the presiding officer, as he ranks the representatives of all other nations; therefore he should be a model man in every respect.

Liberia, as I have said before, is a most beautiful country, and nature has supplied it with all that heart could wish. I never wanted to be a young man so badly in my life. I would come here, and, if I had half as much sense as I have now, I would be worth a fortune in ten years. Nevertheless, as I have said before, I would advise no one to come here without a hundred or two dollars. This is not the place for any one to come without money. Well, if he is a mechanic, viz., carpenter, blacksmith, painter, tailor, watchmaker, or professional, as a doctor or a lawyer, he might do well enough; but a mere laborer should bring some money, for the native African stands ready, ten thousand strong, to snatch up all the mere common labor to be done, at twenty-five cents per day, or five dollars a month; and two native Africans can do more hard work in one day than five of our ordinary men, such is their strength and vigor.

As for the acclimating process, nearly everybody must pass through it, yet all do not have the fever. Men, and women too, who have been here ten and fifteen years, tell me they have never had anything like fever. But if a person comes here, young or old, with any chronic disease lurking in his system, Africa is apt to purge it out, or kill the person in the process of purgation. At all events, the party will get better or worse. But if a person comes here healthy, sound and sober, there is no more danger than in any change of climate.

One thing the black man has here—that is, manhood, freedom, and the fullest liberty; he feels as a lord, and walks and talks the same way.

I notice when the English, or even the cultured Africans, speak of the colored people coming here from America or elsewhere they do not use the terms "emigrate", or "African emigration," as we do in America; but, instead, they invariably say, "repatriate", or use the term, the "repatriation of the black man", or, as some say, the "negro;" nor are the terms "emigrate" or "immigrate" used among the common people, as they say, "coming home", or "When are you all coming home?" The native African, from the kings down, cannot realize that the black man in America is at home across the sea.

Out of the many receptions given in my honor, or the honor of the church, and the eloquent address delivered upon the occasions, I will send the two following, they being the only ones which have fallen into my hands in manuscript. I failed to get the others by reason of having to leave so soon. The first was delivered by Rev. June Moore, of the Baptist Church, the great friend and comrade of Rev. S. J. Campbell, at the opening of the Liberian Conference; the other at the 10 o'clock breakfast tendered to Elder Geda and myself at Monrovia, which was read by Hon. H. W. Grimes.

# Levi Jenkins Coppin,
# 1848–1924

Levi Jenkins Coppin was born in Frederickstown, Maryland. When he was seven his parents took him to Baltimore and later to Delaware. He was largely self-taught. In 1865 Coppin joined the Methodist Church and in 1866 was licensed to preach. The following year he was admitted to the annual conference from the Bethel Church in Wilmington, Delaware. His first pastorate was in Philadelphia. In 1884 Coppin entered the Philadelphia Episcopal Divinity School, graduating in the class of 1887. In 1888 Coppin was elected editor of the *African Methodist Episcopal Church Review*, America's Negro church magazine. In 1896 he returned as pastor to Bethel Church in Philadelphia.

In 1900 Coppin was elected as Bishop of South Africa in the Methodist Church and, as a result of the work done by Bishop Turner, was assigned to the fourteenth episcopal district (Cape Colony and the Transvaal) from 1900 to 1904. Bishop Coppin took with him to South Africa his wife, Fanny Ann Jackson, famous in her own right as Principal of the Institute for Colored Youth in Philadelphia. Coppin's main responsibility was to weld together the Ethiopian Churches into the African Methodist Episcopal Church and to establish new churches among the Cape Colony Colored people. Bishop Coppin founded the Masonic Lodge of Cape Town, and a lasting testimony of his popularity and that of his wife is the existence of the Fanny Coppin Girls' Hall at Wilberforce Institute in South Africa.

Bishop Coppin was a prolific hymn writer; among his best known hymns are "The Church is Moving On" and "Our Father's Church". He also wrote *Unwritten History*, *Relations of Baptized Children to the Church*, *Key to Scriptural Interpretation*, *Fifty-two Sermon Syllabi*, and *Observations of Persons and Things in South Africa*, from which the selections in this volume are taken.

# Letters from South Africa*

## BISHOP L. J. COPPIN

LETTER NO. 4—*A Service with the Natives.*

Sunday, February 24th, was a bright and beautiful day in Cape Town. The cloud waves on Table Mountain were white, having not the least appearance of storm. A delightful breeze swept over the city, which nestles below, making the day quite a contrast to the previous one, which registered 105 degrees in the shade. It was my first Sunday in South Africa. The first thing to attract my attention upon rising was a man driving a cart; he had stopped right under my window to shovel up a pile of sweepings. The first thought that came to me was, that this business should have been attended to before the Sabbath; but upon inquiry I learned that since the appearance of the bubonic plague in Cape Town the authorities have taken every precaution to prevent its spread. Learning this, I recalled the words of our Lord: "The Sabbath was made for man, and not man for the Sabbath." The plague, coming down from the soldier's camp in the interior, has actually reached Cape Town. Several cases have been reported, and a number of deaths. This apparent innovation of the man and cart did not seem to rob the city of its Sunday appearance. The noise of vehicles of every description and the prattle of venders of numerous wares—such as constitute the daily life of the city, were hushed into silence. The hour for service soon came and we were off to Friendly Hall, where at 10.30 a.m. services would be held for natives. We reached the place promptly at the hour. The pastor said, "You are just on the minute". The hall was well filled, and the services began immediately.

Rev. Joseph Spawn, a licentiate and candiate for the deaconate, is pastor in charge. Rev. M. M. Mokane is the presiding elder; but he is out of the city, but Rev. A. B. Ngcayiya, a visiting presiding elder being in the city, acted as senior officer. The presiding elder and pastor proceeded with the service, all in the native tongue. Representatives from different tribes were present, but the services were held in what is popularly known as the Kafir language. It some times hap-

* Bishop L. J. Coppin, *Letters from South Africa.* Philadelphia, A.M.E. book concern, n.d., 210 p.

pens when a large number of persons representing different tribes are present at a meeting, more than one or even more than two interpreters are used. Many of the people present at this meeting, indeed most of them, could speak and understand English fairly well, but as a few of them could not, it was thought best to have an out and out native service. An abridgement of the Church of England Book of Common Prayer, as used by the Wesleyans, has been translated into Kafir, also a Hymn Book and Bible. The Heartiness with which all entered into the service was truly inspiring. A very large number had books in their hands, and those who did not seemed so familiar with the form of service that they readily took part. When the choir would sing a selection from the Gospel Hymns in English, or even an anthem, the congregation would join in just as readily and intelligently as though they had been doing it in their native tongue. What a revelation and a lesson all this was to me. Just think of it, many in that congregation could speak four tongues fluently—English, Dutch and at least two native tongues. Rev. Ngcayiya, who took the lead in the opening service, can speak perhaps as many as a half dozen. He takes an English Bible and reads in a native tongue with perfect ease. What would one mean who would refer to those people as being ignored? or of what service would an "ignorant" pastor be to them? It is not light that they are seeking, but it is more light and greater opportunities. They are hungering and thirsting for more knowledge. They have strong minds as one may readily infer from their ability to acquire different languages, a thing that is generally most difficult in our school and college life. Many a college student who takes the classics as a part of his necessary course and graduates with honors, cannot speak fluently the languages which he has been taught to read. It is exceedingly difficult to so educate the ear as to distinguish readily between so many different sounds.

The opening services being ended, I spoke to them in English. Rev. Ngcayiya translating or interpreting for the benefit of those present who did not understand English at all, or who do not understand well. Many who quite understood me would give vent to their feelings by a hearty "Amen", before my interpreter had reproduced my words. It was to me a delightful service. Fifteen persons were received into full membership; four of whom received the Sacrament of Baptism. The services finally closed with a general handshaking. Many persons held fast on to my hand until they had kissed it. I am now thinking and praying over the subject of how best to reach and help the less fortunate ones, their brothers and mine, many of whom have left the interior and come to town seeking employment, and who are in a very crude state and condition both in body and mind. There are thousands of them in town with but little more than their native blanket as clothing. No one seems to care for their souls while in this crude condition, or, to say the most, but little is being done for them.

A gentleman on shipboard was telling me how the raw native, in coming to town, would first adopt the vices of the town people, especially the cursed, degrading habit of liquor drinking. When I asked him what was being done to help them, he said a law had been passed making it unlawful to sell whiskey to a native after 6 o'clock in the morning and before 6 at night; the presumption is that between these hours they are at work, and the object, therefore, is to keep them sober long enough to do a day's work. If this is accomplished, they may do as they please the rest of the time. Is not that reformation with a vengeance? What is needed is a place of meeting right in their quarters, where services of a social, moral and religious character could be carried on by faithful men and women who would not fear being defiled by coming into close contact with them. They should be taught to wash their bodies and put on proper clothes, and other habits of civilized life; and at the same time have religious instruction given them. It is not necessary to say that this requires money; but if we could get but a small amount of what even Christian people are throwing away daily, while they sing, "Pity them, pity them, Christians at home", we could begin the work at once, and what a blessing it would be. It is not at all likely that any more will be done for this class of natives by the Europeans than is being done. There is already a measure on foot—and it finds many advocates—to remove them to a "location," that is to say, to get a camp outside of the city and place them there, where they will he beyond the reach of civilizing influences. I inquired to learn what, in this case, they would do for a living, and was told that a line of cars would extend to their quarters that they might come into town during the day and find work. The wages they command is small at the very best, so by the time they pay car fare, morning and night, to and from their work, there will be little left for them to purchase food and clothing or to make their homes even partially comfortable. The inevitable result, therefore, will be that under this plan they will remain perpetually in their present condition, though living under the very shadow of a civilized and Christian community. Once they owned all the land by inheritance, and now they are not permitted to domicile on it, or, only upon such portions of it as may be allotted to them out of pity. When we are told that a man in America is denied civil and political rights on account of being a descendant of Africa, we are content to call it unjust, ungodly; but when we are told that an African in Africa is denied civil privileges because he is an African, we feel that besides being unrighteous and unworthy our Christian civilization, it is ridiculous in the extreme. I do not say that civilization should not advance to those who are trampling upon the hidden treasures of earth without making an effort to obtain them, or without having a proper conception of their value; to those whose broad acres are lying without cultivation and improvement; nor should it be expected that those who go to their relief, and that, too, at great sacrifice, should not have ample remuneration; but the least to be expected of those who come and take their inheritance is that they should give them kindness and civilization in return.

It is somewhat amusing to hear the contention that is going on about who are "Africanders". The dictionaries tell us that an Englishman born in America is an Anglo-American; in India, an Anglo-Indian, etc.; but, if born in Africa, he is not an Anglo-African, but an Africanda. Thus we have in South Africa natives, Boers, Africanders and colored people. The native is, of course, the aboriginal; the Boer is the man of Dutch descent; the Africanda, the European, not of Dutch descent, born in Africa; and the "coloured," the man of color who either was not born in Africa or who is of mixed blood. But all these divisions and sub-divisions; except the native, claim the title of Africanda; that is to say, the Englishman born in Africa claims that he is an Africanda, while the Dutchman born here dissents and says he has a right to the distinguishing—or distinguished—title; while the coloured people say it is simply audacious for the white people to take their country and now want to take their name. Personally, I have not entered into the scramble at all; since I hold a passport from my government, I am an American pure and simple, even without the questionable and much controverted "Afro". An out and out Dutchman who is connected with our work here, in paying his respects to me, seemed a trifle embarrassed and finally said that if he could take some paint and blacken his face, he would freely do so; but I told him that it was not at all necessary to resort to such a device in order to be a member in good standing in the A.M.E. Church. We take into our communion, and upon terms of perfect equality, the whole human family, whether it comes "Simon pure" or in parts.

There is, also, a most mischievous tendency to draw social lines sharply between the native and the "Cape coloured people." This would indeed be unfortunate. It is not expected that when the native

248

comes down fresh from the interior, with no training in habits of civilized life, he should take his place in society; but it is expected that he should be regarded as our less fortunate brother and the helping hand should be extended without question. Let it be remembered that the condition of all the natives is not the same; they differ as do we. There are schools in the interior that have carried their pupils in their studies as far as Greek, Latin and higher mathematics, and with their school studies they have been taught a different mode of life from the untutored native. There is but one right thing for the African, Africander, Afro-world wider or colored man by whatever distinguishing title, to do; and that is to unite in an effort to prove that merit does not inhere in color, but with common attributes, the whole human family, under proper conditions, is capable of reflecting the image of God and rising to that dignity of which mankind alone is capable.

LETTER NO. 7—*The Coloured Man of South Africa*\*

The English people have a way of spelling color with an "our"; or, it might be quite as appropriate to say that the American people have a way of dropping the "u". The tendency of linguistic movement is toward abbreviation. The old "programme" is now "program"; and why not? As there is a difference between the English and American spelling, so there is also in the definition. In America, the word colored—or even Negro for that matter—stands for every man, woman or child who has, visibly, or invisibly, a drop of blood coursing through his veins that can be traced back through generations to a native African parentage. This sometimes involves a lot of trouble, and affords much amusement. A conductor on a railroad train in the Southern States will sometimes ask a passenger if he is white or colored; his object is to decide which coach he is entitled, according to law, to ride in. No question is raised as to the class of ticket he holds, nor of his personal appearance, i.e. whether he is clean or unclean; nor as to his behavior; the search is purely and simply for that drop of blood. It is not necessary to say that thousands with the "drop" are never detected, but this does not at all excuse the vigilant conductor from faithfully performing his duty according to his best knowledge and belief. 'Tis the law, and the dignity and majesty of the law must be maintained even in a railroad car, where men may be returning from a lynching bee.

\* *Ibid.*, 66–72.

In South Africa the case is different. A coloured man here is dis-tinguished from a native. One will often hear the expression: "This man is a native and that one is a Cape coloured man." The variety of shade in complexion, however, is quite as various as in America. Taking Cape Town as a sample, we have representatives of about all the darker race-varieties except the American Indian. Then adding to these divisions the sub-divisions that have been caused by the commingling of the Dutch, English, Italian, Dane and others, with both native and coloured, we have indeed and in truth every color of the rainbow represented under this one general title, coloured. It is a case of "very much mixed", and the only reason that the natives are not put into the same classification is that coming fresh from the interior, they are in language and habits so much unlike the Cape coloured people that they naturally form a different class.

Just now, at this writing, the bubonic plague is in Cape Town, and strenuous efforts are being made to stamp it out. Among other measures resorted to by the authorities is a location for the natives, to which place they have already been moved. The object, it seems, is not to compel the more civilized natives to go to the location, but only those who have recently come from the interior to Cape Town seeking work, and who, unable to procure suitable quarters, are being huddled together in large numbers. The object, then, of the location is to provide better sanitary regulations for these new comers and thus prevent the spread of the disease through them. It does not yet appear, however, that the natives have been the most fruitful source of spreading the terrible disease. A census taken by one of our dailies gives the per cent of the afflicted as follows: Europeans, 31; coloured, 31; native, 29. In this summary the natives really have the advantage over the other citizens, but their removal from the crowded quarters in which they are living is a necessary and reason-able precaution. The landlords who have so unscrupulously profited by the over-crowded tenements will be obliged to look out for other tenants. They may also have an opportunity to spend some of their ill gotten gain in putting those places in a proper sanitary condition. This separate classification of the natives, however, is not based upon color, but condition. As fast as the natives are civilized and educated they must take their place in the great mass of people who are denominated "coloured" to distinguish them from the "Euro-pean". Practically, then, there are but two classes, coloured and European; or, as we call it in the United States, colored and white. The third class, or native, is but a temporary classification and cannot endure only to the extent that the native is kept away from civilizing influences.

It is most remarkable how readily the native takes to the life, language and habits of the European when brought into contact with him. I have in my mind now a number of persons whom I have recently met who speak the native, the Dutch and the English languages, and read and write in them. They can entertain an audience in either tongue, turning immediately and rapidly from one to the other. Sometimes English, Dutch and two or more native tongues; not parrot-like but, thinking on their feet, and in many instances showing a superior quality of mind. Many of the natives who have not come into contact with European civilization, whose every word must be interpreted, are really marvels of deep thought and eloquence. We are also told that in the gold and diamond mines they learn readily to manipulate the most difficult machinery, so much so that they are intrusted with most important duties— beneath the ground—though the value of their work is not recognized in the matter of pay. But no education is without its value. Africa is a large continent and has, doubtless, many gold and diamond mines not yet discovered. What the native needs is education, enlightenment, and this is cheap at most any cost. The term coloured man, then, must eventually come to mean all who are not white, or all who are not so recognized.

The practice of drawing the lines sharply between native and colored cannot result in the best of either. The Caucasian has freely mingled his blood with other race-varieties regardless of color, clime or condition; but he stubbornly refuses to incorporate any of the descendants into his own proud family. The colored man need never feel elated when told that there is a difference in his favor between him and a native. But one more step is necessary to disclose the fact that when it comes to a claim for absolute equality for the human race under like conditions, he is then classed with the native and rejected. It is the theory of the English government that under the British flag all subjects are equals as citizens, all things else being equal, of course. This fact has caused the man of color to love the "Union Jack" and feel safe beneath its folds. Many a fugitive from hatred and oppression has, after a weary journey and untold hardships, rejoiced at last to plant his bleeding feet upon British soil and bless the name of the people who had reached the noblest height in civilization. It is to be hoped that this proud history of the Briton will never be vitiated by the inordinate love of power and money that seems to so largely influence the nations of the earth. Already we begin to hear much about "equality for all white men in South Africa, and justice for the native." This is offered to the Boers as a condition of laying down their arms. Concerning such an announcement, we are bound to ask: First, by what rule will justice to the natives be measured? Second, what becomes of the "coloured man" in this summary? The declaration is sufficiently indefinite to be perfectly harmless, but at the same time sufficiently suggestive to cause one to turn it over in his mind. But of one thing we can always be sure, viz: that progress never goes backward; there are many ways by which it can be hindered in its onward march, but never turned back. When once the king of day struggles through the darkness and finally lifts his head above the eastern horizon he never falls back, but goes with straight course to the western skies. Very much like this is the course of nations; once lifted out of a state of barbarity and started out upon civilized life, they may make dark pages which in after years they would unmake if they could, but it is impossible to return entirely to the state and condition whence they came. I think we may safely conclude that the universal tendency of the civilized world is toward a better understanding between man and man. We grant that we have daily contradictory circumstances, on account of which many become pessimistic; but the only way to measure the progress of the world is by periods of time, not by unfavorable circumstances which happen within those periods. Has the world moved a pace since the beginning of the last century? Has that progress been so substantial and permanent that there is no cause for fear of permanent retrogression? Within this period named, human slavery has been swept from the face of the civilized earth. Within half this time, the American bondman has not only been released from his bonds, but clothed with citizenship, by which he has come within a step of reaching the highest position in the gift of the nation. Is it any wonder that with such unprecedented progress he lost his hold and slipped back a few steps? It is only that he might get a firmer hold, and starting again, be less liable to fall. As in America, so also in Africa; the man of color has been lifted up from heathenism and released from bodily bondage; he has been made to see the light of God as it beams from the face of Jesus Christ, and the cry of the slave driver has been hushed as far as the foot of civilized man has trod.

In Africa, more than any other place upon the face of the globe, it will be difficult to withhold from the black man the measure of justice and privilege to which he is entitled as a man. This is his home. Here he is to the manor born. He who would on account of superior strength resolve to rob him of his country and his privileges must feel that to do so would be to take the vineyard of Naboth. Two hundred and fifty years have passed since the Dutch settled for permanent residence in South Africa. Their methods of subjugating the weaker tribes which they found occupying the Cape coast brought upon them many trials and caused them to move further and further north until situated beyond the Vaal, and strong in experience and rich in possession, they came to regard the man who is native to the soil as being the man without a soul. But how pathetic today to see them by the thousands scattered about upon islands, in forts, in locations and upon transports, with homes destroyed and property confiscated. "Be not deceived. God is not mocked."

But the colored man, whether in South Africa or elsewhere, has a duty to perform. He must learn to appropriate the light that comes to him. He must show himself worthy of his place among civilized nations. He must profit by the terrible lessons that others have been taught before his face. He must in every sense be a man. The inducements now being offered to make a distinction between black and blacker, brown and browner, light and lighter, are but nets to entangle his feet and hinder his progress. All must rise or fall together. In the days of Queen Esther, the plots against the Jews would have included her; and today an injustice to the native will in due course of time reach the fairest of those who through the remote ages descend from Ham, for "all ye be brethren".

# Eslanda Robeson,
## 1896–1965

Eslanda Cardoza Goode Robeson was born in Washington into a family of considerable intellectual attainments. Her father was an employee of the War Department and her maternal grandfather, Francis Lewis Cardoza, had been the Secretary of State and the Secretary of the Treasury of South Carolina during the reconstruction.

Mrs. Robeson studied at the University of Chicago and completed her Bachelor of Science degree at Teachers College, Columbia University, in 1923. In 1921 she had married Paul Robeson, who was then a law student at Columbia University. They have one son, Paul.

Almost always with her husband on tour, Mrs. Robeson had had little time to pursue her initial interest in chemistry, but she had devoted herself to writing. Her first book, *Paul Robeson, Negro,* was published in 1930. From 1935 to 1937 Mrs. Robeson studied anthropology at London University and at the London School of Economics. Having had from childhood a desire to visit "the old country", she went to Africa in 1936 accompanied by her son. In these days of frequent travels to Africa, Mrs. Robeson's somewhat pioneering journey provides one of the first views of the modern period.

In 1939 the Robesons returned to the United States and Mrs. Robeson continued her studies at the Hartford Seminary Foundation, from which she was granted the Ph.D. degree in Anthropology in 1945. The family lived in Enfield, Connecticut, where Mrs. Robeson was very active in community work and in Negro rights. After the War the Robesons went abroad where they remained until 1963. Although Mrs. Robeson was a distinguished person in her own right, she was most popularly been known as the wife of Paul Robeson.

# "We Go" *

## ESLANDA ROBESON

I wanted to go Africa.

It began when I was quite small. Africa was the place we Negroes came from originally. Lots of Americans, when they could afford it, went back to see their "old country". I remember wanting very much to see my "old country", and wondering what it would be like.

In America one heard little or nothing about Africa. I hadn't realized that, consciously, until we went to live in England. There was rarely even a news item about Africa in American newspapers or magazines. Americans were not interested in Africa economically (except for a very few businessmen like Firestone, who has rubber interests in Liberia), politically, or culturally. Practically nothing was or is taught in American schools about Africa. Liberia was the only place I had ever heard of, and that was because the United States maintains an American Negro consul there. Of course when I speak of Africa I mean black Africa, not North Africa.

In England, on the other hand, there is news of Africa everywhere: in the press, in the schools, in the films, in conversation. English people are actively interested in Africa economically and politically. Members of families are out in Africa in the civil service, in the military, in business; everywhere you go, someone's uncle, brother, or cousin is working, teaching, administering, or "serving" in Africa. Women go out to Africa with their men, or go out to visit them. There are courses on Africa in every good university in England; African languages are taught, missionaries are trained, and administrators are prepared for work "in the field". Everywhere there is information about Africa.

When we first went to England I remember how startled I was by all this readily available information on Africa. I had thought, somewhat complacently I'm afraid, that I was well informed about the Negro question. My grandfather, the late Frances Lewis Cardoza, was well known for his early awareness of the Negro problem, and was a pioneer in Negro education and in the fight for Negro rights.

* Eslanda Goode Robeson, *African Journey*, pp. 13–19. Copyright © 1945 by Eslanda Goode Robeson and reprinted by permission of The John Day Company, Inc., publisher.

255

I was brought up in a household wide awake to every phase of the Negro problem in America.

There was the hitch: *in America*. There in England I was disconcerted by the fact that the Negro problem was not only the problem of the 13 million Negroes in America, but was and is the far greater problem of the 150 million Negroes in Africa, plus the problem of the 10 million Negroes in the West Indies.

Later on—much later—when I finally began to find out what it was all about, I came to realize that the Negro problem was not even limited to the problem of the 173 million black people in Africa, America, and the West Indies, but actually included (and does now especially include) the problem of the 390 million Indians in India, the problem of the 450 million Chinese in China, as well as the problem of all minorities everywhere.

It is just as well I didn't realize all this immediately. I probably would have been floored. As it was I was pretty much overcome by the fact that I knew so little concerning the problem about which I had always felt so well informed. That would never do.

I began reading everything about Africa I could lay hands on. This proved to be considerable, what with the libraries of the British Museum, the House of Commons, London University, and the London School of Economics. I began asking questions everywhere of everybody. The reading and the questions landed me right in the middle of anthropology (a subject I had only vaguely known existed) at the London School of Economics under Malinowski and Firth, and at London University under Perry and Hocart. It was all very interesting and exciting and challenging. At last I began to find out something about my "old country," my background, my people, and thus about myself.

After more than a year of very wide reading and intensive study I began to get my intellectual feet wet. I am afraid I began to be obstreperous in seminars. I soon became fed up with white students and teachers "interpreting" the Negro mind and character to me. Especially when I felt, as I did very often, that their interpretation was wrong.

It went something like this: Me, I *am* Negro, I *know* what we think, how we feel. I know this means that, and that means so-and-so.

"Ah, no, my dear, you're wrong. You see, you are European.*

* "European," a term which is very widely and somewhat loosely used among anthropologists, usually means "white", not only in colour, but also in culture, in civilization; "European" in their usage generally means a white person with Western (as against oriental and primitive) education, background, and values.

You can't possibly know how the primitive mind works until you study it, as we have done."

"What do you mean I'm European? I'm *Negro*. I'm African myself. I'm what you call primitive. I have studied my mind, our minds. How dare you call me European!"

"No, you're not primitive, my dear," they told me patiently, tolerantly, "you're educated and cultured, like us."

"I'm educated because I went to school, because I was taught. You're educated because you went to school, were taught. I'm cultured because my people had the education and the means to achieve a good standard of living; that's the reason you're cultured. 'Poor whites' have neither education nor culture. Africans would have both if they had the schools and the money. Going to school and having money doesn't make me European. Having no schools and no money doesn't make the African primitive." I protested furiously.

"No, no," they explained; "the primitive mind cannot grasp the kind of ideas we can; they have schools, but their schools have only simple subjects, and crafts; it's all very different. You see, we've been out there for years and years (some ten, some twenty, some thirty years); we've studied them, taught them, administered them, worked with them, and we know. You've never been out there, you've never seen them and talked with them on their home ground; you can't possibly know."

It all sounded nonsense to me. And yet the last bit made sense—maybe. I'd better check it. Paul and I began to seek out all the Africans we could find, everywhere we went: in England, Scotland, Ireland, France; in the universities, on the docks, in the slums. The more we talked with them, the more we came to know them, the more convinced we were that we are the same people: they know us, we know them; we understand their spoken and unspoken word, we have the same kind of ideas, the same ambitions, the same kind of humor, many of the same values.

I asked Africans I met at universities, taking honors in medicine, in law, in philosophy, in education, in other subjects: "What is all this about primitive minds and abstruse subjects, about only simple subjects and crafts in your schools?"

"Oh, *that*," they said with a twinkle, "there's nothing primitive about our minds in these universities, is there? And how can we cope with any but simple subjects and crafts in our schools, when that is all they will allow us to have? Actually, they rarely give us any schools at all, but they sometimes 'aid' the schools the Missions have set up for us, and those we have set up for ourselves with our own money and labor. But they definitely limit our curricula."

I began to see light. It was the old army game every Negro in America will recognize: The white American South says the Negro is ignorant, and has a low standard of living; the Negro says the South won't give him adequate schools or decent wages.

With new confidence I began to ask more questions in seminars. And always I came up against the blank wall: "But I was out there thirty years—I know. You have never been out there—you simply don't know."

"I *am* one, so I know."

And they would say: "You're different; you've met a few European-educated Africans who are different too."

This pattern was familiar to me also. In America Negroes get the same reaction: White America generalizes in its mind about the primitiveness, ignorance, laziness, and smell of Negroes. When we protest that these descriptions are just not true of us, nor of millions of our fellow Negroes, they answer: "But you are different; you are the exceptions." No matter how many facts we marshal to prove their statements untrue, they close their minds against these facts. It is more convenient for them to believe their own generalizations than to face the facts. So the facts become the "exceptions." But we "special" Negroes look closely and thoughtfully at the facts. We know we aren't essentially different from our fellow Negroes. We know also that others' merely saying we are different does not make us so.

So far, so good. But I had no answer to the constant "You have never been out there." Very well, I would go. I'd just have to go out to Africa and see and meet and study and talk with my people on their home ground. Then I would be able to say truly: I have been there too, and I *know*. . . .

And so we began to plan: While I was away, Mother could go to Russia to visit my two brothers who live and work there. Paul would go to Russia later on and spend some time with Sergei Eisenstein who was making a Russian film in the country outside Moscow. The idea of Paul making a Russian film had been discussed; this would give him a chance to perfect his Russian and observe Soviet methods of film making.

That disposed of everybody but Pauli, our beloved only child. He was eight—a fairly tender age; he was sturdy, but Mamma had always most carefully supervised his diet and general regime, which was rather strict. But he was adventurous, like me.

258

What was more important, Paul and I remembered vividly the time when, on the set of the *Sanders of the River* film, Pauli had been astonished and delighted to see all the Africans. "Why, there are lots of brown people," this then six-year-old had said happily, "lots of black people too; we're not the only ones." We had been profoundly disturbed by the realization that he had been living in an entirely white world since we had brought him and my mother to live with us in England, when he was ten months old. The only Negroes he had seen besides ourselves and Larry (Lawrence Brown, our colleague and accompanist) were the occasional ones who visited at our home. His young mind had thought we were the only brown people in a totally white world.

We must do something about that, we had said then. Well, this is it; this is what we'll do. If some Africans on a film set open up a new world to the child, a trip to the heart of Africa itself will be a revelation. He will see millions of other brown and black people, he will see a black world, he will see a black continent. So it was decided that Pauli would go with me.

We made our plans: we would go by sea from England to Capetown and Port Elizabeth, right at the bottom of South Africa. We would try to connect up with Bokwe, our African friend who had finished medicine at Edinburgh University and gone home to Alice, Cape Province, to practice; and his sister Frieda and her husband Zach Matthews, whom we had known in London when he was attending the Malinowski seminars; they and their children also lived at Alice, where Matthews was teaching at Fort Hare, the African college. Then we would go on to Johannesburg and maybe see the mines; and perhaps work in a trip to Swaziland; and maybe I could manage to run up to see Tshekedi Khama, the African regent we had all been so thrilled about. Then we would go down to Mozambique in Portuguese East Africa, pick up a ship and sail up the east coast to Mombasa, and go overland by train to join Nyabongo, an African student of anthropology at Oxford, who would be at home in Uganda for the summer. It was arranged that Nyabongo would meet us at Kampala and take us out to his home in Toro, where I planned to do my field work on the herdspeople. Then we would fly home from Entebbe. All very ambitious.

We got down to brass tacks. There were vaccinations and injections to be taken at the Hospital for Tropical Diseases. There was shopping to do: tropical clothes, mosquito boots, cholera belts for Pauli and me; tropical luggage, my Cine-kodak to check, and a lot of films especially packed for the tropics to buy. Paul gave me a gem of a camera, a Rolleiflex. "You can't take too many pictures," he said wisely. There were ship and rail reservations, passports to be put in order, visits to the Colonial Office, and visas.

The visas were the real problem. It seems if you are Negro, you can't make up your mind to go to Africa, and just go. Oh, no. Not unless you are a missionary. The white people in Africa do not want educated Negroes traveling around seeing how their brothers live; nor do they want those brothers seeing Negroes from other parts of the world, hearing how they live. It would upset them, make them restless and dissatisfied; it would make them examine and re-examine the conditions under which they, as "natives", live; and that would never do at all. In fact it would be extremely dangerous. Something must be done to prevent this "contact". But what to do? It's simple; just keep all other Negroes out of Africa, except maybe a few who will preach the Gospel. The Gospel always helps to keep people quiet and resigned. And how to keep them out? That's simple, too: just don't grant them visas. So they don't grant them visas. *Voilà*.

I had had a fair amount of experience traveling about with Paul and Larry all over Europe and to Russia. On concert tours I always took care of tickets, passports, itinerary, foreign monies for us all. For this trip I planned a rather elastic itinerary, bought steamer reservations at Cooks', hied me to the Colonial Office for visas to Swaziland, Buasutoland, Kenya, Uganda, Egypt (for the air trip home).

The Colonial Office wanted to know why I was going. I was going out to do my fieldwork for a degree in anthropology. When I presented my credentials from the professors at school the Colonial Office was helpful and gave me all the visas.

Then to South Africa House, but no South African visa.

"Why not?" I asked innocently. Well, it seems all visas are granted from the home office in Capetown, and mails take time. "All right, it takes time. I have time; I'll come back."

Our arms swelled up and became stiff and sore from the vaccinations and injections. Our luggage accumulated, and the time for sailing drew near. Back to South Africa House—still no visas.

"Still no word," they said. . . .

"I'll gladly pay for telephone calls through to the Capetown office," I said.

Another few days, and still no visa.

Then Paul and I took counsel.

"They're not going to give us visas," I said. "I recognize the runaround in this 'still no word' business."

We were angry, frustrated.

I said, "They will have to tell me no, and why, before I give up."

"So they will tell you no," said Paul, "and then you can't go."

"But I've got to go," I said. "Pauli and I will just get on that ship, with or without visas. When we get there, all they can do is to refuse to let us land. If they do that, I'll set up a howl there, and you can set up a real howl here, and then maybe they'll do something."

"It sounds crazy," said Paul, "just crazy enough to work. The worst that can happen is that you'll miss South Africa and have to go right on up the east coast without stopping off."

Cooks' said I couldn't sail without visas. It just wasn't done.

"But we've got visas," I said, waving our passports. "Swaziland, Basutoland, Bechuanaland, Kenya, Uganda, Egypt."

"Well—" said Cooks'.

"Well," I said firmly, "we'll go, and if necessary we'll just have to miss South Africa."

# Richard Wright,
## 1909–1960

Richard Wright was born in Mississippi and, after living in many urban areas of the Deep South, ran away from home. Like so many Negroes of his time, Wright migrated to Chicago. His first best seller, *Native Son*, deals with the problem of the urban southern Negroes living in the north. Largely self-taught, Wright, a strong protest writer, deeply felt the problems of American Negroes and sought active solutions, first by joining the Communist Party and finally by leaving this country and becoming a citizen of France, where he died.

As with many Negroes seriously concerned with their situation in America, Wright ultimately turned to Africa. He played an important part in the development of the literary journal, *Presence Africaine*, published in Paris by the Society of African Culture, which he also helped to organize, and in the First International Conference of Negro Intellectuals held in Paris in 1956. As a logical consequence of this African interest and involvement, Wright went to Africa in 1953 to visit Ghana. Like many other American Negroes who are deeply committed to Africa, Wright was not prepared for the reality of Africa. Too long perhaps had he indulged in dreams and fantasies about Africa, or, having suffered so much in the real world of whites, expected too much from the real world of blacks. The open letter to Kwame Nkrumah is at the end of *Black Power*, prophetically perhaps Wright's last well-known work, and it reflects his reactions to Africa as the answer to the Negro problem as he felt it.

# Open Letter to Kwame Nkrumah*

## Richard Wright

Dear Kwame Nkrumah:

My journey's done. My labors in your vineyard are over. The ship that bears me from Africa's receding shore holds a heart that fights against those soft, sentimental feelings for the sufferings of our people. The kind of thinking that must be done cannot be done by men whose hearts are swamped with emotion.

While roaming at random through the compounds, market places, villages, and cities of your country, I felt an odd kind of at-home-ness, a solidarity that stemmed not from ties of blood or race, or from my being of African descent, but from the quality of deep hope and suffering embedded in the lives of your people, from the hard facts of oppression that cut across time, space, and culture. I must confess that I, an American Negro was filled with consternation at what Europe had done to this Africa. . . .

Yet, as grim as the picture is, its grimness is somewhat relieved by the fact that African conditions are not wholly unique. The suffering that your people bear has been borne triumphantly before, and your fellow countrymen have shared that burdensome experience of having had their destinies dictated by alien powers, from above, an experience that has knit together so many of the world's millions in a common consciousness, a common cause.

Kwame, let me put it bluntly: Western lay and academic circles utter many a hard saying against Africa. In defending their subjugation of Africa, they contend that Africa has no culture, no history, no background, etc. I'm not impressed by these gentlemen, lay or academic. In matters of history they have been more often wrong than right, and even when they have been right, it has been more by accident than design, or they have been right only after facts have already been so clearly established that not even a fool could go wrong.

I found only one intangible but vitally important element in the heritage of tribal culture that militated against cohesiveness of ac-

* Richard Wright, *Black Power*, pp. 342–351. Copyright © 1954 by Richard Wright and reprinted by permission of Harper and Row, publishers.

tion: African culture has not developed the personalities of the people to a degree that their egos are stout, hard, sharply defined; there is too much cloudiness in the African's mentality, a kind of sodden vagueness that makes for a lack of confidence, an absence of focus that renders that mentality incapable of grasping the workaday world. And until confidence is established at the center of African personality, until there is an inner reorganization of that personality, there can be no question of marching from the tribal order to the twentieth century. . . . At the moment, this subjective task is more important than economics!

Manifestly, as in all such situations, the commencement of the injection of this confidence must come from without, but it *cannot* and *will* not come from the West. (Let's hope I'm wrong about that!)

Have no illusions regarding Western attitudes. Westerners, high and low, feel that their codes, ideals, and conceptions of humanity do not apply to black men. If until today Africa was static, it was because Europeans deliberately wanted to keep her that way. They do not even treat the question of Africa's redemption seriously; to them it is a source of amusement; and those few Europeans who do manage to become serious about Africa are more often prompted by psychological reasons than anything else. The greatest millstone about the neck of Africa for the past three hundred years has been the psychologically crippled white seeking his own perverse personal salvation. . . .

Against this background one refrain echoes again and again in my mind: *You must be hard!* While in Africa one question kept hammering at me: Do the Africans possess the necessary hardness for the task ahead?

If the path that you and your people had to tread were an old and tried one, one worn somewhat smooth by the past trampings of many people; had Europe, during the past centuries, dealt with Africans differently, had they laid the foundations of the West so securely that the Africans could now hold Western values as basic assumptions—had all this happened, the question of "hardness" would not have presented itself to me. (I know that some Europeans are going to say: "Ah, look, a black man advocates stern measures for Africa! Didn't we tell you that they needed such as that?") But Kwame, the truth is that nothing could have been more brutally horrible than the "slow and sound" educational development that turned into a kind of teasing torture, which Europe has imposed so profitably upon Africa since the fifteenth century. . . .

The accomplishment of this change in the African attitude would be difficult under the best of circumstances; but to attain that goal in an Africa beset with a gummy tribalism presents a formidable problem: the psychological legacy of imperialism that lingers on represents the antithesis of the desired end; unlike the situations attending the eruptions of the masses in Russia, China, and India, you do not have the Western-educated Africans with you; in terms of mechanization, you must start from scratch; you have a populace ridden with a 90 per cent illiteracy; communication and transportation are poor....

Balancing these drawbacks are some favorable features: West Africa, thanks to climate, is predominantly *black!* You can pour a libation to the nameless powers that there are no white settlers to be driven out, no knotty land problem to be solved by knocking together the heads of a landed black bourgeoisie. And, though the cultural traditions of the people have been shattered by European business and religous interests, they were so negatively shattered that the hunger to create a *Weltanschauung* is still there, virginal and unimpaired.

If, amidst such conditions, you elect, at this late date in world's history, to follow the paths of social and political evolution such as characterize the history of the institutions of the Western powers, your progress will go at a snail's pace and both of your flanks will be constantly exposed and threatened.

On the other hand, just as you organized against the British, so will other Nkrumahs organize against you. What Nkrumah has done, other Nkrumahs can do. You have made promises to the masses; in your heart of hearts I know that you wish hotly to keep those promises, for you are sincere.... But suppose the Communists out-bid you? Suppose a sullen mood sets in? Would not that give the Communists *their* opportunity?

On the other hand, I cannot, as a man of African descent brought up in the West, recommend with good faith the agitated doctrines and promises of the hard-faced men of the West. Kwame, until they have set their houses in order with their own restless populations, until they have solved their racial and economic problems, they can never—no matter *what* they may say to you at any *given* moment!—deal honestly with you. Given the opportunity, they'll pounce at any time upon Africa to solve their own hard-pressing social and political problems, just as you well know that they have pounced in the past. And, also, I'm convinced that the cultural conditioning of the Africans will make it difficult for them to adjust quickly to values that are solely Western, values that have mocked and shamed

265

them so much in the past, values that go against the grain of so much in the African heart. . . . After all, you have already been down that road.

Your safety, your security lie in plunging full speed ahead!

But, how? What methods? Means? What instrumentalities? Ay, there's the rub. . . . The neurotically fluttering attempts of missionaries, the money lust of businessmen, the cool contempt of European soldiers and politicians, the bungling cynicism of statesmen splitting up families and cultures and indigenous national groupings at their pleasure—all of these have left the task of the redemption of Africa to you and yours, to us. . . . And what a task! What a challenge! What an opportunity for creation. . . !

One simple conviction stands straight up in me: Our people must be made to walk, forced draft, into the twentieth century! The direction of their lives, the duties that they must perform to overcome the stagnancy of tribalism, the sacrifices that must yet be made—all of this must be placed under firm social discipline!

I say to you publicly and frankly: The burden of suffering that must be borne, impose it upon *one* generation! Do not, with the false kindness of the missionaries and businessmen, drag out this agony for another five hundred years while your villages rot and your people's minds sink into the morass of a subjective darkness. . . . Be merciful by being stern! If I lived under your regime, I'd ask for this hardness, this coldness. . . .

Make no mistake, Kwame, they are going to come at you with words about democracy; you are going to be pinned to the wall and warned about decency; plump-faced men will mumble academic phrases about "sound" development; gentlemen of the cloth will speak unctuously of values and standards; in short, a barrage of concentrated arguments will be hurled at you to persuade you to temper the pace and drive of your movement. . . .

But you know as well as I that the logic of your actions is being determined by the conditions of the lives of your people. If, for one moment, you take your eyes off that fact, you'll soon be just another African in a cloth on the streets of Accra! You've got to find your *own* paths, your *own* values. . . . Above all, feel free to *improvise!* The political cat can be skinned in many fashions; the building of that bridge between tribal man and the twentieth century can be done in a score of ways. . . .

You might offer ideology as an instrument of organization; but, evidently, you have no basis for that in Africa at this time. You might, by borrowing money from the West, industrialize your people in a cash-and-carry system, but, in doing so, you will be but lifting them from tribal to industrial slavery, for tied to Western money is Western control, Western ideas. . . . Kwame, there is nothing on earth more afraid than a million dollars; and, if a million dollars means fear, a billion dollars is the quintessence of panic. . . .

Russia will not help you, unless you accept becoming an appendage of Moscow; and why should you change one set of white masters for another. . . ?

There is but one honorable course that assumes and answers the ideological, traditional, organizational, emotional, political, and productive needs of Africa at this time:

AFRICAN LIFE MUST BE MILITARIZED!

. . . not for war, but for peace; not for destruction, but for service; not for aggression, but for production; not for despotism, but to free minds from mumbo-jumbo.

I'm not speaking of a military dictatorship. You know that. I need not even have to say that to you, but I say it for the sake of others who will try to be naive enough to misconstrue my words. I'm speaking simply of a militarization of the daily, social lives of the people: I'm speaking of giving form, organization, direction, meaning, and a sense of justification to those lives. . . . I'm speaking of a temporary discipline that will unite the nation, sweep out the tribal cobwebs, and place the feet of the masses upon a basis of reality. I'm not speaking of guns or secret police; I'm speaking of a method of taking people from one order of life and making them face what men, all men everywhere, must face. What the Europeans failed to do, didn't want to do because they feared disrupting their own profits and global real estate, you must do.

Above all, Africans must be regimentalized for the "long pull," for what will happen in Africa will spread itself out over decades of time and a continent of space. . . . You know as well as I that what has happened in the Gold Coast is just the beginning; and there will be much marching to and fro; there will be many sunderings and amalgamations of people; there will be many shiftings and changes of aims, perspectives, and ideologies—there will be much confusion before the final redemption of Africa is accomplished. Do I sound gratuitously hard, cruel? How I wished I did not have to think of such measures! Yet, what could make such measures unnecessary? Only a West that could come forth and admit that it didn't do the job, that the job has to be done, and that it was willing to help you to do it. . . . Yet, I cannot conceive of the West acting in that manner, even though all the common sense of history, moral and material, is in favor of it. In its fight against Communism, Europe could bind Africa to her by such an act of help and understanding. . . . Of course, when this is pointed out to Westerners, they shrug their shoulders and say that they have timed African development according to their conceptions of what Africans can do; but, in saying this, they forget that they are not free to indulge in such fantasies. Western time today is being timed by another time; *Communist* time! It would seem that the issue of self-preservation alone would jolt Europeans out of their infantile dreams about Africa. . . .

And in exchange for aiding honest Africans to shake their people loose from their tribal moorings, the West could have all the raw materials it wanted, a larger market for its products. . . . And an Africa deliberately shaken loose from its traditional past would, for a time, be a more dependent Africa than the angry, aimless Africa of the present day. Such an Africa could menace nobody.

Why do I bring up the question of "menace"? Because the mere thought of a free Africa frightens many Europeans. Europeans do not and cannot look upon Africa objectively. Back of their fear of African freedom lies an ocean of *guilt!* In their hearts they know that they have long tried to murder Africa. . . . And this powerful Europe, with atom bombs in its hands, is haunted by visions of an eventual black revenge that has no basis in reality. It is this subjective factor, among others, that makes the West brutally determined to keep Africa on a short chain. . . .

Will the West come forward and head up these nationalist revolutions in Africa? No; it's a dream. If it comes true, I'd be the first to hail it. But since we cannot wait for dreams, let us turn to reality. . . . That is, the militarization of African life.

The basis, concrete and traditional, for the militarization of African life is there already in the truncated tribal structure. The ideological justification for such measures is simple survival; the military is but another name for fraternalization, for cohesiveness. And a military structure of African society can be used eventually for defense. Most important of all, a military form of African society will atomize the fetish-ridden past, abolish the mystical and nonsensical family relations that freeze the African in his static degradation; it will render impossible the continued existence of those parasitic chiefs who have long bled and misled a naive people; it is the one and only stroke that can project the African immediately into the twentieth century!

Over and above being a means of production, a militarized social structure can replace, for a time, the political; and it contains its own form of idealistic and emotional sustenance. A military form of life, of social relations, used as a deliberate bridge to span the tribal and the industrial ways of life, will free you, to a large extent, from begging for money from the West, and the degrading conditions attached to such money. A military form of life will enable you to use *people* instead of money for many things and on many occasions! And if your people knew that this military regime was for their freedom, for their safety, for the sake of their children escaping the domination of foreigners, they will make all the sacrifices called for.

Again I say: Would that Western understanding and generosity make these recommendations futile. . . . But if the choice is between traditional Western domination and this hard path, take the hard path!

Beware of a Volta Project built by foreign money. Build your own Volta, and build it out of the sheer lives and bodies of your people! With but limited outside aid, your people can rebuild your society with their bare hands. . . . Africa needs this hardness, *but only from Africans.*

You know as well as I know that politics alone is not enough for Africa. Keep the fires of passion burning in your movement; don't let Westerners turn you away from the only force that can, at this time, knit your people together. It's a secular religion that you must slowly create; it's that, or your edifice falls apart.

There will be those who will try to frighten you by telling you that the organization you are forging looks like Communism, Fascism, Nazism; but, Kwame, the form of organization that you need will be dictated by the needs, emotional and material, of your people. The content determines the form. Never again must the outside world decide what is good for you.

Regarding corruption: use fire and acid and cauterize the ranks of your party of all opportunists! *Now!* Corruption is the one single fact that strikes dismay in the hearts of the friends of African freedom. . . .

In your hands lies the first bid for African freedom and independence. Thus far you have followed an *African* path. I say: *So be it!* Whatever the West or East offers, take it, but don't let them take you. You have taken Marxism, that intellectual instrument that makes meaningful the class and commodity relations in the modern state; but the moment that that instrument ceases to shed meaning, drop it. Be on top of theory; don't let theory be on top of you. In short be *free*, be a living embodiment of what you want to give your people. . . .

269

You and your people need no faraway "fatherland" in either England or Russia to guide and spur you on; let your own destiny claim your deepest loyalty. You have escaped one form of slavery; be chary of other slaveries no matter in what guise they present themselves, whether as glittering ideas, promises of security, or rich mortgages upon your future.

There will be no way to avoid a degree of suffering, of trial, of tribulation; suffering comes to all people, but you have within your power the means to make the suffering of your people meaningful, to redeem whatever stresses and strains may come. None but Africans can perform this for Africa. And, as you launch your bold programs, as you call on your people for sacrifices, you can be confident that there are free men beyond the continent of Africa who see deeply enough into life to know and understand what you *must* do, what you *must* impose. . . .

You have demonstrated that tribes can be organized; you must now show that tribes can march socially! And remember that what you build will become a haven for other black leaders of the continent who, from time to time, long for rest from their tormentors. Gather quickly about you the leaders of Africa; you need them and they need you. Europe knows clearly that what you have achieved so far is not confined to the boundaries of the Gold Coast alone; already it has radiated outward and as long as the influence of your bid for freedom continues to inspire your brothers over the teeming forests of West Africa, you can know that the ball of freedom that you threw still rolls. . . .

With words as our weapons, there are some few of us who will stand on the ramparts to fend off the evildoers, the slanderers, the greedy, the self-righteous! You are not alone. . . .

Your fight has been fought before. I am an American and my country too was once a colony of England. . . It was old Walt Whitman who felt what you and your brother fighters are now feeling when he said:

*Suddenly, out of its stale and drowsy lair, the lair of slaves, like lightning it le'pt forth, half startled at itself, Its feet upon the ashes and rags—its hands tight to the throats of kings.*
*O hope and faith!*
*O aching close of exiled patriots' lives!*
*O many a sicken'd heart!*
*Turn back unto this day, and make yourself afresh.*
*And you, paid to defile the People! you liars, mark!*

*Not for numberless agonies, murders, lusts,*
*For court thieving in its manifold mean forms, worming from his*
*simplicity the poor man's wages,*
*For many a promise sworn by royal lips, and broken and laugh'd*
*at in the breaking.*
*Then in their power, not for all these, did the blows strike revenge,*
*or the heads of nobles fall;*
*The People scorn'd the ferocity of kings.*

NOTE: Quotation from poem by Walt Whitman in italics.

# Era Belle Thompson

Era Belle Thompson was born in Des Moines, Iowa. She received her B.A. degree from Morningside College in Sioux City, Iowa. In 1938 and 1940 she did postgraduate work in journalism at Northwestern University, and, after working from 1942 to 1947 as a senior interviewer of the United States and Illinois State Employment Service, she joined the Johnson Publishing Company as Associate Managing Editor. She is still an employee of that firm, which publishes *Ebony* and *Negro Digest*. In 1946 she published *American Daughter*, an autobiography written as a result of a fellowship received from the Newberry Library. In 1949 she was a Bread Loaf Writers' Conference fellow, and in 1953, to gather material for the Johnson Publishing Company, she was sent on a tour of Africa. The excerpt in this anthology, written on the basis of her experience on that trip, is taken from *Africa, Land of My Fathers*.

# Africa, Land of My Fathers*

## ERA BELLE THOMPSON

My African safari was prompted by the same desire that prompts other Americans to return to Europe and Asia to visit their "Old Country", or that of their parents or grandparents. I, too, wanted to return to the land of my forefathers, to see if it is as dark and as hopeless as it has been painted and to find how it would receive a prodigal daughter who had not been home for three hundred years. And I wanted to know what my own reactions would be to my African ancestors. . . .

Africa! The strange "Dark Continent", the land of my fathers. And I was coming home. . . .

Until a few months before, Africa had been the last place on earth I wanted to visit. Until a few years before, my knowledge of the

272

continent, like that of most Americans, both black and white, was geared to concepts handed down by Livingstone and Stanley nearly a hundred years ago. And like most American Negroes, I was so busy shedding my African heritage and fighting for my rights as an American citizen that what happened to my 175,000,000 brothers beyond the sea was a matter for the missionaries. Had anyone called me an African I would have been indignant. Only race fanatics flaunted their jungle ancestry or formed back-to-Africa movements—and they were usually motivated more by a king complex than by any loyalty to black genes.

When I saw bare-toed African students walking down Chicago boulevards in their flowing robes and colorful head cloths, I, too, shook my head and murmured, "My people!" If there was the skeleton of a chief in my family closet, he was Cherokee, not Kru; Black Foot, not Yoruba or Fulani. I was proud of my red and white blood, ashamed of the black, for I grew up believing that black was bad, that black was dirty and poor and wrong. Black was Africa. I did not want to be an African. . . .

My first reaction to my aborigine brothers was negative. I was especially loath to accept the half-naked man with the mop of fuzzy red hair, and the bony old ladies who squatted beside foul-smelling shops with their withered bosoms exposed. . . .

As startling as was the nudity, and as pathetic the obvious poverty, what surprised me most were the Syrian and Lebanese proprietors behind the counters. It was a black man's country, but there was the same lack of business leadership found in the Negro neighbourhoods in the States. Even the better-class stores on the hill were owned mostly by white immigrants and staffed by white clerks. . . . The question of white monopoly over a black country's business was a sore one, I soon found. . . .

In this country (Nigeria), I could stop worrying about the black folks and start wondering how the white folks fared. There were only a handful of them, less than 10,000 in fact, and only 4,000 in Lagos against 230,000 Africans. Here, as in Liberia, there were no white settlers. Only Africans were allowed to own property. Nigerians frowned on exclusive organizations, so for whites to segregate themselves would be neither popular nor easy, as they lived in many sections of the city. Furthermore, they never had long to stay in Nigeria, coming as they did on two- or three-year assignments. With so few whites, there were few intermarriages, and when one did occur, the average citizen did not think much about it one way or another. . . .

I was resentful of the superior attitude Europeans displayed toward "My People", but was also flattered by the deference shown me because of my American citizenship. I had been leaning heavily on my nationality, lightly upon my race. But I was coming "home" to Africa. I was coming back to re-establish ties of kinship, not to sever them. Liberia and Nigeria had removed many of my inherent prejudices against Africans, but years of propaganda and ridicule built up against a people is not dissolved in three weeks. Neither is the habit of imitation. . . .

I found Accra disappointing. It lacked the robust progressiveness of Lagos and the friendliness of Monrovia. . . . Business here, too, was predominantly in white hands. Syrians controlled the grocery stores, Indians the dry goods business, and the large concerns were owned by Britons, Swiss and French. Africans were strong in the professions, with the accent on law. . . .

The Gold Coast had objected to my entrance. It had rejected me as a friend or distant relative. The people of Kumasi and Sekondi had been kind, but I was leaving Accra a stranger. . . .

I had not intended to conduct a seminar on the North American Negro; nor had I meant to sit in arbitration on Congo grievances, but my audience had cornered a runaway sister and was determined not to let her go until they had at least some of the answers to their problems. A few exploratory questions revealed that their chief contact with Stateside Negroes had been limited to GI's who had joined our Belgian allies during World War II. They could count the Negro visitors to their land on the fingers of their two hands. . . .

The leader rustled his papers impatiently, then asked, through the interpreter, "Why do you not send us black missionaries?"

American Negro Missionaries, I told them, are no longer admitted to the Congo.

"Why does not our brother come to teach us the things they have learned in America, how to operate our business or to farm our land?" . . .

Remembering what the clerks had said about segregation, I wondered if I would have been permitted to ride up front had I been dressed as an African. And remembering what the clerks had asked about American Negroes wanting to be white, I wondered what kinds of names my brothers back there were calling me. . . .

Early next morning the caretaker drove me to the airport. Just before I got out of the car, I asked him why he had assigned me to the room downstairs when there were much nicer vacant rooms upstairs.

"The missionaries", he answered quietly, "told me." . . .

Charles played the host, half-heartedly, then sat down beside his advisor and lapsed again into his immobile self. I joined the two as we sipped red wine from crystal glasses, for I wanted to know more about these wonderful people, relatives or not. That Rosalie did not care for me was evident, but of Charles I could not be sure. If he looked at me at all, it was with the same sloe-eyed indifference with which he regarded other guests. There is a wider gulf between themselves and the Bahutu, so the Watutsi say, than there is between the Belgians and the Africans. And the gulf between the Watutsi and me seemed even wider. . . .

To the Africans, as to farmers from Alabama to Montana, the arrival of the train was an event. All ages greeted the passengers or just stood grinning up at the coaches. They ignored me completely. Housedresses were quite common among the women, nearly all of whom were in some stage of pregnancy. More men and women wore shoes here; but despite the increasing cold, babies went stark naked, with nothing but their string of belly beads to keep them warm. White men took on a thick-legged ruggedness, sun-red beneath white shorts, hairy-faced beneath white sun helmets. . . .

Two months in Africa had made me feel more at home in the air than on land, and far more welcome. Up there I was not harassed by customs and immigration officials. I was always sure of accommodations and courtesy from the crew, regardless of their nationality or the airlines company or the country I was in. And there was a peace of mind above the earth that dwarfed even the problems of Africa. . . .

Our first stop was an African hut on the edge of a coconut forest. A boy, about seven, and three small children were playing in the yard. A woman came out of the house and tried to talk with me. When a chicken came between us, I backed away because I have a phobia about feathers. That made the woman laugh and her kids laughed too.

As a repatriated African, I was doing just fine! Could not swim, was afraid of a chicken, and did not even speak the language of my people. I had been a member of a majority race, now for two whole months, and frankly I had never had it so bad. Homeland, indeed!

I had started out on my African journey in the West, looking for blood ties between the American Negro and his African cousin. I had wanted to know what it would be like to come "home". So far I had been given the full treatment. I had met with everything from the open arms of Liberia to barred doors in Zanzibar. The return of this native was quickening into a rout. . . .

Nairobi was disappointingly peaceful. Africans, Asians and Europeans went about their business without friction. The tension headlined in newspapers all over the world was certainly not apparent on the surface. I saw only one civilian whose gun was showing, a European farmer whose revolver butt was visible under the tail of his jacket as he bent over in the post office to tie his shoe. The Native Reserve had rifles strapped so firmly to their backs that I wondered how they would ever get to them come an emergency. The only evidence of extra precautionary methods was the barbed wire that hemmed in the police barracks to protect ammunition from Mau Mau raiders. All Kikuyu prisoners had been removed to compounds outside of town. . . .

Uganda was another British protectorate with a paternalistic attitude towards its black subjects, but it had no white settlers. I should not have trouble here, but I knew from recent experience that even such favorable elements had little bearing on the way in which I, an American Negro, might be received. Zanzibar was a protectorate, Mozambique was paternalistic, and there were no white settlers in the Gold Coast. Yet, in all three countries, I was in various degrees rebuffed. So it was with much of the old feeling of apprehension that I approached Kampala. . . .

Yes, I had traversed the length and breadth of Africa, seeking a bond between the American Negro and his African brother; but the African, I found, knows even less about us than we do about him. And small wonder.

Some three hundred years ago we sailed away in slave ships and few of us have returned. Until World War II, when some of our GI's were stationed there, and Africans were sent abroad to fight, few Africans had ever seen a real live American Negro. Even in English-speaking countries, practically no news of us seeps through to their world. In the Union of South Africa, Negro publications—and Negroes—are barred. Few American Negroes travel as far as Africa, and when they do, their destination is usually the west coast. The only Negroes who have the means and inclination to venture farther into the interior are missionaries (and in many sections they are now barred), an occasional State Department representative on a prescribed tour, or a research student looking for the same primitiveness white research students are looking for.

But to those Africans who do have knowledge of us, the bond is real—the blood thick. Come home, they say, all is forgiven. We need your skill and your capital to help us develop the land that we have and to regain the land that has been taken from us.

And how do I feel, now, about them?

I am proud of the African blood in my veins and proud of my black heritage, for I have seen evidences of that ancient African civilization in the excavations of Ife, and I have talked with black kings who are the descendants of African conquerors, and I have walked in the streets of a black kingdom whose Christianity is among the oldest in the world.

Africans are my brothers, for we are of one race. But Africa, the land of my fathers, is not my home.

I am an American—an American by nationality, a citizen of the United States by birth. I owe my loyalty and my allegiance to but one flag. I have but one country.

# Horace Mann Bond, 1894–

Horace Mann Bond was born in Nashville, Tennessee. He was graduated from Lincoln University and received the M.A. and Ph.D. degrees from the University of Chicago. All of his professional life has been spent in Negro universities: Lanston University, Alabama State College, Fisk University, Dillard University, Fort Valley State College, Lincoln University, and Atlanta University. His interest in Africa was most clearly manifest from 1945 to 1957 during his years as president of Lincoln University where he was in a position to know and help many African students who attended that university. Dr. Bond was the first president of the American Society of African Culture. He has been invited to Africa many times as the guest of outstanding African leaders, and he was a member of the special education committee of the University of Ghana which met in December, 1960. He is the author of *The Education of the Negro in the American Social Order*, *Education in Alabama: A Study in Cotton and Steel*, and *Education for Production*. This selection, "The Ram and the Thicket," was an address delivered by Dr. Bond at the Third Conference of the American Society of African Culture.

## Howe and Isaacs in the Bush: The Ram in the Thicket*

### HORACE MANN BOND

*Dean, School of Education*
*Atlanta University, Atlanta, Georgia*

### I

On May 13, 1961, the *New Yorker* magazine published a long (12,000 word) essay by Harold Isaacs, self-advertised as a "special"

---

* Unpublished statement distributed at the Conference of the American Society of African Culture, New York, 1960, and reprinted by kind permission of the author.

inquirer for the Massachusetts Institute of Technology's Center for International Studies, under the title, "Back to Africa". On June 22, 1961, the *Reporter* magazine published an article by Russell Warren Howe, advertised as a reporter for "American, British, and Indian" newspapers. Howe's subject was, "Strangers in Africa".

Both articles had remarkably parallel themes. Africans did not like American Negroes, and American Negroes did not like Africans. American Negroes were mis-fits in Africa, and Africans did not identify themselves with American Negroes.

Howe succinctly stated the inescapable conclusion of the matter: ". . . the policy of using a large number of American Negroes in African jobs is dangerous for all concerned—the employer, the usually discontented or disenchanted Negro, the natives, and the United States." And Howe immediately puts the clincher on this conclusion by pointing to the long practice of missionary bodies. "The U.S. Protestant Missions, who live with 'their' tribes and know them better than British or French colonial administrators, have never encouraged Negro missionaries."

Howe's statement is written with the pontifical certitude one expects from journalists, if not from "special" inquirers on assignment from a university center of supposedly reputable "research". Isaacs' generalizations are no less confident; true specimens of the *ex cathedra* style of the true pundit. But the statement quoted from Howe's article may, in its naive revelation of an arrogant ignorance, be taken as characteristic of the way in which both articles reach extremely questionable conclusions, on the basis of "facts" that are not *facts*.

As a matter of fact, United States Protestant Missions *did* encourage American Negroes to go to Africa, from as early as 1774, to about 1910. They did so, first, on the original theory that African slavery in the American colonies, and later in the United States, was in fact a part of the providential design by which Africa was destined to be evangelized. Two Gold Coast seamen, resettled in Newport, Rhode Island, were sent to Princeton in 1774 to be educated for future service in Africa; they were the first of a long series of efforts by United States Protestant Missions to give the theory concrete realization.

This idea of "Providence" was reinforced when white missionaries began to experience the frightful mortality characteristic for such persons in Africa before quinine came into general use as a malaria preventative, and before modern anti-malarials and anti-biotics were discovered. The major United States Protestant Missions thought that Negroes enjoyed a racial immunity to malaria; and without exception encouraged the recruiting of Negro missionaries. Even in the South, the Southern Baptists, Presbyterians, and Methodists made heroic efforts to recruit Negroes; Bishop William Taylor, of the Northern Methodists, developed a grandiose scheme in the 1880's for chains of "self-supporting" missions in Africa, and the backbone of the plan was to recruit Negro missionaries in Southern Negro colleges.

This period ended about 1910, as Wilber C. Horr showed in his 1945 University of Chicago doctoral dissertation on the subject, *The Negro as an American Protestant Missionary in Africa*. Provoked by numerous evidences that American Negro missionaries were only *too* successful in identifying with Africans, the various colonial governments reached unwritten, but iron-clad agreements with the governing mission Boards of United States Protestant missions, to tolerate American missions only so long as the Boards promised *not* to send American Negroes. The American Negro missionary was widely suspected, and with reason, as a threat to the colonial regimes. In South Africa, missionaries of the (Negro American) African Methodist Episcopal Church were accused of fomenting various uprisings; in Nyasaland, John Chilembwe, educated and supported by American Negro Baptists, who had also sent several missionaries to assist him, actually led an abortive revolt against the white settlers and government. In the Congo, William H. Shepard, an Alabama Negro who had been sent to Africa by the Southern White Presbyterians, and had become their prized foreign missionary, was tried on the charge of libelling King Leopold when he attacked Belgian colonial methods and their accompanying atrocities, and set free only when he was withdrawn by his supporting church. As Horr, and the Scotch historian, George Shepperson, have shown, American Negro missionaries were permitted to operate freely only in Angola, and Liberia. Elsewhere, the Belgian, French, and British governments used every device to exclude them; by refusing visas, by ordering steamship lines not to sell them tickets, and, as noted above, by collusion with United States Protestant churches not to appoint them.

Yet, Howe sustains now, in 1961, his argument that the use of American Negroes in Africa "is dangerous for all concerned", by citing "The U.S. Protestant Missions, who live with 'their' tribes and know them better than British or French colonial administrators, and who have never encouraged Negro missionaries."

For fifty years, United States Protestant missionaries had also to "live with" colonial administrations in daily fear of African revolution. Long ago, the big American Mission Boards decided that it was better to live with the colonialists, than to hire American Negro missionaries.

As is true of the journalist, Howe, the "special" inquirer, Isaacs, is given to making absolute statements that are so obviously untrue that one shudders at the thought of how anyone in his intelligent, supposedly scholarly mind, would put such *erratica* in print. "Africans", writes Isaacs sententiously, "scornfully reject the term 'Negro' ". American Negroes, he says, are distressed to discover "That in Africa 'Negro' is someone with a stigma. African rejection of the term 'Negro' is part of the assertion of African superiority over Negroes."

It happens that in 1949, I was the guest of the African Academy of Arts and Research in what turned into a triumphal tour of Nigeria. My principal host was Kingsley Ozuomba Mbadiwe, who was, and is, a most masterful adept at public relations. I had, at Mbadiwe's request, written out a biography; I had designedly billed myself, as the "first person of African descent" to become President of Lincoln University. My self-made publicity flier was, in most cases, faithfully followed in the numerous scrolls of official greetings handed to me in each of the communities I visited; I personally prefer the term, "person of African descent", as a basis for establishing international relations with Africans, by other persons of African descent throughout the world, in preference to the parochial term, "American Negro".

Hence, I was surprised to note that my favored phrase had been discarded, time after time, by the local scribes, who had substituted for my grandiloquent "person of African descent", the word: "Negro!" This was in widely separated places such as Lagos; Ibadan; Benin; Ohafia; Onitsha; Sapele; and Enugu. I have brought several of these examples of Isaac's "scornful rejection," by Africans, of the word "Negro".

But if 1949 is too long ago—things changing in Africa so rapidly—let me cite an instance that transpired on January 7, 1961, during a meeting of the Commission on University Education for Ghana, at the University College at Legon. I have a cloud of witnesses among the other members of the Commission who were present, when a delegation of the African members of the Faculty came to wait upon us: Laura Bornholdt, then of the University of Pennsylvania; Professor Torocheshnikov, of Moscow; Davidson Nicol, of Fourah Bay, Sierra Leone; Professor Evans-Pritchard, the renowned

Oxford anthropologist; Professor J. D. Bernal, of Birkbeck College of the University of London; Daniel Chapman, Headmaster of the Achimota School; Kojo Botsio, then Minister of Agriculture, Chairman of the Commission; Thomas Hodgkin, of the School of Arabic Studies at McGill, and Nana Nketsia, Oxford D. Phil., co-secretaries of the Commission.

We entertained that afternoon a delegation consisting of the foremost academic lights among the African faculty of the University College. They had come to present their case for an accelerated program of Africanization in the Staff. The spokesman was a distinguished member of the Law Faculty, and a man prominent in the higher circles of the Convention People's Party.

Although pleading for "Africanization", he used the word: "Negro!"

"We *Negroes* in this Faculty," he began, "are being discriminated against. When vacancies occur, invariably we find that Europeans are the ones finally selected in the higher posts, although highly competent *Negroes* are candidates for the job. We *Negroes*. . . . We Negroes. . . ."

Doubtless Isaacs—and Howe—have a ready explanation for this performance; one that will still prove the "scornful rejection"— by Africans—of the term "Negro".

My own explanation is, that Howe, and Isaacs, as interpreters of African opinions and attitudes toward American Negroes, are strictly in, of, and from, the Bush; and this, in all of the African, American, and American Negro meanings of the word.

II

There is, supposedly, a difference in the "method" of study by which the two authors, Howe, and Isaacs, have arrived at their findings. Howe is the admitted journalist; that is to say, the man who arrives at the right to issue encyclicals by the Divine Right of his craft— that sees all, knows all (except some simple historical facts), and therefore can tell all.

Isaacs, on the other hand, is a "social scientist". At the Massachusetts Institute of Technology, and particularly in the Center for International Studies, there appears to have been perfected a new technique for gauging opinion through "sampling interviews". A selected number of subjects are exposed to "depth interviews", which means two or three hours of intensive questioning. A bit of word-association technique is thrown in and a dash of the psycho-analytic "free-flow" recall-lying-in-the-couch methodology is added. Presto! One has it.

If one wants a fairly immediate index as to what "the Negro" is thinking (or has thought), one selects fifty Negro "Leaders" who stand as surrogates for *all* Negro leaders, and, indeed, for all Negroes. You make an appointment with each, in turn; you ask them searching questions; you *probe*! And the man, or woman, tells you their guts—aided by a few search questions and suggestions. Afterward you assemble your notes, you add a few interpretations nicely selected from Freud, Adler, Jung, or what have you; and the thing is done, the mission accomplished, and you know!

One of the great difficulties with this method, of course, is always the selection of a proper sample. Howe, as a journalist, makes no pretension of "disguising" his examples; although two of them are non-existent unless so heavily "disguised" as to be practically unrecognizable. When, for example, he speaks of two American Negro "executives" of an "oil company", it may categorically be stated that no such animals exist in Africa. Likewise, when Howe tells the affecting story of the African affection for the sympathetic English headmaster who visited Africans and drank palm wine with them, while his American Negro successor did not, the internal evidence permits us to recognize the story as a Fictionalized figment of Howe's journalistic imagination. Howe quotes ". . . a West African teacher whose school now has an American principal under the technical assistance program . . ." who had succeeded an "English" headmaster; if the officer was an "English Headmaster", this had to be some country with a British system of education. There is absolutely no American Negro serving as "principal" of *any* West African secondary school in *any* British colony, or former colony; this may be said categorically, George Johnson is "principal" at the University of Nigeria at Nsukka, but he is the First, as the University began with him. Furthermore, if it were in the only other country conceivable—Liberia—there would have been no "English *Headmaster*", and besides, the American ground rules for technical assistance, even in Liberia, require that the "headmaster" *or* "principal" be a national of the country aided by our technical assistance, while the American operated *only* in a counter-part capacity as an advisor; but never as "principal". In short: Howe's style of selection requires the introduction of fictional characters in a fictional situation, and the assurance with which he speaks rests on the ease with which one can deceive the ignorant American reader of the *Reporter*.

As for Isaacs: the cast of characters of his semi-scientific story reminds one of those old theatre crowd scenes, where several ranks of soldiers dissappear through one wing, while the flow continues unabated from the other. In this way you make a squad seem to be an army. This is the Isaacs' method. By actual count, there are 32 members of Isaacs' cast, African, and American Negroes. However, Isaacs' happy method permits him to explain, in his introductory paragraph, that ". . . in my account of these conversations I will use no names and will blur places while I try not to blur what these individuals had to say".

The process of "blurring" results in a curious dwindling of specifics as Isaacs gets into the body of his story. The original cast of 32 includes 27 persons identified as "American Negroes". But when one realizes that Subject No. 7—"an American Negro who is now a permanent resident in Africa"—is also Subject No. 14—one of "the older hands among the American Negroes"; who is also Subject No. 17—the "young man who regards himself as a permanent settler"; who is also Subject No. 26, ". . . one young man who had left America for good, he said, some eight years ago," in short, that all these different sources are all one and the same "subject", the sample becomes less impressive. Likewise, Subject No. 5 is also Subject No. 27; the same young man "who had come to Africa to see", and "had come to find out". Subject 23 is also Subject 24, and the only instance where it is stated that the same subject is being quoted twice. One cannot help but wonder if "the tan American girl in Guinea", the "dark-skinned American", the "very dark American girl", and the "two young American Negroes in Senegal" are not, likewise, doubling, tripling, or even quadruplicating in brass—or should we say ebony? Thus we are led to suspect, that Subject No. 8—"one of these wives" —may also be Subject No. 9—"a woman of great character"; or, almost certainly, Subject No. 25, where a "young American woman describes the views of her Ghanaian husband and her friends".

Incidentally, Isaacs' reference to the "tan American girl in Guinea" reminds me of the "tan American girl" *I* met in Conakry first, and, later, in Accra. There was no question but that Africans liked her, and she, them; her only regret was that the Africans did not have enough money to pay her prices, and so, she was principally obliged to permit Europeans to patronize her, as she floated—trim and demure—down the Coast to Freetown, Monrovia, and then to Accra where I saw her again. I am sorry Isaacs missed her, if, indeed, he did; she had a better story to tell about international relations in West Africa, than M.I.T.'s Center could possibly match.

Indeed, I regret that Isaacs did not resurrect the interview he did of me several years ago, when he was studying the reactions of Negro leaders. Perhaps he did not, because I told him at the time that I thought the interviewing technique nonsensical, especially with Negro subjects; and I asked him not to quote his interview with me.

This was, I said, because Negroes—American and African—are a notoriously polite people; especially when they deal with white people. The late Dr. Robert E. Park, sometimes professor of Sociology at the University of Chicago, somewhat shocked all of us in his Seminar, "The Negro in the Old World", one day in 1924, when he said: "The Negro is the lady of the races; delicately proportioned, small boned, devoted to the arts of music and the dance, with exquisite manners, the utmost in politeness; she cannot bear to hurt anyone's feelings."

Over the years, I have come to appreciate Park's description of the people so named that were, in those days, popularly believed to be the "true Negro", who lived on the coasts of West Africa. Whether in Africa, or in America, it is a people who are agonized at the mere thought of giving hurt to the sensibilities of an acquaintance. (In this respect, at least, I must confess a savage, non-Negroid absence of the trait!)

The Negro—I told Isaacs—knows exactly what is in the mind of a white man, when that white man "probes him" with a "depth interview". He has an acute sensibility as to what his guest believes, and what his guest wishes to hear by way of confirmation of his own already-set convictions. And so this excessively polite man, reluctant to give pain by disagreeing, tells the white man precisely what that white man wishes to hear.

This, in my opinion, is the fatal defect of the M.I.T. technique, as applied by Isaacs to African, and American Negroes.

Had my testimony been admissible, there are many reflections that I would like to pass on to the readers of the New Yorker, and of the Reporter. Principally, to the tales of African brutality to servants, I would like to suggest prolonged exposure to living in many—not one—African homes; and not the hotels and guest houses that are the usual lot of the traveller.

For years, it was my custom, to get off the plane at Ikeja Airport in Lagos, and take a cab, wholly unannounced and unexpected, to the first home I found in that city on my first visit in 1949. This was the compound of the wealthy contractor, Chief Biney, an "expatriate" from the then-Gold Coast, who is a kinsman of Kwame Nkrumah.

Chief Biney would greet me, show me to a room, and let me alone. When I had leisure, I would wander around the compound on my own; through Chief Biney's private Zoo, where many a Nigerian child saw, for the first time, tigers, lions, crocodiles, and an occasional gorilla; out back, to the stables where the Chief kept his string of race horses; but principally, among the houses in the Compound itself, where Chief Biney's retainers lived.

They had a favorite game; it was a draughts game using twenty men on a side, that I have seen played in the United States only at the Negro college I attended, and in such cities as New Orleans, Mobile, Natchez, and Montgomery, Alabama. I liked to find a match, and join it; and, on winning, declare myself the Champion of West Africa, as once, years before, I had crowned myself the Champion of my College.

Brutality to servants?—Many of the "servants" were, in fact, members of Chief Biney's enormous "extended family"; as are, indeed, many African menages.

The African homes in which *I* have stayed (and since my earliest trip, in contrast to former visitors who were entertained by European officials, I have made it a practice to live in African homes, unless a hotel was officially necessary), have been the most harmoniously organized living communities in which I have ever been— Greene Mbadiwe's Day Spring House at Enugu, Nigeria; the house of my old student, Vincent Ikeotyuonye, Headmaster of Zixton Grammar School, near Orlu, Eastern Nigeria; the home of the Minister of Foreign Affairs, Ghana's Ako Adjei; here even the Muslim Chauffeur from Salt Pond was thoroughly "integrated" in this Presbyterian household; and he grew positively excited when he learned that I was an American Negro, and told me: "American Negroes, they have begun the insurance company where I have a policy. American Negroes are honest people! Before them, a poor man could not get insurance; Europeans are no good for Africans."

III

Following the free-association method, a person reared on the daily bread of the Old Testament cannot avoid connecting the name of Isaacs with that of Abraham—and the happy remembrance of how

God in the nick of time, sent the Ram in the Thicket as his token of appreciation for Abraham's faith.

Articles like those of Howe and Isaacs do not just happen, by coincidence. They were, of course, commissioned. The fact that two editors of two such magazines should, at the same time, feel the necessity to commission two such articles—the main burden of which is an alleged "mutual prejudice" between American Negroes, and Africans, is a revelation of something deeper than the current interest in Africa. Obviously, the editors knew that an avid public would welcome such articles; and so, they commissioned them to be written to supply the waiting market. Themes: Negroes don't like Africans, Africans don't like Negroes; there is mutual prejudice between them, it is dangerous to send American Negroes to Africa.

It is not difficult to see that there must be a powerful public feeling, that it *is* dangerous to send Negroes to Africa; and that, whether true or not, American Negroes *ought* to dislike Africans, and vice versa. This is one of the oldest of American stereotypes; and linked to it, is the deep-seated folk-thought, that America must be a better place than Africa, and that every-one here—including persons of African descent—just *must* prefer America to the land of the blacks. In 1858, a Northern "liberal" visited Charleston, South Carolina, to collect material for a book he later published as a comment on Slavery, under the title, *Life and Liberty in America*. The proper Charlestonians gave Reverend Mackey the full treatment. He was taken a few miles from the city, to see General James Gadsden's great plantation, "Pimlico".

On hand, as one of the stock experiences used to regale Northern visitors, was a venerable old Negro, who had been born in Africa, and was now retired from all labor. To the visitor's astonishment, when brought face to face with "Uncle Tom", the old Negro burst into imploring tears, asking the visitor please, please, not to send him back to Africa, breaking into happy chuckles only when solemnly reassured by General Gadsden, that the visitor, indeed, had no intention really of freeing him so that he could go back to Africa.

You find this story or its cousin in all of the magnolia and tuberose treacle novels of the Old South; and you find it, today, as an inveterate part of the mental equipment of a great many Americans. In 1949, I was returning by plane from my tour of Nigeria, that through the propaganda magic of Mbadiwe had truly been turned into a triumphal journey in honor of the "African brother"—the "Negro" —who had returned from overseas to greet his African—his Negro— brethren.

287

On the plane was a cameraman employed by the Southern Baptists, who had been making a film of mission work as part of the fund-raising activities, at home, of the Southern Baptists. We talked for hours about Africa, the Negro in America, and the future of both continents.

On one point his mind was made-up. There was, he said, no identification of the African with the American Negro. They had, he said, nothing in common; and he should know, having just completed a tour of fifteen thousand miles through Southern Baptist mission schools in Nigeria, the Camerouns, and the Congo.

I was too polite to argue with him.

But the notion of American Negro "disenchantment" with Africa; of the "deep pool of mistrust and prejudice" between Africans, and American Negroes, is the Ram in the Thicket. Isaacs unconsciously betrays a hint of it when, speaking of Elmina, the slave castle, where he says the African guide had no interest or information about its uses for the slave trade (the guides told me all about it in 1949, in 1952, in 1953, in 1957 and 1961 when *I* saw Elmina), he says: "I had the small but faintly consoling thought that *my* ancestors, whatever other sins they might have been committing at the time, were sequestered in some Eastern European ghetto, and could not have been among the slavers who waited out there on those ships."

Well, one never knows. The early Sephardic Jews of Charleston, Mobile, and New Orleans, were not ones to let a good thing go by the boards, entirely in default to their Christian fellow-traders. Jacob Cohen was well established as an importer of Africans in Charleston, long before 1807, when the Trade officially came to an end—but not unofficially; and the three Jewish sires of the Cohens, B. Mordecai, and A. J. Salinas, held, in 1859, rank among the ten leading slave-traders of this veritable Capitol of the traffic. Before, the Sephardim and the Ashkenazim of the Hanse and Dutch cities had no insignificant part in the conduct of the slave trade on the Western African Coast.

But the mere confession of the need for consolation reveals the shadows of the Ram in the Thicket; the guilt-fears, the wished for hopes; "They don't like each other, why should we"; and the need for a scapegoat, shared by the editors and the readers of America's most sophisticated magazines.

Isaacs—and Howe—have reported from the Bush; the Ram is still in the Thicket.

# PART IV

# Negro Self-Identity and Pan-Africanism

During the late nineteenth and early twentieth centuries the small intelligentsia among Negro Americans became actively concerned with assisting African development through co-operation between the New World and Old World Negro communities. Initially this concern was cast in the missionary terms of Christianity; the Christian doctrine and church were considered valid mechanisms for assisting the cultural and technological modernization of African societies. The Negro American educated groups were themselves thoroughly committed to Christian doctrine and practice and, therefore, considered it natural that Christianity be used to forge co-operation between themselves and Negro Africans for purposes of Pan-Negro modernization.

Basic to this outlook was the assumption, adopted by Negro American educated elements from white Americans, that Christianity was a superior form of religious expression and organization. For instance, Thomas Fortune, the able and influential editor of the *New York Age*, a Negro newspaper, was explicit about this: "The Christian religion is destined to supplant all other religious systems of belief, because it is the best code of moral philosophy ever given to man as an inspiration or as a development, an evolution of the social life of a people." Thomas Fortune was not unique in holding this view, for other leading Negro American intellectuals expressed it, and the African work of Negro American bodies like the A.M.E. and A.M.E.Z. churches and Tuskegee Institute reflected this outlook. Perhaps W. E. B. DuBois, viewing Christianity with some disdain, was the only member of this group of educated Negroes who approached the problems of Pan-Negro modernization in purely secular terms.

In West Africa, on the other hand, the most effective spokesmen of Pan-Negro thought among the emergent African intelligentsia were generally critical of Christian institutions as instruments for Negro modernization. For instance, J. E. Casely-Hayford, the founder of the National Congress of British West Africa in 1920 and an eminent Ghanaian lawyer at the turn of this century, bemoaned the Negro American's loss of his cultural ties with basically African religions. In comparison with the Jew's religious ties to Palestine, Hayford believed, "the African in America is in a worse plight than the Hebrew in Egypt. The one preserved his language, his manners and customs, his religion and household gods; the other has committed national [cultural] suicide, and at present it seems as if the dry bones of the vision have no life in them."

Whereas Hayford merely lamented the Negro American's loss of his religious heritage, Edward W. Blyden, the prominent Liberian educator during the second half of the nineteenth century, explicitly opposed Christianity as a system of values for the modernization of Negro peoples. Instead, Blyden embraced Islam as nearer to the Negro's indigenous *self* and as representing a truer set of values and codes for guiding Negro transition into modern society. Christianity, moreover, was associated with that ultimate debasement of the Negro's *self* epitomized in the Western slave trade and plantation slavery. For Blyden Christianity could never really free itself of responsibility for this slander upon the Negro's manhood. Though Islam and the Arabs, with a violence seldom used by white Christian slavers, equally racked Africa for slaves, Blyden overlooked this cruel point in Islam's relationship to black men because Islam permitted the Negro, free or slave, to enter Islamic society as a self-determined man, something impossible in Christian society. In a speech made in America in 1875, Blyden compared the ultimate impact of Christianity and Islam upon the Negro as follows:

It is not too much to say that the popular literature of the Christian world, since the discovery of America, or, at least for the last two hundred years, has been anti-Negro. The Mohammedan Negro has felt nothing of the withering power of caste. There is nothing in his colour or race to debar him from the highest privileges, social or political, to which any other Muslim can attain. The slave who becomes a Mohammedan is free. . . . It must be evident that Negroes trained under the influence of such a social and literary atmosphere must have a deeper self-respect and higher views of the dignity of human nature than those trained under the blighting influence of caste, and under the guidance of a literature in which it has been the fashion for more than two hundred years to caricature the African, to ridicule his personal peculiarities, and to impress him with a sense of perpetual and hopeless inferiority. . . . There is nothing in Mohammedan literature corresponding to the Negro—or 'nigger'—of Christian caricaturists.

The foregoing ideas and thinkers had an important influence upon the emergent Pan-Negro thought of the late nineteenth and early twentieth century, and they helped to link the intelligentsia of the Old and New World Negro communities. For instance, John Edward Bruce, a Negro journalist in New York, had many contacts with the emergent intelligentsia in West and Southern Africa. Both Blyden and Casely Hayford were honorary officers of the Negro Society for Historical Research founded by Bruce in 1911 as were other Africans in West and Central Africa. Another Negro American who had intimate ties with African intellectuals and who contributed to early Pan-Negro thought was Dr. Carter G. Woodson, a Harvard-trained historian who was a founder of the Association for the Study of Negro Life and History and founder-editor of its organ, *The Journal of Negro History*. Professor George Shepperson of Edinburgh University has uncovered from Woodson's private papers the following members of the African intelligentsia who were in contact with Woodson and his work: Casely Hayford, Gold Coast; W. Esuman-Awira Sekyi, Gold Coast; Kodwo Nsaaku, Gold Coast; Mojola Agbebik, founder of the first independent Native African Church in West Africa, Nigeria; Dada Adeshigbin, Nigeria; D. E. Carney, Sierra Leone; Isaiah Goda Shishuba, South Africa; the Amanzimtoti Institute, South Africa; and the Ethiopian Church of South Africa.

These links between Old and New World Negroes in the chain of ideas of Pan-Negro thought eventually led to a political Pan-Africanism. Unlike Pan-Negro thought, Pan-Africanism emphasized organized political action in behalf of the social and economic problems confronting Negro peoples living in the white-controlled modern world.

## POLITICAL PAN-AFRICANISM

The first organized expression of political Pan-Africanism was the Pan-African World Conference held in London in July, 1900. A West Indian lawyer, H. Sylvester Williams, initiated the Conference and, as far as is known, he was the first person to use the term "Pan-Africanism." As Williams saw it, the Conference's purpose was to give organizational articulation to the emergent Pan-Negro thought of this period and "to start a movement looking forward to the securing to all African races living in civilized countries their full rights and to promote their business interests."

Among the several Negro Americans associated with Williams at the 1900 Pan-African Conference was W. E. B. DuBois, who was Chairman of the Conference's Committee on Address to the Nations of the World, and who later seized the initiative in the effective international organization of Pan-Africanism. Unlike Thomas Fortune, H. M. Turner, Bishop in the African Methodist Episcopal Church, and Alexander Walters, Bishop in the African Methodist Episcopal Zion Church, all of whom found a place for Christian institutions in the search for Pan-Negro identity and modernization, DuBois viewed this problem in secular and political terms. This was basic to his famous statement in 1900 that "The [political] problem of the Twentieth Century is the color line." Although DuBois' political approach to the resolution of the "color line" was aggressive and stern, it stopped short of being revolutionary. Writing in 1940 a summation of his manifold endeavors on behalf of Pan-Africanism as the main avenue for attacking the "color line", DuBois remarked:

> My plans had in them nothing spectacular nor revolutionary. If in decades or a century they resulted in such world organization of black men as would oppose a united front to European aggression, that certainly would not have been beyond my dream. . . . Out of this there might come, *not race war and opposition, but broader cooperation with the white rulers of the world, and a chance for peaceful and accelerated development of black folk.*

Five years later speaking to the Fifth Pan-African Congress, which he organized along with Kwame Nkrumah, Jomo Kenyatta, George Padmore, I. T. A. Wallace-Johnson (Sierra Leone), and Peter Abrams (South Africa), DuBois reiterated his basically non-revolutionary plea for cooperation of black and white men on behalf of Pan-African modernization:

> . . . We seek to express our will and ideal, and the end of our untiring effort. To our aid, we call all men of the earth who love justice and mercy. Out of the depths we have cried unto the deaf and dumb masters of the world. Out of the depths we cry to our own sleeping souls. The answer is written in the stars. . . . We may yet live to see Pan-Africa as a real movement.

Blessed with a long life of 94 years, DuBois did live to see Pan-Africanism become a "real movement". With the independence of Ghana in 1957 and the inspiration of her former President, Kwame Nkrumah, the organization and control of Pan-Africanism shifted from New World Negroes to Negro Africans; and today Pan-Africanism is moving, however fitfully, toward the fulfillment of DuBois' hope. By the late 1950's, however, DuBois had abandoned his earlier non-revolutionary approach to Negro modernization through Pan-African organization and adopted instead a basically communist approach to this problem, officially joining the American Communist Party at the age of 93 in 1962. His thinking on the communist approach is related in the selection included in this volume. The communist approach is equally apparent in the essay in this volume by James Ford, a prominent Negro leader in the American Communist Party during the 1920's and 1930's.

### CULTURAL PAN-AFRICANISM, NEGRITUDE, AND GARVEYISM

Following World War I there was an outburst of Negro-centered literature by a group of writers who, though of middle-class origin, shunned the anti-Negro proclivities of the emergent black bourgeoisie and turned instead to the Negro lower classes for sources of artistic inspiration. Prominent among these writers were Jean Toomer, Sterling Brown, Claude McKay, Countee Cullen, Robert Hayden and Langston Hughes.

In 1926 Hughes proclaimed the ideological orientation of this group of writers: "We younger Negro artists who create now intend to express our individual dark-skinned selves without fear or shame. . . . We know we are beautiful. And ugly, too. . . . We build our temples for tomorrow, strong as we know how, and we stand on the top of the mountain, free within ourselves." Hughes also sounded the call for a rejection of the way of life of the rising Negro middle class and thus of middle-class America generally:

> But then there are the lowdown folks, and they are the majority— may the Lord be praised! The people who have their nip of gin on Saturday nights and are not too important to themselves or the community. Their religion soars to a shout. Work maybe a little today, rest a little tomorrow. Play awhile, Sing awhile. O, let's dance!

In the same vein Claude McKay, born in Jamaica but educated largely in America where he wrote and lived, immortalized the culture of the lower-class Negro in his novel, *Home to Harlem* (1928). The main character, Ray, was conceived by McKay as the answer to white-controlled, middle-class civilization:

That this primitive child, this kinky-headed, big-laughing black boy of the world, did not go down and disappear under the serried crush of trampling white feet; that he managed to remain on the scene, not worldy wise, not 'getting there,' yet no machine-made nor poor-in-spirit like the regimented creatures of civilization was baffling to civilized understanding. . . . He was a challenge to civilization itself.

Though such graphic acceptance of the naked essence of the Negro *self*, his *negritude* or blackness, had one or two precursors before the 1920's, it did not become an expressive cultural (artistic) and political force until this time. As such, it necessarily entailed a rediscovery of the African roots of the Negro American subculture. Such rediscovery was invariably ambivalent for the Negro intellectual. On the one hand the rediscovery was a confused though eloquent query, as in Countee Cullen's poem, *Heritage:*

> What is Africa to me
> Copper sun or scarlet sea.
> Jungle star or jungle track,
> Strong bronzed men or regal black
> Women from whose loins I sprang
> When the birds of Eden sang?

Or, in the same person the rediscovery appeared complete, reflecting proud acceptance of the Negro American subculture's ties to the African past, as in Cullen's poem *Shroud of Color*:

> Lord, I will live persuaded by mine own,
> I cannot play the recreant to these:
> My spirit has come home, that sailed the doubtful seas.

However ambivalent the rediscovery of Africa was for this important group of post-World War I Negro intellectuals, all agreed with DuBois that "the price of culture (civilization) is a lie!" Taken together, their literary endeavours helped to rid the Negro consciousness of the debilitating effects of self-rejection imposed by the psycho-cultural principle of white supremacy that governed the dominant society's relationship to the Negro. At this point the cultural features of the search for Negro self-identity merged with the political features as expressed in the Pan-African movement.

Indeed, simultaneous with the cultural reaction of the intellectuals and artists a movement emerged which sought to fuse this reaction with political black nationalism. This movement was led by Marcus

Garvey, who began propaganda for a back-to-Africa movement among Negro Americans in 1918 and organized the Universal Negro Improvement Association in New York in 1917 to realize this aim. Like the artists who formulated the cultural reaction to the problem of Negro self-identity, Garvey turned to the Negro lower classes for his inspiration and directed the bulk of his political activity toward them. He differed, however, from the artists, urging the formation of exclusively Negro institutions as the means for merging both the cultural and political reactions to the Negro people's debased lot in modern society. He believed that ultimately such institutions could survive only in Africa itself.

Garvey had little success on the institutional side of his programme, but his movement had an enormous ideological impact upon the self-attitudes of the lower-class Negro. The sensitive Negro artists of the 1920's also found a measure of self-reinforcement in the ideological aspects of Garvey's black nationalism. Even a few leading members of the black bourgeoisie were influenced by Garveyism and embraced it. For example, Emmett J. Scott, private secretary to Booker T. Washington and heir to Washington's mantle of conservative political influence, was deeply interested in Garveyism in his later days and accepted from the UNIA the title of Knight Commander of the Sublime Order of the Nile.*

Far afield in Africa the impact of Garveyism was felt too. As Shepperson has noted, Garvey's

massive propaganda for pride, not shame, in a black skin left an ineradicable mark on African nationalism everywhere, all the criticisms which were made of him by men of his own color notwithstanding. Kwame Nkrumah has stated unequivocally that the *Philosophy and Opinions of Marcus Garvey* influenced him more than anything else during his period in America. And Garvey's pride of colour through his organ, *The Negro World*, reached out into West Africa, its independent church and nationalist movements; into South Africa and Central Africa, where it had some effect on the followers of Clements Kadalie of the Industrial and

---

* It is noteworthy that W. E. B. DuBois, reared in a Victorian Age, was initially negative in his reaction to the literary and intellectual tendencies represented by McKay, Toomer, Hughes, Brown, Cullen, and others. In a review of McKay's *Home to Harlem* in 1928 DuBois expressed what may be taken as his general view of this group of writers: "*Home to Harlem* for the most part nauseates me, and after the dirtier parts of its filth I feel distinctly like taking a bath." DuBois, however, had an intellect that refused no challenge to change; and by 1940 he had adjusted to the meaning of the New Negro Movement in literature to the point of penning a description of the Negro personality which differed little from that

Commercial Workers Union of Africa and the remains of the Nyasaland Chilembwe-ite movement; and into the messianic nationalism of the Kimbangu movement in the Congo.*

## CONCLUDING NOTE

Since World War II the question of Negro self-identity in America has taken on more varied forms stemming from the more intense and immediate contact between New World and Old World Negroes in all spheres of life. The militant stage of the Negro American protest movement since the 1950's gained inspiration from the militant variant of African nationalism, especially that associated with Kwame Nkrumah in Ghana, Sekou Toure in Guinea, Jomo Kenyatta in Kenya, and Patrice Lumumba in the Congo (Leopold-ville). Without recognition of this postwar relationship between Negro Americans and Africa, one cannot fathom the deeper motivations and behaviour of such protest groups as the Student Non-Violent Coordinating Committee (one of whose primary leaders, James

---

he rejected a decade earlier: "This race has the greatest of the gifts of God, laughter. It dances and sings; it is humble; it longs to learn; it loves men; it loves women. It is frankly, baldly, deliciously human in an artificial and hypocritical land. If you will hear men laugh, go to Guinea, 'Black Bottom', 'Niggertown', Harlem. If you want to feel humour too exquisite and subtle for translation, sit invisibly among a gang of Negro workers. The white world has its gibes and cruel caricatures; it has its loud guffaws; but to the black world alone belongs the delicious chuckle. . . . We are the supermen who sit idly by and laugh and look at civilization. We, who frankly want the bodies of our mates and conjure no blush to our bronze cheeks when we own it. We, who exalt the Lynched above the Lyncher, the Worker above the Owner, and the Crucified above Imperial Rome."

* For example, John Edward Bruce responded to a speech by Mojola Agbebi in 1902 celebrating Agbebi's founding of an independent African Church, with a comment expressing utmost pride in his, Bruce's, *blackness*: "I am a negro and all negro. I am black all over, and proud of my beautiful black skin. . . ." Bruce was clearly expressing the sentiment of Negro self-identity that in recent years has been associated with the concept of *negritude*, itself first stated and formulated not by a Negro African but by a new-world Negro, Aime Cesaire, the Negro poet from French Martinique. It is likely that Cesaire himself first encountered this notion in the writings of the New Negro Movement in the 1920's and 1930's; McKay, Hughes, Cullen, and Brown were certainly working with cultural-literary concepts that had all the essential features of what Cesaire termed *negritude* in 1939. They in fact can lay claim to discovery of the concept, basically. Indeed, we agree fully with Professor Shepperson's recent suggestion that future research into the fascinating intercourse between old-world Negroes and new-world Negroes in the last 100 years or more will reveal that new-world Negroes originated many of the ideas and intellectual tendencies prominent in the development of modern Negro Africa. For example, J. E. Bruce not only expressed the essence of *negritude* in 1902, but articulated the related notion of "African Personality" and used these same words, perhaps the first to do so.

Forman, came to militant protest through the study of postwar African nationalism), the Boston Action Group, the Harlem Action Group, and the Chicago Action Group, among others.

The religious-oriented Negro protest groups like the Black Muslims were equally inspired by militant African nationalism, although also influenced by African Islam. The Black Muslims' newspaper, *Muhammad Speaks*, reports extensively on political events of the militant African states, and occasionally reprints articles from the newspaper of the Convention People's Party in Ghana, *The Evening News*.

The postwar philosophical, literary, and artistic tendencies in West Africa have also influenced Negro American intellectuals and artists. In 1956 a group of Negro American intellectuals and artists formed the American Society of African Culture, which became a branch of the Society of African Culture organized by French-speaking Africans in Paris in the postwar period. More recently, the younger generation of Negro intellectuals and artists, generally more politically militant and nationalistic than the group associated with AMSAC, have expressed the impact of postwar African events upon them by forming literary and political organizations like the Liberation Committee on Africa (which publishes a monthly magazine, *Liberator*), The Freedomways Committee (which publishes a quarterly, *Freedomways*), and the Society of Umbra (which publishes a quarterly, *Umbra*).

It should be appreciated, however, that all motivation for Pan-Africanism or negritude on the part of American Negroes cannot be realistically attributed to the more obvious psychological search for identification or security. In point of fact, whenever American Negroes have had the responsibility or opportunity to achieve their security in terms of larger issues, they have done so. If this has meant taking a position on Africa, of whatever persuasion, they have willingly undertaken it.

The communist ideology on the one hand, and the more rightist thinking of neo-colonists or perpetual-colonists on the other, were the polar forces frequently dictating the African orientation of some American Negroes. This is not to say, of course, that these Negroes were always "dues paying, card-carrying members" of the factions of the left or the right, but only that the larger political goals or forces of the right or the left did actually influence the postures of certain American Negroes in their relation to Africa.

While a changing viewpoint has not infrequently been expressed by the writers included in this anthology, such variations were usually a reaction to gradual shifts in the actual position of Negroes in this country and were almost always unrelated to broader ideological persuasions. Others have been less consistent—even less honest—but occasionally more popular. In the African-American picture no figure with the exception of Marcus Garvey has brought more popularity to Africa on the part of American Negroes than Paul Robeson, whose identification with various political streams of the left is well known. His leadership of the Council on African Affairs caused many to impugn its basic American goals. James Ford, whose communist affiliation was widely publicized when he ran on the communist ticket for Vice President of the United States, approached Africa as a communist first and a Negro second.

With American Negroes, there have also been those personalities whose positive relation to any issue changes so rapidly that it is almost impossible, or even useless, to classify. Such a person has been Max Yergan, whose career from Y.M.C.A. worker in South Africa and winner of the Spingarn Medal to that of a key apologist for French and Portuguese colonialism in Africa seems almost unbelievable. Equally incredible perhaps is the career of George Schuyler. As a journalist, however, Schuyler is more of a rebel or iconoclast, the questioning personality who for whatever reasons does insist on his right to query issues others prefer to ignore. In recent years these two men, from whatever motivation, have found themselves more and more in the same camp. In 1965 the recently founded American–African Affairs Association, Inc., the expressed purpose of which is "to search out and to disseminate the truth concerning . . . [Africa] without regard to the prevailing shibboleths and from two viewpoints which we take to be similar in all essential respects: the cause of freedom in its struggle against world Communism and the best interests of the United States of America," has as its only two Negro members Max Yergan as Co-Chairman and George S. Schuyler as one of seven directors.

There is another type of American Negro who has emerged in relation to Africa, and who may indeed become increasingly prevalent. This is the Negro who occupies a position of power nationally or internationally and from time to time can and does become involved in African issues. When Ralph Bunche, earlier as a scholar and more recently as an international civil servant, or Charles Diggs, as a member of the United States Congress, care to comment on questions concerning Africa, their role as Negroes cannot be separated in the minds of black men, at least, from their judgments and their actions. No consideration of Pan-Africanism or the spirit of negritude of American Negroes can ignore these personalities or the alignments and issues they choose to emphasize.

Thus, the quest for Negro self-identity, in both its cultural and political aspects, now enjoys a status hitherto unknown. Its future in America is rather bright. Negro Africans, of course, now control the mainstream of political Pan-Africanism, which is what Bruce, Walters, Williams, DuBois, Garvey and others intended. Nevertheless there will surely be many areas in which Pan-Africanism both as a political and as a cultural process will continue to involve the New World Negro communities in general and Negro Americans in particular.

The formation of the American Negro Leadership Conference on Africa in 1962 and its second session in Washington, D.C., in September 1964 are indicative of this. The Conference was organized by leading Negro political pressure groups like the NAACP, the Urban League, the Southern Leadership Conference, and CORE, and has begun to formulate methods by which the Negro American community can assist the development of a more effective African foreign policy by the U.S. government. Furthermore, the activities of Negro trade union leaders like A. Phillip Randolph have been geared to influencing the American Trade Union Movement toward effective assistance to African trade unionism, as indicated in Randolph's address included in this volume. Similar attempts to influence American institutions toward more effective assistance to African development have been a feature of the political leadership of Negro politicians like Congressman Diggs, as seen in his selection included in this volume.

Finally, it is important to note here the critical and sceptical attitude toward Negro American assistance to African development that characterized the thinking of the late Professor E. Franklin Frazier. He was doubtful about the ability of the Negro élite groups to secure a meaningful identification with Africa and its problems,* and he queried the willingness of white American society to prepare the Negro for the task of adequately assisting modern African advancement. With wit and irony, Frazier barely granted a secondary role for the Negro American in post-colonial Africa—the role of an appendage or vassal to the more powerful interests of white-controlled American institutions. There is undoubtedly much truth in

* Frazier, who was intellectually associated with the New Negro Movement during the 1920's, described the curious dialectic of self-rediscovery as follows: "At first the group attempts to lose itself in the majority group, disdaining its own characteristics. When this is not possible, there is a new valuation placed upon these very same characteristics, and they are glorified in the eyes of the group."

Professor Frazier's argument, but it tends to be a little too ungenerous toward the serious attempts of the more enlightened segments of the Negro élite—of which Frazier himself was a notable representative—who seek to employ their own self-identity and modern experiences on behalf of the new African reality.

# Timothy Thomas Fortune,
## 1856–1928

Timothy Thomas Fortune was born of slave parents in Jackson County, Florida. After the Civil War the family moved to Jacksonville. During the Reconstruction, largely because of the political influence of his father, young Fortune was given several minor political positions. But in 1876 he left Florida and came to Howard University, where he remained for two years. Fortune worked on the *People's Advocate* in Washington and after a year of school teaching in Florida came to New York in 1879. In 1880 with George Parker and William Walter Sampson he started the *Rumor*, which soon was changed to *The New York Globe*. *The Globe* continued until 1884, and in the same year Fortune became the sole proprietor and editor of the *New York Freeman*. *The Freeman*, under the joint ownership of Fortune and Peterson, changed its name to the *New York Age*, and from 1880 to 1907 Fortune established his career by writing for this paper. *The Freeman*, because of its format and the quality of its journalism, has been described as the most popular paper published among Afro-American journals, and Fortune himself as a "brilliant, aggressive editorial writer". He has also been described as the leading Negro journalist before World War I.

While identified with the industrial educational philosophy of Booker T. Washington, Fortune was an independent crusader— "fierce in his condemnation of corrupting principles in both the Democratic and Republican parties". He opposed segregated schools in New York and yet advocated the establishment of the New York Colored Regiment, later known as the 369th. He was a founder of the United Democracy, a voter's group, and in 1890 was an organizer of the National Afro-American League, often described as one of the forerunners of the N.A.A.C.P. In his last years Fortune was the editor of the publication of Garvey's Back to Africa movement. He was the author of *Black and White* and *The Negro and Politics*.

# The Nationalization of Africa*

## T. Thomas Fortune

*Mr. President, and Ladies and Gentlemen of the Congress:*

. . . The map of Africa is no longer a Chinese puzzle. Its geographical mysteries have been solved. Its mighty lakes and rivers have been traced to their source, and fiction and cupidity have unlocked hordes of treasure by the side of which that of King Solomon's mines was as the vastness of the Atlantic's waste of waters to the smallest stream that, like a silver thread, wanders down the mountain side and sighs itself away into the sands of the desert. Railroads are spanning its immense distances, steamboats are navigating its waterways, and the electric wire has brought it into talking distance with Europe and America. Its limitless agricultural and mineral resources are being developed for the comfort and the happiness of mankind. Vast States have sprung into being, as if by magic, controlled by European colonists, so that already a South African confederacy has worked its way into the brain of Cecil Rhodes, whose empire is cemented with more human blood and tears than the East Indian empire wrenched into the British Government by the crimes of Lord Clive and Warren Hastings.

Never in the history of mankind has a continent been so rapidly subdued and its waste places made the habitation of civilized governments and its savage inhabitants brought into contact and under the control of civilization. More has been accomplished along these lines in Africa in the past quarter of a century than was accomplished by European colonists in America in the first one hundred and fifty years of their desperate struggles here to subdue the aborgines. Steam and electricity and gunpowder are responsible for this phenomenon. They are conquering forces against which no other forces can prevail. The savage, with his primitive weapons of defense, falls before them as the mists vanish before the all-powerful and all-searching rays of the sun. He must relinquish his sovereignty and his wealth

* Professor J. W. E. Bowen, Ph.D., D.D., Editor; *Africa and the American Negro.* Addresses and Proceedings of the Congress on Africa held under the auspices of the Stewart Missionary Foundation for Africa of Gammon Theological Seminary in connection with the Cotton States and International Exposition. Dec. 13–15, 1895, pp. 199–204. Atlanta: Gammon Theological Seminary, 1896.

of all sorts when these forces confront him. The heroism of the Ashantee or the Zulu warrior, fighting in defense of his fireside and his country, is wasted when his assagai is opposed to the maxim gun or winchester rifle, or even the old Colt's revolver. We have seen this in the subjugation of the North American Indians, and we are now witnessing it in the case of the Africans.

The extent to which the continent of Africa has been spoliated and delimitated by Europeans is shown in the fact that of 11,360,000 square miles of territory, all of it has been absorbed or is claimed except the 9,700 square miles controlled by Liberia on the west coast. France and Great Britain have already made efforts to absorb this residium, and we have no reason to suppose that when they get ready to absorb it and resolve it into a colony they will not do so. In the philosophy of our civilization might makes right in practice, however much we may disclaim it in theory. In this, as in many other of the Christian virtues, our precept and our example are radically at war.

If the conquest of Africa shall proceed in the next seventy-five years as it has done in the past twenty-five, the whole continent will be as completely under European control, after the lapse of a century, physically and mentally and morally, as it is possible for conquerors to impose their conditions upon the conquered. The vast population of Africa will be brought under Christian influences in new forms of government and habits of thought and of conduct. The whole life of the people will be revolutionized. Ancient beliefs and superstitions and tribal relations and dissimilarity of vernaculars will, in the course of time, be transformed entirely. The demoralizing heterogeneousness which now prevails over the whole continent will give place to a pervading homogeneity in language, in religion, and in government.

## WHAT WILL BE THE RESULT IF AFRICANS ARE BROUGHT UNDER CHRISTIAN INFLUENCE?

The physical and mental forces now dissipated in tribal wars, in savage methods of industry, will give place to peaceful administration of government and to concentrated methods of industry. The nationalization of the continent will proceed along these lines as naturally and as surely as did that of Great Britain and Ireland, and as did the Germanic States under the masterful direction of Kaiser William, Prince Bismarck and Count von Moltke. Experience, as the great Virginian proclaimed, is the only light by which we can be guided in a matter so speculative. We can reason only by analogy. Human development proceeds along a straight line.

A common habitation, a common language, a common religion, are the necessary bases of homogeneous citizenship and of autonomous government. They are not possible without these. No government has successfully prevailed without them. It may be that Rome, whose legions overran the world, failed in the end because of the too rapid absorption of alien races possessing dissimilar languages and religions. Absorption was too rapid for proper assimilation, and the mistress of the world perforce died of strangulation. And what a fall was there when "the Niobe of nations", borne down by the massiveness of its own strength, torn by dissensions from within and surrounded by barbarous hordes from without, her proud eagle, which had circled over the nations of the earth, plucked of his pinions, lay prostrate in the dust, even as Milton's arch fiend which had braved the host of heaven. When so great a giant among the nations of the earth can fall to so low an estate as to furnish the nations of the earth with bootblacks and fruit-venders and organ-grinders, what nation, what people can hope to escape the handwriting on the wall, however vaunting their pride, however herculean their strength? Pride goes before a fall, and death lurks in the frame where health is accounted a heritage. "Oh, why should the spirit of the mortal be proud!"

The surface of the earth is capable of sustaining so many people. The population of the earth today is very little greater than it was a century ago. It will be but a little greater a century hence than it is now. The pressure of population upon subsistence is insistent and relentless. The supreme struggle of mankind is one of life, of subsistence, of preventing death by starvation or exposure. All other objects of life are subordinated to this one. It is the sleepless agent of colonization. It has penetrated the utmost bounds of the globe. It has wrenched from the weak their fertile valleys and luxuriant hillsides; and when they have protested, when they have resisted, it has enslaved them or cut their throats. It has invented all weapons of defence and of offence. It has invented all the machinery to increase the productivity of effort at a minimum cost, of whatever sort.

It was, therefore, but natural that the congested population of Europe should seek an outlet in North and in South America and the islands of the sea and in Asia and in the Australias; and it is but natural that the same congested population, in the desperate pursuit of something to eat and something to wear, should now be

306

seeking an outlet in the virgin continent of Africa, whose vast areas of territory and hordes of population have been the despair of geographers and ethnologists and philologists and antiquarians alike. The book of mystery having been unlocked, mankind has made indecent haste to master its contents. No fear of burning sun and expansive wastes of deserts and savage beasts and black men, the fabled genii of the Arabian Nights' entertainment, has deterred them. They are plunging into the forests and the sandy deserts, braving the deadly miasmas, more fatal than "an army with banners", fearful that the pearl of great price shall escape them. If we are to give credence to the doleful croakings of many ravens in this country, we should stand in wonderment and awe at the spectacle of caravan after caravan of white men and white women, the flower of Europe's children, winding in a long procession into the black continent, ultimately to impose their civilization upon the continent and to mingle their blood with that of the 300,000,000 children of the sun, the despised black children of the family of races. Their conduct should be inexplicable to these ravens, who insist that black blood and white blood will not mix, although it has so far done so in the West Indies and the United States, that these countries have a yellow streak running through them so thick and so long that only those hopelessly inflicted with blindness fail to see it and to properly account for its existence and to deduce from it the fact that reason, sympathy, affection, and not the color of the skin or texture of the hair, are the tests of the brotherhood, of the unity, of the human race.

> "Skins may differ, but affection
> Dwells in black and white the same."

Europe will continue to pour its hungry and ambitious and adventurous children into the continent of Africa in the future as in the past, but there will come a time when self-preservation will dictate a restriction or cessation of the infusion. But even before that time shall have been reached, the white races of Europe who are now subduing savage tribes and laying the foundation of empires upon the ruins of savage villages and imposing their yoke upon the natives, their language and their religions and their forms of governmental administration and their system of commerce and industry—even now the European minority in Africa are beginning to be absorbed and assimilated by the vast black majority. This is inevitable. A minority race in contact with a majority race is doomed to absorption and assimilation. It is the primal element of nationalization.

The minority race must exterminate the majority or be exterminated or absorbed by it. This is an iron law. It has been verified in the history of every race and of every nation. It will be verified in the history of Africa. It will be impossible for France to recover Alsace and Lorraine because the population has become Germanized in blood and language and religion. The minority Frank has been absorbed and assimilated by the majority Teuton, even as the invading and conquering Saxon minority was by the conquered Angle majority, and even as the imported and enslaved African black is being absolved by the heterogeneous white races of the United States. The inevitable destiny of the European whites in Africa is absorption and assimilation by the African blacks as surely as the ultimate destiny of the African blacks in the United States is absorption and assimilation by the American whites. I know that to many this is an abhorrent view of the question, but we are dealing with the philosophy of recorded history and the invariable laws of human conduct and not with the prejudices of men. Men are governed by the laws regnant in their environment. They do not make the laws; they cannot control them. If they do not like them, they are free to take themselves into a more congenial atmosphere. If the whites of America did not want to absorb the blacks, they should have left them in Africa; if the European whites do not want to be absorbed and assimilated by the blacks they should remain out of Africa. The matter is a very easy one to decide before the first step is taken; beyond that point it is controlled by "the divinity that shapes our ends, rough hew them as we may". The rigid laws and rules and regulations already adopted by the English, the Germans, the French and the Belgians in Africa to keep the natives in their place will prove as ineffectual to their purpose as such laws and rules and regulations now prove in the United States. The amalgamation of the European in Africa will proceed as surely towards the development of a national type of man as the amalgamation of alien races has proceeded in the United States for two centuries towards the same end. Here we absorb and assimilate the Indian, the European, the Asiatic and the African and grow strong in mental and physical prowess in the process. Indeed, our national strength is to be found in the homogeneity of its heterogeneous race elements, in its common language and in its common religion. The nationalization of Africa will proceed along the same lines as that of the United States is proceeding. What manner of man will be evolved from the process, what sort of national power he will represent, we are already able to judge, inferentially, by the results being worked out in the nationalization of the people of the United States. The intermingling of so many race elements work for national and spiritual and material strength in Africa as it has done in all the instances with which history has concerned itself.

I believe that the nationalization of Africa will be along English lines, as that of the United States, in its language, from the basic point of view, in its system of government and in its religion. The English language is the strongest of all languages, the most elastic in its structure, the most comprehensive in its use as a vehicle of human thought and expression. The English system of civil government is the best that has been devised, because it allows the greatest possible freedom to the citizen consistent with the safety of the state. The Christian religion is destined to supplant all other religious systems of belief, because it is the best code of moral philosophy ever given to man as an inspiration or as a development, an evolution of the social life of a people.

The English-speaking people are to-day the strongest force in Africa, from the European point of view. They will disappoint the truth of history if they do not ultimately effect a confederation of all the other European forces, including the native forces comprised in each of them. They will be forced into this federation in self-defence, as the American colonists were. History repeats itself. The nationalization of the African confederation which is a foregone conclusion from the facts in the case, will be the first step toward bringing the whole continent under one system of government. Language and religion may not produce a homogeneous people, as stated by the Hon. John H. Smythe yesterday, but habitat, language, and religion will do it in Africa, as they are doing it in the United States.

It is written in the Holy Book that Ethiopia shall stretch forth her hand to God. Is it in the power of men to make of no effect the divine prophecy? Perish the thought. There shall yet be evolved out of the conflicting race elements on the continent of Africa a civilization whose glory and whose splendour and whose strength shall eclipse all others that now are, or that have gone before into the shadows, locked in "the double night of ages", from which no traveler returns in gladness or in sorrow.

309

# W. E. B. DuBois
# 1868–1963

William Edward Burghart DuBois was born in Great Barrington, Massachusetts, and received his higher education at Fisk and Harvard Universities. His doctoral thesis for Harvard, *The Suppression of the Slave Trade*, was published as the first volume in the Harvard Historical Series.

Brilliant, handsome, and austere, DuBois is too well known, perhaps, to require more than a brief biography. Though ever a man of action, notably in the formation of the Niagara Movement in 1905 in New York and in the Pan-African conferences from 1919 to 1945, Dr. DuBois fought largely with the pen as editor of the *Horizon*, a journal of the colour line, the *Crisis*, official journal of the N.A.A.C.P., and as the author of several books such as *Black Reconstruction, The Philadelphia Negro, Dusk at Dawn, Souls of the Black Folk*, and innumerable articles.

DuBois is a unique figure in American Negro history. His lifetime spanned the most historic epoch in the history of the Negro, from the end of the Civil War to the March on Washington. His identification with the commitment to Africa was deep. He died in 1963 in Ghana, where he had become a citizen two years earlier, and was currently engaged with the massive project of editing the *Encyclopedia Africana*. In his own words DuBois has given us an explanation of his relation to Africa in an address to the All African Peoples Conference in 1958. He writes:

About 1735, my great-great grandfather was kidnapped on this coast of West Africa and taken by the Dutch to the Colony of New York in America, where he was sold in slavery. About the same time a French Huguenot, Jacques DuBois migrated from France to America and his great-grandson, born in the West Indies and with Negro blood, married the great-great-granddaughter of my black ancestor. I am the son of this couple, born in 1868, hence my French name and my African loyalty.

As a boy I knew little of Africa save legends and some music in my family. The books which we studied in the public school had almost no information about Africa, save of Egypt, which we were told was not Negroid. I heard of few great men of Negro blood, but I built up in my mind a dream of what Negroes would do in the future, even though they had not in the past. Then happened a series of events: In the last decade of the 19th century, I studied two years in Europe, and often heard Africa mentioned with respect. Then, as a teacher in America, I had a few African students. Later at Atlanta University a visiting Professor, Franz Boaz, addressed the students and told them of the history of the Black Soudan. I was utterly amazed and began to study Africa for myself. I attended the Paris Exposition in 1900, and met with West Indians in London in a Pan-African Conference. This movement died, but in 1911 I attended a Races Congress in London which tried to bring together representatives from all races of the world. I met distinguished Africans and was thrilled. However, World War I killed this move-ment. But before the United States entered the First World War, I visited the West Indies and met more persons of Negro descent and heard more Negro history. I wrote a book on the "Negro".

The selection from DuBois in this anthology gives his personal statement of the development of pan-Africanism, in which he played so important a role, and is an excerpt from an article on a subject of equal interest to Dr. DuBois, namely the function and role of the Negro intellectuals, for whose status as the talented tenth and the main salvation of the Negro he fought all of his life.

# The American Negro Intelligentsia*

## W. E. B. DuBois

In *United Asia*, Vol. VII, No. 2, pp. 23–28, I have written: ( . . . ) at the time of the first world war there came suggestions that American participation in this war should lead to a recognition of the rights of African people as against the imperial powers.

President Wilson was approached on the subject and a memoran-dum was directed to the Peace Congress of Versailles. To implement this the NAACP in sending me to Paris after the Armistice to inquire into the treatment of Negro troops, also permitted me to attempt to call a Pan-African Congress. This was an effort to bring together

* *Présence Africaine*, N.S., 5 (Dec. 1955–Jan. 1956), pp. 34–51.

leaders of the various groups of Negroes in Africa and in America for consolidation and planning for the future.

I had difficulty in calling such a Congress because martial law was still in force in France and the white Americans representing the United States there had little sympathy with my ideas. I was in consultation with Colonel House, who was President Wilson's spokesman, and with others, but could accomplish nothing. Finally, however, I secured the sympathy and cooperation of Blaise Diagne, who was Colonial Under-Secretary in the cabinet of Clemenceau and who had been instrumental in bringing to France the 700,000 Africans who as shock troops saved the nation.

Diagne secured the consent of Clemenceau to our holding a Pan-African Congress, but we then encountered the opposition of most countries in the world to allowing delegates to attend. Few could come from Africa, passports were refused to American Negroes and English whites. The Congress therefore, which met in 1919, was confined to those representatives of African groups who happened to be stationed in Paris for various reasons. This Congress represented Africa partially. Of the fifty seven delegates from fifteen countries, nine were African countries with twelve delegates. Of the remaining delegates, sixteen were from the United States and twenty-one from the West Indies.

The Congress specifically asked that the German colonies be turned over to an international organization instead of being handled by the various colonial powers. Out of this idea came the Mandates Commission. The *New York Herald* of 24 February 1919: "There is nothing unreasonable in the program drafted at the Pan-African Congress which was held in Paris last week. It calls upon the Allied and Associated Powers to draw up an international code of law for the protection of the nations of Africa and to create, as a section of the League of Nations, a permanent bureau to insure observance of such laws and thus further the racial, political and economic interests of the natives."

The National Association for the Advancement of Coloured People did not adopt the "Pan-African" movement on its official program, but allowed me on my own initiative to promote the effort. With a number of colleagues we went to work in 1921 to assemble a more authentic Pan-African Congress and movement. We corresponded with Negroes in all parts of Africa and in other parts of the world and finally arranged for a congress to meet in London, Brussels, and Paris in August and September. Of the one hundred and thirteen delegates to this Congress, forty-one were from Africa, thirty-five from the United States, twenty-four represented Negroes living in Europe, and seven were from the West Indies.

The London meetings of the Congress of 1921 were preceded by a conference with the International Department of the English Labour party, where the question of the relation of white and coloured labour was discussed. Beatrice Webb, Leonard Woolf, M. Gillies, Norman Leyes, and others were present. Otlet and La Fontaine, the Belgian leaders of Internationalism, welcomed the Congress warmly to Belgium.

Resolutions passed without dissent at the meeting in London contained a statement concerning Belgium, criticizing her colonial regime, although giving her credit for plans of reform for the future. This aroused bitter opposition in Brussels, and an attempt was made to substitute an innocuous statement concerning goodwill and investigation, which Diagne of France, as the presiding officer, supported. At the Paris meeting the original London resolutions, with some minor corrections, were adopted. They said in part:

"To the World: The absolute equality of races, physical, political and social is the founding stone of world and human advancement. No one denies great differences of gift, capacity and attainment among individuals of all races, but the voice of Science, Religion and practical Politics is one in denying the God-appointed existence of super races or of races naturally and inevitably and eternally inferior".

The Second Pan-African Congress sent me with a committee to interview the officials of the League of Nations in Geneva. I talked with Rappard who headed the Mandates Commission; I saw the first meeting of the Assembly, and I had an interesting interview with Albert Thomas, head of the International Labour Office. Working with Bellegarde of Haiti, a member of the Assembly, we brought the status of Africa to the attention of the League. The League published our petition as an official document, saying in part:

"The Second Pan-African Congress wishes to suggest that the spirit of the world moves toward self-government as the ultimate aim of all men and nations and that consequently the mandated areas, being peopled as they are so largely by black folk, have a right to ask that a man of Negro descent, properly fitted in character and training, be appointed a member of the Mandates Commission so soon as a vacancy occurs."

We sought to have these meetings result in a permanent organization. A secretariat was set up in Paris and functioned for a couple of years, but was not successful. The Third Pan-African Congress was called for 1923, but postponed. We persevered and finally without proper preparation met in London and Lisbon late in the year. The London session was small. It was addressed by Harold Laski and Lord Olivier and attended by H. G. Wells; Ramsay MacDonald was kept from attending only by the pending election, but wrote: "Anything I can do to advance the cause of your people on your recommendation, I shall always do gladly".

The meeting of an adjourned session of this Congress in Lisbon the same year was more successful. Eleven countries were represented there, including Portuguese Africa. The resolutions declared:

"The great association of Portuguese Negroes with headquarters at Lisbon, which is called the Liga Africana, is an actual federation of all the indigenous associations scattered throughout the five provinces of Portuguese Africa and represents several million individuals. . . This Liga Africana which functions at Lisbon, in the very heart of Portugal so to speak, has a commission from all the other native organizations and knows how to express to the government in no ambiguous terms but in dignified manner all that should be said to avoid injustice or to bring about the repeal of harsh laws. That is why the Liga Africana of Lisbon is the director of the Portuguese African movement; but only in the good sense of the word, without making any appeal to violence and without leaving constitutional limits".

I planned a Fourth Pan-African Congress in the West Indies in 1925. My idea was to charter a ship and sail down the Caribbean, stopping for meetings in Jamaica, Haiti, Cuba and the French islands. But here I reckoned without my steamship lines. At first the French Line replied that they could "easily manage the trip"; but eventually no accommodations could be found on any line except at the prohibitive price of fifty thousand dollars. I suspect that colonial powers spiked this plan.

Two years later, in 1927, American Negro women revived the Congress idea, and a Fourth Pan-African Congress was held in New York. Thirteen countries were represented, but direct African participation lagged. There were two hundred and eight delegates from twenty-two American states and ten foreign countries. Africa was sparsely represented by representatives from the Gold Coast, Sierra Leone, Liberia and Nigeria. Chief Amoah III of the Gold Coast, and anthropologists like Herskovits, then of Columbia,

Mensching of Germany, and John Vandercook were on the program.

In 1929 we made a desperate effort to hold a Fifth Pan-African Congress on the continent of Africa itself; we selected Tunis because of its accessibility. Elaborate preparations were begun. It looked as though at last the movement was going to be geographically African. But two insuperable difficulties intervened: first, the French government very politely but firmly informed us that the Congress could take place in any French city, but not in French Africa; and second, there came the Great Depression.

The Pan-African idea died apparently until twenty years afterwards, in the midst of World War II, when it leaped to life again in an unexpected manner. At the Trade Union Conference in London in 1944 to plan for world organization of labour, representatives from black labour appeared from the Gold Coast, Libya, British Guiana, Ethiopia and Sierra Leone. Among these, aided by coloured persons resident in London, Lancashire, Liverpool, and Manchester, there came a spontaneous call for the assembling of another Pan-African Congress in 1945 when the World Federation of Trade Unions would hold their meeting in Paris. This proved not feasible, and the meeting place was changed to London. Here again we met difficulty in securing meeting places and hotel accommodation. However a group of Negroes in Manchester invited us and made all accommodations.

The Fifth Pan-African Congress, therefore, met from 15 to 21 October 1945 in Manchester, England, with some two hundred delegates representing East and South Africa and the West Indies. Its significance lay in the fact that it took a step towards a broader movement and a real effort of the peoples of Africa and the descendants of Africa the world over to start a great march towards democracy for black folk.

At this meeting Africa was for the first time adequately represented. From the Gold Coast came Nkrumah, now Prime Minister of the first African British Dominion. With him was Ashie-Nikoi of the cocoa farmers cooperative. From Kenya was Jomo Kenyatta; from Sierra Leone the trade union leader, Wallace Johnson; from Nigeria, Chief Coker; from the West Indies came a number of trade union leaders; from South Africa the writer, Peter Abrahams acted as publicity director, while George Padmore was general director.

It was interesting to learn that from the original Pan-African Congress the idea had spread so that nearly every African province now had its national congress, beginning historically with the great Congress of West Africa held in 1920 just after the First Pan-African

Congress in Paris. There are now national congresses in South Africa, Rhodesia, Nyasaland, Tanganyika, and Angola.

The following reports from the Fifth Pan-African Congress are of interest. I thus painted the general scene:

"In a great square Hall in Manchester in the midst of that England of the Economic Revolution where the slave trade first brought Capitalism to Europe, there met yesterday and today the Fifth Pan-African Congress.

"As I entered the Hall there were about 100 Black men present. They represented many parts of Africa; the Gambia, that oldest and smallest of English West African colonies that numbers 200,000 Negroes; Sierra Leone with 2 million, the Gold Coast with half a million and so to Nigeria with more than 20 million. They were mostly young men and full of enthusiasm and a certain exuberant determination. Around the walls were slogans "Africa arise, the long, long night is over"; "Africa for the Africans"; "Down with the Colour Bar"; and then the slogans reached out— "Freedom for all subject people"; "Oppressed Peoples of the Earth Unite"; "Down with Anti-Semitism"; and some specific demands like "Ethiopia wants outlet to the Sea"; "Arabs and Jews Unite against British Imperialism".

"There were at the morning session, Tuesday, 7 speakers. One from the Gold Coast, educated in America, Nkrumah. He demanded absolute independence and a Federation of West African Republics. Nikoi followed, Chairman of the West African Delegation to the Colonial Office. He spoke with force and rhythmic eloquence, charging Great Britain with the beginnings of slavery and speaking as a representative of that Aborigines' Protection Society which obtained from Queen Victoria the dictum "I had rather have your loyalty than your land". He was fierce in his demand: "Down with Imperialism! No Dominion Status—I want to be Free". He represents 300,000 farmers of the Gold Coast, the upper class farmers who raise the greatest crop of Cocoa in the world. He complained of the new Colonial Secretary of Labour Government who refused to remove economic controls. He said that the West African Produce Control monopolises the natural products and fixes prices for a mass of people whose average income is 20 dollars a year.

"Then came Annan, a worker delegate from the Gold Coast Railway Employees Union. He told how in 1944 they had celebrated on the Gold Coast the Centenary of the Bond; that original

316

effort at Black Democracy in West Africa, and a century after that Bond the issue on the Gold Coast is poverty—grinding poverty. He reminded his hearers that the workers must be able to live in order to vote, that the Gold Coast needed industrial development and that sacrifices were necessary if their demands were to be granted. They must be willing to live with the dockers and miners. There is Imperialism among us Negroes, ourselves, and we must remember that we can expect no more from a British Labour Government than from a Tory Government.

"Coker, Delegate of the Nigeria Trade Union Congress, was more measured in his demands. He, too, represents the Cocoa Farmers, but he stressed certain remedies like cooperation and planning, and believed that India's Gandhi had the remedy in non-violence.

"Then came perhaps the best known man in West Africa, Wallace Johnson, Delegate of the Sierra Leone Trade Union Congress and of the Moslem League. He represents 10,000 organised workers and twenty-five thousand unorganised workers, and in order to establish these Unions he has spent 5 years in British West African prisons. Trade unionism in Africa, he said, was developed against and in spite of the Law, and they had a much harder time than unionism in Britain. He drew violent applause from the audience. "I have brought", he said, 'a monster document to the Labour Government. In 150 years Britain, in my country, has made but 5 per cent of the population literate and today instead of sending prepared students to England they cater to reaction and complacency.' He instanced the fact that in Sierra Leone, ginger, bringing 25 a ton in the open market before the War, had to be sold to the merchants for 11 a ton, and after the fall of Singapore when the price rose to t 144 a ton, the Black merchants got only t 30.

"Downs-Thomas of Gambia spoke for the oldest West African colony and demanded the abolition of Crown Colony Government. "How", he said, "can 40 different colonies in all stages of development be ruled by the Colonial office?"

"Perhaps the best and most philosophical speech was made by H. O. Davis of the Nigerian Youth Movement. He said that the long range program was Independence for Nigeria, but the short range program had to meet internal hindrances like poverty, ignorance and disease and the fact that the Negroes were unarmed; that the external hindrance was the British Government itself which would never willingly give up the colonies. The leaders must go down to the masses, and he agreed with the West African States Union that it is idiotic to think of the colonies as liabilities. If they were they never would be kept by the Imperial Government. Atrocities are not confined to German and Japanese prisons. They were all too common in the English prisons before the War and British democracy apparently was not for export."

Later speakers were

"Mr. Kenyatta who covered the six territories Somaliland, Kenya, Uganda, Tanganyika, Nyasaland and the Rhodesias. He gave an outline of the conditions under which the native peoples lived before the advent of the Europeans. A picture of happy and contented peoples enjoying the common use of the land with an agricultural, pastoral and hunting economy. He contrasted that picture with present-day conditions with a landless native people of 14 millions, and a small minority of white Europeans forcing the natives to work at slave rates under appalling conditions. Mr. Kenyatta detailed the conditions obtaining in the territories upon which he was reporting, varying only in detail and all displaying the characteristic pattern of imperialistic capitalism that Mr. Kenyatta condemned. He called for political independance for East Africa, and an end to racial discrimination".

"Mr. George Padmore spoke on Southern Rhodesia, where there was a population of 50,000 Europeans and two million Africans; before Bills concerning the Black people could be made law, they must have the sanction of the Colonial Office. The land had been taken from the Africans and given to Europeans, the natives were then forced to work upon the farms and tobacco plantations at low wages. The Europeans wanted the three states to come together so that the laws now prevailing in Southern Rhodesia would be extended. Of Northern Rhodesia Mr. Padmore told of London and American controlled copper mines where the wages paid to coloured workers amounted to 1s 6d a day. White miners got £1 per day. Profits of the mining companies over the last sixty years averaged £10,000,000 and out of this there had been paid only about £1,500,000 in wages. Profits and income tax are paid to the Exchequer in London, the mining companies being registered in London, and taxes are paid to the country in which they are registered. Mr Padmore spoke of the increasingly progressive element among the younger coloured people and called on the Congress to give all support for the aspirations and demands of the peoples of East African territories."

A final report of the Congress said:

"The Fifth Pan-African Congress meeting in Manchester with 200 delegates representing 60 nations and groups of African descent finished their work today and will adjourn with a Mass Meeting tomorrow at Chorlton Town Hall. On Thursday and Friday complaints and appeals were heard from Ethiopia and the West Indies. Ethiopia demands the return of Eritrea and Somaliland and ports of the sea. She charges that England is occupying and proposing to keep some of the best grain lands of Ethiopia. The delegates from the West Indies, that former Empire of sugar by sugar for sugar, complained of poverty and neglect with land monopoly and low wages in the face of 100 per cent increase in the cost of living. The situation brought revolutionary strikes and riots in 1937, led by Butler, Bustamente and Payne, who were promptly thrown in jail. Reforms followed. Something approaching Home Rule has been granted in Jamaica and other places, but insufficient reforms in various islands. Later a black professor from Londonderry reported on French Africa and its rising Nationalism."

This was the final resolution:

"The 200 Delegates of the Fifth Pan-African Congress believe in Peace. How could they do otherwise when for centuries they have been victims of violence and slavery? Yet if the world is still determined to rule mankind by force, then Africans as a last resort may have to appeal to force, in order to achieve freedom, even if force destroys them and the world.

"We are determined to be free; we want education, the right to earn a decent living; the right to express our thoughts and emotions and to adopt and create forms of beauty. Without all this, we die even if we live.

"We demand for Black Africa autonomy and independence so far and no further than it is possible in this 'One World' for groups and peoples to rule themselves subject to inevitable World Unity and Federation.

"We are not ashamed to have been an age-long patient people; we are willing even now, to sacrifice and strive to correct our all too human faults; but we are unwilling longer to starve while doing the world's drudgery, in order to support by our poverty and igonrance a false aristocracy and a discredited imperialism. We condemn monopoly of capital and rule of private wealth and industry for private profit alone. We welcome economic democracy as the only real democracy; wherefore, we are going to complain, appeal and arraign; we are going to make the world listen to the facts of our conditions. For their betterment we are going to fight in all and in every way we can."

Meantime a greater change was taking place among American Negroes. Up until the close of the First World War, the "talented tenth" among Negroes had recognized leadership and the growing respect of the whites. But with the depression and the "New Deal", the American Negro intelligentsia began to lose ground. An economic and class differentiation took place and the race leadership began to shift to a new Negro bourgeoisie. Garvey, the sincere but uneducated and demagogic West Indian leader, had helped this change during his career in America. He promoted an African movement, but it was purely commercial and based on no conception of African history or needs. It was American and not African, and it failed. But American Negro business expanded. Negroes began to enter white industry. Curiously enough, the propaganda of Booker Washington began with 1900 to change from effort to interest Negroes in "working with the hands" to inducing him to invest in business and profit by exploitation of labor. Thus insurance companies, retail business, distribution of goods and white collar work of all kinds increased among Negroes. By the time the Second World War opened, American Negro leadership was in the hands of a new Negro bourgeoisie and had left the hands of teachers, writers, and social workers. Professional men joined this black bourgeoisie and the Negro began to follow white American display and conspicuous expenditure.

This new leadership had no interest in Africa. It was aggressively American. The Pan-African movement lost almost all support. It was only by my hard efforts that the last Congress in Britain in 1945 got American Negro notice. After that all interest failed.

Today the American interest in Africa is almost confined to whites. African history is pursued in white institutions and white writers produce books on Africa while Negro authors and scholars have shied away from the subject which in the twenties and thirties was their preserve.

As big business gained in power and promoted war, that war ostensibly against Communism was really for colonial aggression in Asia and Africa. In order to appease colored peoples, big business found it to its interest to yield ground on the color line in America. Race segregation in schools and travel was made illegal, although the law was not enforced in the former slave South. But this step toward the integration of Negroes into the American state greatly influenced American Negroes and led them to join in opposition to Communism, the Soviet Union and Socialism everywhere. While the right of the Negro to vote is still curtailed, yet it is growing in power and has to be courted. But big business dominates Negro business, including the Negro press. Negro soldiers form a considerable part of the military forces, and their integration into white units has further reconciled the American Negro to war even with colored peoples like the Koreans and Chinese.

But these fatal trends among us will not, must not, last. Leadership is arising which appreciates at its true value the great role which the Soviet Union and China are playing in the world and are destined to play. This leadership today is suffering persecution, but it will prevail.

As the world turns toward Africa as a great center of future activity and development and recognizes the ancient socialism of Africa, American Negroes, freed of their baseless fear of Communism, will again begin to turn their attention and aim their activity toward Africa. They will see how capitalistic exploitation, led by America, is exploiting and impoverishing Negroes of Africa and keeping them sick and ignorant, and thus indirectly encouraging the color line in America. They will realize how American Negroes are in position to help Africa; not only by their growing political power, but by their educational opportunities in the United States. They can when they will furnish technical guidance to Africa; they can give intellectual leadership working with and not for black Africa. When once the blacks of the United States, the West Indies, and Africa work and think together, the future of the black man in the modern world is safe.

# Emmett Jay Scott,
## 1873–1940

Emmett Jay Scott was born in Houston, Texas. He received his early education at Wiley University in Marshall, Texas, and at Wilberforce University. Scott's first job from 1891 to 1894 was that of a journalist on the *Houston Daily Post*, a white newspaper. From 1894 to 1897 he was editor of the *Texas Freeman*, a Negro paper.

First as personal secretary to Booker T. Washington in 1897, and then as secretary of the National Negro Business League from 1902 to 1922, Emmett Scott was deeply involved in the philosophy and power associated with Booker T. Washington, and he received status in accordance with his relation to the Negro power structure. In 1909 President William Howard Taft appointed him as a member of a three-man American commission of inquiry to investigate conditions in Liberia. This Commission made recommendations that the United States should assist in the boundary disputes in which Liberia was then involved and should also assist in the settlement of certain debts, in reforming the finances, and in the organization of a defense force in Liberia. The selection included here is part of a larger article giving Dr. Scott's personal appraisal of Liberia. Scott was the only Negro member of the Commission.

In accordance with the wishes of Booker T. Washington, Emmett Scott played an important role as Secretary to the first International Conference on the Negro held at Tuskegee in 1915. He was also named to the Executive Committee organized to make arrangements for a second International Conference. As this Conference was concerned with the problems and progress of the Negro race all over the world, much of the discussion related to Africa, and delegates from Africa attended.

During World War I, Dr. Scott served as special assistant to the Secretary of War, advising on matters affecting coloured troops. His publication *The American Negro in the World War*, was the outgrowth of this responsibility. In 1919 Scott was appointed Secretary-Treasurer of Howard University, a post which he held until his death. Dr. Scott was author of several books in addition to the one mentioned above. With Booker T. Washington he wrote *Tuskegee and Its People*, with Lyman Beecher Stowe he wrote *Booker T.*

322

*Washington,* and he was the author of *Negro Migration During the World War,* a monographic study for the Carnegie Endowment for International Peace.


# Is Liberia Worth Saving?*

### Emmett J. Scott

In considering Liberia one is tempted to contrast it with the great powers which have embarked on schemes of colonization in Africa. But this would not be fair, for Liberia must be judged by standards wholly different from those which have commanded limitless resources of money and brain.

In the conduct of their government the Liberians are primitive and crude, when contrasted with the Great Powers, and there are to be found many defects of administration, and yet, I am bound to conclude, they have accomplished much in the face of most depressing handicaps. They have deliberately chosen isolation as a guaranty of continued existence. No white man may own land in the country, and therefore no white man may become a citizen; they have not had that contact with a stronger people which their brothers in America have had and which serves so constantly as an incentive for their strivings; and yet, one cannot forbear confessing that when the early struggles of Liberia are considered . . . it has done well and is deserving quite as much praise as of blame.

The civilization they have carried with them to Africa has been preserved, has been kept, despite the fact that they are surrounded by that great mass of uncivilized natives. One has only to see the towns they have established along the sea coast, Robertsport, Monrovia, Buchanan, Sinoe and Harper, and the agricultural settlements along the Rivers St. Paul's and St. John's, to have his respect for the people heightened. These cities are all peaceful and law-abiding. Person and property in them are safe; there is regard for public authority and for wholesome public sentiment. It was with us a source of constant remark that the streets of Monrovia, the capital city, were as safe and as quiet, night and day, as those of any village we could call to mind in our own country.

* *Journal of Race Development,* Vol. 1, No. 3: Jan., 1911; pp. 284–301.

On Sundays they have a very beautiful custom of raising the Liberian flag, and most of the civilized people attend service in some of the churches, or remain quietly in their homes. Sunday is a day of especial quiet. The adjacent native villages feel the influence of the towns and cities and are also orderly and quiet.

The Liberians are not artisans, and are not at present prepared to cope with the industrial development of their country, but are adepts, many of them, in the conduct of civil affairs. With the beginning of Liberian independence they have had to deal with the business of conducting their government. No one can read their state papers, for instance, without being struck with the adroitness shown in the handling of their foreign affairs. These state papers are both dignified and intelligent. The tact and ability they have shown in a number of critical instances have called for much praise in high diplomatic circles.

It is to be regretted that they have not had models for guidance in other branches of governmental administration. Although they can boast of a number of very superior men in the field of diplomacy, they cannot so boast in other directions. For instance, there is not in sight, at the present time at least, any man sufficiently equipped to guard them against financial entanglement.

It was in 1871, and again in 1906, that the Liberians under the compulsion of pressure saw, or thought they saw, a way out of financial difficulty by securing foreign loans. In both cases, they found offers ready and at hand from English sources, and in each instance it is to be recorded that the Liberian government was deprived of the just proceeds of what they had bargained for. Disadvantageous to the best interests of their country were the terms of both of these loans. And yet, Liberia, despite the miserable fiasco in both of these instances, is at present, from her customs receipts, manfully meeting the terms imposed upon her by the second agreement; and is also paying something on the first one. . . .

My purpose in referring at such length to these loan experiences is to show that the Liberians have not produced, as I have stated, a man, or men, capable of keeping them out of such financial entanglements. They have had to pay dearly for their ruinous bargains.

I must not blink the defects of administration to be found, and I have not, but they can in some measure be accounted for, as I have stated, because of the poverty of men and money. Here is a population of 50,000, about that of such cities as, based on the census of 1900, Harrisburg, Pennsylvania; Ft. Wayne, Indiana; Elizabeth, New Jersey, and Portland, Maine, assuming all of the responsibilities of an independent nation. First of all, well trained men are not easily to be found, for they simply have had no opportunity to be trained, and what they receive in return for their service, however efficient or inefficient it be, is lamentably small. We speak of "sensation-mongers" in this country. Liberia has not escaped them. There also they flourish, and it is probably to them that we are indebted for oft-repeated charges of corruption among public officials and of their willingness to supplement their meagre salaries with bribe money. Of this I can only say that such charges are always more easily made than proven. The loudest protestations of this character have come from those, who, having been checkmated in their efforts to further exploit the Liberians, now turn upon them, and seek to rend them. At any rate no basis could be found for these exaggerated stories of official perfidy and corruption by men as open-minded and quite as disinterested as those who now seek to cultivate a wholly different opinion. Corruption and inefficiency are not synonymous terms.

As a matter of straight fact the internal affairs of Liberia represent the dominance of orderly, constitutional government, and this has been true from the beginning of Liberia's independence. Even the one president they got rid of was deposed by the constitutional method of impeachment. Their election periods breed a certain measure of public excitement, but, in this country at least, probably no censure will rest against them because of that. Sixty years of constitutional government without even one lapse is not a discreditable record. Liberia now, however, finds itself face to face with duties it can no longer shirk. While the Liberians have done well in governing themselves, they cannot, without outside aid, I fear, cope with the tasks now imposed upon them.

Briefly stated, these larger and more complicated tasks grow out of relations with the powerful nations, with unlimited resources, that hedge them about on all sides. These relations, of course, involve boundary disputes and all of the necessary and consequent problems of international contact. They find themselves in conflict in their disputes with the flower of European diplomacy and while not wholly overborne in diplomatic jugglery, are nevertheless powerless to protest against the weight of brute force.

The question of reclaiming the great hinterland, and developing the splendid resources of the Republic contained therein must not longer be deferred. The world nowadays does not recognize "squatter sovereignty". Either Liberia must develop her own resources, or must see others acquire her lands and do it.

And then, the question of a rational solution of the native problem, the civilizing, the Christianizing, the assimilation of that great mass of uncivilized natives must soon be met in the spirit of the broadest sympathy and with a program at least logical and hopefully promising.

If there be those who insist that the relations of the civilized Liberians and the natives is the immediate and vital point of the future, I may, quite respectfully I hope, reply that it is not less the vital point in the continued existence of European sovereignty over other parts of Africa. Certainly there is no more native unrest, I should say, under Liberian domination than under European domination which has followed the partition of Africa by the Powers of Europe. I do not believe that any one contends that Europeans have solved the difficulties in the Belgian Congo, in the French Congo, in the Portuguese colonies, in German Southwest Africa, in South Africa, and in Egypt. I should say that Liberia should seek to attain at least as much success in dealing with the natives as the European governments have with the natives in their colonies. There is a native problem in Liberia it is true, but it is just now rather secondary than primary, more remote than immediate.

The native population of Liberia is made up principally of Mandingoes, Krus, Grebboes, Gorahs, Pesseys, Vais, etc.

This multitude of native peoples has no common language. Each tribe and tribal group has its own dialect. Of these tribes, with dialects peculiar to themselves, only one, the Vais, have a written language. In fact, one of the few examples in the world of the invention of a written language was by Duala Bukere, a member of the Vai tribe, who made this invention something like seventy-five years ago. Although the languages of tribes belonging to the same family have philological relations, it appears that the diversity of the dialect is even greater than that of tribal differentiations. As for example, different villages of the Pesseys have such diverse dialects that they cannot communicate with each other except through interpreters. Men, however, with a knowledge of more than one dialect are not rare and they are much sought after as interpreters. Such men wield a great deal of influence in the affairs of their villages.

The most important characteristic of the native population from the standpoint of the government of civilized Liberia is disunion. Because the native population is split up into so many different languages and ruled by hosts of petty chiefs, they have never been able to offer effective resistance to Liberia's authority. There are no signs that this diverse people have any feeling of solidarity or that their differences will ever be sunk in a common cause. . . .

As to the education of the native: That is a question and a problem yet to be worked out, not in Liberia alone, however, but elsewhere in Africa, as well. Some few schools for the natives in Liberia have been started, but the problems to be met are many. A system of education especially adapted to the native must in time be devised and Liberia will continue for many years to need the benevolence which now finds its way across the Atlantic.

The other complicated tasks before Liberia, briefly, are: those that grow out of the boundary disputes with France and Great Britain, and those that have to do with the organization of the internal finances of the republic. . . .

Liberia in her present extremity is anxious to have the United States as attorney, or next friend, in preventing further territorial aggressions. It was the unanimous opinion of the Commission of the United States of America to Liberia "that considerations of national honor and duty urge that the United States help these people whose commonwealth was founded by the people of the United States with the aid and assistance of its Government," and to this end presented six recommendations which are designed to constitute effective measures of relief. . . .

I have spoken mainly in defence of the Liberians, but not without the keenest appreciation of the faults of the past and the tasks of the future. Hope, faith, confidence, racial ties,—all, lead me most earnestly to hope that there may be preserved this one spot on the African continent where, unhampered, the black man may be permitted to work out his destiny in fear and trembling.

Is Liberia worth saving? I believe that it is. Her people are not revolutionary in character, as are, for instance, those belligerent friends to the South of us. The Liberian republic is not bankrupt despite alarmist reports to the contrary. The Liberians have advanced and not retrograded in civilization. They have helped to uplift the natives—to no considerable degree it is true, but nevertheless to an appreciable degree. Finally, they have given the lie to the statement that "Negroes cannot conduct an orderly form of government," guaranteeing to its people life, liberty, and the pursuit of happiness.

# James Weldon Johnson, 1871–1939

James Weldon Johnson was born in Jacksonville, Florida. He received the A.B. and M.A. degrees from Atlanta University and did further study at Columbia University, Talladega, and Howard University. Having been admitted to the Florida bar in 1897, he practised law in Jacksonville until 1901. In 1906 he was appointed United States Consul to Puerto Cabello, Venezuela, and from 1909 to 1914 he was U.S. Consul at Counto, Nicaragua. Johnson also collaborated with his brother, J. Rosamond Johnson, on the writing of plays and light opera. He was also a contributing editor to the *New York Age* and from 1916 to 1920 he was the field secretary for the N.A.A.C.P. From 1920 until 1930 he was the Executive Secretary of the N.A.A.C.P. Johnson was the recipient of the Springarn medal and a trustee of Atlanta University. He was the author of *The Autobiography of an Ex-Colored Man, Fifty Years and Other Poems, The Book of American Negro Poetry, Along This Way,* and the editor of the *Book of Negro Spirituals.* He was a frequent contributor to *Century, Independence,* and the *Crisis.* As a writer, lawyer, diplomat, and protest leader, James Weldon Johnson was able to influence and direct American Negro thinking on a wide variety of fronts. From many points of view, James Weldon Johnson, by virtue of background and training, belongs in the company of Negro leaders of the nineteenth century rather than of the twentieth.

# Africa at the Peace Table and The Descendants of Africans in Our American Democracy*

## ADDRESS BY JAMES WELDON JOHNSON

There has been some slight criticism of the Advancement Association for the steps it has taken to bring Africa to the attention of the Peace Conference and the civilized world. There are those who profess to see in such a move a danger to the cause of the American Negro. I wish to say that these steps have not been the result of any passing flash of enthusiasm; they were taken after careful thought and deliberation.

As long ago as the spring of 1915, Dr. DuBois published in *The Atlantic Monthly* an article entitled, "The African Roots of War," in which he showed that when we cut down through the layers of international rivalries and jealousies we found that the roots of the great war were in Africa.

As soon as the armistice was signed, the Association received a large number of letters from organizations and individuals all over the country and even from Canada, asking that some step be taken to influence world opinion regarding the disposition of the former German colonies in Africa.

While these letters were coming in, Dr. DuBois was already outlining and developing a program. I have here a copy of his memorandum; the whole of it is too long to read. But in order that you may have a fair idea of what he is bringing to the attention of the delegates at Paris and what he is striving to impress upon public opinion centered there, I shall read the four paragraphs in which the salient points are summarized:

"If the world after the war decided to reconstruct Africa in accordance with the wishes of the Negro race and the best interests of civilization, the process might be carried out as follows: The former German colonies, with one million square miles and

* "Africa and the World", National Association for the Advancement of Colored People, Annual Conference, 1919, pp. 13–20. Reprinted by permission of the Association.

twelve and one-half millions of inhabitants, could be internationalized. To this could be added by negotiation the 800,000 square miles and nine million inhabitants of Portuguese Africa. It is not impossible that Belgium could be persuaded to add to such a state the 900,000 square miles and nine million natives of the Congo, making an international Africa, with over two and one-half million square miles of land and over twenty million people.

"This re-organized Africa could be under the guidance of organized civilization. The Governing International Commission should represent, not simply governments, but modern culture— science, commerce, social reform, and religious philanthropy.

"With these two principles the practical policies to be followed out in the government of the new states should involve a thorough and complete system of modern education built upon the present government, religion and customary law of the natives. There should be no violent tampering with the curiously efficient African institutions of local self-government through the family and the tribe; there should be no attempt at sudden "conversion" by religious propaganda. Obviously deleterious customs and unsanitary usages must gradually be abolished and careful religious teaching given, but the general government set up from without must follow the example of the best colonial administrators and build on recognized established foundations rather than from entirely new and theoretical plans.

"The chief effort to modernize Africa should be through schools. Within ten years twenty million black children ought to be in school. Within a generation young Africa should know the essential outlines of modern culture and groups of bright African students should be going to the world's great universities. From the beginning the actual general government should use both colored and white officials and natives should be gradually worked in. Taxation and industry could follow the newer ideals of industrial democracy avoiding private land monopoly and poverty, promoting co-operation in production and the socialization of income."

When the opportunity arose, the Advancement Association sent Dr. DuBois to France. He went in a three-fold capacity; as the special correspondent of *The Crisis* at the Peace Conference; also to collect first hand material to go into a history of the Negro in the Great War; and as a representative of the Association for the purpose of bringing to bear all pressure possible on the delegates at the peace table in the interest of the colored people of the United States and of the world.

In the latter capacity it is the intention of Dr. DuBois to call a Pan-African congress to meet in Paris and press the question of the internationalization of the former German colonies.

The question will arise in the minds of some as to why the demand for self-determination is not included in this program for the future of these colonies. It is omitted not because of doubt in either the right of the natives to self-government or their ability for it, but because of the very practical reason that the question of the former German colonies will come up before the Peace Conference in only three forms: their return to Germany, their division among the Allies or their internationalization.

It is idle to hope, even in this era of making the world safe for democracy, that any people will secure self-determination by merely petitioning for it or even as a matter of plain justice. Self-determination will be secured only by those who are in a position to force it from their overlords. The internationalization of Central Africa holds the promise of being the quickest and least costly step by which the natives can reach that position.

And there is no man more preeminently fitted to press this matter than Dr. DuBois—not only on account of his individual ability but on account of the experience he gained and the connections he formed at the great Races Congress which met in London in 1911, to which he was a delegate.

There are several reasons that justify the National Association in taking up the question of Africa, and I will give them to you briefly:

In the first place, the race question in the United States is a national question; the peace delegations neither of England, France or Italy, would dare to broach it at the table; and it is hardly probable that the American delegation will voluntarily bring it up. Japan and China may possibly protest against discrimination against Asiatics. But not even these two great colored nations would so far violate international precedent and courtesy as to bring up to the peace table a matter which will be regarded as a domestic question with which only the United States is concerned.

I am not now speaking of what is right and of what ought to be done; I am speaking of what, according to all the probabilities and in accordance with international law, precedent, courtesy and *international red tape*, will and will not be done. I am facing the cold, hard facts.

On the other hand, the question of Africa is an international question; it belongs at the peace table; every nation represented there, from England to Liberia, can freely discuss it. Africa as I have said, is at the bottom of this war and I tell you we may form all the leagues of nations that can be formed, but if the African question is not settled justly, we will have wars and wars. Therefore, the African question being an international question, we had sense enough to know that we could bring it before this international body, and perhaps by that step pursue the very wisest and best means of focusing the attention of the peace delegates and the entire civilized world on the question of the just claims of the Negro everywhere.

There is another reason that justifies our interest in Africa, which is not so practical or material as the one I have just stated, but which is nevertheless vital in its effects. It will be a lamentable condition when the American Negro grows so narrow and self-centered in his own wrongs and sufferings that he has no sympathy for the wrongs and sufferings of others, not even his blood brothers in Africa. When he reaches the state where he wants everybody to be interested in his condition, but has no interest in the condition of others, he will have forfeited the right to demand that others be interested in him.

Still another valid reason for taking up the cause of Africa is the dense ignorance about that land; not only dense ignorance, but criminal ignorance. There has been and still is a historical conspiracy against Africa which has successfully stripped the entire Negro race of all credit for what it contributed in past ages to the birth and growth of civilization.

Makers of history have taught the world that from the beginning of time the Negro has never been anything but a race of savages and slaves. Anyone who is willing to dig out the truth can learn that civilization was born in the upper valley of the River Nile; that in the misty ages of the past pure black men in Africa were observing the stars, were turning human speech into song, were discovering religious truths and laying the foundations of government, were utilizing the metals, developing agriculture and inventing the primitive tools; in fact, giving the impulse which started man on his upward climb; while the progenitors of present-day Anglo-Saxons and Teutons and Slavs were hairy savages living in dark caves and crunching on raw bones; savages that had not yet the faintest glimmer of a knowledge either of religion or letters or government.

Of course, the makers of history take cognizance of Egyptian civilization; but at the same time they claim that the ancient Egyptians were white people. This claim is made for obvious reasons, but it is made in spite of the fact that the features of the Sphynx and other early Egyptian monuments are as Negroid as the features of the typical deck hand of a Mississippi River steamboat.

And in the same manner these makers of history have claimed as white other black and dark races who have accomplished something. The Arabs and the Hindus and the Moors are "white people". Efforts have been made to prove even that the Zulus on account of their bravery and prowess in battle are not really Negroes. We can all remember how, shortly after the close of the Russo-Japanese war, a number of scientifics and pseudo-scientifics sought to show that the Japanese people, after all, were a branch of the white race. It is a wonder that somebody didn't try to prove, after he licked Jim Jefferies, that Jack Johnson was a white man. Perhaps in the far future, when pugilism is a lost and forgotten art, some writer on the subject will try to prove it.

By these methods and means the Negro has been raped of all credit that is due him as a contributor to civilization. The truth is: the torch of civilization was lighted on the banks of the Nile, and we can trace the course of that torch, sometimes flaming, sometimes flickering, and at times all but extinguished—we can trace it from Egypt around the borders of the Mediterranean, through Greece and Italy, and Spain, on into Northern Europe. In the hands of each people that held it, the torch of civilization has grown brighter and brighter, and then died down until it was passed on to other hands.

The fact that dark ages fell upon Africa and her people is no more of a discredit than the fact that dark ages fell upon the buried empires of Asia Minor, of Asia, and of ancient Greece. Races and peoples have in their turn carried this torch of civilization to a certain height, and then sunk back under the weight of their own exertions.

It seems that there is more truth than mythology in the story of Antaeus and Hercules. Hercules in wrestling with Antaeus found that each time the giant was thrown he arose stronger. The secret lay in the fact that the earth was his mother, and each time he came in contact with her he gained renewed strength. Hercules then resorted to the strategem of holding him off the earth until his strength was exhausted. So with races and peoples; it seems that after they have climbed to a certain height, they must fall back and lie close to the earth.

And this reminds us of the truth that all things in the universe move in cycles; so who knows but that in the whirl of God's great wheel the torch may not again flame in the upper valley of the Nile?

We ought to know more about Africa, and if we did we would not be ashamed of it but proud of it. A knowledge of its history would give the background which would enable the Negro to hold up his head among the peoples of the world.

And it is only just that in the settlement to follow the war provisions should be made to secure the soil of Africa and the resources thereof for the benefit primarily of the natives; and for the establishment of governments that may insure them self-determination as rapidly as possible.

But the main interest of the Advancement Association, notwithstanding its broad sympathies for all oppressed peoples, is not in Africa and Africans, but in America and colored Americans. And the Advancement Association knows enough to realize that the problem of the Negro in the United States is not going to be settled around the peace table at Versailles. It knows that the Powers of Europe are not going to do very much, even if they could, to change the laws and the disregard of laws in Georgia and Alabama and Mississippi.

And so, although the Advancement Association is willing to accomplish as much as is possible by bringing Africa, which is an international question, before this international body, it realizes that the fight for the democratic rights of the American Negro must be fought at close quarters right here at home.

In fact, the fight for democracy for native Africans and the fight for democracy for people of African descent in the United States are not on the same plane. The truth of the matter is, the question of the democratic rights of the American Negro has no recognized place at the peace table. The Negro in the United States is not a subject race and does not accept the status of a subject race. He is a citizen of the United States, with all the rights of American citizenship guaranteed him by the Constitution. Subject races all over the world are today struggling to have certain rights of citizenship written for them in the laws of the nations to which they bear allegiance; therefore their cases naturally go for consideration before the international tribunal which is now assembling. But the American Negro is contending for the fulfillment of rights already guaranteed him by the Constitution and for the impartial interpretation and application of existing laws.

In other words, the American Negro is not asking a favor; he is not asking for something that belongs to somebody else; he is demanding only that which is legally his; he is laying claim to that of which he is being wrongfully deprived. The question as to the wisdom of writing the Negro down in the Constitution as a citizen is aside from the point; what is written is written, and these laws are law. And the righteousness, the morality, the self-respect and the common decency of the nation are involved in seeing that these laws are carried out.

This is the battle ground on which the forces of the Advancement Association are entrenched, and it is on this front that we intend to fight it out without hesitation, without fear and without compromise until the end is achieved.

The National Association realizes that our fight is here at home and must be fought at close quarters—not over there, but right here. And that is the big job before us; that is the job which we have been tackling for ten years, with increasing force and increasing earnestness. It is a big job. There are many phases of it; it is complicated; it is complex. There is an economic side. A great many people hold that all of this question is economic; that it is simply a question of exploitation, just as the European countries exploit natives in Africa. That is good as far as it goes but it does not entirely cover this problem of ours in the United States.

I cannot take up this whole question but there are two phases of which I shall speak. There is a bitter race hatred and there is a national apathy and indifference with which we have to contend. I hardly know which is the more dangerous and which works the greater damage. Bitter race hatred is limited but makes up in activity for its limitation. But the apathy on this question of human rights as it concerns the American Negro is general, it is widespread. It is a sort of inertia, it is a thing difficult to move. But that is one of the jobs this Association believes it has before it, and that is a job we are tackling.

To do this, we are using every rightful means that we can command. This nation is indifferent; it is not thinking about us as it should be made to think and as it was made to think sixty years ago. The country is very much concerned about democracy abroad, but not very much interested in democracy at home, so far as it applies to more than ten million Negro citizens. But I will tell you what we are going to do. . . . It is our intention to carry on an intelligent, persistent and aggressive agitation until we educate this nation, more than educate it, until we whip and sting its conscience, until we awaken it, until we startle it into a realization that we know what we want, we know what we are entitled to, and that we are determined by all that is sacred to have it and be satisfied with nothing less. . . .

# Ralph J. Bunche,
# 1904–

Ralph Johnson Bunche was born in Detroit, Michigan. He received his early education in Los Angeles, his B.A. degree from the University of California, Los Angeles, and his A.M. and Ph.D. degrees from Harvard University. Bunche did post doctoral work in anthropology at Northwestern University, the London School of Economics, and the University of Capetown, South Africa. He received post doctoral fellowships from the Social Science Research Council and the Rosenwald Foundation to pursue studies in South and East Africa and in Malaya. In 1939 Bunche was a staff member of the Carnegie Corporation Survey of the Negro in America, whose findings were later published as *The American Dilemma*. He has taught at the University of California and Howard University, and for two years he was Professor of Government at Harvard University. For some years Dr. Bunche was a social science analyst in charge of research on Africa and other colonial areas in the British Empire section of the Office of Strategic Services. From 1944 to 1947 he was with the U.S. Department of State. He was assistant secretary to the U.S. delegation to Dumbarton Oaks in 1944, and adviser to various other U.S. delegations. From 1946 to 1954 he was Director of the Division of U.N. Trusteeship, and during that period acted as Principal Secretary for the United Nations Palestine Commission and as United Nations Mediator in Palestine; in 1960 he was sent as Special U.N. Representative to the Congo. Dr. Bunche has been a member of the board of higher education in New York and winner of the Spingarn Medal and of the Nobel Peace Prize. Since 1958 he has been Under Secretary for Special Political Affairs at the United Nations.

# A World View of Race*

## Ralph J. Bunche

### RACE AND IMPERIALISM

Modern imperialism has given added impetus to the tendency to classify human peoples as "superior" and "inferior" for race has been a convenient device for the imperialist. Under imperialism's zone of conquest the population of the earth has been arbitrarily divided into "advanced" and "backward" races or peoples. Imperialist propaganda has taught the world to regard certain peoples as helplessly backward and incapable of keeping step with the modern industrial world. In fact, strenuous efforts are made to make these peoples think of themselves as backward. But this classification is not a mere theoretical one. It is used as the basis for justifying conquest and exploitation and for dividing the world into dominant and subordinate peoples. Thus imperialism has attempted to mask its cruelly selfish motives under high-sounding titles. Powerful industrial nations have raped Africa under the false pretense of shouldering "the white man's burden". It has been held to be the particular mission of the dominant peoples to bring civilization to the backward peoples of the earth; to convert them to the Christian religion and to expose them to the benefits of an advanced European culture. A new "moral" philosophy is invented which holds that some peoples are naturally backward and therefore properly may be kept in a more or less permanent state of subjection to the advanced peoples. But since the backward peoples have often been reluctant to receive these blessings they have been forced to accept them at the point of the bayonet. In this way Italy is bestowing the "blessings of civilization" upon the hapless Ethiopians today. After the conquest has been completed, the backward peoples bitterly learn that the "blessings" consist of brutal suppression, greedy economic exploitation of the natural and human resources of a country which is no longer their own, forced labor, the introduction of previously unknown diseases, vice and social degeneration. . . .

* Ralph J. Bunche, *A World View of Race*, the Associates in Negro Folk Education of Washington, D.C., pp. 38–39, 41–43, 46–48, 61–65. Reprinted with permission of the author.

### AFRICAN IMPERIALISM

Africa, and particularly West Africa, may be taken as an excellent illustration of how the dominant and "superior" races of Europe have conquered peoples less expert in "civilized" methods of warfare. It also demonstrates how race has been employed as a device not only to justify the conquest to the world, but how in some instances it has proved an effective means of emotional appeal in order to make the exploitation of the conquered peoples more acceptable to them. The technique of governing subject races and minimizing racial conflict in West Africa is both revealing and fairly typical of the methods employed elsewhere in the Far East, Australia and the Caribbean.

In considering the impact of Western imperialism upon the African it must be borne in mind that the partition of the Dark Continent among the nations of Europe is an affair of only the past half-century. The penetration of Africa actually began much earlier, but the imperialism of today is a product of modern capitalism, and the beginning of its application to Africa coincides with the deep penetration into the hinterland and the partition of the continent in the last quarter of the nineteenth century. Back of this partition of Africa were the compelling economic forces of modern industrial capitalism. The need of industrial countries for expanded markets, for raw materials found in the tropics and sub-tropics, the accumulation of "surplus capital" and the resultant demand for overseas investments, all tended to force European imperialist nations to invade completely the African continent. In addition, it should be remembered that until the twentieth century the colonizing nations had little to offer Africa but imperialist exploitation in its crudest form, accompanied by greed, hostility and misunderstanding. It has been this brief but unsavory early history of Europe in Africa which has impelled some writers to indict the general effects of European policy as "almost wholly evil," and to regard the process in its entirety as one of fraud and robbery.[1]

It should not be surprising that a defenseless people, regarded as members of an "inferior," primitive race by invading conquerors, should be as much victimized in their own country in which they are in the great majority as where they are a minority racial group, as is the case of the Negro in this country. Moreover, there is in both

---

[1] Leonard Woolf. *Empire and Commerce in Africa*, p. 352.

instances the same lack of serious effort to work out a just and intelligent policy for the government and control of these peoples.

The representatives of Western civilization in Africa from the beginning set about considering the new country mainly in relation to their own needs and interests. The fertility of the soil, the richness of natural resources, the salubrity of the climate, the industry and health of the primitive population are all important to the European only in terms of potential exploitation. Commonplace as the observation may be, seldom, if ever, has the welfare of the native population been given front rank in these considerations.

The European administrator in Africa is generally quite indifferent to the conditions of native life. Forced to take many precautions to preserve his health in a severe and trying climate, he finds it difficult to exert an interest beyond the immediate demands of his job. For example, the West African administrator quite often forgets that many of the West Africans are culturally in a transitional stage: in reality they are neither primitive nor civilized in their present mode of living. Residing in the coastal towns of West Africa are thousands of natives who have become detribalized, who have picked up many European customs and who have forgotten many of their own. There are many of them who wear fine European clothing, speak polished French or English, construct beautiful homes and send their children to school. Yet they may worship fetishes, marry several wives, eat without cutlery and sleep on the floors in bare bedrooms despite elaborately furnished parlors. They will scorn the authority of chiefs whose education is often inferior to their own. Their conception of property is private, no longer communal. . . .

#### HOW THE AFRICAN IS GOVERNED

By what devices is the African governed? In the history of the contact of Europe with the African two extremes of policy have been applied to him. The one, based entirely on greed, regarded him as the essentially inferior, sub-human, without soul, and fit only for slavery. The other, based entirely on sentiment, regarded him as a man and brother, extended to him the equalitarian principles of the French Revolution and attempted to "Europeanize" him overnight. Both desired to get as much from him as possible. Both were unscientific and devoted little attention to the needs and desires of the African.

The basic weakness of the policies which have so often been applied to the African is in the fact that these policies still remain so vague as to the actual objectives aimed at. Where is the African headed? Is he to have eventual independence or is he to remain forever a subject race in "harmonious cooperation" with his administrators? Or is he to be completely absorbed by the conquering people? These questions the French have attempted to answer, on paper, at least, much more clearly than the other colonizing nations. But a colonial policy which aims to do justice to the native must embody much more than platitudes and vague assurances that the "welfare of the natives is paramount." It must exhibit a definite program for native development which will lead the native toward an ultimate specific political and social status. Few, if any, existing colonial policies have gone that far.

It would seem that the only sound objective of African colonial policies should be to prepare the Africans for membership in the community of the civilized world, not as individuals but as communities. Any other policy applied to regions of Africa such as West Africa, for example, where extensive white settlement is definitely proscribed by nature, leads to the inescapable inference that the native is to be kept forever in political bondage, even though of a milder sort, by a handful of his "superiors." Second only to this first principle of colonial policy toward subject peoples should be the premise that the social and political development of the native in the African colony must at least keep pace with the economic exploitation of his country and whatever economic development may be presumed to accompany that explotation. An analysis of the colonial policies in effect in present-day Africa, however, indicates clearly that they fall far short of meeting either of these desirable ends.

In general, particularly insofar as West Africa is concerned, it may be said that there are two policies of native administration in vogue among the colonial powers. One of these is commonly identified as the "French system," and the other as the "British system." Neither nation employs one or the other system exclusively, however, and there are certain fundamental factors which each has in common with the other. In the first place French and English alike are in Africa primarily for economic exploitation and not from motives of philanthropy. In the second place both powers intend to retain control of their respective possessions and their subject populations indefinitely. England and France are not thinking in terms of native independence or self-government for the West Africans except in its most meager local sense. For the English the objective is what is styled "harmonious cooperation"; for the French what is called "association." Colonial authorities like the noted Englishman, Lord

340

Lugard, doubt that the African race, whether in Africa or America, can develop capability for self-government.

## WHITE SETTLEMENT

Segregation is particularly acute in areas of white settlement. Many English writers have defended the British practice of encouraging white settlers to establish themselves permanently in Africa, particularly South and East Africa. The South African General Smuts takes the view that any enduring civilization in Africa must be based on intensive permanent white settlement wherever that settlement is possible.[1] Coupled with this doctrine is a rigid policy of separation of white and black populations. That is to say that any civilization in Africa which is desirable and progressive must have a "white backbone."

White settlement does not exist to any great extent in the French African dominions. But in British South and South Central Africa it is the dominant feature of English influence, and is now making rapid progress in British East Africa. Wherever it has been pursued as an extensive policy it has created problems which seem to defy solution. It has been the cause of much hard feeling between the races and a great deal of injustice to the native populations who have been shoved off their most fertile lands, compelled to work on plantations owned in many instances by absentee landlords, and robbed of valuable mineral lands contrary to treaty agreements.

## WHAT HOPE FOR THE NATIVE?

Thus the concepts of race and race difference play a significant role in the control of subject African peoples by the French and British. The French have so far been able to use the emotional appeal of race brotherhood as a very helpful device in keeping down unrest in their African dominions. The British find race a sore problem. The Englishman might say with some grace "If I were a cultivated native I would prefer to live under the French system, where the cultivated natives have undoubted equality. But if I were a primitive native of the masses I would prefer the English system." The French might retort with equal cause: "The African can never be more than a *good native* to the Englishman and the best native is never thought by the

[1] General J. C. Smuts. *Africa and Some World Problems.* p. 50.

English to be as good as even a bad Englishman." To all of which many educated Africans will aver that neither French nor English offer very much of fundamental benefit to the native, though both take a great deal from him. Probably the greatest error is the mistake of assuming that the African and his problems are so essentially different from the problems confronting the peoples of the Western World. In truth the African is confronted with the same difficulties encountered by any people in process of social development. There is nothing particularly unique about either the African or his problems. The African native today is comparable with the peasants and work-men of England and France of a century ago and with other workers and peasants today in less advanced countries of the modern world.

The "race-problem" has reared its ugly head in Africa as elsewhere in the modern world, but there as everywhere else, with increasing clarity, it can be identified as one sordid and acute aspect of the class problem. Both France and England will sooner or later have to face a day of reckoning with their Negro populations which are daily becoming more intelligent and articulate. The French may be able to postpone this day longer than will the British, because France finds it possible to mollify the native elite by giving them racial and social equality. But even for the elite native, racial and social equality without economic and political equality on a broad scale, can offer no real solution to the problem of native life. . . .

The contemporary international order, characterized by its capita-list-imperialist organization, has no possibility of effectively control-ling the destiny of such peoples and areas. For the international order cannot override the existing vested capitalistic interests which muster the forces of the state for their protection. As the world is now organized these interests cannot be overcome, for they are intimately tied up with the class-relations of capitalist society. The same forces which protect them are the exact forces which protect and promote the interests of the capitalist within the capitalist state to which he claims allegiance. Just as the capitalist state in its internal affairs maintains a legal and constitutional system designed to protect absentee ownership and safeguard those property rights which make the capitalist supreme, just so, in the realm of external affairs, the state's authority, by the very nature of his relationship to it, must be employed to impose that type of supremacy over other peoples.

It is only when this supremacy and privilege are dissolved and when it is no longer within the power of the privileged property-holding class to determine the institutional life and habits of the modern state, that there can be hope for the development of an international order and community which will promise the subject peoples of the world genuine relief from the heavy colonial burdens of imperialist domination. At the present their outlook is not bright: the international order and their race are both arrayed against them.

# George S. Schuyler, 1895–

George Samuel Schuyler was born in Providence, Rhode Island, and was educated in the public schools of Syracuse, New York. His early years were spent with the United States Army, and in 1923 he joined the editorial staff of *The Messenger*, a monthly published by A. Philip Randolph. In 1926 he joined the editorial staff of *The Pittsburgh Courier*. From 1937 to 1944 he was business manager of the *Crisis*. In 1931 Schuyler acted as special correspondent for *The New York Evening Post* and associated newspapers which were investigating the charges of slavery in Liberia. He also participated in an investigation of labour conditions on the Mississippi Flood Control Project for the N.A.A.C.P. He covered the first Negro Conference in Brazil and was a delegate to the Congress for Cultural Freedom in Berlin in 1950.

Throughout his life Schuyler has been a controversial writer, always prodding the Negro community according to his own tenets. He feels his interest in Africa is understandable, as his great-grandmother was from Madagascar. He has, however, been associated with numerous conservative groups. He was Director of the America-China Policy Association and later its President. Some years ago he issued a special supplement of *The Pittsburgh Courier* in which he tried to indicate that the French Community, which encouraged the closer co-operation of the African countries with France, was the only means for those countries to make any progress. In 1961, after a trip to the Portuguese areas of Africa, Mr. Schuyler again issued a special supplement of *The Pittsburgh Courier* in defence of Portuguese colonial policies. George Schuyler and Max Yergan are the two Negroes whose recent activities regarding Africa have aimed largely at pointing out the Africans' unreadiness for independence; an attitude more in keeping with the conservative attitude and philosophy of colonial powers.

In addition to his regular column in *The Pittsburgh Courier*, "Views and Reviews," George Schuyler has written *Slaves Today*, *Black No More*, and *Racial Intermarriage in the United States*, and he has contributed rather regularly to several American journals, such as *American Mercury*, *Readers Digest*, *The Nation*, *Opportunity*, and *Crisis*.

# Slaves Today*

## MISSIONARIES "WINK AT CONDITIONS IN LIBERIA"

### Domestic slavery and "boy" traffic an old story to natives

Schuyler says products of seventy-year-old missionary system are shiftless and untrustworthy—ruling class grafters.

The findings of the recent international committee, startling as they were to the outer world, were really old stuff to Liberians. It was like announcing in Chicago that Al Capone's men had "bumped off" another rival gangster.

The Fernando Po "boy" traffic had been in operation for almost a score of years, pawning ante-dated the settlement of the country by the freed-men from America, domestic slavery had been practiced since the earliest days when the recently-landed colonists turned right around and virtually enslaved the unfortunate Negroes taken off slave ships by British men of war and dumped on the beach at Monrovia, and forced labor was as ordinary as the annual rains.

If these practices are so shocking and reprehensible, and have been going on so long, one wonders why there has never been an outburst of protest from the missionaries who overran the country. As a class, they have sat serene and complacent and observed the forced labor of whole tribes on the government roads. They have stood with closed mouths and seen "boys" returned from Fernando Po who were unable to walk because of sleeping sickness and elephantiasis. They have never seen fit to protest to the outer world about the debauchery of native women living as concubines in the homes of many of the leading Liberians. The spectacle of hundreds of little children enslaved as drudges in households has never aroused their pity to the point of protest. If they observe the socially harmful custom of pawning, they kept it quietly to themselves.

### NONE WOULD PROTEST

If these missionaries were the representatives of some savage cult that favoured slavery, pawning, concubinage, and forced labor,

* *Pittsburgh Courier*, October 17, 1931. Reprinted by kind permission of the editor.

there would be no occasion for comment at their long silence. But they are Christian missionaries, most of them are good Baptists, Methodists, Catholics, Lutherans and Episcopalians, and almost all of them come from the land of the Free! With the exception of the Catholics, they are running back and forth to the United States all the time. It does seem that during the past seventy years, during which time they have been operating in Liberia, at least one prominent missionary might have protested effectively to the world against the evils easily observed in the black republic.

There is no use asking where they have been, for they have been right here in the midst of what elsewhere they are hot to denounce as sin and iniquity. Representative of the very Protestant sects who in the United States are foursquare behind the Anti-Saloon League and the Lord's Day Alliance, actually seek in Liberia to smooth over and apologize for the acts of the Americo-Liberian ruling class.

### "POOH-POOH" CONDITIONS

When I spoke to a venerable Bishop of a powerful church about the terrible sanitary conditions in Monrovia, where the new Sanitary Officer from the Gold Coast actually had raked together 1,000 motor truckloads of trash, tins and bottles in a town of 6,000 people, he pooh-poohed the whole matter and went on to compare conditions today with those forty years before when he had first come out to this country.

Back in the hinterlands near the French border, I was telling the missionary with whom I was dining what I had discovered about the huge quantities of rice, amalo, chickens and cattle exacted from the natives by Liberian officials. He immediately launched into a half-hearted defence of the government men after advising me that he had been stationed here for ten years.

During my stay in Liberia, I can remember but two missionaries out of the large number I met who did not sound like Americo-Liberians when discussing the aborigines. They were eager to tell how shifty were the chiefs and how watchful they had to be to keep the natives from taking advantage of them. Some of them expressed regret that the evils disclosed by the International Commission were in existence. I met none who was full of Christian zeal to do anything about it. "Our hands are tied," they would say. "What can we do about it?" Then they would tell of their work in bringing Jesus to the savages.

## MISSIONARIES CALLOUS

Missionaries of the Lord sent out to the wilds of Africa to Christian-ize the so-called benighted natives struck me as being singularly callous and indifferent about the fate of the aborigines. They are eager for his soul, but apparently not interested in his body. At least, they have never been sufficiently concerned to protest to the world his enslavement and mistreatment. It is significant that the reports of conditions in Liberia have been communicated to the outside world, not by these disciples of Christ, but by individuals having no connec-tion with the Church.

It is these missionaries who have been in charge of Liberian educa-tion for the past three-quarters of a century. Today, the various denominations support some sixty mission schools and stations with a total annual budget of a half a million dollars, all coming from the United States. With the exception of five or six small stations in the interior, all of these schools are inside the forty-mile strip which marks so-called civilized territory, and they serve principally Americo-Liberians and the two thousand civilized natives. Primary and grammar school courses and some sort of industrial training are given, but most attention is naturally paid to molding good Christian character.

## SCHOOLS LIMITED

Since the number of Liberian public schools does not exceed 10, which number includes Liberia College, a glorified high school graduating mainly lawyers and receiving $8,000 annually from the government, it is no exaggeration to say that Liberian education is missionary education. The foreign churches are supporting such prominent secondary schools as Monrovia College, the College of West Africa, Muhlenberg Academy, Brierly Memorial School, Kate Palmer's Seminary, Cuddington College, and St. John's Academic and Industrial School.

Thus, whatever be the character and training of the Americo-Liberians, the missionaries are largely responsible. After seventy years of this excessively Christian education, which begins and ends the day with hymn-singing and long prayers, we find products of the system to be, the most shiftless, untrustworthy, incompetent and grafting ruling class to be found today anywhere. With some excep-tion, they display an amazing lack of industry, originality and ingenuity except in the field of intrigue, evasion, sponging, double dealing, excessive litigation, and exploitation of natives, but are very adept at annoying and interfering with the foreign businesses, eager to assist in the development of the country.

INCIDENTS CITED

The following incidents illustrate the point: the wife of an important official of the Firestone Company asked a group of Liberian boys to stop throwing stones on her veranda. They continued until she grew frantic. Then one of them ran up on the veranda and made faces at her. "Just push me", he yelled, knowing that it is an offence to lay one's hands on another in Liberia. "I wish you would push me, I want to get some of the Firestone money too".

The Firestone Company built an excellent garage and machine shop in Monrovia for the care and repair of passenger automobiles and trucks. It filled a great need, as there was no other of its kind in the Republic. Liberians and farmers began to patronize it regularly. Soon the company had to close it down because not a single Americo-Liberian would pay his garage bill. The garage is still closed.

President Barclay, I was told, purchased a limousine from the United States Trading Company and hadn't paid the first cent on it when I was there. Another Government official wanted to purchase automatically from the same company, but having no ready money, suggested that he allocate to the Company his July, August, and September salary as part payment. Wary, the Company officials made a private investigation and discovered the applicant had already drawn his July salary. Confronted with this information, the Liberian blandly apologized, saying it was an oversight on his part.

# Views and Reviews*

## George S. Schuyler

When it comes to advancement in race relations, it must be conceded that the French have it all over the USA, which has been boasting, not without justification, of the progress it has made since the end

* *Pittsburgh Courier*, November 16, 1957. Reprinted by kind permission of the editor.

348

of World War II. We have racially integrated our defence forces since 1949, have eliminated considerable color discrimination from government contracts, have liberated transportation and voting from Jim Crowism, and made a brave step towards ending racially segrated schools and tax-supported recreational facilities. We have three Congressmen from Negro districts.

During the same period, the French made all of their former black subjects citizens of the Republic. Prior to 1945, all blacks were subjects except those in the West Indies, Cayenne, Senegal, and Reunion, who had all the rights of citizenship since 1848. Now the French black Africans have universal suffrage and dozens of them sit in the National Assembly in Paris as deputies, senators, and delegates to the French Union. There have been various colored ministers in French cabinets since the appointment of Blaise Diagne of Dakar, Senegal, during World War I. Today, Houphouet-Boigny is Minister of State as well as being head of the powerful African Democratic Party and Mayor of the big city of Abidjan, Ivory Coast.

Gaston Monnerville, a French West Indian Negro, is President of the French Senate (Council of the Republic) and has been for ten years. Ya D'Oumba is vice-president of the Assembly of French Union. There are numerous Negro assistants in the various Ministries. In Africa itself, (French West Africa, French Equatorial Africa, and Madagascar), almost all local, territorial and federal officials are black. The people have been given increasing control during the past decade over the administration of affairs under the tutelage of experienced men and women from metropolitan France, to an extent almost inconceivable in our South. There has been nothing like it in Portuguese or Spanish Africa, or in British East Africa, and certainly not in South Africa, where a reverse situation has become intensified since Malan and Strijdom took office.

There has scarcely been a French delegation to the United Nations which has not included one or more Negroes. For every American Negro handling large administrative affairs, there are a score of Negroes in French West Africa in such positions, both by appointment and election. French mistakes in Indochina and North Africa have not been repeated in black Africa where the French record in education, sanitation, industrialization and modernization has been most impressive.

Real interracialism obtains everywhere in the French union, and of course its prerequisite, integration. It is more than we can say even for the "good" parts of the USA.

# Alain Locke,
# 1886–1954

Alain Locke was born in Philadelphia and educated at the Philadelphia School of Pedagogy, Harvard and Oxford Universities, and the University of Berlin. He was selected as the first Negro Rhodes Scholar and studied in England on this fellowship from 1907 to 1910. For most of his life he taught philosophy at Howard University, where he was chairman of that department. Dr. Locke edited the *Bronze Booklets* and was the author of numerous articles and works. As a writer and teacher, and the first Negro ever to receive his Ph.D. in philosophy, Dr. Locke was an important moulder of Negro opinion. His analyses of the dynamic factors in American life, which produced changes in the American Negro and his self-image, inevitably involved the significance of Africa in this development. The selection included in this anthology originally appeared in *Opportunity*, for which he also wrote the annual retrospective review of literature on the Negro. It is not only of significance in itself but also as it prompted the sensitive letter to him by Captain Harry Dean, also included in this anthology (p. 129).

# Apropos of Africa*

## ALAIN LOCKE

I

Except from the point of view of religious missionarism, it has been until recently almost impossible to cultivate generally in the mind of the American Negro an abiding and serious interest in Africa. Politically, economically, scientifically, culturally, the great concerns of this great continent have engaged the Caucasian and primarily

* *Opportunity*, February, 1924, pp. 37–58. Reprinted by kind permission of The National Urban League.

the European mind. The sooner we recognize as a fact this painful paradox, that those who have naturally the greatest interests in Africa have of all peoples been least interested, the sooner will it be corrected. With notable exceptions, our interest in Africa has heretofore been sporadic, sentimental and unpractical. And,—as for every fact, there is of course a reason: the dark shadow of slavery has thrown Africa, in spite of our conscious wishes, into a sort of chilly and terrifying eclipse, against which only religious ardor could kindle an attractive and congenial glow of interest. The time has come, however, with the generation that knows slavery only as history, to cast off this spell, and see Africa at least with the interest of the rest of the world, if not indeed with a keener, more favored, regard. There are parallels, we must remember, for this: Except for the prosperous Tories, England was a bogey to the American colonists; from the thirties to the nineties, the average Irishman was half-ashamed of Erin in spite of lapses into occasional fervent sentimentalism; and even with the sturdy Jewish sense of patrimony, Zionism has had its difficulties in rekindling the concrete regard for the abandoned fatherland. Only prosperity looks backward. Adversity is afraid to look over its own shoulder. But eventually all peoples exhibit the homing instinct and turn back physically or mentally, hopefully and helpfully, to the land of their origin. And we American Negroes in this respect cannot, will not, be an exception.

The very same facts that have frustrated the healthy, vigorous interest in Africa and things African, have focused whatever interest there was upon the West Coast,—erroneously regarded because of the accidents of the slave-trade as our especial patrimony, if we ever had any. But the colored millions of America represent every one of the many racial stocks of Africa, are descended from the peoples of almost every quarter of the continent, and are culturally the heirs of the entire continent. The history of the wide dispersion of the slave-trade and trading-posts will establish this in the mind of any open-minded person, and an anthropological investigation of American Negro types would conclusively prove this. If the Negro is interested in Africa, he should be interested in the whole of Africa; if he is to link himself up again with his past and his kin, he must link himself up with all of the African peoples. As the physical composite of eighty-five per cent at least of the African stocks, the American Negro is in a real sense the true Pan-African, and certainly even apart from this, on the grounds of opportunity and strategic position, should be the leader in constructive Pan-African thought and endeavor. Enlightened imperialism,—but who can visualize enlightened imperialism,—would have seen in the American Negro just those resources of leadership and devoted interest which it would have needed, and could have utilized if its real aims had been the development, and not merely the exploitations of this great continent and its varied peoples. But it is rather against than with the wish of the interested governments, that the American Negro must reach out toward his rightful share in the solution of African problems and the development of Africa's resources.

II

With a more practical and enlightened vision, the question of the redemption of Africa has become with us the question of the regeneration of Africa. We now see that the missionary condescension of the past generations in their attitude toward Africa was a pious but sad mistake. In taking it, we have fallen into the snare of enemies and have given grievous offence to our brothers. We must realize that in some respects we need what Africa has to give us as much as, or even more than, Africa needs what we in turn have to give her; and that unless we approach Africa in the spirit of the finest reciprocity, our efforts will be ineffectual or harmful. We need to be the first of all Westerners to rid ourselves of the insulting prejudice, the insufferable bias of the attitude of "civilizing Africa,"—for she is not only our mother but in the light of most recent science is beginning to appear as the mother of civilization in general. On the other hand, the average African of the enlightened classes has his characteristic bias,—his pride of blood and bias of clan,—so that the meeting of mind between the African and the Afro-American is dependent upon a broadening of vision and a dropping of prejudices from both sides. The African must dismiss his provincialism, his political-mindedness, his pride of clan; the Afro-American, his missionary condescension, his religious parochialism, and his pride of place. The meeting of the two will mean the inauguration of a new era for both. Above all, it must be recognized that for the present the best channels of co-operative effort lie along economic and educational lines, and that religion and politics, with their inevitable contentiousness and suspicions, are for less promising ways of approach and common effort. America offers the African his greatest educational opportunity; Africa offers the Afro-American his greatest economic opportunity. So we may truly say that the salvation of the one is in the other's hands. I am aware that this is not to many a self-evident proposition, but sober thought

352

will prove to the far-sighted what the logic of the course of events must ultimately justify for the multitude.

But here on this point we have, strangely enough, the feeling of the masses, more ready and ripe for action than the minds of the leaders and the educated few. The Garvey movement has demonstrated that conclusively. Perhaps in the perspective of time, that will appear to have been its chief service and mission,—to have stirred the race mind to the depths with the idea of large-scale cooperation between the variously separated branches of the Negro peoples. This is without doubt the great constructive idea in the race life during the last decade, and must become the center of constructive endeavor for this and the next generation. Unfortunately obscured by the controversy between its radical exponents in the Garvey movement and its liberal exponents, Dr. Du Bois and the sponsors of the Pan-African Congress, and still more unfortunately but temporarily discredited by the financial mal-administration of Mr. Garvey's over-ambitious ventures, the idea has seemed to suffer a fatal setback. But each branch of the movement has done yeoman service, in spite of great obstacles and unfortunate mistakes,—for publicity for the idea is for the present the main thing; its successful working out is a matter of painstaking experiment and endeavour. Each has temporarily failed in what it considered to be its main objective, and what, if realized, would have been a great service both to the cause of the race and humanity at large. The establishment of a great tropical African state, under international mandate, was one of the most constructive and promising proposals in all the grand agenda of the Peace Conference. If Mr. Wilson had sponsored it, fewer of his fourteen points would have been shattered by selfish European diplomacy, and not only America, but the American Negro would have had an official share and a responsible opportunity in the guardianship and development of this great continent. Many forces combined to crush the idea; but when the secret history of the Conference becomes public, General Smuts will probably appear as the most blameworthy opponent of the scheme. Time will, however, eventually justify this idea and acclaim this brilliant sponsor, and out of the desperate exigencies of the near future we may yet see it brought forward in altered form in the councils of the League of Nations, although the greatest practical opportunity, the disposal of the German colonies in Africa, has been irrevocably missed. Similarly, but for internal rather than external causes, the main objective of the Garvey movement has foundered. Wholly self-initiated and self-supported trade intercourse with Africa would have been in itself a wonderful demonstration of practical economic ability on the part of American Negroes as well as of a modern and constructive interest in their African brethren. It is more of a pity, more of a reproach, that this was not realized. But in both cases the idea has survived its initial defeat. Journalistically the Garvey movement has made a permanent contribution to the Afro-American press, and has built bridges of communication for the future. The first great span in the archway, communication, exchange of thought and information between American Negroes and their brothers in the West Indies, can be optimistically regarded as already established. With greater difficulty, three Pan-African Congresses have been trying to construct the broader spans of communication and publicity between us and Africa. The greatest difficulty is in bringing African interests together; that task once achieved, it will be comparatively easy to link up with the American groups. This is especially the problem of the Third Pan-African Congress, which has just concluded its sessions. In the present situation when national feeling, especially that of the French and Belgian contingents, threatens to disrupt the feeble unity of action already achieved, it is very necessary that the American Negro, the most disinterested party, should assume very direct leadership and responsibility for the movement, insisting upon keeping dominant the Pan-African character of the scheme. This is Dr. DuBois' purpose in holding the conference at what is considered by many formerly enthusiastic members as a singularly inappropriate time. Quixotic as it may seem to run counter to the wishes of many African delegates, such a course is undoubtedly right; but pending its justification, the Pan-African idea is just now at the most critical point of its career. The European press and public opinion have always shown keenest interest, appreciating the important potentialities of this movement; it is the apathy and disinterestedness of the American, and especially the Afro-American press, which is the strange and disappointing feature of the situation. If the movement should lag, it will be an indictment of the intelligence, perspicacity, and race-mindedness of the American Negro.

### III

The great reason for this unfortunate apathy of interest is the lack of widespread and matter of fact information about Africa. Our interests are fed on sentiment, and not with knowledge. Our first duty is to cultivate every opportunity for the diffusion among us of the knowledge of Africa both of today and of the past. Travel, exchange of students, the spread of journalistic and academic information are for the moment of paramount importance. In a decade in which the study of African art and archeology has come to the very forefront of scholarship, it is both a reproach and a handicap to have no recognized experts of our own in these fields. Instead of being reluctant, our Negro colleges should be eager to develop special scholarship in these directions; in the cultural field, here is their special and peculiar chance to enter the academic arena and justify themselves. The pioneer work of the *Journal of Negro History*, under Dr. Carter G. Woodson, and of Howard University in the courses of the history of African civilizations, under Mr. Leo Hansberry, deserve not mere passing interest and praise but the financial support of the people and the active participation of the talented tenth. And both must eventually culminate, the sooner, the better, for the present is a very psychological moment in African studies, in well-planned and well-supported research investigation in Africa. Later I shall write more specifically about the problems and opportunities of research in this field as they have come under observation in the *reconnaisance* trip I have been able to undertake; for the moment it will suffice to quote, by permission, the following representative opinion from a letter of Mr. Arthur Weigall, former Chief Inspector of Antiquities for Upper Egypt, to that most eminent of archeologists, Sir William Flinders-Petrie: "The study of the history and traditions of the African races by their own students is, I think, most interesting, and I am sure you will find the idea of an African mind applying itself to ancient African manners and customs a very promising one." Out of over a score of most eminent authorities interviewed on this subject, all save two have substantially concurred in this opinion, and these two were investigators who strictly relegate ethnological matters to the findings of anthropometry and, naturally enough, consider physical anthropology too scientifically neutral for there to be any advantage or peculiar point to our participation. On the other hand, even they were willing to admit that in the question of folk-lore and comparative study of customs, psychological *rapport* and *entree* to the groups studied were of paramount importance, and that with respect to the study of African peoples, the employment of trained colored investigators would inaugurate a new era in this important, but admittedly unsatisfactory, field of research. . . .

IV

While our active interests in Africa must of necessity and of reason remain educational and eventually economic, there is every reason why we should be keenly interested in the political fortunes of all African peoples. The apathy of our general public opinion in the matter of the proposed American loan and economic protection to Liberia was a shameful dereliction, which should not be allowed to repeat itself on any matter of African politics. Assessing at the lowest value, the motives of this project, and supposing even that it could have militated somewhat against Liberian sovereignty—a too pessimistic and undeserved assumption, especially in view of the moral force of the League of Nations, we may warrantably ask, what better guarantee of fair and considerate treatment could the Liberians have had than the force of the American Negro electorate, if properly awake and intelligently directed? Minorities have as their best protection today the court of world opinion; if they do not live on an international scale and in the eyes of the world, they are doomed even in the twentieth century to medieval conditions and hardships. Witness the effectiveness of that fine voice in the League of Nations, the former Haytian representative, Monsieur Bellegarde, who ought to have the esteem and gratitude of the entire world of colored people. European statesmen and publicists felt and acknowledged the force of this man; his recall was a calamity to our larger international interest. The success and strength of the Jew, still very precariously situated in some parts of the world, has been his international scale of organization, promoted first of all by his religion, and latterly through many other channels of cooperative race effort, of which Zionism is only one phase. Mr. Ford's phrase is true,—the international Jew: but it is an unwarrantable calumny because his inferences are wrong. In the first place, the Jew has been made international by persecution and forced dispersion,—and so, potentially, have we. In the second place, as a minority threatened here and there, its only intelligent safeguard has been international appeal and international organization. To relieve pressure in one place very often pressure has to be strategically applied in another, and the Jewish people have perforce become masters in this intelligent and modern strategy of group action. And if the international mind is to be for all people the eventual achievement, the Jew has simply the temporary advantage of having acquired it a little in advance of the rest of the world.

356

There is much value to us in this great example. We have for the present, in spite of Mr. Garvey's hectic efforts, no Zionistic hope or intention. But for protection and mutual development, we must develop the race mind and race interest on an international scale. For that reason, we should be most vitally interested in the idea of the League of Nations and all kindred movements. . . .

# Canada Lee,
## 1907–1950

Canada Lee (Lionel Corneliou Canegata) was born in New York City and was educated in the public schools of that city. His first occupation, at the age of fourteen, was that of a race horse jockey; later he became a prize fighter and won the Metropolitan Inter-City and Junior National Championships (popularly known as the Golden Gloves). For a brief period he organized a band, and he expressed an early interest in the theatre. Because of his inability to make a living in the theatre, he became a stevedore at the age of twenty-eight, alternately returning to the stage to play many significant roles. The first role to attract attention was in Orson Welles' production of *Macbeth*. Later he played Christophe in *Haiti* and the feature role of Drayton in *Mamba's Daughter*. He also played Bigger Thomas in Orson Welles' production of *Native Son*, Danny in *Anna Lucasta*, and Caliban in *The Tempest*. He was selected for the principal role in the motion picture version of Alan Peyton's *Cry the Beloved Country* which was produced in Africa.

## Africa and a New World A-Coming

### ADDRESS BY CANADA LEE

*Chairman, Patrons of the African Academy of Arts and Research, Ladies and Gentlemen:*

It is an honor for me to participate in such a program as this, designed to broaden the visions of men and women entering a new epoch in our eventful human history. I have followed the work and aspirations of the African Academy since its debut at Carnegie Hall up until the present time. I am appreciative of the splendid work that it has done in educating the American public about the people of Africa, their contributions and their responsibilities in the new coming order. I am speaking tonight as co-chairman of its Production Division.

One of the objects of this meeting is to pay tribute to our late beloved and illustrious Wendell L. Willkie. Many things have been said and written about this great personality whom we all loved; but to my mind, the greatest way to mourn our Willkie is to champion those things he stood and fought for—yes, to complete the unfinished task which he left behind him. And along these lines, what I am indicating is that we look at Africa as Willkie might have looked at it if he were among us today. My talk, therefore, boils down to Africa and a "New World A-Coming."

Africa represents one of the world's oldest civilizations, as attested by historians biased or unbiased. During the period of its grandeur, it made several significant contributions, for which the world today has found no better substitutes, but which it has improved whenever necessary. To cite one illustration: it was an African who performed the first successful operation for blindness, at which time Europe was still in feudal bondage and America was yet to be discovered. I will not belabor my audience by giving countless illustrations, let me pass from here to discuss Africa as it applies to myself.

Let me say I am an African of African descent, though a loyal and devoted American. Some people say that they have been so far removed from Africa that they have lost all connections. Some say they have been intermixed for a long period of time. For my part, I do not care how far removed they are, or in how many generations they have been mixed or unmixed. In a few years hence, these same people will re-echo "me too am African," for they will find it the land to draw inspiration from, and strength when the struggles of this life are toughest on them. I say, therefore, without apology or hesitation, that it is through Africa that American Negroes can revive their pride and then be proud of their heritage. This recovery of pride is a forerunner to total freedom.

WHY NOT ME?

It is for this reason that the Jews today are determined to rebuild Palestine. It is for this same reason that our white friends in America trace their ancestry to all parts of Europe. Why cannot we then follow the same course of action? Why cannot we then look forward to that land that had been an asylum for all things worthy of a good report. It was an asylum for Jesus Christ, and if that land was good for Him, it is then more good for us. The time has therefore come for American Negroes and the Africans to unite in bonds of fellowship and in bonds of common brotherhood. I look at Africa as a house which a young man builds in his youth, so that he can take shelter in his old age.

Coming to Africa in its relation to international politics, I must here touch on Willkie's idea—One World. The idea of one world which permitted Willkie's thinking cannot come about until there is total freedom for all people of all nations.

Statesmen of today amaze me when they talk about freedom, it is not the same freedom you and I know and cherish and would fight and die for. They talk about freedom for Europe, but not freedom for Asia, India or Africa. Let it be known today to the world that Negroes of America resent that type of approach, and let it be further known in this respect we cannot be indifferent to the fortunes or misfortunes of Africa. What we stand for and will always stand for is freedom for all.

There are many parts of Africa that are over-ripe to control their own governments. I refer to Nigeria, the Gold Coast, and Sierra Leone, to mention just a few. Some of these places have been governing themselves for thousands of years, and to tell us today they cannot now do so is just a lot of nonsense. That statement comes from vested interests that would rather see the whole world bled white than yield one iota of the sources from which they derive their ill-gotten gains.

Today we are asking: What form will world organization take? How can peace be maintained? The answer is that a world organization for a durable peace will collapse unless Big Powers renounce the domination of weaker Powers as an instrument of national policy. Let us further remember that Europe has been much more burdensome to the world than Africa, for it has refused to remain peaceful even for a continuous thirty years. The world should be humble to acknowledge this fact, and courageous to take the lead from Africa.

Let us look at the military picture of Africa in this war. When France fell, African people under Governor General Eboue still raised the banner of freedom in their determination to fight to the end. The French Equatorial African Army, formed by the late Governor, were the first Allied soldiers to arrive in Paris when the liberation movement struck. West African troops are fighting in India and are leading the fight in jungle warfare against the Japanese military might. And yet, we hear so little about this military feat and these heroic, forgotten and forsaken allies of ours.

My friends, let us reassure Africa of our sincerity. The best way to demonstrate this type of cooperation is to embrace the Africans who are here and who have extended their hand of friendship. Since my contact with the African Academy of Arts and Research, I have come to learn more about these people, their aspirations and their plans. Since my contact with Mr. Mbadiwe, I have become more convinced of the leading role which Africa is destined to play. The cause of Africa is our cause and before we leave here tonight, let us demonstrate our interest by concrete financial contribution toward the work of the African Academy of Arts and Research. Let us reassure Mr. Mbadiwe that we are behind this project. What then does Africa mean to me? Let me re-echo it in the words of Pearl N. Robinson:

AMERICAN NEGRO

What is Africa
 To me
With its tall palms
 And Mystery
I am part of this land—
 Its throbbing night and day,
Its temples where men come
 To kneel and pray.
I am part of its music
 Its laughter and its call;
Its boundless wide pavements
 Its buildings tall.
I am part of its movement,
 Its science and skill;
Its giant factories making planes
 With dauntless will.

Ladies and gentlemen, I therefore say again, the cause of Africa is our cause. The work of the African Academy of Arts and Research is our work. We must act now or never.

# E. Franklin Frazier,
# 1894-1962

Edward Franklin Frazier was born in Baltimore, Maryland. He spent his early life in that city, where he also received his primary and secondary education. After receiving the B.A. degree from Howard University, he taught at Tuskegee Institute, St. Paul's Normal and Industrial School in Lawrenceville, Virginia, and in the Baltimore high schools. His subsequent degrees were an M.A. from Clark University and a Ph.D. from the University of Chicago.

For almost forty years, beginning in 1920, Edward Franklin Frazier studied the Negro in the United States and race relations throughout the world critically and with great concern. As the author of ten books, innumerable chapters in books, and many articles, he manifested the rare quality of examining and criticizing those aspects of life close to him objectively but still with concern and often with wit.

As a sociologist, Dr. Frazier viewed the Negro community fundamentally as a product of the American experience. Because Negroes had been deprived of opportunities for nourishing more than remote memories of their history and life in Africa, he did not see Africa as a panacea or an answer to the problems of the American Negro. But he did believe that Africa provided the American Negro "with a new identification and a new image and a new sense of personal dignity".

The selection included in this anthology is part of a speech Dr. Frazier made shortly before his death, in which he reiterates his favorite theme of the general irresponsibility of the American Negro intellectual toward the Negro masses, and the opportunity for African intellectuals to correct this deficiency.

# The Failure of the Negro Intellectual*

## Dr. E. Franklin Frazier

In recent years there has been much talk about the integration of the Negro but hardly any attention has been given to his assimilation. There have been some wild guesses about the amalgamation or absorption of the Negro and his disappearance in 300 to 500 years. It is to the question of the assimilation of the Negro that I want to devote the remainder of this talk.

It may seem strange if I tell you that the question of integration and assimilation of the American Negro has not been considered or raised by American Negroes but by African intellectuals. Only recently at a luncheon in Washington an African intellectual spoke on the subject and afterwards asked me to write an article on the subject. But the contrast between the attitude and orientation of American Negro intellectuals and African intellectuals was revealed most sharply at the congresses of Negro writers held in Paris in 1956 and in Rome in 1959.

At these congresses the African, and I might add the West Indian intellectuals, were deeply concerned with the question of human culture and personality and the impact of western civilization on the traditional culture of Negro peoples. It was to be expected that African intellectuals would be concerned with such questions.

*But the amazing thing was that American Negro intellectuals who were imbued with an integrationist point of view were not only unconcerned with this question but seemingly were unconscious of the implications of the important question of the relation of culture and personality and human destiny. . . .*

In my *Black Bourgeoisie* I have considered this phenomenon and it is unnecessary to go into the question here. There are certain phases of this phenomenon which are relevant to this discussion.

The first aspect is that the new Negro middle class is the stratum of the Negro population that is becoming integrated most rapidly because of its education and its ability to maintain certain standards of living. In its hope to achieve acceptance in American life, it would slough off everything that is reminiscent of its Negro origin and its Negro folk background.

* *Negro Digest*, February, 1962, pp. 26–36. Reprinted by kind permission of the editor.

At the same time integration is resulting in inner conflicts and frustrations because Negroes are still outsiders in American life. Despite integration, the middle class, in escaping from its sheltered and privileged position in the Negro community, has become more exposed to the contempt and discriminations of the white world. Thus, the new Negro middle class is confronted with the problems of assimilation and their intellectuals have not provided them with an understanding of the problems.

This lack of understanding on the part of the so-called intellectual fringe of the new middle class is due partly to the general anti-intellectualism of this class and partly to the desire to achieve acceptance in American life by conformity to the ideals, values, and patterns of behavior of white Americans.

This is no speculation on my part. Every study that has been made reveals that they think very much the same as white Americans, even concerning Negroes.

Moreover, so-called Negro intellectuals continue to repeat such nonsense as "No race has made as much progress as the American Negro in the same period and that his remarkable progress has been due to oppression."

Yet, anyone knows that after 250 years American Negro intellectuals can not measure up to African intellectuals. . . .

The great difference between the orientation of the African intellectual and the American Negro intellectual is striking when one considers their starting point in their analysis of the position for whom they are supposed to provide intellectual leadership.

All African intellectuals begin with the fact of the colonial experience of the African. They possess a profound understanding of the colonial experience and its obvious effects upon not only their traditional social organization but the less obvious and more profound effects upon the culture and the African-personality.

The American Negro intellectual goes his merry way discussing such matters as the superficial aspects of the material standard of living among Negroes and the extent to which they enjoy civil rights. He never begins with the fundamental fact of what slavery has done to the Negro or the group which is called Negroes in the United States.

Yet it is as necessary for the American Negro intellectual to deal with these questions as it is for the African intellectual to begin with the colonial experience.

The American Negro intellectual is even more remiss in his grasp of the condition and fate of American Negroes. He has steadily refused to recognize what has been called the "mark of oppression." It was the work of two white scholars that first called attention to this fundamental aspect of the personality of the American Negro. Moreover, it was the work of another white scholar, Stanley M. Elkins, in his recent book on *Slavery*, who has shown the psychic trauma that Negroes suffered when they were enslaved, the pulverization of their social life through the destruction of their clan organization, and annihilation of their personality through the destruction of their cultural heritage.

Sometimes I think that the failure of the American Negro intellectual to grasp the nature and the significance of these experiencies is due to the fact that he continues to be an unconscious victim of these experiences. After an African intellectual met a group of Negro intellectuals, he told me that they were really men who were asleep.

All of this only tends to underline the fact that educated Negroes or Negro intellectuals have failed to achieve any intellectual freedom. In fact, with the few exceptions of literary men, it appears that the Negro intellectual is unconscious of the extent to which his thinking is restricted to sterile repetition of the safe and conventional ideas current in American society.

This is attributable in part, of course, to the conditions under which an educated and intellectual class emerged in the American society. This class emerged as the result of white philanthropy. Although the situation has changed and the Negro intellectuals are supported through other means, they are still largely dependent upon the white community. There is no basis of economic support for them within the Negro community. And where there is economic support within the Negro community it demands conformity to conservative and conventional ideas.

. . . Most Negro intellectuals simply repeat the propaganda which is put out by people who have large economic and political interests to protect.

Of course, Negro intellectuals are in a different position from the standpoint of employment. If they show any independence in their thinking they may be hounded by the F.B.I. and find it difficult to make a living. At the present time many of them find themselves in the humiliating position of running around the world telling Africans and others how well-off Negroes are in the United States and how well they are treated.

One is reminded of the words of Langston Hughes in his recent book, *Ask Your Mama*, where he says that the African visitor finds that in the American social supermarket blacks for sale range from intellectuals to entertainers. Thus, it appears that the price of the slow integration which Negroes are experiencing must be bought at the price of abject conformity in thinking. . . .

In a chapter entitled, "What can the American Negro Contribute to the Social and Economic Life of Africa" in the book, *Africa Seen By American Negroes*, I pointed out that the American Negro had little to contribute to Africa but that Africa, in achieving freedom, would probably save the soul of the American Negro in providing him with a new identification, a new self-image, and a new sense of personal dignity.

I want to emphasize this by pointing out that if the Negro is ever assimilated into American society his heritage should become a part of the American heritage, and it should be recognized as the contribution of the Negro as one recognizes the contributions of the English, Irish, Germans and other people.

But this can be achieved only if the Negro intellectual and artist frees himself from his desire to conform and only if he overcomes his inferiority complex.

It may turn out that in the distant future Negroes will disappear physically from American society. If this is our fate, let us disappear with dignity and let us leave a worthwhile memorial—in science, in art, in literature, in sculpture, in music—of our having been here.

# James W. Ford,
## 1893-1957

James William Ford was born in Georgia, the son of a tenant farmer and the grandson of a man who had been lynched by a white mob in a dispute over a pig.

Ford was never very far from the working classes of American Negroes. When his family moved to Alabama, he and his father worked for a coal company. After working his way through three years at Fisk University, Ford joined the army in 1917. Because of racial prejudice, he was unable to enter the United States Army Radio School. He undertook similar training with the French government and served at the front with great distinction.

Upon the completion of his military duty, Ford went to Chicago and joined the Postal Service. He was very active in the Postal Workers' Union and in 1926 joined the Communist Party and rapidly rose to prominence in its ranks. In 1932 he ran as a vice presidential candidate on the Communist ticket.

It has been generally agreed that, while the Communist Party actually made little headway among American Negroes, Ford, as one writer has suggested, "personified grievances of the Negroes in the United States—lynching, the cropping system, discrimination, exploitation, exploitation in Southern industries, limited vocational opportunities in the North, and lack of recognition." To that extent he played a useful role as a writer and speaker in the Party's efforts to expand its Negro membership.

# The Negro People and
# The World Situation*

## JAMES W. FORD

*Candidate for Vice President;
First Negro to run for this
office since Frederick Douglass*

. . . "On June 22 Hitler fascists unleased an unprovoked military attack upon the Soviet Union.

Once again the enslaved peoples of Africa, the peoples of Asia, the semi-dependent countries of South America and the Carribean and the Negro people of America were given an object lesson in the mad drive of the Hitler fascists to conquer the world and to enslave nations and peoples everywhere. The masses of Negro people everywhere, toilers in the mines, mills and factories and in the fields, down in the South and far away in the heart of Africa, along with the toilers throughout the world are drawn together in the realization that Hitler's attack against the Soviet Union is calculated to bind the chains of slavery on people in all lands in the most brutal domination in the history of the world. Nothing can stop this threat except the complete military defeat and annihilation of the German fascist monsters. . . .

The oppressed Negro people are not, cannot be indifferent to this threat to the Soviet Union, to the threat of world domination by the Nazi beast.

The Nazi rulers despise the peoples of the Negro race. If German fascists are not destroyed their theories of Aryan superiority doom the Negro people to eternal slavery, "hewers of stone and carriers of water". In Hitler's scheme of a so-called "new Order" the Negro people are assigned to be beasts of burden; their aspirations for natural freedom and liberty are threatened with complete obliteration.

The Negro people have already had terrifying experiences with Hitlerism and fascism. In 1936 Ethiopia was invaded by Hitler's vassal, the Italian fascists. Disregarding all international law and the

* James Ford, *The Negro People and the World Situation*, 1941. Reprinted by permission of New Outlook Publishers.

368

covenant of the League of Nations, the territory of Ethiopia was violated by Mussolini's fascist legions, under the cover of seeking out Communism in the economically undeveloped territory of Ethiopia. The leaders of the Ethiopian people appealed to the conscience of humanity for aid against the violation of their borders. The Soviet Union almost alone fought for sanctions against Italy in the League of Nations.

Negro peoples throughout the world were aroused to the greatest indignation and hatred against fascism by this unprovoked attack on Ethiopia. From the United States a delegation, including Communist leaders, was sent to Geneva to interview the Ethiopian Ambassador. The spokesman for the delegation, in setting forth the menace and character of fascism, stated to the Ambassador as follows:

"The ideals which motivate the Negro masses to stand solidly behind Ethiopia are those of racial ties and the desire to aid a small nation whose independence and national and economic existence are threatened by big powers and megalomaniac fascism, and this it seems not only in the case of Liberia and Ethiopia, but in the case of a great nation like China, nations like Czechoslovakia and Central and South American countries, Cuba, Haiti, etc.

"Our racial ties are remote but our mutual fight for national existence in a world of big bandit nations is clear and tangible, and we stand ready to defend the long history and fine cultural and national growth of the Ethiopian people, so that Ethiopia, by maintaining its freedom, may have the possibility of progressive growth, unhampered by the destructive forces of the so-called "civilized nations.""

## The Vital Problem of the Right of Trade Unions in Countries in Africa*

### JAMES W. FORD†

The right of Africans to establish trade unions for the betterment of their economic lot deserves world wide attention. If they cannot be secure in this right there is no assurance of enduring world peace.

* The Journal of Negro Education, Vol. XVI (Spring, 1947), pp. 251–256. Reprinted by permission of the editor.
† This account is based on one written by the author in October, 1945, for Inkululeko, journal of the Communist Party of South Africa. Inkululeko is from the African language. It means Freedom.

An examination of the problem of the freedom of trade unions in Africa generally and with special reference to South Africa will show that the economic, social and political policies of the white ruling circles in regard to the right of Africans to organize trade unions, threatens the destruction of the peoples of Africa. It is therefore a world problem.

In August of last year 50,000 miners led by the African Mine Workers' Union went on strike to increase their starvation wages from 3 shillings (60 cents) to 10 shillings per day. The strikers were met with brutal attacks and the Chamber of Mines which dominates the mining industry claimed that Africans "are not advanced enough" for labor unions. Nine miners were killed and more than a thousand were injured. Fifty-two persons, including leading members of the African Mine Workers' Union were arrested. At this writing they are appearing before the courts of Johannesburg. Lately eight members of the Central Committee of the Communist Party of South Africa were arrested in connection with the strike. They are charged with sedition.[1] Strikes of Africans are a crime by South African law.

As the principal organizer of the First International Trade Union Conference of Negro Workers, held at Hamburg, Germany, in 1930, and also editor of the journal *The Negro Worker*, this article affords me even if belatedly the opportunity to summarize for American public opinion some experiences in the struggle for trade unionism in countries of Africa. It is intended to give a sketch of the desperate and magnificent struggles which Africans have made to establish unions, and also to expose the fascist-like claims of the white ruling circles in South Africa.

Up to 1930 African workers had faced many difficulties in organizing trade unions. All organized struggles of African labor for its rights were subject to repression. No labour legislation to speak of existed in any part of what is known as Black Africa. The foreign industrial enterprises which controlled the economic life of the continent, strangled all attempts of African workers to organize and secure betterment of their lives. Nonetheless, by 1930 trade unions and even federations of African workers were already in evidence in a number of countries of Africa. They were more highly developed in South Africa, as for example, the Non-European Federation of Trade Unions.[2]

[1] The items enumerated in this paragraph appeared in The New York *Times*, November 17, 1946.

[2] The Non-European Federation of Trade Unions was organized in Johannesburg, South Africa, in 1929. It was composed of The African Laundry Workers' Union, Clothing Workers' Union, Furniture Workers' Union, Metal & Mechanic

The existence of these trade unions coupled with hundreds of thousands of American Negro proletarians who had ties in the trade union movement of the USA, led to the convening of the First International Trade Union Conference of Negro Workers.

The purpose of this conference, according to the program outlined by it, consisted of developing trade unions among the scattered workers in Africa and the West Indies, and among unorganized Negro proletarians in the USA; of raising their living standards; and improving their working conditions; of cultivating the spirit of fraternity between workers in Africa and workers in Europe and America; and of fighting against imperialism and imperialist war.

The conference did not confine its work alone to elementary trade union questions. The scope of its work went far beyond the narrow framework of trade unionism in the ordinary economic sense. Economic struggles were regarded as political and as having important bearing on social problems. This was in contrast to the position of conservative trade union leaders who even at that time had some influence in the trade union movement of South Africa.

The organizers of the conference were from countries where the relation between exploitation of workers and of national oppression expressed itself in a most glaring form. The organizers were of varying political viewpoints. Some few of them were strengthened by their knowledge of the science of Marxism. All of them had acquired a knowledge of the history and the laws of the development of the trade union movement, evolved over a long number of years in Europe and America. They were workers and they had experience in trade unions and workers' struggles. They were in the main African and American Negro workers. But they knew that they were not dealing with an isolated "African" or "Negro" question. They understood that they were concerned with a world-wide problem.

South Africa was found to be typical of the problem and needs of what is known as Black Africa. We found, for instance, that South African workers were restricted by pass laws and other regulations which barred the path of trade union organization. It was found also that African workers occupied a position of the most degraded class of labor in South Africa. There was also the class of so-called "colored" labor. Above both stood "poor white" workers.[3]

---

Workers' Union, African Bakers' Union, Transport Workers' Union, Food Workers' Union, Meat Workers' Union, Rope Workers' Union, Steel Workers' Union and the Dairy Workers' Union.—From the "Negro Worker," Jan.–Feb., 1929, p. 2.
[3] The Durban riots, the increased number of strikes, the development of

Two factors therefore determined our approach to the problem of labor in South Africa, namely, (a) African labor and the relation which existed between organizations of white workers and those of African workers, and (b) the deteriorating influence of the International Federation of Trade Unions (IFTU) in the South African labor movement.

Beginning in 1922 the strikes which had been lost by trade unions that excluded African workers made the conditions of white workers progressively worse. This was because of the attraction to the mining industry of ever larger numbers of skilled and semi-skilled African workers who were without trade union protection. The most urgent problem was the right of African workers to organize.

The entire economic life of South Africa rests on the mining industry. And this industry is manned almost wholly by African labor. For a number of years due to the chaotic condition of the mining industry and to the white supremacy policy of the South African ruling class, unemployment and wage cuts had been causing wide spread discontent among white workers. The average yearly wage of white workers in manufacturing industries had had the following downward trend: in 1925 their average yearly wage was £239; 1926, £238; 1928, £221; in 1929 it was still lower.[4] The central question here was the relation between organizations of white workers and those of African workers and the fact that African workers were not allowed to organize trade unions.

Trade unions of white workers never raised the question of African workers. The adherents of the Amsterdam International (IFTU) similarly ignored the problems of African labor. Instead of helping African workers to organize trade unions, they either held themselves aloof from them or they took the standpoint of the local white ruling class and of the foreign imperialists. There was only one sound approach to this situation, namely, the right of Africans to organize trade unions and the single organization of African and white workers.

The conference also found that the entire African population lived under the most oppressive economic and social conditions. Expro-

African trade unions under Communist influence, the joint strikes of African and white workers, the recent demonstrations on Dingaan's Day prove without a doubt that we are on the verge of great national and class battles and struggles in South Africa.—From news release of the International Trade Union Committee of Negro Workers, New York, N.Y., January 15, 1930. (In private files of the author.)

[4] "The International Negro Workers' Review," Vol. I, No. 1, January 1931, p. 4, Hamburg, Germany.

priation of communal lands, heavy taxation (head taxes, etc.) and oppressive legislation forced the population to supply cheap labor for mines and other industrial enterprises, and also for the big farms of white landlords. This method, by which imperialist penetration forced Africans to become proletarians, made their condition hardly distinguishable from plain slavery. It had a deteriorating influence on all labor, white and African. This situation obtained and still holds throughout the continent of Africa.

In a somewhat different social aspect was the position of Negro labor in the United States and the West Indies. In the USA the Negro people were deprived of full civil rights. They were exploited in mines and factories under Jim Crow conditions at lower wages than white workers for the same kind of work. And they worked under pre-Civil War feudal conditions on cotton and sugar plantations. They were victims of race prejudice. They were subject to mob-rule and lynch-law.

There were seventeen accredited delegates and three fraternal representatives at the Hamburg conference. They came from South Africa, Nigeria, Gambia, Sierra Leone, the Gold Coast, Jamaica, Haiti, and the USA.

They represented 20,000 organized workers, from eleven different trade union categories. Two national trade union centers and one national political party were represented. The latter was the Nigerian Democratic Party. Its national membership however was over-overwhelmingly working class in composition. There was also representation from the African National Congress of South Africa. This gave the conference a people's character. The delegations from South Africa and the USA were composed of both colored and white members.

The conference was persecuted by enemies of trade unionism and of the people's movements. For instance, the Non-European Federation of South Africa and the African National Congress held meetings of their organizations "attended by thousands of Negro workers for the purpose of electing delegates to attend this Conference."[5] But several of the delegates elected at these meetings did not arrive at the Conference. They were detained and prohibited from traveling out of the country by the South African Government.

The conference had been scheduled originally to be held at London, England. But the British Labor Government banned it from England. That is why it had to be shifted to Hamburg, Germany. The shift of

[5] From the Proceedings of the International Trade Union Conference of Negro Workers, Hamburg, Germany, 1931, p. 29.

our plans caused no little confusion. Transportation difficulties were created as many delegates had already arranged to travel by boat to England. They were not allowed to land at British ports. They were harassed by operatives of Scotland Yard. Several West Indian delegates entered British ports, and they were detained and held until the conference had finished its work.

Notwithstanding all these difficulties most of the delegates arrived at Hamburg and carried through their deliberations with great success.

The conference had an order of business including "Economic Struggles and Tasks of Negro Workers," "Struggle against Forced Labor," "the War Danger and Its Significance to Negro Workers."

The first point served as a basis for discussing the economic, social and political position of the Negro people in relation to trade union organization. A "trade union program of action" was adopted which included a shorter working day; higher wages; social and labor legislation; defense of the interests of women and youth workers; organization of agricultural workers; abolition of restrictions against trade unions, such as pass laws, etc; full civil rights; struggle against trade union reformism; and the right of self-determination.[6]

The First International Trade Union Conference of Negro Workers also directed its attention to the relationship between white and Negro labor on an international scale. It dealt with the burning questions of international solidarity and the ideology of white supremacy and chauvinism. This ideology divided the workers along racial lines and placed them in opposition to each other. The Conference exposed the chauvinistic position of Social Democracy and its influence in the European and American trade union movements.

The conference also dealt with Negro petty bourgeois nationalism also described as middle class ideas in the ranks of the Negro people. This type of ideology utilized the mutual interests between Negro workers and the people's movements for the purpose of promoting utopian ideas. The conference pointed out how the ruling class encourages these ideas for its own interest of exploitation.

The conference closed its sessions with the election of a staff of officers and the adoption of the following resolutions: (1) Economic Struggles and the Tasks of Negro Workers, (2) Struggle against Trade Union Reformism and the Divide and Rule ideology of the Exploiters, (3) Negro Workers and the War Danger, (4) Against

[6] From Proceedings of the First International Trade Union Conference of Negro Workers, Hamburg, Germany, 1930, p. 31. In private files of author.

Lynching and Terror, (5) Struggle against Forced Labor and (6) Negro Workers and International Solidarity.[7]

The International Trade Union Conference of Negro Workers performed a memorable task. It stimulated trade union organization in countries of Africa. It prepared Negro toilers for the struggle against Nazism and fascism. They were not caught in the false trap of Japanese imperialism. African and Negro trade unionists were a part of the forces that matured and shaped in the war against fascism. They helped to create the world trade union federation.

The World Trade Union Federation, founded at Paris, France in 1945, took measures to raise the living standards of workers, to achieve democratic rights in all countries and to secure the freedom and liberties of all nations. African and Negro workers were accepted as equals in the international trade union movement.

The World Federation of Trade Unions took note of the mutual interests between colonial peoples and the workers of Europe and America. It supported the right of trade unions and the right of self-determination for colonial and dependent peoples.

It acted to eliminate the causes of war and to guarantee that fascism should never again dare plunge the world into war for the destruction of democratic rights and the liberties of nations.

The World Federation of Trade Unions was strengthened by the trade unions of the Soviet Union. And their representatives understood above all, because of the tremendous contribution of their country to the military defeat of fascism and Nazism, that only a broad and solid international federation of trade unions without race prejudice and discrimination would guarantee progress and the well-being of the working class.

The Government of the Union of South Africa and the foreign imperialists by suppressing the right of trade unions to African workers threaten the existence of the peoples of Africa.

By its denial of the right of trade unions, the South African Government headed by General Jan Smuts, violates the principles of the Charter of the United Nations, in the assembly of which it is a member.

Trade Unions are logical developments wherever men and women are engaged in industrial enterprises, and they may be expected to grow up wherever men and women work.

Africans must be secure in their right to organize trade unions. It is a reactionary policy for governments to punish workers for organizing to secure redress of their grievances.

[7] *Ibid.*, pp. 29–40.

# A. Philip Randolph,
# 1889–

Asa Philip Randolph was born in Crescent City, Florida. He was educated at Cookman Institute in Jacksonville, Florida, and the City College of New York. Randolph became the general organizer and one of the founders of the Brotherhood of Sleeping Car Porters, which was established in 1925. Long identified with the Negro labor movement, Randolph has emerged as one of the senior leaders of the Negro community. By threatening to organize a March on Washington during World War II, Randolph played an important part in urging President Roosevelt to sign Executive Order 8802, which led to the formation of the Fair Employment Practices Committee, a milestone in the establishment of equal job opportunities for American Negroes. Randolph is a writer and speaker as well as a man of action. He was editor, publisher, and manager of the *Messenger*, a periodical devoted to the progress of the Negro, which was published in New York. He was co-author of *Terms of Peace and Darker Races*, the *Truths about Lynching*, and *Political Socialists*.

In the 1950's and 1960's A. Philip Randolph has played a significant role in the Negro community and in the labour movement. He is the only Negro vice-president of the American Federation of Labor Congress of Industrial Organizations, was one of the leading figures in the American Negro Leadership Conference on Africa in November, 1962, and was the director and inspirational force in the August 28, 1963, March on Washington.

**Proceedings, Second Constitutional Convention of the American Federation of Labor and Congress of Industrial Organizations, Atlantic City, December 11, 1957\* on Resolution No. 150 for a Program for World Peace and Freedom**

VICE PRESIDENT RANDOLPH: Brother, Chairman and delegates:
I want to say a few words on this resolution. But before I do, I think it proper that I make a few remarks concerning the African

\* Reprinted by kind permission of the Federation.

scholarship program which the AFL-CIO has sponsored, but recently abandoned.

May I say that I was largely responsible for this program, having submitted it to the Executive Council following my visit to Kenya. I was surprised and greatly disappointed when the program was abandoned.

For the record, I want it to show that I did not participate in the meeting in which the program was discussed and where the decision was made to abandon it. I did participate in a subsequent meeting, but in that meeting the decision concerning the program was a fait accompli. It had been decided.

A substitute program has been initiated to provide for the establishment of a school in Tanganyika. I am not offering any criticism of that program. As a matter of fact, I naturally would not oppose any program to establish a school for the training and education of African workers. However, I do think that the abandonment of the scholarship program was a mistake. I do not claim complete knowledgeability of the African problem, and certainly I have the highest respect for those who handled the program and I know that they handled the program in good faith. I have no criticism to make of those who handled the program.

I want to say a word about the resolution, that part of the resolution dealing with colonialism. I think the reason for different approaches to this question probably stems from a difference in emphasis upon the relationship of the AFL-CIO to the International free trade union movement. I am of the opinion that the same revolution which was responsible for the transition of world power from Europe to the North American continent is the revolution which is responsible also for a transition of power and leadership from the British Trades Union Congress to the American Federation of Labor and Congress of Industrial Organizations. In other words, in my opinion history has changed the relationship of America to the free world. America today is the leader of the free world. America must accept the responsibility of leadership. Just as America is the leader of the free world, in my opinion the AFL-CIO is the leader of the free world of labor. As the leader of the free world of labor, I believe that there is a basic challenge and that challenge may be divided into two parts. One is to halt the march and expansion of Russian communism in the world. The second is to tear down and break up and throw into the ash can of history African colonialism.

Africa today is the last stronghold of colonialism in the world. Ninety percent of the land and over 80 percent of the people are still under the yoke of colonialism. Colonialism is an abomination; it is a sin; it is an evil. It brings about the degradation and the demoralization of the human spirit, of the personality of the people who are the victims of it.

No one can countenance colonialism who believes in the principle of the solidarity of the human family. No one can support colonialism who believes in the dignity of the human personality. Consequently, the hope of the free world lies in the abolition of colonialism in Africa, because Africa today is the battleground between the forces of justice and the forces of injustice.

May I say in this connection, fellow delegates, that in my opinion the American Federation of Labor and Congress of Industrial Organizations in many ways has a comparability of relationship to the free world such as the United States has to the free world. In other words, the United States of America does not always function through the United Nations. At the same time, it is dedicated to the United Nations. The Marshall Plan did not emanate through the United Nations. The Truman Doctrine in the interest of Turkey and Greece did not emanate from the United Nations. The Eisenhower Doctrine in the interests of the Middle East did not originate in the United Nations. Nevertheless, the United States is committed to the principle of the United Nations, and the United States is one of the big forces for the stabilization and consolidation of the United Nations.

It would be a mistake were the United States to take the position that all of its international activities should be channeled through the United Nations, and in my opinion the same position must be taken by the AFL-CIO. I do not believe that an international activity of the AFL-CIO is ipso facto and per se incompatible with the philosophy, the program and progress of the ICFTU. The AFL-CIO has been the means of bringing about conditions that have given strength to the ICFTU. I have only to point to the time when the AFL led the fight against the World Federation of Trade Unions. The fight of the AFL against the World Federation of Trade Unions was the foundation for the building of the ICFTU. When that fight was carried on it was led by George Meany, Matthew Woll, and Dave Dubinsky, with the cooperation of Irving Brown in the field and others here at home who were giving technical and theoretical advice with respect to this question.

Following that, the AFL was responsible for the exposure of forced labor by the Soviet Union. This was an initiative taken by the AFL. Following that, the AFL-CIO led the van in rousaing world opinion against the horrors of the crushing of the freedom fighters of Hungary in blood and tears and death. I say that in order that you might understand that world leadership requires initiative. It requires vision. It requires dynamism. It requires faith. The American Federation of Labor and Congress of Industrial Organizations, being a part of a nation which was born in revolt against colonialism, being a part of a nation which is itself committed against colonialism, is spiritually and morally and psychologically more prepared to lead the fight against world colonialism than any other trade union in the world.

I hope what I am about to say will not be of any offense to any of our foreign brothers. I have the highest respect and admiration for our British trade union leaders, because the British Trades Union Congress is the oldest national trade union center, perhaps, in the world. Be it said to the credit of the British Trades Union Congress that its leader, Sir Vincent Tewson, was largely responsible for bringing together the AFL and CIO in the international field in order that the AFL and CIO might participate in world conferences together. They were not together on the international field before that.

But in my opinion, it is just as impossible to expect the British Trades Union Congress, which is a part of the British Empire, to lead the fight against colonialism as it is impossible to expect the State of Mississippi to lead the fight for civil rights. In other words, though the question before us of making a drive against colonialism is basic, I do not believe we can arrest the drive of world communism until we arrest and destroy colonialism in Africa.

Africa is the battleground of three great struggles. One is the coming struggle for power between democracy and communism. We have Ghana, a new state, following the democratic creed. Then we have the beginning of forces that will bring Nigeria into the community of free peoples. But at the present time Africa has a living yoke of colonialism and is the victim of the most uncivilized persecution mankind has ever known.

Look at Kenya. In the Legislature of Kenya there are 16 white settlers. They represent 55,000 people, white settlers of Kenya. There are 6 representatives of the Asians. The Asians represent 500,000 people in Kenya. There are 8 representatives of Africans. These are Africans, and they represent 7 million Africans.

Here you have an inequity which cannot be explained by reason, and consequently no ordinary drive can be made to destroy colonialism. It must be an organized, systematic drive of world proportions in order that we may be rid of this stigma upon mankind.

Look at the Central African Federation, covering northern Rhodesia and southern Rhodesia and Nyasaland. Ninety-seven percent of the people are Africans, and yet 3 percent dominate the Legislature and control the life of the people.

The same thing is true in South Africa. Ten million Africans are under the domination of two and a half million white settlers.

Here, my friends, you have a land where these three struggles are going to take place—the coming struggle for power between democracy and communism, and the coming struggle for power between races. You may, my friends, be shaken by the fact that unquestionably the thunder and the lightning of conflict in Africa is going to come between the races unless there is some basic concession of rights and power and responsibility to the Africans—as a matter of fact, not only a concession of power, but a recognition of the rights of these Africans to rule in their own land.

Finally, the third crisis as a result of a struggle for power will come on the basis of difference in religion. Moslemism and Christianity are in conflict in Africa. The Cairo radio is beaming its voice to the Moslems of Africa.

And, of course, Christianity is at a disadvantage because it is associated with colonialism. Christianity, however, has this advantage, and that is it has established mission schools and out of these mission schools the leaders of Africa are coming. Nkrumah of Ghana came of the Catholic Mission schools of West Africa; then we have Mboya of Kenya coming out of the mission schools. But in addition to coming out of the mission schools they came over to the United States of America and entered the universities and colleges here, and Mboya went to London to Ruskin College.

In other words, here you have in Africa the scene of three great world conflicts, and that is the reason why I am greatly concerned and interested in not only leadership but the nature of the leadership of the African trade union workers.

I hope, my friends, that we will recognize the great position of Africa in the world crises, because if Africa goes down the path of China, if Africa goes down the path of Red Communism, the free world is doomed. Therefore, the hope of the free world is the hope of keeping Africa in the free world, and the hope of keeping Africa in the free world lies in the building of strong trade union organizations by the Africans themselves who know the difference between communism and democracy and who are dedicated to the dignity of every human being who believes in the worth and the value and who will give respect and reverence to the life of every man, whether he be white or black or brown or yellow. And with this concept of humanity I believe that Africa is a wave of the future and means much more to the free world than our being able to compete with Russia on the terms of a Sputnik or on the basis of science and technology, although we must not permit them to surpass us in any field.

Thank you very much.

# Charles C. Diggs, Jr.,
## 1922–

Charles Diggs was born in Detroit and studied at the University of Michigan and Fisk University. He also studied to be an undertaker at Wayne University. He served as Second Lieutenant in the United States Army Air Force (USAAF) from 1943 to 1945. He is president and treasurer of the Detroit Metropolitan Mutual Insurance Company and vice president of Diggs Enterprise. From 1951 to 1954 Diggs was the first Negro member of the Michigan State Senate. He was elected to represent the Thirteenth Michigan District to the 84th, 85th, 86th and 87th United States Congresses. He still serves in the Congress and is the first Negro from the State of Michigan to be so honoured.

# The Role of the American Negro
# in American-African Relations*

### CHARLES C. DIGGS, JR.

The American Negro should have as much interest in the development of Africa as the American Jew has in the development of Israel. Not only will a renaissance of concern uncover the missing link between the American Negro and his African heritage, but it should further substantiate, among other things the rich contributions Africans have made to the culture of the world.

There has been a colossal conspiracy to minimize and even obliterate these contributions. Partly, this is due to the fact that many languages in that vast complex land are spoken but not written, which precludes a proper chronicle of achievement. Partly, it has been caused by centuries of isolation and general inaccessibility. But largely, it was the objective of a calculated scheme to expedite the

* Address given at the Second Annual Conference of the American Society of African Culture, June 26–9, 1959. Reprinted by kind permission of the Society.

exploitation of black people by slave traders and white supremacists. They knew it would be easier to subjugate Negroes, both in Africa and America, if they imposed a badge of inferiority on them based upon an alleged lack of cultural heritage and group achievement.

The resurgence of interest in Africa today presents a unique opportunity for American Negroes to forge an unbreakable chain with their African brethern. They should not only be inspired by great yesterdays in Africa but even more motivated by its great tomorrows. As was so aptly stated last December at the Accra Conference, Africa is the continent of the future. All segments of the Western world, regardless of background, should be interested in the kind of continent Africa will become under pressures of her mid-twentieth century problems. But they will make a grave mistake if they underestimate the African intelligence by displaying an interest based merely upon the power struggle with the Sino-Soviet bloc. It must be a genuine interest based upon the dictates of human decency which demand that Africans stand equal before the bar of world justice. It must be based upon a sincere desire to seek not just trade and industry, but improved mankind. It must be based upon the highest human ideal: that the rise of all men is a menace to no one—and is the one road to world salvation.

Unfortunately, too few Americans below a select leadership group appreciate the important implications involved in our relations with Africa. It is true that our policies toward Africa have changed considerably during the last two years: We have expanded our diplomatic representation there; we have increased our direct aid through the mutual security funds and our participation in international economic agencies; we have interested more private enterprise investments; we have sent numerous and helpful technical missions to Africa; we have stepped-up our student exchange program; and we have entertained scores of African governmental officials and important private citizens. In the United Nations, we have for the first time officially joined the forces who seek the elimination of the extremist racial problems in South Africa, although we are not nearly as vocal on this subject as we were relative to Hungary and Tibet. The role of the American Negro should be to accelerate this progress relating to African peoples.

No other group as a whole should be more sensitive to the aspirations of the African peoples for freedom, equality, and recognition, more understanding of the underlying factors of motivation, and more determined that the United States make a significant contribution to Africa's uplifting.

The American Society of African Culture is making a particularly unique contribution by broadening our country's knowledge and appreciation of African culture. If the true facts of African culture are properly disseminated, it will help change a derogatory image of the so-called Dark Continent which has even victimized many American Negroes. I have just recently prepared a communication to be sent to all major motion picture studios, radio and television networks urging that they re-examine their portrayal of African characters in light of valid history and contemporary realism. They are presently doing a very fine job of recasting oriental characters and culture, eliminating the bowing, grinning, sneaky Chinese or Japanese stereotype. The same treatment can be applied to broaden the "bushboy" concept of Africans here in America. I hope that AMSAC will see fit to associate itself with this appeal. It is this kind of mass medium of communication which must be enlisted if we are to reach within a reasonable time the grass roots elements in America to whom the words Accra, or Lagos, or Leopoldville, or Nairobi or Johannesburg have comparatively little meaning.

It should also be the role of the American Negro in concert with our friends of other groups to establish aid to Africa as a federal political objective. Aside from the fact that as an important underdeveloped area it meets our prime criteria for economic assistance, there is no question that the coveted Negro vote can serve as an impetus to underscore proper attention to Africa's needs. Our Jewish friends proved only recently in connection with the mutual security bill before Congress that aid to Israel has political undertones to which the State Department is not insensitive. You will recall that an announced drastic reduction in aid to Israel was quickly retracted within a short period of time. Not only must we launch an offensive to build up assistance to Africa, which presently is only a small and disproportionate fraction of America's total foreign aid program, but we must prepare ourselves for the probability of an intensified negative attitude on the part of opponents to foreign aid, which includes practically the entire Southern delegation in Congress.

In today's *New York Times*, Milton Braker reports from Tanganyika that white settlers have already begun to equate American aid to Africa with the potentialities of the Negro vote in 1960. Aside from moral considerations, let us not be less politically wise about our own political effectiveness than our discerning enemies thousands of miles away. I suggest, too, that it might help the State Department clear up the blurred vision of its policy toward Africa which is best described as a diplomatic tight rope walk between African independence aspirations and the principles of continued African ties with Western Europe. Although I recognize the delicacy of this problem, I see no reason why we cannot have a clear-cut policy in support of the African quest for nationalism. This is not only consistent with America's historical origin, but could not possibly cause a serious rupture with our NATO allies. They have no choice but to maintain their marriage to us. On the other hand, Africa's policy of positive neutralism indicates a long courtship before she will even consider being engaged to anyone.

Africa has such tremendous requirements for technical assistance and general education benefits that the role of the American Negro must certainly encompass participating in the fulfillment of these needs. There are already many who are presently serving with distinction in these capacities, and with the present rate of inquiries about opportunities in this area, we may expect a considerable amount of future activity.

There are those who challenge the ability of the American Negro to contribute through his own private investment to the African economy, on the premise that he has not demonstrated such a capacity in this country. Unfortunately, it is true that we do not control a share of the American economy comparable to our purchasing power. This is our principal weakness. Outside of the insurance company organized by New Yorkers in Ghana, a lumber company organized by Detroiters in Liberia, and a mining company also in Liberia in which some American Negroes have an interest, I am not aware of any other major investment by us in Africa. There is a group of Negroes who plan an exploratory conference, immediately following the National Negro Insurance Convention this summer, on the possibilities of starting another insurance company somewhere in Africa. Our Jewish friends, on the other hand, have invested millions of dollars in private capital into all kinds of projects in Israel during its short existence, and whereas they admittedly possess considerably more assets than we do, their successful activity should serve as an inspiration and guide.

Finally, I believe part of our role should be to absorb and practice the lessons our African brethern are teaching us—the lessons of solidarity, despite tremendously diverse backgrounds, and a passionate determination to succeed, including the capacity to sacrifice even their lives, if necessary, in pursuit of just goals.

# APPENDIX

The foregoing anthology of responses by Negro American leaders to Africa was not meant to be an exhaustive treatment of this phenomenon, for many individual Negroes wrote of Africa without being leaders in any sense of the word. In "A Bibliographical Checklist of American Negro Writers about Africa," published in 1958, more than 400 titles by 143 Negro authors writing on Africa specifically are included. In general, Negro writings on Africa have been either travel accounts or historical works of Negro American life that include introductory accounts of the African past.

Accounts of travel to Africa were the first type of published writings by Negro Americans relating to Africa. Paul Cuffe's *A Brief Account, etc.*, included in this volume (see p. 14), was one of the first travel accounts of this sort. But by the middle of the nineteenth century innumerable accounts had been published. Two of lasting interest are Daniel H. Peterson, *The Looking Glass: Being a True Report and Narrative of the Rev. Daniel H. Peterson, a Colored Clergyman: Embracing a Period of Time from the Year 1812 to 1854 and Including his Visit to Western Africa* (New York, 1854), and Samuel Williams, *Four Years in Liberia: a Sketch of the Life of Rev. Samuel Williams with Remarks on the Mission, Manners and Customs of the Natives of West Africa* (Philadelphia, 1857).

Of special value among the nineteenth century travel accounts is Charles Spenser Smith's *Glimpses of Africa, West and Southwest Coast, Containing the Author's Impressions and Observations during a Voyage of Six Thousand Miles from Sierra Leone, St. Paul de Loanda and Return, Including the Rio del Ray and Cameroons River, and the Congo River, from its Mouth to Matadi* (Nashville, Tennessee, 1895). Smith, Bishop of the African Methodist Episcopal Church, served as resident Bishop of that Church in South Africa, a post established by Bishop Turner (see p. 43), from 1904 to 1906, and he later wrote a book on British administration in South Africa. This book, entitled *The Relation of the British Government to the Natives of South Africa*, was printed, like his earlier book and like those of other Negro American travellers to Africa, on presses owned and

386

operated by Negro groups. In Bishop Smith's case the press was owned by the African Methodist Episcopal Church's Sunday School union at Nashville, Tennessee.

Several of the nineteenth century travelogues touched on more serious matters of African history. Occasionally, these took the form of ethnographic accounts of traditional African life. The best work of this genre was that of Martin Delany, especially his *Official Report of the Niger Valley Exploring Party* (New York, 1861) included in this volume (see p. 26). But also making a contribution in this field was his *Principia of Ethnology: the Origin of Races and Color, With an Archaeological Compendium of Ethiopean and Egyptian Civilization from Years of Careful Examination and Enquiry* (Philadelphia, 1879). Ethnographic accounts also appeared in several missionary journals, notably the *African Repository*, the journal of the American Colonization Society from 1875 to 1892, and the *Southern Workman* between the years 1873 and 1930. The *Southern Workman* was particularly noted for its accounts of the work experiences of Negro American agriculturalists who were sent out to Africa in the late 19th and early 20th centuries from Hampton Institute and from Tuskegee Institute. A typical article was one by J. N. Callaway, entitled "African Sketches," appearing in Volume XXXI of the *Southern Workman* (1902). The article describes the work of Tuskegee trained agriculturalists who were hired by the German Colonial Economic Society to train Africans in German Togoland in modern methods of cotton production. It appears that the first monograph on African tribal life published by a Negro American was George Ellis's *Negro Culture in West Africa: A Social Study of a Negro Group of Vai-speaking People* (New York, 1914). Ellis spent much of his life in American foreign service in Liberia and was thus able to observe the traditional life of the Vai and other Liberian tribes.

Ethnography, however, was only a small part of the early writings by Negro Americans on Africa. More common were the general histories embracing broad features of African cultures, normally in the context of a survey history of new world Negroes, and Negro Americans particularly. While many of these early historians were poorly trained, and often unable, therefore, to sift fact from myth, they were concerned, and understandably so, with refuting the charge of white American scholars that black men in Africa or America were incapable of viable civilized existence. A number of books written before the Civil War attest to this fact; among them are Robert Benjamin Lewis, *Light and Truth* (Boston, 1836), J. W. C.

Pennington, *A Textbook of the Origin and History of the Colored People* (Hartford, 1841), James Theodore Holly, *A Vindication of the Capacity of the Negro Race for Self-Government* (1857), and William Wells Brown, *Emancipation: Its Course and Progress from 1481 B.C. to A.D. 1875* (Hampton, Virginia, 1882).

None of these writers was concerned with African history as such; they viewed a study of Africa as a necessary background to a study of the history of Negro Americans. Furthermore, the tendency was to take the rather advanced Amharic culture of Ethiopia, and occasionally Egyptian civilization, as presumably representative of Africa, neglecting the largely neolithic and early iron age cultures of Negro Africa. This tendency was, no doubt, related to the scarcity of material written in English at that time on the History and cultures of so-called Black Africa.

The most reliable account of the origins of the new world Negro community published by a black man in the nineteenth century was *The History of the Negro Race in America from 1619 to 1880* (New York, 1883) by George Washington Williams. Williams, like Cuffe, Delany and several others, is also included in this anthology (see p. 98), for, as a minister and politician, he was indeed a leader, but this book establishes for a him a particular position in the development of Negro scholarship. Less well known than Williams's history, but following its general format, was *The History of the Colored Race in America, Containing Also their Ancient and Modern Life in Africa, The Origin and Development of Slavery, The Civil War, Emancipation* (Kansas, 1888) by William T. Alexander.

It was the appearance of W. E. B. DuBois's *Suppression of the African Slave Trade to the United States of America, 1638–1870* (New York, 1896) that marked the beginning of a school of Negro historians whose work claimed scholarly acceptance among established American historians. DuBois's monograph was somewhat in the tradition of the writings of earlier Negro historians in so far as Africa was not the main focus of the inquiry. The monograph, which was published as the first in the Harvard University Historical Series, was largely an inquiry into the role of the United States in limiting and suppressing trade in human cargo. In his other scholarly works, however, Africa became a major focus in DuBois's writing. In his book, *The Negro* (New York, 1915), he set out to describe "the history of the darker part of the human family, which is separated from the rest of mankind by no absolute physical line, but which nevertheless forms, as a distinct mass, a social group distinct in history, appearance, and to some extent in spiritual gifts." Thus,

Africa was a subject of eight of the book's twelve chapters. These chapters were written and revised in *The World and Africa* (New York, 1947), which also dealt with the modern colonial and international status of Africa. Sources for the study of traditional and modern Africa were also included in DuBois's *Encyclopedia of the Negro* (New York, 1945).

The success of DuBois's first book paved the way for a new crop of Negro American historians whose work gained a wide appreciation. William H. Ferris, a graduate of Yale University, saw the history of the Negro as a situation of the black man in the diaspora and in 1913 published his two volumes, *The African Abroad*, Part IV of which is entitled "An Epitome of Deeds, Achievements, and Progress of a Colored Race in Africa, Europe, Hayti, the West Indies, and America"; all in 93 pages. John W. Cromwell, a lawyer and educator, and the co-founder with Alexander Crummell of the Negro American Academy, published his work, *The Negro in American History, Men and Women Eminent in the Evolution of the American of African Descent*, in 1914; in it data on Africa, colonization, and slavery were included in the introductory chapters.

Carter Godwin Woodson (see p. 148) was undoubtedly the Negro historian who established for scholars, both black and white, the study of the Negro as an area of respectable research. And, as he traced the history of Negroes in this country, Woodson never failed to see the relevance of Africa to their development. In addition he wrote and edited several books solely concerning Africa; among these were *African Myths together with Proverbs* (Washington, D.C., 1928), *The African Background Outline* (Washington, D.C., 1936), and *African Heroes and Heroines* (Washington, D.C., 1949). Woodson also founded and edited the *Journal of Negro History*, which, beginning with its first issue, frequently included papers on African topics.

Two other persons merit attention for their role in bringing the facts of African history to the Negro American public—Joel Augustus Rogers (1880–1966) and William Leo Hansberry (1894–1965). Rogers, while probably not qualifying as an academic historian, did, nevertheless, search with diligence for those little known facts of African life which, when appreciated, served to strengthen the Negro American's pride in his heritage. Suffering from the difficulties of getting the interest of publishers in this little known material, Rogers usually paid for the publication of his books out of his own pocket. Illustrative of the kind of writing Rogers did are *The Real Facts about Ethiopia* (New York, 1936) and *World's Great Men of Color* (*3,000 B.C. to 1946 A.D.*) (New York, 1946).

Rogers's last book, *Africa's Gift to America* (New York, 1961), was published when he was eighty years of age and had been, as one reviewer described him, "an astute interpreter of Africa and Afro-American life and history for over forty years".

William Leo Hansberry was first and foremost a teacher; yet he pioneered in the study of African civilization. Continuing the interest and emphasis of the earlier Negro historians in Ethiopian and Amharic culture, but providing more thorough documentation, Hansberry sought to uncover the facts of early, pre-European civilization in Africa. He received his graduate education at Harvard University. While his long awaited five volume work on the Pre-History and History of Africa was not completed before his death, Hansberry will be remembered by his students, Negro American and African alike, for the stimulus they received from his lectures for over a quarter of a century while he was the Director of the African Civilization Section of the Department of History at Howard University. He was co-founder, in 1953, of the Institute of African-American Relations, the predecessor of the African-American Institute. In appreciation of his long interest in Africa, Africans, and African history, the University of Nsukka in Nigeria named its Institute of African Studies in his honour.

This note on Negro scholars writing on Africa is not meant to be complete. Indeed, almost every book on Negro history published in this country has included some reference to the African background of the Negro American people.